The Eldorado Network

by the same author

GOSHAWK SQUADRON
ROTTEN WITH HONOUR
KRAMER'S WAR

The Eldorado Network

Derek Robinson

W · W · NORTON & COMPANY
New York · London

Library of Congress Cataloging in Publication Data
Robinson, Derek, 1932–(Apr. 12)–
   The Eldorado network.
   I. Title.
PZ4.R6617E 1980   [PR 6068.01954]   823'.9'14
ISBN 0–393–01322–7   79–23640

1 2 3 4 5 6 7 8 9 0

For Tim and Natasha

*'Scratch a Spaniard
and
start a fire.'*
– old Spanish saying

Part One

Chapter 1

When Luis Cabrillo awoke he did not open his eyes.

It was seven o'clock; the sunshine had just reached his face, easing him out of sleep and warming his skin most pleasantly. He knew what he would see when he opened his eyes: a sky of such a clean and tranquil blue that it would seem illuminated, lustrous, a soaring reminder that heaven was indeed more than a priest's promise; not that Luis believed in heaven, but in Spain even agnostics acknowledge that God makes a good case for His existence. Good, but not good enough.

The sunlight bathed his eyelids while he enjoyed the excellence of the sky in anticipation. It was going to be another good day: no cares, enough comforts, all the enjoyment and entertainment he wished. His eyes opened and he saw, through the high, half-open casement window, a sky of infinite sweep and tenderness. He stretched his arms above his head, grasped the brass rails of the bed-head, and breathed the beautiful air deep into his lungs.

Luis Cabrillo was twenty-two years old. He was securely locked in an apartment on the third floor of a house in the middle of Madrid. It was 27th May 1941, and he was as happy as any young man who had been locked in a third-floor Madrid apartment for over two years could be.

Distant feet sounded on the stairs, climbing slowly. To Luis Cabrillo the sound was as comforting as an old, familiar tune: he recognised the steady rhythm, the pause for rest on the landing below, the slowing of pace as the stairs became steeper, the change of tone when linoleum gave way to wood. There were five steps to the board that squeaked, then three to the one that creaked, and two more to the top. (That final footfall always came slightly later and heavier, as if to celebrate its arrival.) Shuffle. Clink of crockery. Pause while one might count to six, before the key rattled into the lock. A click, a clank. The door opened. In came breakfast.

'I finished *Stamboul Train* last night,' Cabrillo said. 'Excellent,

3

most enjoyable. Get me more Graham Greenes if you can.'

The old man put the breakfast tray on the table, carefully, so as not to spill the coffee. His breath was whistling softly in his throat, and he could see little red sparks drifting across his eyeballs. 'She told me to tell you something,' he wheezed. 'But I've gone and forgot.'

'I still have a few of Ernest Hemingway's short stories to read,' Cabrillo said. 'Try and get me some more of his stuff too. Hemingway. Can you remember that? Also a man called Joyce, James Joyce. Can you remember? I'd better write them down.' He got out of bed.

'I can remember, I'm not that stupid.' The old man went over to the window and looked down at the street. His body, once thick and powerful from a life of labouring, was now thin and shrunken, so that the front of his trousers had to be gathered in a big tuck under his belt. Only his fists remained their old size, and the skin on his heavy fingers was mottled like the margins of an old book.

'I'll write them down,' Cabrillo decided. 'There's a couple more I want you to look for. Russians in translation. You can't be expected to remember them.' He sipped his coffee. 'Hey!' he said. 'No eggs. You forgot the eggs.'

'That's it. That's what she told me to tell you. You don't get no eggs today.' The old man perched on the windowsill and rested his head against the glass. 'I told you I'd remember it.'

Cabrillo looked for an explanation. None came. 'What went wrong?' he asked. 'No eggs . . . That's never happened before. Did somebody drop the bowl, or something?'

'Drop the bowl?' The old man chuckled wheezily. 'Nobody dropped the bowl, my lad. We've got plenty of eggs downstairs. *You're* the one without the eggs.' He yawned as the sunlight warmed him.

'What d'you mean? I don't understand.' Cabrillo split open a roll and buttered it. Rolls and coffee: that was all the tray held. 'You know I always have eggs for breakfast. What's up? What's the matter with you all?'

For a long moment they looked at each other. Both were chewing: Cabrillo on his buttered roll, the old man on his gums. Cabrillo was puzzled, a little annoyed; the old man was thinking. 'Nothing the matter,' he muttered.

'Well . . . For God's sake go and get me my eggs, then.'

4

Cabrillo pulled off his pyjama top. A seam split. He bundled the garment and tossed it in the old man's lap. 'And get me some more pyjamas too, while you're at it.'

The old man opened the bundle and found the split seam. His fingers clumsily fitted the edges together. 'It'll mend,' he said. 'Besides, you can't have new pyjamas. That's what she told me to tell you. The money's all gone.'

Luis Cabrillo stopped eating. For a few seconds he stopped breathing. So did the old man, startled by the impact of his own remark. His words seemed to fill the room, expanding in power and meaning until they made him afraid of what he had said. 'That's why you got no eggs,' he explained nervously. 'No money, see. All gone.'

'But that's impossible!' Cabrillo put down his cup without looking and slopped coffee over the table. 'I gave you enough to last for three years, at least! What have you done with it all? Where's it gone? You can't be serious, I don't believe you, it's too . . .' He began pacing about the room, searching the walls for an answer, pounding pieces of furniture with his closed fist. 'Three years! God in heaven, what's become of it? I gave you a fortune, you said yourself when . . . This is absurd, it's crazy. How can you have the gall to try and tell me—'

Cabrillo turned angrily, accusingly, and saw that the old man was gazing absently at a little dribble of coffee running off the edge of the table. Cabrillo slammed his palm against the spillage and made it spatter everywhere. 'Listen!' he shouted. The old man twitched and turned his head. 'What the hell's going on here? Three years, we agreed! Now you wander in and park your ancient backside on my windowsill and casually tell me my money's all gone! *Where* has it gone? Because it certainly hasn't all gone on *me*, has it?'

'Yes,' the old man said. He eased himself from the windowsill and used the pyjama top to mop up the spilt coffee. 'Yes, my friend, it's all gone on you. Every last peseta.'

'Gibberish! Junk! Poppycock! That's utterly impossible, and you know it.' Cabrillo found himself gasping for breath. His heart had started thudding like a badly tuned engine. There was a taste in the back of his mouth which he had almost forgotten: panic, or fear, or was it the excitement of risk? 'Go and fetch my eggs, damn you!' he ordered.

'Every last peseta,' the old man said. Slowly he refolded

5

the pyjama top so that the dry part was outwards, and he polished the table. 'See . . . things have changed while you've been here. Prices have gone right up. Food's not as cheap as what it was. Oh no. Nothing's cheap any more. It's the war, see. Money won't buy what it used to, not even yours, and you can't blame us for that. Blame the war.'

'Blame the war? You think I'm feebleminded?' Cabrillo cried. 'The silly bloody war's been over for years, you doddering old fool!'

The old man licked a finger and tried to rub out a scratch. 'No, no, no,' he said patiently. 'Not *that* war, not *our* war. I'm talking about the one they've got going on now. The Adolf Hitler war. The big one.'

'My God,' Cabrillo said. 'Is that still happening? I thought the Germans beat everybody. I thought it was all over.'

'Oh no,' the old man said. 'It's still going on. They say it's only just really begun.'

'I'll be damned.' Cabrillo sat on the bed and massaged his face.

'It's your own fault, isn't it? If you won't read a newspaper or listen to the radio, how do you expect to know what's happening?' The old man shuffled towards the door.

'Has the money really all gone? Truly all?'

'Every last peseta.'

'Jesus . . . You might have given me some warning.'

'Well, funny you should say that. I've been meaning to mention it. As a matter of fact she kept asking me to tell you there wasn't much of it left. Every morning she mentioned it.'

'So why didn't you?'

'Must have forgot,' the old man said. Cabrillo listened to the sound of his footsteps going downstairs: an old, familiar tune, being played backwards for the last time.

He went over to the mirror.

'No money,' he told himself accusingly. 'So what the hell are you going to do now, idiot?'

6

Chapter 2

On this day—27th May 1941—Louis Cabrillo was certainly the best-read 22-year-old Spaniard in Madrid, probably in Spain, possibly in Europe. Throughout the previous two years and one month he had been in hiding, never leaving his third-floor apartment, and reading on average a book and a half a day, say ten books a week, which came to about eleven hundred books in all. The old man—he was the building's caretaker—bought the books for him at secondhand bookstalls or from foreigners he accosted outside hotels or railway stations. All the books were in English; Spain's censors automatically banned anything in Spanish that seemed interesting, whether it was subversive or not; or perhaps they defined subversion as anything interesting; so Cabrillo read whatever British and American books the old man brought him. The old man knew no English, so the result was extreme variety : everything from Zane Grey to Bertrand Russell, and from P. G. Wodehouse to Walt Whitman. In one memorable week Cabrillo read sixteen novels, plus an 1896 book on how to play rugby football, a veterinary guide to pig breeding, and the Royal Automobile Club's Handbook for 1923. Of them all he found the pig-breeding manual by far the most interesting. He was impressed to learn that a boar's penis is shaped like a corkscrew, and the more he read about the sexual habits of the domestic pig the more he came to understand that animal's challenging yet slightly cynical expression.

This two-year feast of reading was an attempt to repair his education, which (he now saw) had been a disaster.

Luis's father had been a traffic manager with Spanish Railways : a restless, questioning, dissatisfied man who wanted to make sweeping changes in the running of the whole Spanish railway system. His ideas were good but his manner was abrasive; he was too impatient to spare the time to try to persuade people; he had a talent for turning a discussion into an argument and an argument into a scathing denunciation.

What's more, he was bad at his job. Routine work bored him. He let the daily chores pile up until the backlog created an exciting conflict which was worth tackling, at which point he tackled it with enormous skill and enthusiasm. Meanwhile, rail traffic in the rest of his section moved sluggishly in fits and starts. Whenever this poor performance was pointed out to him, Luis's father struck back with an angry, brilliant analysis of how superbly the entire railway network could be operated once his ideas were adopted. He was not a popular man.

The trouble with Luis's father was that he was too difficult to be tolerated and yet never quite incompetent enough to be sacked. (Also he had an uncle who was a director of the company.) So he constantly got transferred.

The Cabrillo family rarely stayed longer than a year in any one town. By the time young Luis was fifteen they had lived in Barcelona, Seville, Cadiz, Ayamonte, Badajoz, Cordoba, Bilbao, Madrid (twice), Valencia, Valladolid, Alicante and Zaragoza. Luis had been to twenty-seven different schools in thirteen towns, and he had been kicked out of twenty-three of them. The other four schools were actively considering expulsion at the point when Señor Cabrillo announced that he was transferred yet again and thus saved them the trouble of deciding.

What was wrong with the boy? 'Luis is highly original,' wrote one headmaster, 'and this must be curbed if he is to make any progress.' Many tried; all failed. Trying to curb Luis's originality was like trying to train a butterfly to travel in a straight line.

He had inherited his father's restless, questioning nature. There were many aspects of education which he refused to accept, starting with history. When he was nine he wrote an essay on the Spanish Empire which pointed out, amongst other things, what good luck it was that the U.S.A., not Spain, got California, because now America made all those terrific movies in California, and everybody agreed that Spanish movies were fucking abominable. This was a phrase which Luis had just picked up without bothering to examine its meaning too closely. His teacher beat him and burned the essay in the school yard. Luis was hurt, not so much by the cane as by the school's refusal to discuss his case or even to define his crime.

From that day on, he knew that school was a battlefield,

and he was determined never to surrender.

The battles were fought in every classroom. When he was twelve, Luis refused to read *Don Quixote* because, he told the teacher of Spanish literature, he found Cervantes unreadable.

'How fascinating!' the teacher said. 'And how privileged we are! Luis Cabrillo, despite his inky fingers and his scabby knees, knows better than Spain's greatest writer!'

'I didn't say that, sir,' Luis replied. 'I said I can't read *Don Quixote*, because it's boring.'

'But this is a revelation!' the teacher said. 'One wonders how all those millions of intelligent men and women who have read and enjoyed Cervantes' masterpiece could have been so mistaken, so misled, so misguided.' The class tittered. 'Were they all just poor hoodwinked fools, Cabrillo?'

'That's not the point, sir,' Luis said. 'What other people like is none of my business. All I know is *Don Quixote* bores me, and I can't read a book if it bores me. Can you, sir?'

'We're not here to discuss my tastes, Cabrillo.'

'There you are, then. If it bores you too, sir, why don't we chuck it out and read something interesting?'

'Because I'm not *paid* to be interested, Cabrillo.'

'I'm not paid at all, sir.'

For that remark Luis was beaten; but he still refused to read *Don Quixote*.

Next year, at a school run by nuns, he got into deep trouble over the teaching of the Catholic faith.

The subject was the apparently miraculous revelations at Fatima in Portugal, in 1917. Luis's class was told that the Blessed Virgin Mary appeared, in an oak tree, to three peasant children while they were tending sheep. She gave them important messages from God. Fatima, the nun said, had now become a place of pilgrimage for thousands, millions of devout Catholics, who attend the Basilica and Chapel of the Apparitions, which was built on the actual spot where—

'Why didn't God just tell the Pope?' Luis asked.

Sister Theresa was elderly, heavy, benign except when opposed, and slightly deaf. 'I beg your pardon?' she said.

'Why didn't God just tell the Pope?' Luis, repeated, more loudly. 'If God had something important he wanted the Church to know, why did he send the Virgin Mary to tell three little kids in Portugal?'

9

'Why does the sun rise in the east and not in the west?'
Sister Theresa replied, with a rather tense smile. 'Because God
knows which way is best.'

'Yes, but they might have got it all wrong,' Luis said. 'I
mean, they were only kids. Suppose they didn't understand?
Or maybe they had rotten memories. They might have forgotten the really important bits.'

Sister Theresa's tense smile was losing its grip on her
stony face. 'God selects His messengers with care,' she said.

She and Luis exchanged stares, while the rest of the class
hid behind its hands and willed the argument to go on.

'It still strikes me as a funny way to do a simple job,' he
said.

'It strikes you as funny, does it?' Sister Theresa said icily.
'I hope you will remember that remark when you are older
and you discover that God is infinitely wiser than you are.'

Luis grunted.

'Now then. To return to the Basilica—'

'What were the messages?' Luis asked.

'Don't interrupt, you discourteous little thug,' Sister Theresa
barked.

'I apologise, Sister. It just seemed to me that if God went
to all that trouble, we ought to know what's on His mind.'

Sister Theresa clenched her jaw and pursed her lips until
her sparse moustache bristled. 'When it is necessary for you
to know, then you will be told,' she declared. The class
shifted restlessly and looked at each other. 'There is no great
urgency about the matter,' she added. Luis shrugged his
shoulders, and she could see that several other children were
looking puzzled or sceptical or, even worse, amused. 'Which
is not to say that the divine messages were not extremely important *at the time*,' she said sternly. 'Our Lady announced the
end of the Great War. She also warned us against the evil
spread of Godless Russian Communism, which despite the
valiant efforts of the Catholic Church has come about, and
she predicted that unless men cease from sinning an even
worse war will follow.' Sister Theresa gave Luis a look of
grim satisfaction: *Make something of that if you can, you
little fiend.*

'I heard there was another message,' Luis said. 'A secret one.'

'That need not concern us,' Sister Theresa said firmly,

'as it was written down by one of the children, at the instruction of Our Lady, and placed in a sealed envelope which is now entrusted to the care of the Bishop of Leiria.'

'Why doesn't he open it?' Luis asked.

'The time is not yet right.'

'Who says?'

Sister Theresa stiffened. 'Cabrillo, I give you leave to reconsider your question,' she said, snapping her fingers nervously.

Luis thought about it. 'It doesn't make any sense, Sister, that's all,' he said. 'What's the point of God going to all that trouble to send us a message in 1917 if some Bishop won't tell us what it was?'

'The Church knows greater mysteries than your weak faith can comprehend, my son,' said Sister Theresa. Her finger-clicking grew louder.

'Yes, of course,' Luis agreed. 'I have never questioned that, Sister. I just wonder who is really in charge: God, or the Bishop of Leiria?'

'God *through* the Bishop,' Sister Theresa ruled.

'I bet he's opened it,' Luis said. There was a sharp intake of breath by the rest of the class, but Luis could not stop himself. 'I bet he opened it and read it and it's not a message from God at all, it's just a load of old Portuguese rubbish, and that's why he won't tell—'

'Foul-mouthed wretch!' Sister Theresa shouted. She crashed her leatherbound Bible against Luis's head and knocked him off his seat. 'Evil, poisonous brute!' Her large shoes kicked him to the front of the class. Another beating was on its way. Sister Theresa died of a stroke the following year, and all the other nuns blamed Luis Cabrillo; but by then Luis was in another town, another school, and another battle.

As he grew older, his conflicts became more dogged. He refused to learn any geography because the school could give him no good reason *why* he should memorise the principal rivers of Australia. He was in trouble in the art class, where his nude studies were considered too explicit. 'Unhealthy' was the word the art teacher used. 'But this same human body was good enough for El Greco and Goya and Rubens and Raphael,' Luis argued. 'There's acres of flesh hanging in the Prado, isn't there?' For once he was not beaten, but was sent out to play soccer. That didn't work either. He tripped opponents and he handled the ball so often that the teacher who was refereeing threatened to send him off. 'But tripping and handling are difficult skills,' Luis claimed. 'Besides, how can the game ever develop unless new techniques are introduced?' 'Shut up, Cabrillo,' the referee said. 'Free kick against your team.' Two minutes later, Luis tripped the referee.

That was the day he left school for good. He possessed only one academic skill: he could read and write English and (to some extent) speak it, no thanks to any of the schools he had passed through. Luis Cabrillo had taught himself English so that he could get his moneysworth out of the American movies, which were his big interest in life. He was about thirteen when he realised that Spanish subtitles were far briefer than the dialogue on the soundtrack. This was not only a swindle but also an insult. In Luis's experience the only things worth his attention were stuff the authorities wanted to hide. He bought a teach-yourself-English book and studied it all day in school: through geography lessons, algebra lessons, divinity lessons. The book was confiscated. He bought another. Eventually he knew enough English to identify what the Spanish subtitles were avoiding, and sometimes he took it upon himself to fill in the gaps for the benefit of others. When a cowboy punched a gambler through a saloon window, and the Spanish caption offered only a terse '*Be gone!*', Luis loosely but loudly translated the soundtrack's actual *Beat it, you fourflushing sonofabitch or I'll kick your teeth past your tonsils*. He was thrown out of so many cinemas that he became known to the police. Also to the secret police.

At first that didn't much matter. It was 1934, he was only fifteen, the disapproval of the police or the secret police meant no more to him than had the disapproval of a whole series of teachers and headmasters. And young Luis had no politics, unless chronic dissatisfaction with everything counts as politics. His parents had other things to preoccupy them: railway timetables for his father, piano-playing for his mother. She was convinced that she had talent, perhaps great talent, if only she could bully her fingers into expressing it. One of the perquisites of her husband's job was that every time he got transferred the company moved all their belongings, free; so Luis became accustomed to travelling with her scratched and scarred grand piano. He never got accustomed to her tirelessly bad playing. Señora Cabrillo attacked the keyboard as if it were a lengthy combination lock, a bit stiff, a bit grudging, which had to be struck scientifically but ruthlessly in the correct sequence before it would deliver up its treasure. Day after day she kept striking it, year after year, with chords like village carpentry and cadenzas like heavy rope, and still no treasure showed itself. To Luis each of his parents was lost on some endless, pointless search. His father was the Flying Dutchman of the Spanish railway system, and his mother had a stranglehold on her piano if only she could find its jugular. They fed, clothed and housed him, but otherwise took little interest. When the incident of the tripped referee brought about angry and tedious repercussions, he decided to leave school and get a job. Neither parent interfered.

Chapter 3

They were living in Barcelona at the time.

The man who wrote film reviews for Barcelona's biggest evening paper, Luis noted, was also the bullfight critic and sometimes covered football matches. The editor got a letter from Luis proposing himself as the newspaper's first full-time film critic. Attached was a review of a film currently being shown in the city. It was a miracle of compression: Luis managed to libel the star, the director, the film critic of a rival newspaper, and the owners of the cinema, all in 250 words. But he had a certain style—'the trouble with this film is that it goes on long after it has finished', he wrote—and so the editor offered him a job as a copy boy. 'I have a nose for talent,' the editor said. 'Work hard, learn all you can, and maybe one day you'll be sitting in this chair.'

That was fine and very encouraging, except for one thing: Luis was fifteen and the editor (as he discovered by looking up his file in the obituary department) was fifty-three. Luis took the job but he wasn't willing to wait thirty-eight years. For a couple of weeks he trotted about the building, carrying copy from writers to sub-editors, from subs to typesetters; taking proofs in the reverse direction; fetching coffee; finding taxis; listening to arguments over pictures, headlines, expenses; getting a sense of the way a daily newspaper gradually winds itself up from a slightly bleary sluggishness through a brisk professionalism to a manic, mannerless, get-the-hell-out-of-my-way rush, as if the paper itself were a wild beast which had to be set free; and then the slump, the anti-climax, the taste of flatness when there was nothing left to do but read the damn thing.

He quite enjoyed it but after a couple of weeks he was still just a copy boy.

The paper published its film reviews on Tuesdays and Fridays. The following Tuesday, as he picked up the cinema critic's copy, Luis respectfully asked him which film he intended to honour with his comments on Friday. When Friday came round, Luis again collected the man's words, took them to the entertainments editor, and hung around until he was given the pages to be set. He went away and hid them inside his shirt. The typesetters, he knew from observation, would need about twenty minutes to do their work. He delayed until the last possible moment, and then gave them his own film review.

It almost got through. The printers accepted it—Luis's version looked convincing, even to the extent of a few corrections in the entertainments editor's green ink—and after that, time was so short that nobody bothered to read the proof very closely. This was not unusual : the film critic was stiflingly tedious. In fact Luis's rogue column was actually printed in a few thousand early issues meant for the suburbs. As the bundles were being loaded onto the vans, they were recalled for pulping. His headline had given him away.

New French Film Is Good News For Insomniacs, the editor read as he glanced through his rush copy. He read it again. It looked odd; not like the usual stuff : too crisp, too sharp. He read the opening paragraph and laughed aloud, twice. Then he picked up the phone, killed the column, (they put in a picture of swans at sunset instead) and fired Cabrillo on the spot.

Luis found out later where he had gone wrong, and it taught him a lesson. 'You can be *too* good,' he told his father. 'Now if I'd written a dull, boring headline, the kind of thing they run every week, my piece would have gone through.'

'So why didn't you?' His father never went to the cinema and rarely read a newspaper.

'Because the whole point was to show them how much better it can be done.'

'For God's sake,' his father complained, 'I thought you said that's why they sacked you.'

'So it is,' Luis said angrily. 'And I lost a week's pay.'

'Well, serve you right. You knew your job, didn't you? You should have stuck to it. Suppose I needed a locomotive—'

'I'm not a damn locomotive,' Luis said. His father stared. 'Oh, to hell with them,' Luis muttered. 'It was a lousy job anyway.'

'Then get yourself another. I can't keep you in cinema-tickets.'

He went to work for a wine merchant and for ten days he corked bottles. Next morning he arrived with both hands heavily bandaged. 'Broke my fingers in a boxing-match,' he announced. 'Can't cork.'

The owner swore a bit, found him a fairly clean white coat and put him in the front office, to help attend to customers. At first the arrangement worked well. Luis was quick and courteous. He was old enough and grown enough to have the beginnings of a presence, yet he still conveyed some of the innocence and vulnerability of youth. And he was handsome as only a young Spaniard can be, with a trace of melancholy, a hint of tragedy, and a glimmer of amusement that anyone should be taken in by either. His eyes were a cool, dark brown. His skin was flawless, shaded olive and stretched over high cheekbones and strong brows in memory of some distant Moorish ancestor. He had a brief but brilliant smile for the customers' wives which made them forget their boring husbands. For the husbands, sampling wines, he had an attitude of interest and respect which made them feel like Baron Rothschild. Luis rarely spoke, he simply attended; but he was a definite asset to the front office.

On the afternoon of Luis's second day in the white coat, the owner received a semi-important local politician and his wife. For half an hour they tasted samples which Luis poured, holding each bottle in a white napkin and demonstrating a small flourish of pride, while the owner released his limited wine-vocabulary a word at a time, like toy balloons: *mature . . . discreet . . . robust . . . challenging . . . brave . . .*

He opened a fresh bottle and handed it to Luis.

'Now this is something different,' he said. 'Those others are good wines, excellent wines some of them. But this I have kept apart for several years, awaiting . . .' He leaned forward and watched closely as Luis poured. '. . . awaiting a palate which can appreciate the gift of time.'

Luis stiffened. The politician's wife noticed this, and glanced at him. Luis finished pouring, but omitted the usual small flourish.

They raised their glasses and examined the wine. 'Once in a lifetime,' the owner said. 'Perhaps, if God wills it, twice. Ten years ago, when I was privileged to make this discovery, it was so small and so rare that I made the decision that I must bottle it all myself, with these very hands.'

'No you didn't,' Luis said.

Three heads turned and stared. The owner's eyes were sick with rage. Luis tightened his grip on the bottle and breathed deeply.

'Explain yourself,' invited the politician's wife.

'He didn't bottle this stuff ten years ago,' Luis declared. 'I bottled it last week. There's enough of it downstairs to drown an elephant. '

'Get out,' the owner ordered. 'The boy is feeble-minded,' he told them, smiling savagely.

'Two elephants,' Luis said. His heart was galloping, squeezing all the air from his lungs.

'Ignore him, the child is drunk,' the owner said. He wanted to grab Luis but Luis had moved behind a table and the owner was afraid of a humiliating chase. 'He is a halfwit, you see. I took him on as a favour, a halfwit, he says these things, stupid meaningless things.' The owner was sweating like old cheese. 'And when I am not looking he drinks. A drunken halfwit.'

'I am not a child,' Luis said evenly. 'I am fifteen years old.' He pressed his thighs against the edge of the table to stop them trembling.

The politician and his wife looked at each other. 'Well, my dear,' he said. 'Shall we taste the wine?' They tasted the wine and gazed past each other, lips pursed. The owner stood

16

with his fingers curled and straining at his cuffs. His jaw muscles flickered with tension, and Luis could hear his teeth make a faint squeak. Luis began to be afraid.

At last the politician swallowed, and looked into his glass. His wife swallowed, and he glanced sideways at her.

'The boy is wrong,' she said quietly. 'This is not fit even for elephants.'

They put their glasses on the table in front of Luis, and she gave him just the beginnings of a smile. They went out, escorted by the owner, who was thunderous with silence. As he closed the door behind them he turned and snatched up a walking-cane. 'You stinking little bastard streak of whore's-piss,' he whispered in case the politician and his wife heard. 'I'm going to cut your ass into strips for that!'

Luis showed him four bottles of the firm's irreplaceable five-star brandy, each bottle individually numbered, dated and signed by a monk who was long since dead. He held two bottles in each hand, like Indian clubs. 'You come near me and I'll smash them all,' he said.

'I'll kill you!' the owner hissed. He realised that the politician and his wife were out of earshot. 'I'll kick your filthy guts out!' he roared.

'You were going to do that anyway,' Luis said. His arms were starting to ache. The owner took a sudden step forward and Luis twitched, so that the bottles clinked. The owner froze.

'I want a taxi,' Luis said. 'Get it outside the front door with the engine running. When I'm inside it, you can have these back.'

The owner cursed and stamped about the room, while Luis braced himself and prayed that his fingers would not lose their grip. Eventually the man stormed out and shouted furiously for a taxi. Luis followed, cautiously, and eased himself into the back seat, never taking his eye off the owner. 'When I say go,' he told the driver, 'please drive like hell.' He thrust the bottles out of the window and into the owner's arms. '*Go!*' he shouted. The taxi leaped forward with a scream of wheelspin, flinging Luis back against the cushions. The last he saw of the owner was a contorted figure desperately failing to stop one bottle slipping through his arms and smashing on the cobblestones.

Luis had to interrupt his mother's piano-practice in order

to borrow the taxi-fare. She wasn't interested in hearing about his experience and she was annoyed at the interruption. She was also very annoyed at Chopin, who was resisting her with more than his usual stubbornness. To punish them both, she made Luis stand beside her and beat time. He wasn't much good at beating time, so she soon had the satisfaction of correcting him. That left only Chopin to be overcome, and Señora Cabrillo was fairly confident that one day she would beat him too. She had the stamina, and Chopin wasn't getting any younger.

Chapter 4

The following week Luis's father was transferred to Valencia, where Luis got a job as a waiter and kept it for almost a month.

He quite enjoyed being a waiter, and he learned a lot, especially from serving tourists.

'They say they want coffee,' he complained to José-Carlos, the head waiter, on his third day. 'I just gave them their soup and already they want coffee!'

José-Carlos identified the table. 'Americans,' he said approvingly. 'Give them coffee now. Give them what they want. They ask for coffee, water, ketchup, ice-cream, more coffee, hot rolls, cold rolls, stale rolls, cheese before beef, fruit before fish, soup with jam—*any*thing, as long as we have got it, you give it to them. Make 'em happy.'

'Yes, but coffee on top of soup . . .' Luis shook his head.

'Listen: don't tell people what they like.' José-Carlos gave him a shove. 'You give them what they want and they'll give you what you want.'

The Americans got ample coffee and Luis got a good tip. Thereafter his whole attitude changed, and nothing was impossible. He learned to anticipate: hungry patrons need food at once, if it's only bread and olives; when the steak is tough make sure the knives are sharp; to the man who pays the bill goes the tastiest portion. And so on.

Towards the end, Luis discovered a harmless little ruse which boosted his tips appreciably. He had just presented a bill and he was halfway back to the kitchen when he realised he'd overcharged them. Included an order of mushrooms which got cancelled. Tiny mistake. For a second he hesitated, looking back at the table where a large, bald man was laughing at somebody else's joke while he spread banknotes over the bill. Luis knew what to do: say nothing, cross out mushrooms and pocket the difference. That's what anybody else would do. So he went back and corrected the bill. At first the bald man was irritated; he thought Luis had forgotten something and was now adding it on. Then he was pleased—more pleased than the few pesetas' saving was worth. In the end most of it went to swell Luis's tip.

After that Luis regularly forgot to cancel the mushrooms.

José-Carlos observed how frequently Luis had to return to his tables and adjust the bill, and he commented on it. 'I try to make people happy,' Luis said.

'I don't mind that,' José-Carlos told him. 'Just make it eggs mayonnaise once in a while.'

It was neither mushrooms nor egg mayonnaise that got Luis sacked, however, but cherry ice-cream.

He had begun to make something of a personal crusade out of giving customers exactly what they wanted. Coffee between courses was too easy; he nagged the kitchen into stocking hot mustard for the English, pumpernickel for the Germans, escargots for the French. Most of these extras went to waste; too few foreigners used the restaurant. Luis ignored this. Just serving people from the menu was boring; he wanted to surprise them, to bring them the impossible.

One evening the kitchen was going full blast—the chef cooking with one hand and slicing with the other, worrying over what his girlfriend might be doing at that moment, sweat stinging his eyes—when Luis breezed in.

'My friend the rich American wants cherry ice cream,' he announced.

'He's out of luck,' the chef growled. He began cooking an omelette while he sautéd some kidneys and tried to work out where the fish soup had gone wrong.

'Come on, chef, I promised him,' Luis urged. 'He's homesick, he said he bet we didn't have cherry ice cream.'

19

'He's right. *Hot plates*!' the chef bawled.

Luis stood and stared. He hated to go back to the American and lose face. On the other hand the chef was obviously choosing to be completely unhelpful. He saw him wince as he slid the omelette onto a plate which was so hot it made the food sizzle.

'You've got cherries, haven't you?' Luis asked.

'Yes.' Kidneys came off, veal went on, another waiter claimed the omelette.

'And you've got ice cream.'

The chef nodded and basted a chicken.

'Well then, make me some cherry ice cream.'

'*Sweetbreads*!' the chef shouted. 'Piss off,' he told Luis evenly.

Still Luis hesitated. He had thought the chef liked him, responded to his charm, was amused by his eccentric demands. How to overcome this new indifference? Be even more outrageous? 'What's the problem?' he asked, half-grinning. 'Even a tenth-rate dump like this can afford a spare mixing-bowl, can't it?'

For an instant the chef was motionless, frozen in time. Then he turned with the tray of sweetbreads in his hands and hurled it at Luis. Lumps of bleeding meat rained against his face and splattered the kitchen. The tray just missed his right ear and smashed into a stack of serving-dishes. Luis gaped in astonishment while cold blood ran from his chin to his collar. '*Piss off*!' the chef howled, and flung a chopping-block at him. Luis fended it off with his hands and the bruising pain aroused him. He backed away, dodging a small loaf, a half-cabbage, a coffee-pot, a ladle, not dodging a nearly-full tin of English mustard. The uproar brought the proprietor at a run. He hustled Luis out by a back door and kicked him—literally kicked him—into the street. 'Imbecile!' he shouted. 'Maniac! Cretin!'

'But you don't know what happened,' Luis protested. An old man, picking through a bin of kitchen waste, paused to listen.

'You have enraged my chef! What else is there to know?' The door slammed. Luis stood trembling with shock, pain, anger, shame.

'You shouldn't have done that,' the old man reproached.

20

'Good chef, he is.' He held up the remains of half a roast chicken. 'Have a taste of this, friend. Exquisite flavour. Out of this world.'

This time Luis said nothing to his parents. It was the beginning of his true growing-up: from now on he would make his own decisions without informing or consulting anyone. Luis had made the great adolescent discovery—not only do parents not know everything; if you don't tell them, they never get a chance to find out.

During the next year he had seventeen jobs and was fired from all except three, which he quit.

He walked the streets, selling peanuts. Fired because he got into a fight with a rival peanut-vendor and lost. Worked as a window-cleaner for a few days until the paralysing boredom made him quit. Sacked for incompetence or insubordination as a stable-lad, bookshop assistant, roadmender, bellhop and delivery boy. Got a job gutting fish and rapidly came to hate the smell so much that he quit and went to work as a florist's assistant, until one day a rich and elderly customer came in and ordered a dozen red roses for her dog.

'When did he die?' Luis asked as he wrapped them.

'He isn't dead,' the customer said stiffly. 'These flowers are for his birthday.'

'His *birthday*?' Luis stopped wrapping. 'Flowers don't mean a thing to dogs, you know, madam. Not a thing.'

'I beg your pardon?'

'Dogs are colourblind. That's a scientific fact. And they can hardly smell flowers at all. Food, yes. Roses . . . Well, you might as well give him a photograph. Or a book.'

'Young man, you are being extremely impertinent.'

'Madam, I'm only telling you the truth. I mean, if *you* want red roses because *you* like red roses, that's different, that's understandable, take these. But if all you want is to make your animal happy I can think of many better ways: nice juicy bones, scraps, perhaps hot gravy—'

'All right, all right, Cabrillo . . .' The florist had arrived, flushed and flurried. 'I'll take care of this.' He thrust Luis into the back room. Luis didn't wait to be told; he knew by now what that grating tone of voice meant. He moved on and got a dreadful job clearing tables in a sleazy hotel dining-room, quit after three days and was hired as a room-service waiter by a much grander hotel. There, at the age of slightly more than sixteen, he lost his virginity.

The event took place in an expensive suite on the fourth floor. Breakfast had been ordered. Luis took up the tray and found a youngish woman, still in bed. She was astonishingly beautiful, like the glossy stills of filmstars he'd seen displayed outside cinemas: lustrous red hair tumbling around a fresh, provocative face; brilliant eyes; shining lips; dazzling teeth. She told him, huskily, to put the tray on a bedside table, and as he walked across the room he felt enormously elated, as if a vast audience of tens of thousands was watching him.

'Can you stay for a little while?' she asked, turning towards him.

'Yes, of course.' Luis noticed that her shoulders were bare, and his heart began to hurt his ribs. 'Do you want me to . . . Do you need something . . .'

She smiled so happily that he found himself instinctively smiling back.

'Oh, I think so,' she said. Her long, slender naked arm came out and tugged at his trousers. 'I want you to take off those silly clothes.'

His fingers trembled and stumbled. The waiter's uniform was disapproving and awkward. A button sprang off the jacket. A shoelace locked itself in a knot. Sunlight flooded the room, and street-sounds reached him distantly and harmlessly, as if from another world. Luis, trying to step out of his underpants, got his left foot caught and had to hop strenuously to save himself from falling over.

At last he was out of those silly clothes, shivering a little for no reason of temperature, breathing more deeply than necessary. He stood for a moment, toes worrying the carpet, and felt his skin make a million tiny shifts and adjustments to the touch of the air and the pleasure of her gaze.

The sheets were silky, cool as liquid. She was unexpectedly warm, almost glowing, and thrustful. Luis was not very good but that didn't matter because she soon took charge, and she was more than good: she was astonishingly, outstandingly marvellous. She led Luis on a grand tour of her universe: first gliding, then flying, then falling, then climbing; diving, racing, strolling, teetering, shimmering, stalling, flaunting, brawling, storming, pounding, blasting, bounding, surging, soaring and,

22

at last, bursting. It was magnificent but it was not what Luis had imagined it would be like. There were no overwhelming spiritual insights, for instance. He had expected a new vision or two, yet the image which swamped his brain at the end was of himself plunging into a colossal bowl of melting cherry-ice-cream. Still, he was grateful.

'Are you hungry?' she asked.

'Yes.'

'Good.' She stretched that slender, naked arm again and touched the coffee-pot. Not hot. 'Go into the bathroom and get dressed,' she said. 'I shall send for more breakfast.'

They ate together, she propped against a hill of pillows, he sitting on the side of the bed. He watched her all the time, seeking a flicker of animal passion in her delightful face and finding nothing but loveliness. They talked, but it was all about Luis: where he had lived and what he wanted to be. It was easy and utterly enjoyable, a taste of life at a level of luxury and confidence that Luis had never before known.

After half an hour she held out her hand. He stood, feeling adult and serious, and they shook hands. 'Goodbye,' she said.

And that was that. She had not told him her name, nor asked his. He went back to work, gave them some excuse for his absence which they clearly didn't believe, but he didn't care. He knew that he was utterly changed, his whole life was changed; he could think only of her, remembering and reviving every glorious detail. For the rest of that day he went about in a slight daze. The kitchen staff decided that he had fallen down some stairs and concussed himself.

He went home, shut himself in his room and indulged his impatience in an orgy of anticipation, mentally rehearsing their next meeting in every possible mood and manner—witty, intense, casual, noisy, brooding, friendly, dramatic. Each would be a wonderful, incomparable experience. He tried to sketch her and made such a hopeless hash of it that he burned the paper. He studied his face in the mirror, wondering which part she found attractive and testing different expressions for impact. He took a long, hot bath, scrubbing his body until it tingled with purity, and then he examined it in his wardrobe mirror. He suffered a moment of despair when he noticed that his legs were not quite as strong as his stomach and chest; but it passed. He lay on his bed and made glorious plans, while dusk slowly drained all the light from the room and his limbs grew cool as earthenware.

Next morning he was at the hotel early, before the other room-service waiters arrived. This reinforced the concussion theory. As the breakfast orders came in he worked with fearful speed, hastening back to the kitchen in a constant panic in case he missed the call from the suite on the fourth floor. Sweat made his shirt dank and his face sticky. Normally talkative, today he was silent. The kitchen staff watched him uncomfortably: if he wasn't working he was looking for work. It was unnatural. They preferred the old, argumentative, back-chatting Luis.

By nine o'clock no order had come. Luis was in despair. He refused food and straddled a chair in a corner, chewing his nails and watching the telephone. His legs ached from pounding up and down stairs.

9.05. No call.

9.11. The telephone rang. Luis felt all his gloom and misery lift like a theatre curtain, turning the kitchen into a place of colour and light. A businessman on the second floor wanted breakfast. The curtain thudded down.

Luis took the man's tray and was back by 9.20. No other orders had come in. He began to feel slightly lightheaded with uncertainty. The obstinately dumb telephone became a hateful object; the whole kitchen was oppressive, unbearably squalid. The thought of that sun-splashed heaven waiting on the fourth floor made him feel as if he were trapped in a greasy tomb.

Waiting and stillness were impossible any more. He slipped out and began prowling the corridors. His shoulders were hunched, his eyes were strained, his fingers kept up a running battle with his thumbs. For the first time in his life Luis was sick with love, and it had sapped his wits.

His legs carried him upwards, floor by floor; his brain was too swamped with desire to have an independent opinion. Groups of guests walked past him, talking of leisurely, pleasureful things; and when Luis met a curious glance from one young man—snowy blazer draped fashionably about the shoulders—he wanted desperately to explain that he didn't really belong in this silly uniform, that he deserved to be one of *them*, if only . . .

24

The door to the suite on the fourth floor was shut. Luis stared, unblinking, trying to see through the wooden panel and summon the mistress of his delight who lived and breathed so easily on the other side. His stomach muscles kept clenching and relaxing and suddenly clenching again, as they used to do at school just before he went into a boxing-match. He raised an arm to knock, lost his nerve and walked away. *Stupid feeble fumbling braggart!* he shouted silently. *Last night you were spilling over with big plans. Now look at you. Gutless. Brainless. Useless!*

For ten minutes he paced up and down the corridor, thinking up things to say when she opened the door. 'I was afraid you might be feeling unwell, and so . . .' Or: 'It would give me great pleasure to know your name . . .' Or: 'I just came to say thank-you,' plus an irresistible smile which would add: Please . . .

The sound of a door opening made him twitch guiltily. It was the wrong door. Somebody placed a breakfast tray in the corridor and went back inside.

Luis walked over and looked at it. He had no reason to look at a used breakfast tray, God knows he'd seen plenty of them, but by now he was beyond reason. Grapefruit, boiled eggs, rolls, coffee. Rind, shells, crumbs, dregs.

These people had eaten. Why hadn't his goddess eaten? She needed food. How could she give unless she also took? He shook out the napkins, covered up the debris, and lifted the tray. Without actually making up his mind he reached a decision; or maybe a decision reached him. He walked to the suite and knocked quite firmly, one-two-three. His balls ached pleasantly with desire.

The sound of the door handle raised a broad, brash grin to his face. *Flowers*, he thought, *should have brought flowers!* The door swung open and a black-bearded man with a wrestler's chest stared down. He had gangster's eyes and he was wearing only a bath-towel. 'What?' he snapped. Luis wet himself a little.

'Room service, sir,' he said in a voice which cracked. His grin had fallen off and left his face vacant.

The man's black and heavy brows drew together: gunsights searching for a target. Despair descended on Luis like a sudden sickness. He knew at once that the man knew everything: he knew when Luis had been here before and what had happened and why he had come again. The man reached out and Luis flinched, but all he did was lift a napkin, to reveal a gutted half-grapefruit. Inside the suite Luis briefly glimpsed the woman before she moved quickly away. She was still very beautiful but now she looked nervous.

The man took the ruined grapefruit in his fingers and collapsed it. His other hand clasped the back of Luis's head. He rammed the grapefruit into Luis's mouth, prodding the edges home until Luis's lips were stretched and his cheeks were bulging. He dumped the dregs of milk and coffee onto Luis's head and flung the sugar after them. He hooked his fingers around Luis's belt, tugged savagely enough to bend his spine, and dumped a dish of marmalade inside his trousers. Then he placed one enormous bare foot against Luis's quivering stomach and heaved him ten feet backwards until he hit the opposite wall with a mingled crash of body and crockery. The door slammed.

Even then, Luis didn't think of giving up. He pulled out and spat out the tattered grapefruit, found an empty bathroom, cleaned himself up. And the more he thought about it, rinsing shreds of marmalade from his pubic hair, the more he saw that duty now reinforced desire. Obviously this big bastard was a bully and a brute; he kept the poor girl in a state of terror. If Luis could somehow liberate her, he would get his reward in heaven *and* on earth. He didn't believe in heaven, but she might, and now he was doing all this for her.

Having the job was going to be a great advantage. It gave Luis access to the fourth floor at any time, and sooner or later blackbeard would have to let her out. Or else go out himself. That would be the moment for youth and gallantry to strike a blow in the cause of chivalry and true love. Luis dragged on his soaking trousers, combed his sticky hair and took the tray down to the kitchens. He was ready to begin his crusade. Instead, he got fired.

'Cabrillo, damn you, where the hell have you been?' an assistant manager demanded. 'Every time you're wanted you disappear. You're sacked, get out.'

Luis was appalled. 'It wasn't my fault,' he protested. 'I . . . Something went wrong, I had to . . . I had an accident, that's all.'

'So I see,' the assistant manager said glumly. 'Oh God . .
You'd better tell the housekeeper when you hand in your
uniform.'

'Not that sort of—'

'Look, I don't care. I'm fed up, understand? Just clear off.'

'No! You can't do that!' Luis cried. His voice was harsh
and his eyes were leaking tears. If they fired him he would
never see her again: unbearable: like being sent to prison.
'Give me another chance. I'll work for nothing. Please let me
stay. *Please.*'

The assistant manager gave him a profoundly cynical look.
Any room-service waiter who wanted to work for nothing
had to be mixed up in some kind of racket. 'You're out,
Cabrillo,' he said.

Luis fumbled in his pockets. 'Look, I'll give you fifteen
pesetas,' he pleaded. 'Twenty-five, thirty . . .' The grubby
notes trembled in his outstretched hands. 'That's all the
money I have. Just let me—'

'If you're so much in love with this damned place,' the
assistant manager growled, 'book yourself a room.'

Luis did just that.

He turned up an hour later, in his best suit and with all
his savings, and took a cramped and stuffy room on the top
floor. He calculated that he had just enough money to stay
for three nights, provided he spent nothing on food. Hunger
did not worry him: there were always scraps to be scavenged
from trays, and besides, a little starvation would be a good
test of his love.

Nothing rewarding happened on the first day.

The hotel was busy, which allowed Luis to stroll on or near
the fourth floor without looking conspicuous. All the same
it was not possible to keep a constant watch on the suite. He
heard nothing as he loitered near the door. The couple failed
to appear when he was nearby. The long, repetitive hours
drifted past in a daze of resolute plans and erotic fantasies.
Get a revolver, charge in and rescue her . . . Push him down
the stairs and break his legs . . . Sound the fire alarm and
when they got separated in the panic and confusion, gently
steer her into a vacant room and . . .

No, smuggle a note: *Meet me in my room at midnight.*
Pitter-patter; gentle finger-tap; trembling kiss; flimsy gown;

27

silky skin; radiant embrace; liberty, triumph, sunburst! Luis let out a soft groan which was heard by a group of residents on their way down to dinner. He thumped himself on the chest and cleared his throat loudly, but they were not fooled: he looked as lovesick as he sounded. Lovesick and obstinate: it was 2 a.m. before he grudgingly gave up and went to bed.

On the second day nothing happened, except that Luis began staring after, and lusting after, every desirable woman he saw.

On the third day, privation and obsession began to tilt the balance of his mind. He had eaten very little, spoken to nobody, and continuously flogged his brain like an overloaded donkey up his mountain of infatuation. Still he heard nothing from the suite; still the couple did not appear. By mid-afternoon Luis was trembling with tension and anger, but it was boredom and hunger that drove him to action. Abruptly he abandoned his vigil and went down to the tea lounge, a chattering arena of potted palms and beige music. He saw her as soon as he went in.

She was sitting alone, reading a magazine; coffee and cakes stood on a sidetable. Luis did not hesitate, did not even think; he strode over, bowed and said: 'Good afternoon. May I join you?' He felt quite marvellous; exhilarated.

'If it pleases you,' she said lazily, and went back to her magazine.

Luis sat down and studied her. Even more beautiful than he remembered. Ravishing. Overwhelming. His unfed stomach made a noise like a distant lion in a cave.

'My name is Luis,' he said.

She nodded without looking up.

He rested his arms on his knees and wondered what to say next. Why was she behaving so coldly?

'I am staying at the hotel at the moment,' he announced. The lion rumbled again.

Without looking, she offered him the plate of cakes. He took one. 'Have them all,' she said. He took the plate. 'Now let me read my magazine,' she told him.

While Luis ate a cake he began to feel offended. 'We have met before, you know,' he remarked.

She turned a page.

'Inside your suite,' he added.

The magazine slowly sank to her lap, while a finger kept her place. She looked ahead and slightly upwards, over the crowd.

'In those days I wore silly clothes,' he mentioned, helpfully. Her expression did not change. 'Only sometimes I didn't wear them.'

She raised her left index finger as a signal of recognition. 'Yes. From the florists. You delivered flowers.'

'No.'

'The electrician, then.' The finger was still raised. 'You changed a fuse or did something of that sort.'

'No, I—'

'As I recall, the young man from the dry cleaners had a moustache.'

'I was room service,' Luis said sulkily. 'I brought you your damned breakfast.'

She retracted her finger. 'I don't remember. Have another cake.'

'I don't want your damned cake,' snapped Luis. 'I don't suppose it interests you, but the only reason I'm staying here is that I want to save you from that raving gorilla of a husband.' His face was stiff with dedication. A crumb clung to his lower lip.

'Gorillas do not rave,' she said, 'and my husband is in Rio de Janeiro. Wipe your mouth.'

Luis dragged his knuckles across his lips. 'Then who the hell was that?' he demanded.

She looked at him as if he were ten years old and asking for more pocket-money. 'Just a toy,' she said. A waiter strolled by, paused, smiled enquiringly, glanced at Luis, and moved on, elegant as a shark. 'And I suppose *he's* just a toy as well,' Luis said bitterly.

'All men are toys.' She reopened her magazine.

Luis heaved himself to his feet and trudged away. He felt hopelessly weighed down by disappointment and disillusion: everything he had lived for was wasted. His life was in ruins. At the same time the scorch-marks of insult and rejection hurt, they stung, they scarred. She hadn't even given him the status of a *toy*. Blackbeard was a toy. Luis was nothing, *nothing*! He reached the door and turned for a final look. That flaring red hair glowed like the treacherous bloom of a poisonous plant. He marched all the way back and stood staring down.

'The trouble with you,' he told her in a low, thick voice, 'is you can't tell a toy from a man.'

'And the trouble with you,' she replied in a clear, calm voice which several other people could hear, 'is you think a free fuck is as good as an introduction.'

Luis turned brick-red and walked from the room on legs that felt like stilts. He walked out of the hotel, and then he walked out of Valencia too. The whole town was a disaster, a shattering and humiliating disaster. Escape, escape! That was all he could think of.

Four hours of hard, unbroken walking took him deep into the countryside. From time to time he tormented himself by remembering in relentless detail exactly how she had delighted him and destroyed him, until the sunny suburbs blurred and streaked before his eyes and he had to blow his nose. Then at other times it was all remote history, and the day became blank and ordinary. But distressed or composed, he kept on walking, tramping steadily westward until his feet throbbed and his knees ached and the setting sun made him squint into a kaleidoscope of splintered reds and yellows.

The prolonged effort purified him. When he stopped, he felt empty and weary; but whole again.

It was a little village: San Luis de something; a good omen maybe. Church with a busted clock; white cottages; dirt square; fountain with a piddling, plashing jet and a tiny thicket of bamboo growing out of the water. He sat against a wall and uttered a long sigh of relief.

The village was coming to life in the early evening. Kids chased each other to the point of breathlessness; regrouped; plotted; chased each other some more. Orange blossom scented the air. Five black-shawled women sat around a threshold and cracked almond-shells. Their little hammers made a soft stuttering. Somewhere out of sight a donkey manufactured its painful *eeee-aw, eeee-aw*, sounding more like the rusty straining of a village pump than the real thing. Luis fingered the cool, fine dust and watched the sky grow purple, the deep smooth purple of an over-ripe plum. This, he knew, was where he wanted to live. San Luis de whatever-it-was had an easy, comforting atmosphere. Strength was seeping back into his limbs. Yes, this was the place to be. Luis gradually realised that he had left home. Good. He had grown up at last.

A man strolled over and looked down at him. The man was a strong, middleaged peasant: clumping boots, blue overalls, beret, a face as work-worn as old harness.

'Why are you sitting here?' he asked. There was no threat, only curiosity.

'Because I am tired,' Luis replied.

'Your fine clothes will get dirty.'

'True.' His best suit made Luis conspicuous. 'I don't care,' he said.

'Are you from the police?'

Luis started. 'Certainly not.' He was half-flattered, half-alarmed.

'The secret police, then?'

'No, no.' Luis glanced up nervously at the man's powerful silhouette.

'Then why have you come to our village?'

Luis quickly considered four or five dishonest explanations and fell back on the truth. 'To escape a woman,' he announced with dignity and feeling.

The peasant laughed and helped Luis to his feet. 'That's a good reason, a very good reason. Come and have a drink.' Halfway across the square he paused. 'If you had been from the secret police I would have beaten your brains out,' he said.

'If I had been from the secret police I would have had no need of brains,' Luis replied. The peasant laughed all the way to the bar. That night Luis got monumentally and ecstatically drunk.

He stayed five days in the village. They were wonderful days. He had enough money to buy meals for himself and wine for anyone—money he owed for his hotel room—and he slept in the nearest heap of straw. By day there was always someone to talk to, some gentle job to help with: picking oranges, gutting fish, plucking chickens, collecting eggs. By night there was wine and food and more wine. He became unwashed, unbrushed, unworried, unhurried. Fifty or sixty villagers were his friends. He belonged there, like the piddling fountain and the rusty donkey and the church with the busted clock. Until his money ran out.

There was no question of living off his new friends; he knew how poor they were. The alternative was work. But work meant getting up at dawn and doing somebody else's drudgery all damn day. Picking oranges for an hour was amusing. Picking oranges for a living would be deadening.

Luis gave it some thought, and next morning he said good-bye and set out westwards, away from Valencia. He walked steadily for an hour. His tongue began to feel dry, and his belly grumbled for food. He wanted a bath. His underwear itched. He felt lonely for someone to talk to. The world seemed huge, and hugely empty. A bus hurried towards him, destination Valencia, and roared past. He stood and watched it diminish in a cloud of dust and diesel fumes, until it twitched over a short bridge and was lost to sight. Now the countryside seemed even huger and emptier. A butterfly ambled down the road, also heading for Valencia. Luis gave in and followed it.

It was seven in the evening when he slipped through the back door. His mother was busy playing the piano—Beethoven, for a change—and there was no sign of his father. Luis went quietly upstairs and took a long hot bath. An hour later he came out smelling of half-a-dozen urban oils and unguents. The sheer luxury of fresh, crisp clothing made him smile at his reflection. He looked older, he decided. Older and stronger.

On his way downstairs he met his mother, coming up. She had a headache: he could tell by the way she pressed a handkerchief to her forehead. 'We must get a better piano,' she said, not stopping. 'I simply cannot go on playing that thing, it's intolerable.'

Luis watched her limp up the stairs. 'Where's father?' he called.

'Working late, I expect.' She went into her room.

They had not missed him.

Later, Luis realised that this was not so very surprising: his life and theirs had ceased to touch at many points. If they failed to see him at breakfast or at night, they assumed he was working strange new hours at some strange new job. He had not sought out their company when he was briefly at home, so why should he expect them to seek out his? In a way perhaps it was flattering, perhaps it showed that they trusted him. Nevertheless he felt unexpectedly saddened. Of course he wanted complete freedom, but did it have to come so fast? Why could he not have a choice? Or a fight, even? He felt like going to his parents and saying *Look I know I took my independence but that doesn't mean you had to give it to me, does it? Anyway I'm not sure I'm ready to be a damned adult. I'm not sure I even like the idea* . . .

But it was too late now to begin that sort of discussion.

His experiences at the hotel had taught Luis that it was possible to get more out of a job than just money. He did three months as a van-boy for a delivery company: boring work, jumping in and out of a truck all day and getting nipped by dogs twice a week and being raped by lovely lonely housewives never. After hours he hung around and helped the mechanics service the vehicles. That was the extra reward. In six weeks he knew how a truck engine worked and what to check if it didn't. In two months he could drive around the parking area, slowly.

Then, in the summer of 1935, with their usual unsurprising suddenness, Spanish Railways transferred Señor Cabrillo to Granada. Valencia was glad of it and Luis was not sorry. There was little more for him to learn about the racketing guts of a delivery truck, and in Valencia the danger always existed that he might turn a corner and meet the demon redhead and her toy gorilla.

In Granada he talked a small garage into hiring him, and quickly mastered the basic secrets of Ford and Citroen and Fiat. On the strength of that he moved up to a bigger garage which specialised in Alfas and Mercedes. After six months there, he borrowed a sober hat and dark glasses, lied about his age, and got a driving licence. A week later he was a taxi-driver, specialising in English and American tourists.

Thus Luis Cabrillo: now seventeen and a half years old, taller than average, not unattractive, with no visible scars but plenty of invisible ones, mis-educated, self-taught, physically fit, few family ties, restless for change, impatient with authority, hungry for excitement, and eager to achieve . . . well, something, God-knew-what, anything, as long as it won him admiration, popularity and fame. Also money. Driving a taxi was better than draining sump-oil into an inspection pit, but it did not exercise his imagination, enthusiasm and courage which (he felt) were limitless. Above all he wanted to test his courage. He was afraid that perhaps courage decayed, like muscle, unless it got used. Sadly he saw precious little prospect of excitement and adventure in Granada, or anywhere else in Spain. He was thinking moodily of becoming a racing driver, or a diamond prospector in South America, or a deckhand on a whaler; when overnight the Civil War broke out and saved him.

Chapter 5

The car raced down the hill and slithered into the village square, its wheels carving out brown wings of water, and coasted to a halt. Luis Cabrillo played a cheerful tattoo on the horn. 'Home of the heroes of Jarama!' he announced. 'A great Government victory! For you, this is big news.'

In the back, three newspaper correspondents peered through the rain at the broken buildings. A mongrel dog came to a doorway, looked once at the car, and went back inside.

'You mean the dog?' asked Milton Townsend of the *Chicago Daily News*. 'I never interview a dog unless he comes from Illinois. Either that or he's a wounded machine-gunner.'

'Or, ideally, both,' said Nicholas Barker, London *News Chronicle*.

'For both, the dog gets his picture taken too.' The American wiped mist from the window. 'My God,' he muttered. 'I've seen some picturesque enchanting fairytale Castilian villages in my time, but this is one hell of a dump. No bar even.'

'I told you war was hell,' said Barker.

'Listen, let's go back to Madrid. Luis, drive us back to Madrid.'

'Big story,' Luis said enthusiastically. 'Heroes of Jarama. In the church.'

'Heroes of Jarama,' Townsend grumbled. 'How can you have heroes without a victory? What kind of a big story is that?'

The third journalist was a French-Canadian freelance named Jean-Pierre Dru. 'Let's go look in the goddam church,' he said. 'I need some heroes and there may be booze, too.'

They ran through the rain and shouldered open the creaking, iron-studded doors. The air inside was warm. The church was half-full of soldiers, sprawling on the floor or sitting against the walls. They seemed relaxed and happy. A fire shimmered on the chancel steps, wavering from soft red to light purple to gold as the draught from a shattered window played on it. There was no smoke: it had been good, hard wood from the broken pulpit which lay nearby. Except for the massive baptismal font, every other sign of religion had been destroyed or defaced long ago. An officer—the only man whose cap and trousers matched his tunic—stood on the font. He was making a speech.

'. . . and this valiant attack,' he said as the journalists and Luis came in, 'was also preceded by a long and powerful artillery bombardment.'

The men cheered, drowning his flat, insistent voice. His face remained expressionless.

'Latest reports confirm,' he went on, 'that the entire rebel fascist forces are in retreat at all points along the Andalusian front.'

Cheers again.

'The situation in Madrid is extremely good. Fresh reinforcements of tanks, planes and artillery are arriving daily.'

More cheers.

'Everywhere in Spain the illegal and anti-democratic forces of repression are bleeding to death on the bayonets of our courageous and freedom-loving fellow-workers . . .'

Prolonged, excited and deafening cheering. The soldiers lay on their backs and roared approval. They hammered their mess-tins against the flagstones. They hooked their fingers in their mouths and whistled until their eyes bulged.

The officer stood on the font and waited. Despite the uproar he was still boot-faced. He opened his mouth. The racket immediately redoubled. After a few moments he climbed down. At once the cheering subsided like a collapsing marquee. Within seconds it was just a gentle rumble of conversation. Soldiers began standing and stretching and walking about.

The visitors came forward and introduced themselves. The officer said he was Harry Summers, political commissar for the 2nd English Battalion of the 15th International Brigade.

'Battalion?' said Jean-Pierre Dru. 'This is a *battalion*?' There were fewer than two hundred men in the church.

'Jarama was a severe test,' Summers said.

'Is that why they pulled you out of the line?' Townsend asked. 'Because you took such a beating?'

'On the contrary. The battalion is being re-equipped and brought up to strength. As you must have noticed, morale is excellent.'

Nicholas Barker said: 'Is it all right if we ask your chaps some questions?'

Summers hesitated. 'I can tell you everything you wish to know.'

'Tell us what it feels like to get hit by a bullet,' Dru said, looking at a man whose arm was bandaged.

'That's not . . .' Summers began; then he changed his mind. 'You must remember they are still feeling the effects of the fighting. Very intensive fighting.'

'Okay,' Dru said.

Summers led them over to the wounded soldier. Luis edged his way to the front. He wished very much to learn what it felt like to get hit by a bullet.

The man was sitting on the floor and examining his left foot, which was bare and black with dirt. It was so uniformly black that to Luis it looked like a negro foot, poking out of the ragged brown-corduroy trouser leg.

'What did you do at Jarama?' Dru asked.

The man got to his feet, stood lopsidedly, and gave the clenched-fist salute. He was about twenty-five, short and skinny, and he smiled cheerfully at everyone. 'No two ways about it,' he said.

'His name is Davis,' Summers told them. 'From Liverpool.'

'What do you remember about Jarama?' Nicholas Barker asked.

'Solidarity, comrades.' Davis saluted with the clenched fist again and gave a little, delighted laugh. Luis noticed that his head kept twitching, as if with eagerness.

'We heard you were very heavily outnumbered,' Barker told him. 'So where did the enemy go wrong?'

'They certainly did!' Davis exclaimed. He rested his left foot against his right leg and began to fall over. Luis grabbed him. 'See?' Davis said. 'Sol'dar'ty! See what I mean?'

36

Townsend came back, stuffing his notebook into his pocket. 'All pissed,' he announced.

'Oh Christ,' Dru groaned.

'You really mean all?' Barker asked.

'Every damn one, my friend. Tanked up and ready to fly to the moon. Pissed as assholes, the whole battalion.'

'Not really drunk,' Summers put in quickly. 'Just reaction after battle . . .' Nobody was listening. Luis saw the discontented faces and realised there was no story here. Davis laid his head on Luis's shoulder. His body jerked to a gentle belch, and Luis breathed the hot and fruity fumes of cheap red wine. 'We're gonna win,' Davis whispered. 'Gonna win 'cus we're right. Right?' Luis lowered him gently to the floor.

As they drove back to Madrid the correspondents argued about Jarama. Townsend argued that it must have been a victory for the Government because Franco's forces had failed to knock the International Brigade off the heights. Dru argued that any unit which lost two-thirds of its men was beaten, and it didn't matter a damn who held the heights anyway. Barker suggested that maybe Jarama might not turn out to be a victory for either side, but the others flatly rejected that. 'My paper wants a victory,' Townsend insisted. 'They didn't send me four thousand miles to report a lousy draw.' Luis listened, and learned.

Chapter 6

Two days later the weather cleared, the sun came out, and the correspondents told him to drive them to Jarama.

The countryside was calm and pleasant, with gentle hills and wide views. There was no sign of war. Men and women working in the fields paused, half-bent, to watch the car dash by. Mule-carts and donkeys made up most of the traffic, and left a tang of fresh dung in the morning air. Luis felt good. He drove briskly, spinning the wheel and accelerating out of corners so that his tyres sprayed gravel against the drystone walls,

Brigade headquarters was in a farmhouse at the end of a rutted lane. Two ambulances and a dozen motorcycles were parked in the farmyard, which also contained a group of soldiers washing their clothes at a cattle trough, a small boy plucking a chicken, and the wreckage of an aeroplane.

'Jarama,' Luis announced.

'Horrifying,' said Townsend, picking his way between the puddles and the cowdung. 'Inconceivably dreadful. Look: dead chickens everywhere. My God, will this bloody war never end?'

'Inside they can tell us,' Luis told him.

'That I take leave to doubt,' Barker said. Luis looked at him uncertainly, but Barker did not seem displeased, and so Luis went over to the sentry on duty at the farmhouse door.

'*Correspondentes*,' he announced. '*Muy importantes correspondentes*.'

The man stopped trimming his fingernails with a clasp-knife and looked the visitors over. He had thick black stubble and bad teeth. He gave a grunt which could have meant anything.

'Show him identification,' Luis suggested. 'Anything, it does not matter. This is just an ignorant peasant.'

'Not true,' the sentry said. 'Ignorant, yes. Peasant, no. Beneath this dirty shirt there beats an indelibly bourgeois heart, I'm sorry to say.' He put the knife away. 'I know you,' he said to Barker. 'We were at school together. Templeton.'

'Were we?' Barker tried to stare beyond the stubble and the grime. 'Wait a minute. You're not Charles Templeton? The cricketer?'

'None other.'

'Good God.'

'Ah, now there I can't agree with you.' Templeton gave a rueful grin. His teeth were not bad; just dirty.

'Listen: can you let us in?' Townsend asked. 'We want to find out what's happening in this damn war.'

'Well, you won't learn anything here,' Templeton said. 'They're holding a brigade conference. It's like the Chelsea Arts Ball gone wrong. Still, you can go in if you like.'

He led them into the farmhouse. 'Weren't you an artist? A painter?' Barker asked.

'I still am an artist,' Templeton said with conviction. 'But

38

here in Spain I can fight for truth as well as paint it. Mind your head.' He opened a door and they ducked into a long, dim room in which forty or fifty soldiers were engaged in half a dozen arguments.

The correspondents stood against the wall while their eyes and ears adjusted to the gloomy uproar. They could see a whole theatrical wardrobe of uniforms, ranging from khaki overalls to black flying jackets, and from red cavalry cloaks to blue tunics. They could hear most of the languages of Europe. Everyone seemed to be talking, no one seemed to be listening. They all had two things in common: fervour and sidearms. Every man present was wearing a large automatic or a revolver on his gunbelt.

'This is a conference?' said Barker. 'It sounds more like a difference.'

'Oh well, everybody is free to give his point of view, in the International Brigade,' Templeton said. 'We are, after all, fighting for democracy.'

'What happens when they don't agree?' Townsend asked.

'It depends. Sometimes the Brigade commander orders lunch. Sometimes the enemy attacks. Something always happens.'

'Doesn't sound very organised.'

Luis felt that the conversation was lacking spark. 'Sir, how many fascists have you killed?' he inquired.

'Oh, hundreds. Hundreds and hundreds and hundreds. Perhaps as many as three. Of course, some may have been dead already.'

Luis flushed. He thought that Templeton was mocking him. 'Perhaps it is so easy to kill fascists that you cannot remember?' he said.

'I can remember killing,' Templeton said, looking openly and easily into Luis's stiff face, 'but thank God I can't remember counting while I did it.'

Barker's pencil skidded wildly off his notebook as the door swung open and banged his arm. A tall and very fat man with angry eyes and a shaggy, mistrustful moustache strode into the room, picked up a stool and hammered it thunderously against a table-top. He wore tunic and trousers of workingmen's blue, with a giant pistol tugging down his belt, a flaring red kerchief, and an absurdly large black beret, so big that it fell over one ear, almost to the collar. Even before his table-battering had created silence, he was shouting. The language was French, but the style was universal. The fat man was hysterical with rage. His jowls wobbled, his nostrils flared, his voice and his gestures ripped the air.

This hulking, howling harangue went on for several minutes, while the atmosphere grew unhappier. Townsend nudged Dru and Barker. They backed out, Templeton following, and shut the door.

'André Marty,' Dru said. 'Three hundred pounds of mouth. The moustache is camouflage. Low-flying aircraft mistake him for a horse's ass, and fly on.'

'Marty the Commissar?' Townsend asked. Next door, the ranting seemed to have gained in fury. 'I understood he *was* a horse's ass.'

'You didn't see anyone in there laughing. Marty is Chief Political Commissar of the International Brigades. You want my advice? Don't mess around with that particular horse's ass or he's liable to dump a load of horse's poo-poo all over you.'

'He sounds a bit mad,' Barker said.

'Oh, he's crackers,' Templeton told them.

'What was he raving about?' Townsend asked Dru.

'Treason. Traitors in the ranks. The revolution betrayed. Firing squads. Summary executions. All Trotskyite spies will be purged.'

'He's always on about that,' Templeton said. 'Never stops.'

Luis had been standing with his head bowed, looking very serious. Now he addressed Templeton.

'Sir, I offer my apology for what I said to you earlier. It was bad manners.'

'Oh, that's all right, chum.' Templeton was scratching his armpits, hard. 'Sorry, everybody. I'm afraid I'm a bit lousy.'

Luis was not ready to allow lice to distract him from his views on war. 'It is bad courtesy to criticise a soldier when one has not experienced the truth of war for oneself,' he declared.

'Please don't worry about it.' Templeton slapped his trousers. 'Sometimes violence seems to stun them, and other times it just wakes them up. One never knows what to do for the best.'

For a moment everyone stood around in slight embarrassment, listening to the strident bellow of the brigade conference.

'Well, we're not going to get anywhere here, are we?' Barker said. 'Why don't we trundle off and take a squint at the Front?'

'Show you the way, if you like,' Templeton offered.

As they walked up the hill, Milton Townsend took Luis aside. 'Listen, Luis,' he said. 'The stories I've been getting from Republican Army Headquarters are no damn good to me. Frankly, it's all bullshit propaganda. Now what I need, see, is a nice, simple, gung-ho bit of action. Keep your ears open, okay?'

'Okay.'

'I mean, this is war. Right? So there's got to be a chance for glory *some*where, you know what I mean? Some guy has got to save his wounded buddies, or capture a strongpoint singlehanded, or shoot down three fighter planes with four bullets, or *some*thing. I mean it *happens*, for Chrissake. We've just got to find it, that's all.'

'Sometimes these damned heroes get themselves killed, that is the difficulty,' Luis remarked.

'That doesn't necessarily matter. We just have to find a good witness. This fight for democracy and freedom and all that crap is fine, terrific, but we need action. You go to the movies? You like westerns?'

'Sure! Gary Cooper, Lone Ranger—'

'Okay, you got it. Find me the Lone Ranger of the International Brigade. Dead or alive.'

They found the Front a mile and a half up the track, in trenches dug just short of the crest; and defending this stretch of the Front they found the 2nd English Battalion, now sober, dirty and glum.

Harry Summers came out to meet them. 'I take it you've got permission from Brigade H.Q. to be up here?' he asked.

'We just left there,' Dru said. 'Your lot didn't get much of a break, did they?'

'The men are quite refreshed. They voted to return, as a matter of fact, as soon as they heard we were preparing for a counter-attack.'

Townsend said: 'Preparing to make one or to meet one?'

'The former.'

'Terrific! Maybe you can show us the target?'

Summers took out a very used handkerchief. The fabric crackled as he pulled it unstuck. 'We fight for Spain,' he said. 'For the loyal, free and democratic republic. It is the fascist rebels who are seeking to capture targets. We fight for freedom, not for property.' He blew his nose.

There was a short silence. Luis looked uncertainly at Townsend, who rolled his eyes at him. 'Sir,' Luis said to Summers, 'where is the bloody enemy?' Everyone brightened up. Summers turned and led them forward.

The trenches were crumbling and filthy. Bits of food, rusting tins, broken rifles and stained clothing lay everywhere, and now that the sun was high the flies were loud: the trenches had been used as a latrine as well as a dustbin. The men of the 2nd Battalion were hard at work, cleaning out the mess and strengthening the walls; they pressed themselves against the mud to let the visitors pass; they looked tired and sad, and they said little. Dru caught one man's eye, and smiled. 'It's not the Ritz, is it?' he said.

'Soddin' French did this,' the man said. 'Bleedin' spotless, we left this place.'

They turned into a communication trench which led forward to an observation post: a walled pit with sandbagged slots looking down the steep and bare hillside to a flat valley, almost a thousand feet below. 'Down there you see the Jarama River,' Summers said, 'and beyond the Jarama you see the enemy.'

The soldier on duty stood back to make room for them at the slots. There was no difficulty in seeing the enemy, only in counting them. There were hundreds of troops, probably thousands, with cavalry and horse-drawn artillery in separate encampments. Their many small sounds travelled clearly up the windless air: a motorcycle's buzz, a man singing, the tiny clang of a hammer on steel, the nervous whinny of a horse. Smoke climbed from a dozen fires like softly unravelling wool.

'Who's in command down there?' Dru asked. 'Still General Mola?'

'Mola is the henchman of the fascist rebel Franco,' Summers said, Dru took this to be confirmation.

'How on earth did you manage to hold them off?' Barker

asked. 'I mean, Mola's got a fully equipped professional army. Your chaps are just . . . well . . . volunteers.'

'Exactly. Every man in the International Brigade is fighting for a cause. The fascist mercenaries are merely fighting for pay. Another thing is our superior position. We forced the enemy to attack uphill, with no cover. But above all we succeeded because of our international solidarity. The English battalion fought alongside the Balkan battalion, the Franco-Belge battalion, the Lincoln battalion. Jarama was a political as much as a military victory.'

'I see what you mean about the hill,' Barker said. 'Damn steep.'

'Don't look out so far.' Barker jerked his head back. 'There are snipers in a farmhouse, halfway down the slope,' Summers warned.

'Are there really?' Barker said.

With a sharp and savage bang a sandbag erupted, and dirt sprayed everywhere. The visitors drew back, startled rather than frightened, for the sandbag itself had seemed to explode, without cause. It formed part of the slit where Barker had been looking out. 'I didn't do that,' he said stupidly.

Summers allowed himself a brief, bleak smile. 'No, that was an enemy bullet. They go off with a loud bang when they hit.'

Townsend looked interested. 'I thought explosive bullets were outlawed,' he said.

Summers merely glanced at him. 'Now I think you have seen everything. There is probably lunch waiting for you at Brigade H.Q.'

As they filed out, the American lingered to examine the shattered sandbag. He scorched his fingers on a fragment of bullet, and cursed himself softly: 'Damn idiot.'

'You are, if you believe all that codswallop,' the soldier said. He was squatting in a corner, eyes half-shut, arms resting on knees, hands dangling.

'Is that so?' Townsend sucked his fingers and looked more closely. 'Wait a minute . . . You're the guy we talked to in the church, right? David . . .'

'Davis.'

'Well, I was close. Anyway, you've changed somewhat since then. What hit you? A Pontiac or a Plymouth?'

Davis raised his face. One eye was a shiny red, half-hidden by swollen flesh as black and puffy as an old mushroom. There were cuts and scrapes all over his forehead and jawline. His upper lip was lopsidedly bloated, and his nose looked crooked. 'There's a war on,' he said. 'Haven't you seen a casualty before?'

'You didn't get that collection from General Mola.'

'No.' Davis took an empty sandbag and began scraping dirt into it, using an old saucepan as a shovel. 'No, I didn't. When we came back here I found a Frenchman with his trousers down, right where I made my dug-out. Talk about smell! They eat snails, you know.'

'So I hear.'

'It's true, I seen 'em do it. So I smashed his face in and his friends didn't like it. We got quite lively for a while. That's how I came to be out here. Bloody old Summers's doing.'

'Solitary confinement?' Townsend suggested.

'That and a bit more. He wants them to drop a shell on me, shut me up for good.' Davis dumped the sandbag on its base, packing the dirt down hard. 'My Jarama doesn't tally with his Party Line fairy tales.'

Townsend had his notebook open. 'Tell me about your Jarama.'

Davis gave it some thought while he scraped up more dirt with his saucepan. 'Ready?' he asked. 'Bloody shambles. Got that?'

'Yes.'

'Well, that's what it was. Bloody shambles from start to finish.' Davis spat into the sandbag and closed its neck. His fingers were shaking as they tried to unknot a piece of string.

'How did it start?' Townsend asked gently.

'It started . . .' Davis sniffed, and blinked, and a tremendous weariness seemed to come over him. He stared, frowning at the muddle of footprints in the dusty dirt. 'It started without any breakfast,' he said. 'Imagine that. We'd spent all day in the train and all night in the truck, and it was cold, I'm telling you. You don't know what it's like to be cold till you've been tired out and starving at the same time. The cold soaks right into your guts, and your guts are empty, and you get to the state where your hand hasn't the strength to pick up a piece of bread.'

44

'This was when they brought your Battalion up to the Front,' Townsend said.

'Certainly!' Davis relaxed his hands, and began picking at the hard knots again. 'And about time too, or so we thought. First-class, fully trained, crack fighting men, we were. All in uniform made out of high-grade cheesecloth. Nothing fits, but that's democracy, isn't it? The main thing is, we're fully trained, we know exactly what to do.' He chewed on a knot and looked sideways at Townsend.

'What did they train you to do?'

'Attack,' Davis said. He walked his fingers down his thighs. 'Advance and defeat the enemy.'

'How?'

'Fire the rifle at him. We knew all about the rifle, we'd all fired it, once, on the range. Five rounds. Crack bloody marksmen, we were. Irresistible.'

'But what if the enemy resisted?'

'Then we threw the grenade at him, and he ran away, and we won. We were on the right side, see? We just had to attack and he would run away.' Davis beamed at Townsend, his bruised face distorting under the strain.

'Ahah! Señor Townsend!' Luis cried, bounding down the trench. 'The others sent me to—'

'Sure, sure. Sit down and shut up.'

'But they want—'

'The hell with them. You never found me. Okay, Davis, so you got here and no breakfast. This was what time? Dawn?'

Luis looked from Townsend's notebook to Davis's crooked grin, and suddenly realised: the American had found his Lone Ranger. He sat down and listened.

'It was daylight,' Davis said. 'There was some sort of food, bread, coffee, I don't know what, nobody could stay awake to eat. We all just got out of the trucks and fell asleep. Must've looked like a massacre: bodies everywhere.'

'What about the fighting?' Townsend asked him. 'Was there any fighting going on?'

Davis shook his head. 'That came later. They let us sleep for a couple of hours and then woke us up. Time to attack. The funny thing is, we all felt good. Couple of hours sleep, nice sunny morning, birds singing, and here was our chance to win the war. So, up the hill we went.'

Luis listened carefully. He deeply regretted his earlier criticism of Templeton. Then, he had spoken out of impatience and ignorance. Now was his chance to learn the truth about the gallantry of action, from this battle-scarred yet good-humoured veteran.

Townsend wanted to know how many went up the hill.

'The whole damn battalion, about six hundred. You could hear the bullets fizzing overhead as you got to the top of the hill. Everyone was grinning, we were all excited. Now and then we heard things going off bang, guns firing or shells landing, we didn't know and we didn't care. We just wanted to attack. We knew exactly what was going to happen. The enemy was going to run like hell.'

Luis felt his blood pulse faster, and his thigh muscles were tense with excitement.

Townsend flipped a page. 'What about support? Where was your covering fire?'

'All arranged.' Davis pulled the string through his mouth to straighten the kinks. 'Brigade HQ was sending tanks and artillery and bombers. French artillery, Russian tanks, Spanish planes. Solidarity, see? The people versus the fascists. We couldn't go wrong, could we?'

'Okay,' Townsend murmured. He was wondering if Davis would get into action before that bastard Summers came back. 'Okay. What next?'

'We charged.' Davis leaned back and rested on his elbows.

'You charged.'

'We charged and we charged and we charged, not very fast because most of us weren't very fit, and the ground was a bit rough. Also we hadn't had much sleep and no breakfast. If you want the truth, we charged bloody slowly. More of a limp, if you know what I mean.' Davis hooked the string behind his head and glanced seriously at the American. Luis moved to where he could watch the soldier better.

Townsend looked at his notes, looked at Davis, looked at his thumb. 'And where was the enemy meanwhile?' he asked.

'Meanwhile,' Davis said with a sudden, lunatic smile, 'meanwhile the enemy was lying doggo halfway down the hill and shooting his funny bullets at us with complete disregard for expense.'

'Which means you lost a few men.'

'We lost about two hundred.'

'What happened to your covering fire?'

'Never came.'

'So then you withdrew?'

'Some did. Most of us found a little rock to hide behind. Then they started dropping shells on us, mortar bombs, Christ knows what. And every time we twitched, some bastard had a go at us with his funny bullets. Later on, it got hot, blinding baking hot. A thing I've learnt,' Davis said to Luis, 'is you get twice as thirsty four times as fast when you're under fire. Promise me you'll never go into battle without a full water-bottle.'

'Certainly,' Luis said, nodding hard.

'None of us had water.' Davis turned back to Townsend. 'They hadn't given us canteens, see. There were a lot of wounded out there, too, all wanting water. Another thing I've learnt,' he said to Luis, 'is don't get yourself wounded on a hot hill. Much better to be shot dead and have done with it.' Luis nodded again. 'I think they all died in the end,' Davis said. 'They all shut up, anyway.'

'What happened to you?' Townsend asked.

'I got back at night.' Davis stood up and began piercing holes in the top of the sandbag. 'Next day we attacked again and another two hundred got killed and that was just about the end of the battalion.'

'Two-thirds killed in twenty-four hours,' Townsend said. Luis began to worry. Maybe this was not such a good story. Now Davis was poking the string through the holes and blinking a lot; whether from tears or from the effort of focusing Luis could not be sure.

Townsend went over to an observation slit and glanced out. 'I don't understand why you didn't just plaster this hillside with bullets,' he said. 'Hell, you had height and—'

'Didn't I tell you about the rifles?' Davis cried. 'Our famous Russian rifles! They were not really meant to fire bullets, and they all broke. One thing I've learnt—' He turned to Luis, but Townsend got in first: 'But you had grenades, you said.'

'Did I? I wonder.' Davis closed the neck of the sack and knotted the string. 'I really wonder. Can you call this a grenade?' He took a short length of steel pipe from his tunic pocket. 'There's half a stick of gelignite in there. See the fuse? Now, watch this. As the enemy rushes towards me I light the fuse, so.' He patted his pockets until he found a flint-and-steel lighter, the no-petrol kind used by Spanish shepherds. It consisted of a steel wheel, a flint, and a length of yellow tinder-cord. Davis thumbed the wheel doggedly. Sparks flew and died. 'Never mind,' he said, 'the fuse is probably too wet, anyway.' He gave the grenade to Luis. Luis weighed the weapon in his palm. It felt smoothly sinister.

'Rifles and grenades,' Townsend said. 'That was all they gave you? No mortars, no machine-guns?'

Davis heaved the sandbag over to the damaged slot and sat on it. 'We each had a shosser,' he said.

'Shosser?' Townsend repeated. 'Is that a make, or a nickname, or what?'

'It's French,' Davis said. 'It must be a very dirty French word. The French invented it, anyway.'

'What does it do?' Townsend was happier; even if Summers came back now, the gist of the story was down on paper. 'Is it automatic?'

'Completely automatic. Fires two rounds and automatically jams.'

Luis studied the way Townsend and Davis were looking at each other: the American serious and questioning, the Englishman slouched, sombre, dull with anger. Luis sensed a violence that was beyond warfare, a despair beyond death, and it made him uncomfortable. He wished to help, if only he knew how.

Townsend asked: 'Didn't you know about the jamming?'

'None of us had fired the shosser before we made that attack. Not many of us fired the bloody silly thing after it, either.'

'Sounds like someone made a sweet little deal . . . I'd like to see one of your shossers.'

'Help yourself.' Davis waved an arm. 'They're all out there.'

'Ah.' Townsend put his notebook away. 'In that case I guess it's time for lunch. Can I get you any—'

'Sir, please!' Luis interrupted. 'You wish to have this weapon?'

Townsend shrugged. 'Sure. Maybe there's a name on it, something to identify . . . You know where you can lay your hands on one?'

Luis dodged past him, put one foot in the observation slit, and heaved himself onto the rim of the pit. Townsend shouted and Davis grabbed, but Luis jumped onto the hillside and began running. The slope seemed vaster and far steeper now that he was a part of it; he had a jumbled impression of rocks and scrub plunging to a distant, hazy flatness where a river gleamed, everything about him seeming huge and hanging high after the snugness of the observation post.

Then the bullets came.

He was dodging from rock to rock, and the harsh and startling *crack! crack!* from behind made him think that Davis was firing. At *him?* Luis stopped, looked back. Immediately the rocks in front detonated a string of blasts. Luis saw the stony splinters fly, and remembered the explosive bullets. He fell flat, and a steely whine raced overhead and made a crisp bang higher up the hillside.

The ground felt awkward and unhelpful, poking into his ribs and thighs and twisting one foot against the wishes of its ankle. A tangy fragrance reached his nose from a shrub crushed by his fall. Luis elbowed himself towards a larger rock. The shrub slowly swung upright and shivered to a tunnelling bullet which blew up far behind him.

The rock sheltered Luis as long as he lay flat and kept still. 'You didn't have to do that, son,' came Davis's voice. 'I'd have washed my feet, if only you'd asked nicely.'

'Where is a shosser?' Luis shouted. 'I cannot see any damned shossers.' As he squinted around him, he realised that he would not recognise a shosser even if he saw one.

'Are you crazy?' Townsend called. Under stress, his accent twanged like a big bow. 'Forget the sonofabitching shosser! Get your ass the hell back in here!'

Some ants were crawling up Luis's right leg. He half-raised it to knock them off and instantly attracted another bullet.

'Don't for Chrissake move!' Townsend shouted.

'One thing I've learnt. . .' Davis began conversationally.

Luis rolled onto his back and gazed in wonder at the sky. *I have been under fire,* he thought, *and I have not disgraced myself!* He beat his heel on the ground to dislodge the ants, failed, and decided to tolerate them; he and they had much in common, exposed to sudden death in strange surroundings.

'Listen, Luis!' It was Townsend again. 'Stay put, you hear

me? Wait there till dark. You got that?'

'Sure, sure,' Luis murmured. Lie behind a rock for eight, nine hours? Absurd. Who would drive the correspondents back to Madrid? Townsend was still shouting instructions. 'Yes, yes, okay,' Luis answered irritably. There was a moment of silence, during which Luis admired a hawk, poised high above the crest of the hill, balanced on the rising air currents, searching for prey: another war within a war.

Thirty yards from him, urgent voices were being raised, overlapping and blurred. The hawk sideslipped away. Luis rolled onto his front. He was bored with this stupid hillside which kept sticking into him. He shifted his hips to avoid a hard lump and discovered that it was in fact inside his pocket. It was Davis's steel-pipe grenade.

'Magnificent,' he whispered. 'Utterly and outstandingly magnificent.'

The dull grey tube was about the size and shape of a kitchen candle. He twirled the wick and sniffed the other end. He had a box of matches. He struck three together. Flames spat and soared and he held the wick in their fire until it glowed gold. Gripped gently by the fingertips and poised in front of his face, the grenade seemed innocent and friendly, its wick hissing softly as the fibres were consumed.

Luis rose on one elbow, lobbed the grenade and flattened his face in the dirt. It fell halfway to the observation post, slightly downhill. He braced his arms and legs. An ant, pushing on above the knee, explored his inside thigh. The explosion was immense: a crack like a lightning-strike, a crash like trains colliding. The ground quivered, and the noise pounded over him like a big sea. Then his hands forced him up and his feet thrust against the broken stone and slippery heather, and he was running into a mist of smoke and dirt.

The funny bullets sang as they searched for him, erupting in a harmless crackle, far uphill. Then he was out in the sunshine again. Bullets whined and droned, whined and buzzed. He dodged sudden bits of litter: a bayonet, a knapsack, a broken weapon . . . His feet were too slow for his brain: they skidded as he turned to grab that weapon and he nearly fell. The post was ten feet away. He threw the weapon into it, forced his legs into a last, lurching dash, and flung himself over the wall. The place was crammed with people and he landed on half of them.

Summers was there, bleeding slightly from the head where the broken weapon had hit him. Barker and Dru were there. Townsend and Davis were still there, and they had been joined by three or four officers. The whole packed assembly had been shouting at each other when Luis fell from the sky and briefly silenced them. Summers was one of the men he felled, and Summers was already angry at having been struck on the head. By the time he struggled to his feet he was shaking with fury. 'What the hell are you doing?' He kicked Luis. 'How dare you?'

Townsend dragged Summers away. 'Cut that out, you maniac,' he growled.

'I'll have you shot.' Summers' face was white with loathing. 'I'll have you both shot.'

'What with?' Davis mocked. He held up the broken weapon which Luis had found. 'This junk?'

'Shosser?' Luis panted eagerly.

'Half a shosser,' Davis said.

'You came here to spy,' Summers accused. 'You're all spies, fascist traitors—'

'Oh, shut up,' Barker said.

'Sir, do you have what you need?' Luis asked Townsend. He felt bewildered; everyone was so upset. He desperately wanted to be told that he had done well.

One of the officers said: 'Is that what all this row is about? A broken shosser? For God's sake . . .'

'It's a useless piece of shit,' said Davis, 'and whoever got it for us ought to be shot.'

'Give that thing to me,' Summers demanded.

Davis handed the broken shosser to Townsend. 'Tell the world, friend,' he said. 'They won't like it, they won't believe it, but for Chrissake tell them anyway.'

Summers' trembling fingers drew his pistol and thrust it at Townsend's face. 'Give that thing to *me*!' he demanded again.

'Go get your own,' Townsend snapped.

The muzzle was twitching and trembling. 'That equipment is military property.'

'Shit!' Davis shouted. 'It's shit!'

'Milton,' said Dru gently, 'this guy is very, very inexperienced at handling firearms. Believe me, it's not worth it. Give him the shosser.'

Townsend twirled the weapon and looked straight into Summers' furiously blinking eyes. He gave him the shosser.

Summers threw it out of the post with all his strength. It clattered far downhill. Townsend held Luis by the arm. 'I've seen it, Luis,' he said. 'That's good enough. Leave it be, okay?'

'Hey! Why not chuck everything out there?' Davis asked. 'You chucked the battalion down the hill, why not—'

'Silence!' Summers roared. His voice was not made for roaring and it broke.

'Chuck everything!' Davis hurled his battered saucepan out of the post. 'Everything!' His ropesoled shoes went flying, then his cap. He wrenched Summers' pistol free and sent it spinning away. *'Every . . . bloody . . . thing . . .!'* he sang, stretching the words like a dedication, and raising his arms to the wide blue sky.

'You're under arrest, Davis,' Summers said. He spoke flatly, not trusting his voice: everything betrayed him now. 'You'll be court-martialled.'

'Really? With tanks, and planes, and guns?' Davis taunted. 'Promise?'

'Get him out of here.' Summers turned to one of the officers. Davis grabbed the sandbag and slammed it hard against the side of Summers' head. Summers lurched and thudded against the wall, folded at the knees and slid to the floor, bringing a little rain of dirt and pebbles down on top of him. It coated his head and shoulders and trickled down his arms.

'Clear off!' one of the officers snapped. At once Davis vanished up the communications trench.

Summers lay stunned; his eyes kept opening and closing; each time they opened he was looking in a different direction.

'I guess we ought to be going too,' Townsend said, but at that moment Davis came back. Behind him tramped the huge, unhappy figure of André Marty. The trench was too narrow for both of them.

At the sight of Summers, Marty stopped. He gave the little circle a glare of scalding contempt; then he stooped, seized Summers by the tunic and hauled him semi-upright. 'Zis man,' he growled, 'equals fifty of you!' He thrust

52

Summers at the nearest officer and dusted his hands.

Davis had backed out and escaped again. Marty went to an observation slit. He took out his pistol and blasted off the complete clip in the general direction of Mola's camp. *'Sales boches!'* he spat. Summers moaned.

The correspondents slipped out, and filed through the trenches in silence. As they emerged onto the hillside they saw Davis talking to Templeton. He waved cheerily.

'You ought to lie low, you know,' Townsend called.

Davis shrugged. Townsend walked on, worrying, and then turned back. 'That bastard is liable to have you shot,' he said.

'Oh well.' Davis scratched at his scabby face. 'Isn't that what bastards are for?'

'You're crazy.' Townsend was angry and concerned; if he hadn't stayed to talk, Davis wouldn't be in this mess. 'Listen, come back to Madrid with us. Lie low for a bit. Take a break.'

'No thanks. I didn't come to Spain to lie low.'

'Why the hell *did* you come to Spain?'

'Can't remember. But it seemed a good idea at the time.'

Townsend ran to catch up with the others. 'Get a good story?' Dru asked.

'Dunno. The International Brigade got screwed at Jarama. Is that a good story?'

'But they *won*,' Barker said. 'I mean, they really did win. Mola got badly beaten. That's what those officers told us.'

'The man Davis is very funny,' Luis remarked.

'I laughed till I cried,' Townsend said.

*

Three days later Dru was back at Jarama—but on the other side of the lines.

Townsend and Barker had lost interest in the battle. Dru, however, now hoped to get a good pro-Franco story out of it. Victories usually made better news than defeats, and Dru couldn't see the Republicans winning this one. So Luis drove all around the flank of the war zone, approached Jarama through the Franco lines, and delivered Dru to the flat roof of General Mola's headquarters in good time to watch Mola's men go up the hill to attack the International Brigade. This battle had gone on long enough; Dru wanted a good, clean-cut result. He rested his binoculars on the parapet and searched for signs of success in Mola's men. 'These guys look like they know what they're doing,' he told Luis.

They did. Six batteries of Spanish artillery had lobbed shells at the Republican positions; German gunners of the Condor Legion had been pounding away with their 88-millimetres; and a unit of the Italian Air Force had bombed the crest. Now Mola's infantry were climbing to take the hills: professionals from the Army of Africa, lithe, agile, Moorish-looking riflemen in grey blanket-capes. They seemed to flit up the slope like a plague of moths climbing a brown curtain, pausing every few paces to find cover where even Dru, using binoculars, could see no cover. Their shots sounded like someone breaking up firewood, a busy, irregular snapping which nibbled away at the quiet of the valley. Once they had broken the Line, Mola said, he would launch his cavalry at the retreating remnants.

A German captain of the Condor Legion came onto the roof to watch the assault. Dru nodded to him, and said: 'Those eighty-eights of yours pack quite a punch.'

'In Germany we make the best artillery in the world.'

'You enjoying yourself in Spain?'

'It is good training for my men.' The German accepted a glass of beer from an orderly, and grimaced at it. 'See: no guts. That's the trouble with this country. They make bad beer. And bad bread. And bad governments.'

'Do they make anything good?' Luis asked him.

'They make good targets.' The German turned away and called down to a friend who was walking by and spilled some beer over the edge to make him dodge.

Luis was about to reply when Dru nudged him. 'Forget it,' he said.

'Spain does not need these foreign mechanics to save herself,' Luis scowled. 'I wish they would all go home.'

'How about *those* foreign mechanics, up there?' Dru asked.

'At least they are dying for Spain.'

'Uh-huh. You've got to die for something before you're accepted into the club. Is that it?'

There was an answer to that but Luis could not immediately produce it. He folded his arms and stared sullenly at the hill. At length he made a statement. 'It is all a matter of courage and sacrifice,' he said. 'That is what matters in Spain.'

When they went downstairs for lunch, the assault had been

54

halted by raking machine-gun fire from the top: the Republicans' elderly, armour-plated Maxims were clattering away as regularly and implacably as farm machinery. Mola was in good humour, however. He welcomed Dru and asked him about his impressions of the Republican forces. 'I'm told those curious volunteers up there actually have no maps,' he said. 'Is that right?'

'It's possible. I saw no maps.'

'Their commander does not believe in using maps. It seems he associates maps with treachery.' Mola spread his arms in a gesture of mild amazement. 'How can one win a war without a map?'

Dru put his finger to his lips. The muted clatter of the Maxims came down the hot midday air, soft and steady, like someone lazily popping the stitches of an endless, metallic seam. 'They don't think they're losing,' he said.

'Nor does the bull when he charges the matador,' Mola replied, and there was a ripple of laughter from his aides.

'Is that how you see this war? A kind of ritual blood-letting?' Dru asked. 'An act, a dramatic performance?'

Mola sipped his wine while he thought about his answer.

'In Spain everything is a dramatic performance,' he said. 'It's always the same drama: life against death. Every Spaniard is half in love with death. Here we have a civil war because so many Spaniards wish to kill Spain, and only a great deal of death will satisfy them. It must be death met with courage and resolution and all the other dramatic virtues, of course, otherwise the performance will not be considered adequate. Our friends from Germany and Italy,' he smiled at those present, 'are not full participants in our drama. They are, if they will forgive the expression, stage-hands rather than actors.'

The German captain did not look as if he could forgive the expression.

'And how do you think today's battle will go?' Dru asked.

'I hope the enemy will counter-attack,' Mola said. 'One cannot have a drama without dialogue.'

It took another three hours before he had his wish. The International Brigade counter-attacked at half-past four, a long, thin line of men strung out as they appeared over the skyline and ran downhill, their weapons sputtering like stale firecrackers. Dru watched through binoculars and saw the skilled

55

marksmanship of the Moorish soldiers pick off their stumbling attackers, at first by twos and threes and then, as the range shortened, by dozens. The counter-attack faltered, halted, and turned back uphill. Dru watched several men get knocked on their faces as if smashed between their retreating shoulders by an invisible battering-ram. He gave the glasses to Luis and turned away in disgust. 'What the hell was that meant to accomplish?' he asked.

'Dialogue,' said Luis brightly.

'Lousy dialogue. Jesus Christ, any dummy can get himself killed.' He clenched his teeth and swallowed to suppress a feeling of nausea. 'Get the goddam car, Luis. I'll go say my farewells to the Big Man.'

As they drove out of the camp, slowly so as not to startle the horses, Luis asked: 'How does the general feel?'

'He says tomorrow is another day.'

They bounced past the batteries of the Condor Legion, and Luis waved at the blond men sunbathing, naked, by their guns.

'I don't understand Mola,' Dru said. 'He keeps attacking straight up the face of those hills. That's a thousand feet from the river to the top.'

Luis waved at the sentries and put on speed.

'I just had a look at Mola's map,' Dru said. 'Half a mile to the right, those hills come to an end and another river runs into the Jarama.' He fished out a piece of paper and read his notes. 'The Jajuna. Nice wide, flat valley with a good road beside the river. So Mola could send his cavalry around there, outflank the Republican position, and capture the whole damn lot inside an hour.'

Luis sniffed. 'One does not kill the bull by sticking the sword in its rump.'

'What the hell's that supposed to mean?'

'It means battles are for fighting.'

'Then you're all crazy.'

Luis was not listening. 'You do not understand Spain,' he said, and put his foot down hard.

*

When they got to Madrid the city was under fire. Luis swerved expertly around reeking craters, and hooted his way through the rescuers and onlookers who milled about the dusty ruins of newly shelled buildings. From time to time they heard another curt *crump*, as random as a thunderclap. After one unusually loud explosion had rattled the car windows, Luis grinned and said, 'Boom! Boom! Good story for you.' Dru slumped in his seat and braced his feet against the dashboard.

They found Barker and Townsend at their hotel. With them was Charles Templeton, the ex-cricketer-painter from the 2nd English Battalion. He was buoyant and breezy and slightly drunk.

'Get anything new?' Townsend asked at once.

Dru made a sour face. 'It's like a bad prize-fight on a wet Tuesday in Alberta. Nobody has the punch to win or the brains to lose. What the hell's he doing here?'

'I deserted.' Templeton looked briefly woebegone. 'You are harbouring an outlaw. I can't tell you how delicious it feels.'

Dru looked at Barker. 'Is there a story in this?'

'Unfortunately, there is,' Barker said. He went around with the brandy bottle, and gave Templeton a good four fingers. 'Can you bear to relate the awful facts once more, old chap?'

'I'll tell you what,' Templeton said, 'I'll relate the awful facts, if you'll order up some grub. Quails' eggs and avocados and Beef Wellington and knickerbocker glories and lots of brown-bread-and-butter. You see . . .' He rinsed his teeth in brandy and swallowed pleasurably. 'I've eaten nothing but filth and sludge for weeks.'

'I'll try,' Barker said. He picked up the telephone.

'And get lots of wine. Tell them to send up a few firkins of decent claret and a couple of carboys of fine hock. You've no idea how abrasive Spanish homebrew can be. Even after it's been cut with ditchwater. One's palate remains scourged, simply scourged.'

'So what happened to you?' Dru asked.

'Nothing,' Templeton said. 'But poor old Davis got shot stone dead, and that kind of thing is very infectious these days.'

He told the story quickly and brightly. Templeton and Davis had shared a dug-out. In the early hours of the morning after the correspondents' visit, two men had awoken Davis and taken him away to Brigade Headquarters.

When Davis did not come back, Templeton had volunteered to fetch ammunition from Brigade Headquarters. He sniffed around the farmhouse and found what looked like a fresh grave. He got a shovel and opened it. Davis was three feet down. He had been badly beaten up and shot, or perhaps shot and beaten up, although the latter was less likely.

'Any ideas?' Dru asked.

'Oh, it was André Marty,' Templeton told him. 'I met a despatch-rider who told me he saw Marty taking Davis into a barn, before breakfast. Any luck?' he asked Barker.

'I've got you some ham sandwiches and a half-bottle of Beaujolais.'

'Wonderful.' Templeton shut his eyes and swallowed loudly, in anticipation. 'Absolutely spiffing. You're a gent.'

'Well, we were at school together.'

'So then I pinched a motorbike and beetled off to Madrid.' He held out his glass for more brandy.

'Poor old Davis,' muttered Townsend.

'Well, he knew what was coming, the silly man,' Templeton said briskly. 'He didn't have to stay.'

'It sounds as if Marty really is mad,' Barker remarked.

'Of course he is,' Dru said. 'He goes around shooting people. He's shot about two hundred already.'

'I'll tell you what, old boy,' Barker said, 'why don't you have a bath? You smell a bit fruity, you see.'

'What a noble thought!' Templeton began taking off his clothes and throwing them out of the window.

Luis had been following the discussion closely. Now he sat staring into his brandy and looking morose. He glanced up and caught Dru's eye. 'This is not war,' he muttered with sad conviction.

'You may be right,' Dru said, 'but it'll do until something worse comes along.'

Chapter 7

Jarama fell. Madrid was isolated. Franco's armies moved on, and with them went the war correspondents.

Luis Cabrillo was still their driver but now he was also something more, a cross between a researcher, a translator, a courier and a spy. Because the correspondents found it easier and safer to report the struggle from the Nationalist side, they paid Luis to cross the war zone and bring back Republican accounts of the fighting. This was difficult work, wearying and dangerous: he drove long distances, around or between the battlefronts, guessing at unguarded areas, bluffing and lying when he guessed wrong, perfecting a display of craven horror when stopped by sentries: *The war . . . ? you mean the war is here already? . . . God in heaven . . .* And with trembling hands Luis would turn the car, and accelerate away in such a panic that the rear wheels fish-tailed dramatically, and the guards laughed so much that they forgot to note his registration number. Or so he hoped.

Eventually, inevitably, somebody remembered him. Or suspected him. Sooner or later somebody, Republican or Nationalist or both, was bound to notice the young man in the big car who always took the wrong turning and turned pale when he ran into the war. Meanwhile, Luis was bringing back rich information, the kind which nobody could invent and which only a Spaniard could discover. He knew what made a good story for each of his employers: Dru needed anti-Republican scandal, Townsend needed straightforward blood-and-guts, Barker needed pro-Republican politics. It was always the same story, but Luis learned how to serve it up three ways. Everyone was pleased and Luis got well rewarded. The extra money compensated for his loneliness, and not just on the trips through the Lines. Suddenly Luis was an orphan.

He learned about his parents' death several days after it happened, too late for him to do anything about attending their funeral. They had been travelling in a train, in Valencia, when it was bombed and went tumbling down an embankment at speed. The news reached Luis by a slow and roundabout route, through colleagues of his father. He never discovered which side's aircraft had done the bombing.

At first he was calm. *What a surprise*, he thought. *How very very curious.* He thanked the man who had brought the news. 'A terrible shock,' the man said. 'We all knew your father. He was . . .' It was difficult, in the circumstances, to say just what Señor Cabrillo was. Or had been. Luis smiled gently, and nodded. They shook hands and parted.

Later, when the day was dying and the dusk had the texture of old velvet, he wept. It was as if his calmness had been a paper screen of no strength, only a certain position; almost anything could make a hole in it. Luis was in his room, brushing his hair, when someone across the street picked out the first notes of a Chopin waltz on a piano. He stopped brushing. It was a piece which his mother had always played stiffly and resolutely. The unknown hand stopped, and after a moment Luis heard the soft thud of the keyboard cover. He stood with his lungs full of useless air, his fingers squeezing the hairbrush, and tears crept from his eyes like agents of betrayal. He wept not so much for what he had lost as for what he had never had. Throughout his childhood, through all the changing schools and homes and towns, and later when he went from job to job, his mother and father had always been there, too busy to bother with him perhaps, but always *potentially available*. One day, when everything got straightened out, Luis had planned to approach his parents again, as an equal, of course, so that they could be true friends. Now they would always be strangers. Luis wept with a passion which took him by surprise. What had he lost? Nothing. Then why this grief? He was furious at his own weakness. All his life he had asked nothing of the world, and yet here he was, still painfully vulnerable. It was unfair. Okay, so life was unfair; everybody knew that. To hell with life! He remembered the slogan of Franco's Moroccan troops: *Viva el muerte!* Long live death! Luis leaned against a twilit corner of his room, hugging himself for want of anyone else to hug, and cried not like a child but like a man.

Next day Mola opened a new offensive in the north, and Luis drove the correspondents up to Burgos. The Republicans, it seemed, were fighting a rearguard action as they fell back through the Basque country. That was supposed to be the broad theme, anyway; as usual, hard news was scarce. When they reached Burgos, Luis volunteered to go ahead and find out what exactly was happening.

When he got back, three days later, he had seen so many corpses that death was as familiar as daylight.

He found the correspondents in the hotel bar. They were delighted to see him because there was a powerful rumour that a small harmless Basque town had been knocked to bits by bombers, and for some reason there was a most satisfactory international uproar.

'It's nowhere special,' Townsend said. 'Just some half-assed little dump.'

'The story is true,' Luis announced. 'I myself was there only yesterday. Much destruction, many dead.'

'Who done it?' Barker asked.

'Oh, the bombers of the *Legion Condor*, without doubt. There are many witnesses.'

'Right! That's what we heard.'

Townsend clinked the ice in his glass. 'Any idea why the krauts picked this particular place?'

'For the arms factory, presumably.'

'*Arms* factory!' Dru rubbed his hands. 'It's a goddam munitions dump! What did I tell you? Did they hit it?'

'No. Every day for four days the *Legion Condor* bombed the town but every day it missed the arms factory.'

'Pity,' muttered Dru.

'On the third day they machine-gunned two nuns,' Luis offered. 'And on the fourth day several horses—'

'Wait a minute, wait a minute,' Townsend interrupted. 'The way I heard it, they only bombed this place but the once.' He spread a map on the bar, 'We ought to get up there now and check it out. See, it's not all that far and—'

'Pardon,' Luis announced firmly. 'That is the wrong town.'

'Guernica,' Townsend said.

'No! Durango.' Luis tapped another town, fifteen miles to the south of Guernica. 'Durango has been bombed. Not Guernica. Durango.' He smiled reassuringly.

'When?' asked Barker.

Luis shrugged. 'A week ago, two weeks.'

'Sorry, Luis. Guernica just got it.' Dru told him. 'The dust hasn't settled, and already Berlin denies that the Condor Legion had anything to do with it, so it must be good and juicy.'

'Oh.' Luis felt defeated. 'So you are not interested in Durango?'

'It's not Guernica,' Townsend pointed out.

'It's just as big,' Luis said, 'and Durango got bombed four times. Two hundred civilians killed.'

'Forget it, Luis,' Dru told him amiably. 'Right now it's Guernica or nothing. Durango's dead.'

'Well,' Luis said, 'I can't argue with that.'

Chapter 8

From a nearby hillside, Guernica did not look as if it had been bombed. It looked as if someone had just decided to build a ten-lane highway across Spain, and Guernica was where they had begun. A broad strip of demolition trampled through the town, its edges as ragged as torn newspaper. The savaging of Guernica looked (from a distance) less like a military assault than a bureaucratic blunder.

The correspondents got back in the car and Luis drove them down the hill.

A close sight of the havoc was not much more harrowing than the distant view. But what took the correspondents by surprise was the smell. The harsh fumes of explosives and incendiaries mingled with the sad aromas of a hundred fires—charred mattresses, scorched paintwork, burnt clothing, ruined food—to form a miserable, inescapable stench which made the sunshine seem stupid.

'God damn it,' Townsend said, sniffing. 'Someone forgot to empty the ashtrays.'

Nobody laughed. Even Luis wished that Townsend had not spoken.

They split up and went off to make separate inspections of the town. The Nationalist forces had occupied it but Luis knew better than to waste time asking questions of Mola's men. Instead he found the priest.

This was a short and stocky man, aged about fifty, whose face was rigid with a determination not to reveal the shock which still flickered behind his eyes. He was in the crypt underneath his gutted church; it was being used as an emergency mortuary. His parishioners lay all around him in ragged rows.

Yes, he told Luis, *he had seen the bombing. He had seen the aeroplanes.*

What sort of planes?

German, of course. The markings on the wings had been unmistakable. One flew so low that he had taken a photograph of it.

Were people expecting the raid?

The priest shrugged. The town was full of soldiers. They had fallen back from Durango. Everyone knew what had happened there . . .

But was there anything worth destroying in Guernica?

Obviously there was the arms factory, the Astra-Unceta arms factory. Think of all the pistols and rifles and machine-guns made there!

And did the bombers damage this factory?

No. Anyone can go and see. The buildings are intact.

How many soldiers were killed?

Not many. The soldiers knew about bombing. But the refugees . . .

There were many refugees in Guernica?

Thousands.

Where are they now?

Look around you.

Luis talked to more townspeople as he picked his way between the craters and the collapsed buildings: a barman, a nurse, a garage mechanic. By the time he got back to the car he had a clear picture of what had happened to Guernica.

The correspondents were sitting under a tree, drinking wine mixed with lemonade.

'Don't tell me,' Dru said to Luis. 'The Stukas did it. Right? The krauts flattened Guernica with their Stukas as a cold-blooded experiment in divebombing, period. Am I right?'

'How did you know that?' Luis made himself comfortable on the ground.

'Bilbao Radio's been yelling and screaming all morning, and Franco's people monitor the bulletins. I just got a full briefing from them, and I'll tell you something else: Guernica never saw a Stuka in its life!' Dru pulled out a magazine and displayed its cover: a picture of a Stuka, gull-winged and wheel-spatted, tipping sideways into a dive. 'I must've shown this to fifty people today. Not one of them recognised it. Not one.'

'Proves nothing.' Townsend yawned and stretched. 'You're getting the shit bombed out of you, you don't hang around and rubberneck.'

'Could it perhaps have been a different type of German bomber?' Luis suggested.

'No,' Dru said firmly, 'but it could have been a different kind of *Republican* bomber. The two-legged kind.'

'My God, Jean-Pierre,' Barker said, 'when you're smug you're intolerable.'

'The Republican army dynamited Guernica and set it on fire when they retreated through it,' Dru declared. 'Then they turned round and blamed everything on the mythical Stukas. Simple as that.' Dru's hands depressed an imaginary plunger. '*Ba-room!* Guernica's a great big propaganda news swindle, and I'm gonna blow the racket sky-high.'

'I expect it was done by the miners of Asturia,' Luis said.

'You see?' Dru turned to Barker and Townsend in triumph. 'Luis knows all about it. How d'you spell that name, Luis? As-what?'

Luis told him. 'It is a big mining area. Very tough. The miners are expert with dynamite. The Republican army is full of them. They fight with dynamite.'

'You're a genius,' Dru said. 'He's a genius,' he told the others.

'Get that in writing,' Townsend advised Luis.

'Okay, okay.' Dru lay back and relaxed. 'You make the wisecracks and I'll make the news, and we'll see who makes more money.'

That was unanswerable, and the others sat in silence for a moment. Behind them, Guernica smoked listlessly. A distant shout was followed by a grumbling rumble as, somewhere, a ruined wall was pulled down.

'I can't honestly believe the Nazi air force did all this,'

64

Barker said. 'Look at the shape of the damage: it's all too precise, too tidy. And it's what *didn't* get blown up that's most interesting. The railway station, the bridge, the arms factory. Things that Franco's people would prefer to capture intact . . . I wonder if . . .'

Luis thought hard about what Barker might be thinking.

Townsend shaded his eyes and squinted at the ruins. 'I wish to hell they'd dig out some unexploded bombs made in Düsseldorf,' he muttered.

'Señor Barker,' Luis remarked cautiously, 'perhaps the explosions were made by men of Franco's army, agents of Mola . . . Saboteurs, or . . .'

'Infiltrators,' Barker said.

It was a new word to Luis. He tried it and liked it. 'Infiltrators . . . who made chaos . . .'

'Spread panic,' Barker said. 'Disrupted communications. Yes, indeed.'

'Perhaps,' Luis went on, more confidently, 'they even pretended that they were Republican soldiers with orders to . . . you know . . .'

'Bogus miners!' Barker exclaimed. 'Of course! Franco's infiltrators pretend to be Republican soldiers, they blow up the town, then Franco simply waits for the Republicans to blame him for it, and he trots out his ready-made answer.'

'Which is half-true,' Luis added.

'Is it?' said Barker. 'Yes, in a sense, I suppose it is.' He sighed. 'Funny thing about working for newspapers: you always get two sides to every story.'

'I covered lots of two-sided stories in Chicago,' Townsend said. 'Guys found in speakeasies with a dozen bullets in the back. Turned out to be suicide. I tell you, working as a crime reporter in Chicago teaches a man humility. Also modesty and courtesy.'

'Why is that chap so very interested in our car?' Barker asked. They suddenly became alert, and stared. A Nationalist officer was walking around the car, his hands clasped behind him, his head tipped to one side. 'If he decides to requisition the bloody thing, we're in queer street,' Barker said.

Luis jumped up and made for the car. Halfway there, he suddenly realised why the officer was interested in the car, especially its numberplate, and his lungs jumped to a little

65

gasp. His legs kept walking forward, but each pace felt uncertain, as if his feet suspected a hidden trapdoor ahead.

The officer saw him coming, and straightened up. He was in his forties, broadshouldered, with serious grey eyes, a square jaw, and a forehead ribbed like corduroy. He was eating a sweet, and he held it between his front teeth for a moment while he studied Luis. He looked very calm and very fit.

'Is something wrong with the car?' Luis asked.

'Is it your car?'

'No.'

'Then why do you ask?'

'I was requested to keep an eye on it, that's all.'

'Ah.' A fly buzzed annoyingly in front of the officer's face; he caught it with one swift snatch, and held it. 'And who requested you?'

'If there is nothing wrong with the car,' Luis said, amazed at his own daring, 'then it does not matter.'

The officer slightly widened his eyes. The fly droned in his fist. 'You are Luis Cabrillo,' he stated.

'No,' Luis said. 'But if you want him, I know where he is.'

'Where is that?'

'I shall have to show you.'

The officer opened his fist. The fly charged away and banged into the side window of the car. It fell to the ground, buzzing weakly. The officer trod on it and followed Luis.

They walked into Guernica. Luis had no idea where they were going except that it must be away from the correspondents, and he had to keep walking purposefully, because if the officer decided to search him and found that he really was Luis Cabrillo, they would shoot him inside ten minutes. That was how it was on both sides, Republican and Nationalist: whenever they captured a place, they always shot people. He strode on, making it seem that he knew exactly where he was going.

Guernica was never a big town and the bombing had made it smaller. Luis soon reached the centre. If he kept going they would rapidly end up in the bare countryside. He stopped at a corner and stared around, as if searching for a landmark in the ruins. The only thing he recognised was the gutted church, so that was where they went.

The idea came to him as they were going down the steps

to the crypt, and it came with such force that his head jerked and he almost stumbled. It was such an easy, obvious idea that he was ashamed for not thinking of it much earlier. He stood aside to let the officer look across the morgue. 'I forgot to ask,' Luis said. 'Is there a reward?'

'Just find him,' the officer said. He looked bored and disappointed now. As they walked between the rows of bodies, he unwrapped another sweet and held it between his teeth while he balled the wrapper with his fingertips and flicked it away.

Luis found what he was looking for at the end of the second row : the severely mutilated corpse of a slim young man. The head was in a bad way, and one arm had come off. '*Voilà*,' he said.

The officer nodded gently and thought about it. 'And that's Luis Cabrillo,' he said.

'Well, it isn't the king of England.'

The officer walked to the other end of the corpse and put on a pair of hornrim spectacles. 'How do you know that this is he?' He took off the spectacles and waved them at the meaningless face. 'In the circumstances.'

'I recognise the hands,' Luis said. 'If I am right there should be a distinctive scar just about . . .' He stooped, paused, looked up. 'With your permission?'

The officer nodded. Luis exposed the torso. It was a mess of dried blood and torn skin. 'Never mind,' Luis said, turning his back on the officer and stooping again, 'perhaps there is something in the pockets . . .'

'Leave it!' the officer snapped. Luis stood back, quickly and respectfully. The officer straddled the body and searched it. In a side pocket he found a Madrid hotel bill made out in the name Luis Cabrillo. He read it, and grunted. 'Fetch two soldiers. Also a stretcher. *Any* two soldiers,' he said as Luis opened his mouth.

Luis shrugged and turned away. 'And that is my reward,' he muttered loudly and rebelliously. He slouched out of the crypt, and sprinted all the way to the car. The correspondents were waiting. 'Who was that?' Barker asked. 'Just a soldier,' Luis said. 'Looking for a friend.' Two hours later they were back in Burgos.

Chapter 9

That evening, they all went to eat in a bar-restaurant just outside the town.

'Hey, Luis,' said Townsend, while they were waiting for their food. 'Did you know that Guernica got bombed on market-day?'

'There was no market that day,' Luis said. 'The country people were afraid of an attack and so they stayed at home.'

Townsend frowned. 'For God's sake,' Barker complained, 'how many damn bodies d'you need?'

'It's not just a question of bodies,' Townsend snapped. 'It's a question of *innocence*. You know—market-day, smiling peasants streaming into town with their fresh country produce, when bang! Out of the blue, without warning, the sinister hail of death. It's twice the story with market-day.'

'Print it, Milt,' Dru urged. 'You like it, you use it. The bigger you build up your bombing, the louder my dynamite's going to be. Hullo! What's this?'

A large party of young men was tramping into the restaurant from the bar. They were in civilian clothes which looked as if they had all been bought in the same department store. Many were blond; all looked fit and strong and tanned. One of them said: *'Ich möchte einen grossen Wiener Schnitzel, ja?'*

'Asturian coal-miners,' Barker said.

'Now's your big chance, Jean-Pierre,' Townsend told Dru. 'Get over there and grab yourself a few eye-witnesses.'

Dru merely smiled.

The young Germans settled down around a circular table. Their legs were too long and they kept scuffing and kicking each other, which led to laughter and denunciations and insults. Somebody rocked the table, somebody retaliated. Half the cutlery fell on the floor. A couple of drinks got spilled. Much laughter.

'They're like undergraduates on Boat-Race night,' Barker

68

observed. 'Hard to believe they . . .' He shrugged.

'One of us should get up and go over and ask them about it,' Townsend said. 'I can't go. My German is lousy and anyway I'm too hungry to move.'

'They'd never talk to an Englishman,' said Barker.

Dru ate some bread and looked at the flies circling the lighting fixture.

'Would you like me to speak to them?' Luis asked.

It had been a long day, full of travel and questions and typing and then arguments with the military censors, and now that the stories were filed everyone was weary. The German table was boisterous and already slightly drunk.

'Don't waste your time,' Dru said.

'They must be from the airfield. Maybe some are pilots.'

'You won't get anything out of those guys, Luis.'

That was a challenge; or perhaps Dru was afraid of what those guys might say. Luis stood up and walked over to the German table.

He waited until the nearest man had stopped talking; bowed, smiled, and said: 'Excuse me . . . Does one of you gentlemen speak English?'

'English . . .' The man turned in his chair and looked up. His elbow was on the table, his jaw propped against his hand. He examined Luis closely. Luis was struck by the untroubled self-assurance in his clear grey eyes. The man was only a few years older than himself yet he seemed enormously more competent. He must surely be a pilot.

The German spoke a few words in German, and all his friends laughed.

Luis, still smiling, glanced across the table. Another German made a remark, obviously referring to Luis, and everyone laughed again. After that the comments came from all sides, until the table was rocking with laughter. Luis stood like a dummy, not smiling any more, and felt his anger building like steam in a kettle. It was not their making fun that enraged him; it was the fact that he did not understand them and they knew this and they did not give a bloody damn. Eventually one of them, bigger and more red-faced than the rest, lurched to his feet, marched up to Luis, and stamped his boots in a mock-flamenco beat. He gave Luis a patronising pat on the cheek and shouted 'Olé!' His friends roared.

Luis went back to his seat, feeling murderous. 'One day I shall kill them for that,' Luis hissed.

'Forget it, old boy,' Barker said. 'They're just pissed, that's all.'

The food came and they ate, while the Germans kept up their gusty, guttural good cheer. Sometimes they sang, sometimes they argued, always they drank. They did everything loudly.

When the correspondents were finishing their coffee, one of the Germans returned from the toilet and came over to their table. He had a keen, intelligent face, and an athletic-looking body.

'Newspapers? You work for newspapers?' His English was awkward but adequate.

Townsend took out a pencil and showed it.

'Ah. You write. My question: what you say about Guernica?'

Luis hunched over his cup and refused to look up.

Barker said: 'According to Berlin your Condor Legion had nothing to do with it, so what do you care?'

'*Ja,*' agreed the German, 'but does Berlin tell exactly *how* we did not bomb Guernica?'

Townsend pulled out a chair. The German sat.

'Here is Guernica.' He tried to draw a square in the middle of the table with his finger, but the surface was wood and nothing showed. He poured some coffee onto the table and, using his finger, shaped the pool into a rough square. 'Here— the river.' He found some hot milk in the bottom of a jug and poured a curving trail past the square of coffee. 'Also, the railway.' He searched about and saw mayonnaise on a nearby table. The correspondents raised eyebrows at each other while he dumped spoonfuls of mayonnaise between the milk and the coffee in a globular, glistening line. 'Is all a matter of communications,' he told them cheerfully. 'Of roads, yes?' This time he used a bottle of tomato ketchup and laid two rich red tracks of the stuff, meeting outside the river of milk. Then he poured an even wider strip of ketchup across the river, over the yellow railway, and into the black town. 'You see?'

The correspondents watched with grudging fascination as the colours contaminated each other. Some of the other airmen had strolled over and were watching. 'Watch closely,' the German said. 'Three squadrons of Junkers fly over, drop their bombs, and *bang*!' He slammed the palms of his hands down on the mess. A multicoloured spray spattered the correspondents' heads and shoulders and arms. Even Luis, leaning back, got his share of the muck.

The Germans fell about laughing.

'So now you know what did not happen to Guernica,' the man said, and went away, mopping his front.

Luis drove the correspondents silently back to their hotel. Next morning, after breakfast, he took Barker aside.

'I can get you a photograph of a German bomber flying very low over Guernica,' he said. 'Do you want it?'

'You get it,' Barker said, 'and I'll give you whatever it costs.'

'It will cost you nothing,' Luis told him stonily.

'All right.'

Barker watched Luis get into the car. *Touchy bloody people*, he thought. *Who can understand them?* He never saw Luis again.

Chapter 10

Driving north, Luis felt confused and depressed. For the first time, he did not care who won the war. Before, he had been impartial but interested, ready to see merit in either side, and wondering how the fate of Spain would affect his own future. Now he knew that his past had been a failure (bad schools, makeshift homes, lost jobs) and he saw nothing better in his future.

Unusually for him, he drove slowly. The day was overcast, neither sunny nor threatening, and lacked all urgency or enthusiasm. Why was he going back to Guernica? It was a stupid thing to do. He was going back to get a blurred photograph of a clumsy aeroplane which had helped to destroy an irrelevant town and kill a lot of people nobody would ever miss. Why? Because it was evidence. Which meant that it would convince those who wanted to be convinced, and the rest wouldn't even look at it. So why bother? Because it made a story, and that was now his job, his skill, his craft: making good stories, whether they were true or not.

No. Luis knew that was not a good enough reason either. It wasn't worth going back into Guernica just to get a good story for Barker. So there had to be something else. His honesty had been getting Luis into trouble all his life, and now it worried and nagged him all the way up the road from Burgos until it made him give in and own up. He didn't care a damn about Spain, about Nationalist lies or Republican propaganda, about truth or loyalty or skill or success. He was doing this stupid thing purely to get his revenge against those Germans who had mocked and humiliated and finally insulted him. That was all. It was an act of spite. This whole war was an act of spite, wasn't it? All right, then. Getting the photograph would be the first shot in Luis Cabrillo's private campaign.

He drove down the hill and crossed the bridge into Guernica, feeling better now that he knew he was acting foolishly for his own selfish reasons. He saw fewer refugees but more soldiers: Mola was getting ready for another push towards Bilbao. Rubble had been cleared from the streets. The fires were out. The smell was fading.

Luis drifted around the main square, looking for a discreet spot to leave the car. He found a gap outside a scruffy-looking barbershop, between a truck and a bus, and backed into it. His fingers were turning the doorhandle when the officer came out of the barbershop, flicking bits of hair from his tunic.

Luis made three bad mistakes, one after another.

First, he let this mild coincidence panic him. He assumed—without checking—that the officer must see him. In fact the man was deep in thought and failed to notice the car until Luis's hand jumped from the door to the ignition key and made the engine bellow. Even as he did this, Luis knew that he had wasted a stroke of good luck: if he had kept quiet, he could have watched where the officer went and then gone the other way. Too late now. Luis swore, and swung the wheel.

That was his second mistake. The officer had failed to recognise the car at first. Now he saw the numberplate, and he let out a shout.

Luis's third mistake was to hit the back of the bus.

72

With the engine roaring in protest he heaved on the wheel and ripped his way out, shedding bits of torn metal and shattered glass. The officer came running alongside, his mouth gaping to reveal a flash of gold, and grabbed at the door just as Luis worked both front wheels free and rocketed into the wide open spaces. The car howled along one side of the square, nearly hit a mule cart at the corner, swerved, and racketed along with two wheels on the kerb, soldiers dodging and whistles blowing. He smashed into and over a parked motorcycle, got the car back on the road, and at last found a split second in which to change gear. The engine responded lustily, but as Luis bowled out of the square the officer, in a commandeered Mercedes, was already after him.

He began catching up before they were out of town. It was inevitable. Luis was clearing the way, blasting the traffic to one side, making the road easy. By the time Luis blared over the bridge, the officer was only fifty yards behind; and in the mirror Luis glimpsed an army truck bucketing along in the Mercedes' wake.

The road forked, right to Burgos, left to Bilbao. Luis saw a long, slow convoy hogging the Burgos road and he flung the car, tyres screaming and spitting stones, hard to the left, then let the wheel kick back and spin through his palms while his foot slammed the accelerator to the floor. Rear wheels dithered, skittered, at last gripped and heaved the car forward with a thrust that made his head jolt.

The Mercedes came around the same corner as if on rails, and gained ten yards doing it.

Over the next couple of miles Luis began to be afraid. His hands were slippery, his eyes were stinging with sweat, his calves and thighs and biceps were bunched and twitching. The officer's Mercedes had more power and better tyres, and probably more petrol. The road was getting worse: twisting and switchbacking through woods. One bad gear-change, one mis-timed corner, and Luis would be dead.

Then a piece of luck won him an extra hundred yards. He panicked a herd of goats browsing at the roadside, and they scattered in the path of the Mercedes.

He risked a glance in his mirror and saw the car skid broadside. Then he lost it completely behind a bend. Suddenly encouraged, he put his foot down even harder and went flat-out along the next straight. The corner grew near, grew nearer; he delayed braking and changing down to the last possible moment, and then waited an instant more. His high-speed four-wheel drift into the bend was perfect. It was the camber of the road that was all wrong.

Luis felt the car come unstuck and fly out like a fairground ride, while the road swung the other way and abandoned him. He was flying, then he was falling, diving into a steep and flickering world of trees. Something rose up and bashed him violently in the backside. Before he could recover, something even more violent clubbed the front of the car and smashed it sideways. Luis's hands were torn off the wheel and he was flung across the front seats. His head rammed the door. He lay stunned, glimpsing wavering treetops soaring away, as the car plunged backwards, ricocheting off rocks and bouncing between treetrunks, until it tried to charge through a two-hundred-year-old oak and failed. The crash was a single, shattering hammerblow. The car crumpled like wet cardboard. The tyres sighed. The springs wheezed. Silence.

It took Luis a quarter of an hour to make his eyes focus, and another ten minutes to train his legs to get him out and hold him up. After all that, his stomach decided to be sick; but eventually he was able to look around and take stock.

He was not alone.

The officer and the Mercedes were nowhere to be seen. Higher up the slope, however, was the wreck of a small grey car. Obviously it too had left the bend at speed, but it had made the mistake of coming down head-first. Both front wheels and the radiator were firmly wrapped around a sturdy pine tree. Most of the engine was in the front seat, and a great deal of the steering column was in the driver.

He was a balding, chubby man in a brown suit and black gloves. He wore a thin, careful moustache like a small-town bank manager, which was what the cards in his wallet declared him to have been. On the back seat was a jumble of heavy cardboard boxes sealed with strong brownpaper tape. They were all stamped *Banco de España*, *Guernica*, and they were all full of money.

Evidently the peasants had not been the only ones to suspect that Guernica was a good place to get out of.

74

Finding the money did not mark the end of Luis's problems, but it was a good start.

He knew that the Nationalist officer would soon turn back and organise a search of the woods, and he knew that the *Banco de España* would one day come hunting for its funds.

He prised the dead driver off the steering column and dumped him in the other car: that would give the officer something useless to chew on. He unloaded the cardboard boxes and hid them a mile away, in the heart of a thicket of laurels. Then he walked into Guernica.

He had a curious feeling that the money was a gift and a test. It was a comment on the nonsense of war: he might well have been killed in the crash, but instead he was rich; yet rich only if he could contrive to keep and spend the money.

So the first thing he had to do was find out whether or not the Guernica branch of the *Banco de España* was still in business.

It was not. The site was a heap of battered bricks and broken beams. Splendid.

Next, he made careful enquiries about the manager. Nobody had seen him since the day of the bombing. Quite possibly he was still buried in the ruins somewhere. Anywhere. When the bombs fell, people took refuge and often their refuge became their tomb. Luis nodded sombrely, and rejoiced in his heart. If nobody had missed the manager, probably nobody had missed the money. Yet.

At a stables on the outskirts of town he bought an old donkey with an even older saddle, a dozen sacks and a pair of secondhand overalls, and went back to the woods. For an hour he pottered about, collecting bundles of firewood. When he was sure he was alone he went and looked inside the laurel thicket. Then he threw the firewood away, half-filled a few of the sacks with dead leaves, and shoved the chunky wads of banknotes deep inside. The cardboard boxes burned to a fine grey ash in fifteen minutes.

For the rest of 1937 he and the donkey pottered across northern Spain. They wandered in an apparently random, zigzag fashion: first north-west to the port of Santander, then back across the mountains and down the valley of the Esla to Leon, followed by a spell of criss-crossing the plain between Palencia and Zamora and Braganca. Luis and the donkey travelled by tracks and trails; he named her Fred Astaire because she had big ears and she never fell over, even on steep and stony paths. The only time they used roads was to go into a town. Once or twice a week Luis entered a town, found a bank, changed a bundle of notes into bills of larger denomination, and got straight out again. He rarely spoke to anyone; he bought his food in little villages; he and Fred slept in empty, quiet places.

By the end of summer he looked like what he wanted to be mistaken for: a poor peasant. His face and arms were sunburned the colour of mahogany, his hair was lanky, his clothes were patched and stained. Nobody bothered him; few people even noticed him. If by chance the *Banco de España* were still looking for anyone, Luis reckoned to be about as forgettable as a dead tree.

From time to time he picked up news of the war. Franco was winning, bloodily; but the details of the battles interested Luis no more than the results of last year's football matches. He was waiting for only one event: the fall of Madrid, where he had decided to spend his next few years. He could avoid the secret police there. He could enjoy his money there.

Madrid surrendered in March 1939, by all accounts in a very bad state. Luis allowed the capital a couple of months to make itself fit for his return. He killed the time pleasantly with Fred Astaire, strolling around the western Sierras between Salamanca and Alcantara. When the period was up he was, in every sense, a very different person from the impetuous youth who had nearly killed himself while fleeing from death. It was over a year and a half since he had slept inside four walls, or taken a bath, or put on completely clean clothes. When he left Burgos for Guernica that would have been an unthinkable prospect. Now he had a different set of values.

He sold Fred at a slight profit and took the train to Madrid. He knew with certainty what he had to have and what he could do without. He could do without people, politics, sex, tobacco, news, alcohol, uniforms and work. He had to have privacy, physical comfort, and a good book. A suitcase full of pesetas should buy quite a lot of all three.

The first thing he saw when he got off the train was a poster showing pictures of twenty men wanted by Franco's police. Second row, third from the left, was Luis Cabrillo. He looked young and cocky. Luis walked away from him and, within an hour, had rented a spacious two-room apartment on the third floor of the Calle Santa Isabel, in the old quarter of the town. He called himself José Antonio Hernández, and two years passed before, unwillingly, he came out again.

Part Two

PART TWO

Chapter 11

Luis Cabrillo shaved, dressed, sat near the window and tried to read a short story by Somerset Maugham. After three minutes he threw the book across the room, not in anger but in despair.

He was flat broke, and that was inescapable. The fact pursued him like a cold draught. Pointless to sit and pretend that he could entertain himself with fiction, as if today were yesterday. Tomorrow was on its way, very fast. Tomorrow would be a bitch without money. Today was going to be a real bastard, but tomorrow would be an absolute bitch.

No money. It was shocking, like waking up to discover that you had no feet, or no eyes: suddenly everything was enormously, frighteningly more difficult. Life was not pleasant any more. The world outside was an enemy. He had no friends to help him; none that he could trust, anyway. Food: what in hell's name was he going to do for lunch? He sucked in his stomach and immediately it sent him a message of a large omelette, firm yet juicy. 'Christ, what's the matter with you?' he cried aloud. 'You've only just had your damned breakfast!'

But no eggs, his stomach reminded him. This is degrading, Luis thought. What am I: a man, or a stomach on legs? His anger carried him to the door and before his fear could do anything about it he was going down the stairs, two at a time. *No money . . .* Well, hanging around in a third-floor room wasn't going to improve things. If there was any money to be got it had to be out there, in the streets. Where he hadn't set foot for two years. He ran down the last flight and strode across the hallway, heels clicking on the shiny tiles, nostrils twitching to old nostalgic smells: washed floors, the trace of hot bread, a hint of maybe orange blossom. Then he was out in the Calle Santa Isabel.

It felt good. Even without money, it felt good. Madrid was having a sparkling, spanking day, and after all that time beneath a twelve-foot ceiling Luis saw the streets as grand and glittering canyons. The traffic whizzed and dodged, bold and cavalier, and the people took it all for granted, like the sublime creatures they clearly were. By the time he had walked to the railway station this sudden intoxication was beginning to wear off, but he still felt like a peasant, gawking at the big city, and he made an effort to look more confident and urban.

His picture was not on the police posters in the railway station because there were no police posters in the railway station. So that was good.

A newspaper headline caught his eye: Germany had attacked Crete. He picked up a copy and glanced at the opening paragraph while his hand felt in his pocket and found (of course) nothing, not even a button; zero, emptiness. He put the paper back and turned away while the owner of the stall came over, straightened the pile of papers and squinted at him. Luis frowned and checked his watch against the station clock. Two minutes slow. He grunted briskly. Not good enough. He must have money!

For the rest of the morning he walked around the centre of Madrid. The layout was familiar but the impact was startling: for the first time he saw how damned *rich* the city was. The Prado had always been just a big art gallery; now he climbed its broad exterior staircase and stroked one of the massive pink columns propping up the noble façade, and he worked out the bill for this whole colossal effort. A fortune!

This one column alone must have cost ten thousand pesetas. And after that they had to buy all the pictures on the walls inside. Two fortunes, right here in one building! But there were riches everywhere you looked. Next to the Prado was the Neptune Fountain, with a couple of rather slap-happy seahorses galumphing boisterously in the huge pool, and the shaggy old man waving a generous arm towards the Palace Hotel, worth a few million as it stood, and it seemed to be doing good business, too. The whole of Madrid seemed to be doing good business. Most of the damage from the Civil War had been removed or repaired, and Luis saw uniforms everywhere. He stood on the corner of the Calle de Alcalá where it joined the Gran Via, and marvelled that so many countries could afford to send so many military representatives to Spain, and in such big cars, too. The *Banco de España* had its headquarters on the corner, sturdy and splendid, and Luis felt pleased to see that his financiers were still prospering. The whole of the Gran Via seemed to be awash with prosperity: he went along in a happy tide of well-dressed shoppers, past stores which were brilliant with goods, and eventually reached the Plaza España, a great and tranquil plain of trees and flowers. In the middle stood the Cervantes Monument. Luis strolled over and stared. Posterity had done very well by Cervantes, he thought, but the publishers must be doing even better out of him. There was money in books, if only you could come up with the right book . . .

Around the corner, then, to the Sabatini Gardens and good God in heaven above, the Royal Palace! *What a size!* The damn place stretched for ever. Everything was squared-off and balanced, balconies and windows and pilasters multiplying themselves with great discipline, but it was all so bloody *big*! And then Luis realised that he was looking at the end of the Palace. To see the front—the entire front—he had to walk across to the far side of the Plaza de Oriente. The view dazed him: how could there be enough money in the world to put up a building like that? How could he have driven a taxi around Madrid and not seen all these fantastic riches? All this phenomenal wealth?

A combination of fresh air, sunshine, hunger and architectural magnificence began to work on his brain. He walked through the backstreets to the most spectacular square in Madrid, the Plaza Mayor, and stood in its centre, like a drunk in a distillery. The terraced houses rose five storeys high on all four sides, with a colonnaded piazza running around the base. He was in a stadium of balconies far bigger than any bullring, and as vivid as a theatre. *If I owned one-tenth of this,* Luis thought, *one-hundredth even* . . .

He moved on, restless with envy, and found himself in the Puerta del Sol, the Times Square of Madrid. The pulse of the crowds was stronger here, everyone heading for lunch. Only Luis, it seemed, had nowhere to go. He looked for and found the zero-kilometre landmark, the spot representing the nominal centre of Spain, starting-point for all the radial roads. 'This is where it all begins, then,' he said. He looked for, and found, the statue of the symbol of Madrid: the bear and the *madrono* tree. The beast was standing on its hind legs and eating the fruit. Luis patted a massive bronze paw. 'You have the right idea, friend,' he murmured. 'There is money to be made here. I shall make a lot of it. You want to know how? I shall spy for the British.'

Chapter 12

'Now, exactly what sort of agency do you represent, Señor Cabrillo?' asked the British Embassy's assistant commercial attaché, unscrewing the cap from his fountain pen.

'Military intelligence,' said Luis.

The cap went back on the fountain pen. 'Wrong department,' the man said.

'Yes, I know,' Luis told him. 'You see, I did not trust the man who met me when I arrived here. He looked . . .' Luis wobbled his hands and tried to think of the English word. 'What is . . .?' He fluttered his fingers. 'Not quite criminal, but . . .'

'Shifty?' suggested the assistant commercial attaché, getting to his feet.

'Yes, shifty! You have noticed it too.'

'I must remember to tell him. That was Williams, our head of security.'

Luis smiled. 'He has a sense of humour, then.'

'Absolutely none. Stiff as a plank. Wait here, please.'

Fifteen minutes later a woman looked into the room and offered Luis a cup of tea. He accepted.

After another ten minutes a tall, thin man came in and introduced himself as Cameron. He wore a doublebreasted blue blazer and very dark grey trousers. 'Now, Mr Cabrillo,' he said, 'I understand you have some secret knowledge of the German war machine which you wish to share with us.'

'No,' said Luis.

Cameron stiffened, and gave him a hard look. 'That is not the impression you gave my colleague.'

'He makes his impressions, Mr Cameron, and I make mine. I did not completely trust him. He looked . . . shifty.'

84

Cameron grunted. 'Like Williams, you mean?'

'More or less, yes.'

'You will tell me, won't you, if I start looking shifty?'

'Yes. At once.'

'You're very kind. If you have no military information to share, why come to the British Embassy?'

'I wish to spy for Britain,' Luis declared. 'In Germany, preferably. Or in Italy, if you wish.'

'The grub's better in Italy,' said Cameron thoughtfully. 'There's probably more business to be had in Germany, but I'd pick Italy for the food, and of course for the climate . . . Not that I know the first thing about it.' He got up. 'Not my department, thank God. Wait here, would you?'

Luis waited for another half-hour, during which a different woman brought him another cup of tea.

The next man to arrive was a friendly squadron-leader in the RAF, called Blake. He shook hands warmly and smiled jovially, and Luis felt greatly encouraged. At last he was getting somewhere.

'Right! Now, let's find out something about you. I take it you're . . . Spanish?'

'Yes.'

Blake wrote that down. 'And I'm told you're offering us your services as a sort of a . . . That is to say, you'd be involved in . . . well, in a sort of intelligence capacity. So to speak. Mmm?'

'I wish to spy for the British,' said Luis. There had been enough confusion already.

'Of course,' beamed Blake. 'Jolly good.' He wrote that down. 'Now, I hope you won't be offended, old chap, if I ask you why?'

Luis frowned. He had not expected that question. *How* or *when*, yes; but not *why*. This was probably not the time to raise the subject of money. He moved his cup and saucer an inch to the right, crossed his legs, tugged the lobe of his left ear.

'*Porqué?*' Blake added, helpfully.

'It is a matter of style,' Luis told him. 'I very much admire style, and from what I have seen, British style is second to none.'

'Style?' Blake looked surprised, but he made a note.

'I do not mean taste,' Luis said. 'Taste is not style.'

'Isn't it?' Blake chewed his pen. 'No, I suppose it isn't.'

'On the other hand, style is never in *bad* taste.'

'No. I mean I couldn't agree more, old boy. Not that I know much about that sort of thing, but it's always good to hear someone say something nice about the old country . . . Really, though, what I meant was: why come to us instead of to the Germans?'

'As I have said—'

'Yes, I know, style and all that; but let's face it, your government is much chummier with them than it is with us, isn't it?'

'I do not support the government,' Luis said. 'As we say in Spanish: I shit on fascism.'

'Oh.' Blake thought for a moment, wrote something, crossed it out, wrote something else. 'Sounds as if you might have been on the other side in the recent Civil War,' he remarked.

'I shit on Communism too,' Luis said.

'Ah. Well, that seems to take care of the political situation, then.' Blake grinned cheerily, and Luis's confidence in him increased yet again. Clearly this was a man who understood men, who saw facts clearly and made decisions quickly. It would be a pleasure as well as a profit to work for the British.

'In any case, it would be pointless for me to go to the Germans,' Luis said. 'They are winning, they don't need spies. Your country, however, is not winning, and so you need all the help you can get.'

'That's very interesting,' Blake said thoughtfully. 'I've never heard it put quite like that before.'

Blake asked him about his background, and smiled sympathetically when Luis revealed that he had no previous experience in espionage, although his work for the newspaper correspondents could be described as a sort of apprenticeship. 'That does not worry me,' Luis said. 'It means I have nothing in my past to hide, so I cannot be exposed by anybody. My inexperience will be a great advantage, in fact.'

Blake snapped his fingers in admiration. 'I must remember to tell that to the Air Ministry,' he said, and scribbled a final note. 'Perhaps they'll make me a wing commander. Look, thanks awfully for being so helpful.' He shook hands again and clapped Luis on the shoulder. 'You don't mind stooging about here for a sec? I'll get you a spot of tea.' He winked reassuringly, and stepped bouncily out of the room, whacking his notebook against his thigh as he went.

Intellect, competence and decisiveness, Luis thought. Ability and clarity. Above all, *style*. What an admirable people the British were. Admirably dependable too: the tea arrived almost at once.

*

On the floor above, a greyhaired naval commander named Meredith looked out at the Calle Fernando el Santo, listened to Blake's report, and wrinkled his nose.

'What it boils down to, Freddy, is he's a dago spy. What do we want with a dago spy?'

'No idea, sir. I've only been here a week, remember, so it's all Greek to me.'

'All right, listen. Point one: London's not keen on local recruiting. Point two: if we encourage him he'll want money and we haven't a budget. Point three: in any case we don't need a dago spy, we need a victory. Greece has gone down the drain, Crete's going fast, North Africa's bloody dodgy, and look at the havoc the U-boats are doing to our convoys! Have you any idea how much tonnage those bastards sank last month, Freddy?'

Blake creased his brow. 'Quite a lot, sir?'

'A hell of a sight more than we can replace,' Meredith said bitterly. 'And no amount of dago spies is going to alter that awful fact.'

'Tell you what, sir,' Blake suggested. 'I'll stagger down and tell him to buzz off, shall I?'

Meredith leaned forward and squinted into the sunlit street. 'There go those frightful Hungarians,' he grunted. 'Thank God they're not on our side.'

'No style, sir?' Blake asked.

Meredith turned away from the window and heaved a sigh. 'He's got a bloody nerve, hasn't he? Wandering in here without an appointment and . . . Are you sure he hasn't got any connections or . . . or influence? What university did he go to?'

'None, I think,' Blake said, 'but I'll find out.'

Meredith followed him downstairs. When Blake opened the door, Meredith peered through the crack. He saw Luis stand up and smile.

'I say: you didn't go to a university, did you, old boy?' Blake asked amiably, shaking his head: and Luis confirmed this. Blake smiled his gratitude and shut the door.

'How old is he, for God's sake?' Meredith asked.

'Mid-twenties, I'd say, sir. A handsome lad, though.'

Meredith made a face. 'He doesn't look like my idea of a spy. Not a bit like.'

'Sometimes that's all to the good, sir. We don't want our spies to look like spies, do we?'

'He's had no experience, he doesn't *know* anyone, and he hasn't been to a decent university. Not even an *in*decent one. The fellow must think we're absolutely desperate. Damn cheek. See him off, Freddy.' Meredith tramped upstairs.

Blake opened the door and gave Luis a friendly grin. 'Sorry, old chap,' he said. 'None today, I'm afraid.'

•

On his way out of the embassy, the shock and the many cups of tea caught up with Luis. 'May I use your bathroom?' he asked.

'Be my guest,' Blake said. He pointed to a door.

Luis went inside and discovered that the room was indeed a bathroom: it contained a bath and a washbasin. He was too weak to argue. He pissed down the side of the bath to minimise the noise, ran the taps for a moment, and walked out into the glaring heat of the street, trembling with relief and chagrin.

At right angles to the Calle Fernando el Santo was the Calle de Fortuny. The German Embassy occupied number eight. Luis Cabrillo was ringing its doorbell less than a minute after leaving the other place.

Chapter 13

The British Embassy had been like a gentlemen's club on a quiet weekend: spacious, quiet, with an occasional glimpse of a uniformed porter taking something to somebody at no great pace. By contrast the German Embassy bustled like a railway station.

It was in a huge and rambling four-storey building, once the town house of some eighteenth-century grandee. The entrance hall was slightly smaller than a tennis court, but it was big enough to be used as a waiting room. The man who opened the door for Luis gave him a form to fill in, and indicated the rows of chairs. They were well filled.

Luis found an empty seat and studied the form.

Name. Address. Nature of enquiry/business/request. At the bottom, three little boxes marked *Department. Officer. Action.* In very small print, down in one corner, *IG Mad 7/40—50,000.* They'd had fifty thousand of these things printed in July 1940.

Fifty thousand people ringing fifty thousand doorbells to fill in fifty thousand forms and sit on fifty thousand chairs. For how long? Judging by all these expressions of boredom and slumped weariness, fifty thousand years.

Depression seeped into him and stole his energy, his will, his purpose. He had not eaten since breakfast, and his legs ached from too much walking. He stretched and relaxed, and watched the busy Germans hurrying along the corridor that crossed the hall, or trotting up and down the double staircase leading to the other floors. What industry! What organisation! What possible use could these Europe-conquerors have for a dusty, hungry, penniless ex-journalists'-assistant with throbbing feet?

He rested his head against the chairback and caught sight of an astonishing woman sitting in the row in front.

One glance erased all thought of his feet, his poverty, and even his hunger. A prolonged stare made his head tingle with an enthusiastic charge of blood, and he straightened up as if someone had poked him in the ribs with a pointed stick.

She was young: over twenty, under twenty-five. What startled Luis was not so much her looks as—he could find no other word for it—her style. He was accustomed to women who were proud or vain, flirtatious or submissive. This was the first time he had seen a woman so obviously in complete control of herself and her emotions; a woman who knew what she wanted and didn't give much of a damn whether anyone else liked it or not. Those wide grey eyes surveyed the people in the waiting-room as calmly as a contented leopard watching a herd of gazelle. Yet there was humour in the curve of her mouth, and even a suggestion of sympathy in the tilt of an eyebrow.

Or was he finding humour and sympathy only because he was looking for them? She fascinated Luis; she generated an unconscious sexual challenge: how could anyone be so utterly desirable yet so completely self-sufficient? She wasn't Spanish, that was sure. German, perhaps? Healthy-looking enough; confident-looking enough. But long black hair. No, not exactly black: very very dark red. All right, so what? All Germans aren't blondes. Look at Adolf Hitler.

He glanced at Adolf Hitler, whose picture was on the wall, and when he looked back she had half-turned and was examining him in a detached but not unfriendly fashion. He gave her a tight smile and a stiff nod. His heart was playing ragtime and his lungs couldn't keep up with the beat. She returned a small part of the smile with devastating ease. He fumbled open the form and searched for his pen, his face rigid with indifference.

Nature of enquiry/business/request.

Luis crossed out *enquiry* and *request*, thought hard, his brain still alive with excitement, and wrote: *I have technical information concerning the new secret British weapon code-named 'Elephant'.* He signed: *Luis Cabrillo, Count de Zamora y Ciudad-Rodrigo.*

The official who took the form gave him a numbered disc and said automatically, 'Listen for your number.' No number had been called since Luis had arrived. He stalked slowly and aristocratically back to his seat, watched with stoicism by the crowd; whether or not the astonishing woman was watching too he did not dare find out. *'Espérese un momento!'* called the official in a bad accent. *'Count de Zamora?'*

Luis turned. The crowd shifted suspiciously, and when Luis was beckoned back, looked cheated and disapproving and helpless. The official finished murmuring into a telephone and replaced the instrument.

'Por favor, Excelencia,' he said, inviting Luis to precede him.

In a very short time Luis was seated in a small, comfortable room, facing a pleasant young man who said his name was Otto Krafft.

'Well, you're not the Count de Zamora y Ciudad-Rodrigo, are you?' said Krafft in good Spanish, putting aside a copy of the *Almanach de Gotha.*

'No,' Luis said, 'but then you're not the assistant commercial attaché, are you?'

Krafft steepled his fingers and hid behind them. 'So what?' His eyebrows were so blond they were almost silver.

'Suppose I'd written "Nature of business: espionage" on that form,' Luis said. 'What would the German embassy have thought?'

Krafft shrugged. 'Another crank, another halfwit.'

'Yes. So instead of "espionage" I might put down something tedious like "import-export". That would get me as far as the assistant commercial attaché.'

'More likely the deputy assistant.'

'Even worse. Then I tell him what I really want, but of course he knows nobody in that department.'

'Of course. The less he knows, the better.'

'And two hours later, after another three abortive meetings, I might reach your office. If I'm lucky.'

Krafft regarded Luis thoughtfully over his arched fingers. 'Is there a moral to all that, d'you think?' he asked.

'Perhaps nobody expects a spy to be honest.' Luis was amazed at the calm and competent way he was handling this discussion. Evidently that skirmish with those unprofessional buffoons in the British Embassy had done him good.

'Do the British have a secret weapon called "Elephant"?' Krafft asked.

'I haven't the faintest idea. But I'm perfectly willing to find out.' Luis buffed his fingernails on his sleeve and glanced about him at the furnishings of the room, trying to disguise his mounting exhilaration. Now he was out of the shallows and into deep water. Nobody had made him do it; nobody would try to save him. It was a hell of a long way down, and that knowledge made his loins tingle with joy and dread. Terrific. Onwards!

When he looked again, Krafft was leaning back, hands cupped behind his head. This time he spoke in English.

'You wish to spy for Germany,' he said.

'It has been my ambition,' Luis told him, also in English, 'ever since I was a toddler.'

That enormously amused Krafft. 'A toddler! Imagine that!' He jumped up and dragged open a filing cabinet. 'And now, Mr Cabrillo, you want to toddle over to England and toddle around their army camps and toddle lots of lovely secrets back to us. Is that right?' He came back with a thick buff form.

'Oh no,' Luis said. 'Certainly not. I'm not a toddler any more, Mr Krafft. I might slink, I might snoop. I might even, at a pinch, sneak. But let me assure you, Mr Krafft: my toddling days are over.'

Krafft chuckled. 'Surely you wouldn't *sneak*, Mr Cabrillo. That would be very un-English.'

Luis gave himself the luxury of not smiling. He then gave himself the extra reward of not even replying. He merely looked at Krafft: an I'm-ready-when-you-are look.

'I take it you have previous experience in the intelligence field, Mr Cabrillo.'

'During our own civil war, of blessed memory, I made my living as a spy.'

'For whom?'

'For the Nationalists, naturally.'

'And you reported to . . .?'

'To Colonel Juan de la Vega,' Luis said flatly. Vega had died in an air crash in 1938.

'Humm. You must then be skilled in the use of shortwave radio, invisible inks, and so on.'

'No. I always reported in person. One of the luxuries of a civil war, you see.'

Krafft asked him several more questions: family background, marital status, education, where he learned such good English, police record, state of health, experience of firearms.

92

'Not much,' Luis said. 'They're too noisy and too messy. You can't pick a lock with a gun, and—'

'Absolutely. Couldn't agree more.' Krafft rapidly completed the form, blotted it briskly, and slapped the pages shut. 'And it doesn't matter in the slightest, because nobody ever looks at these things.' He slung the form into a wire basket. 'I don't mind telling you, the German reputation for thoroughness can sometimes be a pain in the head.'

'Neck,' Luis said. 'Pain in the neck.'

'So? You suffer from it too.' They laughed, and Krafft opened the door for Luis. 'You don't know it, Mr Cabrillo, but you arrived here at exactly the right time. We need a man with your qualifications,' he said, as they strolled along the corridor, 'and we need him urgently.'

'I'm glad to hear it.' Luis had been considering how much money to ask for; he doubled his estimate. 'I'm ready to start work as soon as we can reach an agreement.'

'Splendid.' Krafft led him down two short flights of stairs and around a corner. 'Wonderful. I can't believe my luck. This morning I was very, very worried, but now . . .' He opened a steel door and signalled Luis to go in. A plump, middleaged man in new white overalls got up from a steel chair behind a steel table. The whole room was steel. 'This is Mr Cabrillo, Franz,' Krafft said in the same optimistic voice. 'He is a British spy. Shoot him.'

He went out and closed the door. It shut with a firm, well-made *chunk*.

＊

It was a joke, of course; Luis saw that at once from the expression on Franz's face: a gentle, reassuring smile, like that of a father about to take his child down a toboggan run for the first time. He reminded Luis of the railway official who had brought him the news of his parents' death : both men blinked too much.

'Now please don't worry about anything young Otto may have told you,' Franz said, fumbling in a deep desk drawer. 'He gets carried away sometimes. This won't hurt a bit, I promise.' He came up with a black automatic pistol so heavy that it bent his wrist.

'I don't understand,' Luis said. His voice was calm but his

stomach was twitching. 'I told Otto that I have no use for firearms. None at all.'

Franz made a wry, apologetic face, and began screwing a silencer onto the pistol. 'It's my fault,' he said, 'I should have had everything ready for you. Would you like to shut your eyes?'

Involuntarily, Luis did shut his eyes for a second, but he opened them wide, and stared. 'This is insane!' he cried, 'You're behaving like lunatics!'

Franz thumbed a clip of ammunition into the weapon, wincing at the effort. 'I merely do as I'm told,' he said. 'Now if you wouldn't mind stepping over—'

'Listen, I'm not a goddam British spy!' Luis told him furiously.

'Well now,' Franz said mildly. 'You would say that, wouldn't you?' He pursed his lips and narrowed his eyes, and Luis realised—with a jolt that made him inhale sharply—that Franz was inspecting him for execution.

'But I'm *not*!' Luis insisted; and even to his own ears the claim sounded childish. 'For God's sake, I came here to work for *your* people!'

'That's as may be, my love.' Franz carefully disengaged the safety catch, and Luis felt himself slipping and sliding helplessly to his doom. *Why didn't you knock the silly bastard down before he got that thing loaded?* he asked himself, bitterly and uselessly. 'I just do what they tell me,' the German said. A touch of heartburn made him beat a chubby fist against his breast. 'Would you mind standing up against that wall?'

'But what good does it do you to kill me?' Luis pleaded. He was acutely conscious of his clothes thinly protecting his body, of his skin shifting wretchedly under his clothes.

'I can't see that a British spy is any use to us alive,' Franz pointed out. 'Can you?' He braced his legs and bent at the knees.

Tell him anything, Luis's brain ordered frantically. *Tell him you're a British spy, tell him you know all their secrets, tell him anything, everything, don't let him kill you!* But the rest of his body seemed to be locked in paralysis. He stood with his chin up and his teeth clenched, and counted the pulse beating in his head, booming away like a clock that was trying to strike infinity. Franz held the pistol in both hands, at arms' length, raising it steadily to shoulder height. 'You really should stand against the wall,' he murmured. Luis clenched his teeth until the muscles hurt. He was afraid, but he was also stiff with rage at the colossal stupidity of these people. He saw the barrel stop climbing. It wavered fractionally. The German closed one eye. Luis felt sick. There was a bang like a book falling off a shelf. Something smashed Luis in the chest and he fell backwards, arms flailing; but already darkness had driven out light. Franz had been right: it didn't hurt a bit.

*

'All right, then, I didn't get a bulls-eye,' Franz said. 'But I got an inner. Definitely.'

Otto made a thoughtful, noncommittal noise and drummed his fingers on Luis's ribcage. 'You're quite sure the heart is all the way over there? Almost in the middle?'

'Yes, of course it is.'

'So why do most people think their heart is on the left, I wonder?'

'No idea. Does it matter?'

'Probably not.'

Luis was stretched out on the steel table, face upwards, his feet overhanging the end. A wide dribble of saliva was rapidly drying on his chin and neck.

'Come on, come on,' Franz said. 'I've got work to do.' He took a pin from his lapel and pricked Luis on the wrist. A shining seed of blood grew on the spot. Luis twitched and his throat made a gruff growl. After a moment he opened his eyes and turned his head.

The two Germans appeared to be standing horizontally, with their feet attached to the wall. They were fuzzy in outline and shimmering, as if seen through water. He watched Franz lift one foot from the wall and take a pace forward without falling on his head. Clever people, these Germans. Very well organised. Then he remembered the pistol, the bang, the smash in the chest, and he sat up. Otto and Franz swooped through a quarter-turn and stood erect, less fuzzy now but still wavering whenever the breeze ruffled the water. He looked at them and they looked back. Already a part of him

95

was in panic, screaming at his brain to wake up and start running, because he was late for the race and the others wouldn't wait, they'd race off and leave him lumbering behind, lumbering like this stupid brain, which was too stupid to know how stupid it was, so he could never win, which made him wildly angry with it, and with them, and with everyone; and at last the blood came pumping vigorously up into his head, driving the panic away and clearing his senses like a flag slowly unfurling. 'Now I expect you could do with a glass of brandy,' Krafft said.

'Schnapps,' Luis said croakily. He had never drunk schnapps but this seemed like a good time to start scoring points. His shirt was open and there was a small bruise in the middle of his chest. He thought hard and said nothing.

Otto gave him a glass of clear liquid. It smelled like nail-polish-remover and tasted like hot nothing. He drank it and buttoned his shirt. The schnapps trickled south and slowly burned itself out. He got to his feet and knotted his tie and smoothed his clothes. 'I see you searched me,' he said.

'How can you tell?' Franz asked.

'Handkerchief's in the wrong pocket.'

'Ah.' Franz looked gratified. 'We wondered if you would notice, Mr Cabrillo.'

'You're doing very well,' Otto said. 'Very well indeed.'

Luis put his handkerchief in the right pocket, and gave Otto a grim, sideways glance. 'I don't like the sound of that,' he said.

They laughed politely, and led him upstairs.

Chapter 14

Colonel Christian's office was on the third floor, and as an office it made an elegant drawing-room: embossed lime-green wallpaper, pale lemon-yellow sofas and chairs, a light grey rug, and a white baby grand piano tucked away in a corner. Cream-coloured venetian blinds sifted the afternoon sunlight and admitted a few select rays of gentle birth and good manners. It was all very civilised and soothing and it was completely wrong for the man.

Christian was about fifty, tall, craggy-featured, with shoulders that might have been happier heaving barrels off a brewer's dray. His face was so hard and square that the moustache and eyebrows seemed unnaturally bushy, like clumps of grass rooted in a rockface. Because he was incapable of keeping still for more than a minute, his well-cut brown suit was as rumpled as an old parcel. But his voice was quiet and quick, and he shook Luis's hand without crushing it. Then he set off on an endless tour of the room. 'So Mr Cabrillo is not in the employment of the British government,' he said.

'No, sir,' said Krafft.

'That's good.' Colonel Christian waved Luis to a seat. 'I don't need you,' he told Franz. 'Go and organise some coffee . . . And you want to spy for us. What is your opinion of spying?'

'It's a job,' Luis said.

'Very boring job. I was a spy, you know. In the Great War. Dreadful hours, but it wasn't the hours, it was the *hanging around*, waiting, waiting . . . How do you know if a troop train has gone through Paris? Or if a squadron has left Boulogne?'

'Wait and see,' Luis said.

'Boring hours. And you meet such boring people. Soldiers don't want to talk about war. So you have to talk about football. Hours and days and weeks of football, just to pick up some gossip about a new rifle.'

'I know football,' Luis said. 'Centre-forward, goalkeeper, offside, corner kick.'

'Sailors are even more boring. Sailors talk sex. Endlessly.'

'I don't know sex,' Luis said. 'But I'm willing to learn.'

'And the paperwork. It's like being a travelling salesman.' Colonel Christian prowled over to the baby grand, sat, played the opening chords of the funeral march, got up, resumed his tour. 'But perhaps you enjoy paperwork?' he asked.

'No, it bores me,' Luis said.

'Rotten food, out in all weathers, and the surroundings are drab as drab can be. Garrison towns. Factory towns. Seaports. Dockyards. All grim.'

'It's a job,' Luis said.

'Rotten job.'

'Perhaps that is what makes the money so good,' Luis suggested.

Colonel Christian paused by the fireplace. 'Are you interested in money, Mr Cabrillo?'

'I'm interested in a *lot* of money.'

Franz came in with the coffee. 'Thank you,' said Christian, 'and goodbye. What sort of information will you give us for our money, Mr Cabrillo?'

Luis was almost trapped into a foolish answer. He was thinking of saying something impressive, like *new aircraft performance figures* or *locations of ammunition dumps.* 'I'll give you what you ask for,' he said. 'You know what you need, I don't.'

Otto poured the coffee. 'How will you get to England?' he asked.

'If that means you don't want to make the arrangements,' Luis said, 'then I would travel as a neutral businessman. Presumably England and Spain are still allowed to trade?'

'We might want you to recruit another agent once you get established in England,' Christian said. He took a cup of coffee in passing. 'Maybe even two.'

'Provided the money is available to pay them, I see no difficulty.'

'I do,' said Otto Krafft. 'I see the British secret service. They will be looking for people like you. What will you do if they start to suspect?'

Luis sipped his coffee. 'That depends. It is best to carry on normally, if possible; otherwise a change in one's pattern of behaviour simply confirms their suspicions.'

'Things get worse,' Christian said. One-handed, he turned a chair upside down and examined its legs. 'They're on to you.'

'Then it's all over. I get out.'

'How?'

'That's my problem.'

Christian reversed the chair and put it back. 'You are an independent soul, Mr Cabrillo.'

'I'm an independent businessman, colonel.'

Otto suddenly clapped his hands. 'I have a wonderful idea!' he cried. 'We make Mr Cabrillo a captain in the German army! Then his pay can safely accumulate here, and if he has to return prematurely he will still be employed.' He spread his arms, eagerly.

'Why not a major?' Christian asked. 'Major Cabrillo. Yes?'

'No,' Luis said. 'I don't want a salary. You pay me by results. And you pay on delivery.'

'Let's get one thing straight, Mr Cabrillo,' Otto said coldly. 'Colonel Christian has no shortage of volunteers. Many men would be willing to pay for the honour and privilege of serving Germany.'

Luis said nothing, but he helped himself to more coffee and loaded it with sugar to pacify his hunger. There was a perpetual trembling under his heart, and from time to time a pulse in the side of his head throbbed so powerfully that he was afraid the others might notice it. Yet his hands were steady, his voice was even. He wished Christian would stop bloody well tramping around the room. And he wished he knew exactly what, if anything, they had done to him downstairs. If he had been drugged, the drug seemed to be doing him a power of good; if not, he was tougher than he thought . . . The silence persisted. He glanced up and saw that they were watching him. He watched them back. That was something he could do without strain. Otto had a mole on his neck. Christian's ears were lightly freckled.

Otto grunted. He sounded a little weary. 'I see,' he said. 'Devotion to duty, patriotism, sacrifice—all these things mean nothing to you.' He turned away. Christian still stared, his eyebrows occasionally working.

'I am not going to argue about it,' Luis said. 'If you think your splendid volunteers can do a better job than I, and also pay you for the privilege, then why waste your time on me?' *Oh, oh, that's a bit reckless*, he thought as the words left his mouth.

Christian stretched a long arm and pointed a slightly crooked finger. 'Why do *you* waste *your* time on us? We have already won. We control Europe. Go and spy for the British. They are desperate for help.'

'Desperate men make bad employers. And you have not quite won, colonel, have you? There is still Britain.'

'A matter of time.'

Christian let the finger go slack, the arm fall. He began

99

bouncing on the balls of his feet, like a long-distance runner loosening up. Otto's back was still turned. He seemed to be slumped in gloom : head down, shoulders bowed. Luis watched curiously, and received the surrealist impression that Christian's jogging was meant to revive Otto. It was a sort of psychic pump-action. At any moment, Otto's shoulders would straighten, his head would rise, and Christian would have to ease off before Otto began snapping his fingers and tap-dancing onto the furniture.

No such luck. Otto remained slumped, and Christian slowed to a bored halt.

Luis stood. The over-sweetened coffee had left a tacky after-taste. He wondered where he had gone wrong. He wondered whether or not there was any point in trying the Italian Embassy. Or the Japanese Embassy. Or the Abyssinian Consulate. Or anywhere. 'If you'll excuse me, then,' he said, as if he had somewhere to go.

'Before you leave . . .' Christian took a deep, important breath. 'Think of this. If you were to accept a commission, you could end up a hero of the German nation, one of the most decorated men in Europe. You could be a powerful force for good once you had helped us to total victory. Now that is worth something.'

'I could also end up dead long before that,' Luis said. 'Which is why I want to be paid on delivery. You may keep the medals until later,' he added.

Colonel Christian paced over to the fireplace, nodding sombrely. 'You're making a great mistake,' he said. 'Money is a poor reward.' Luis shrugged. 'How much do you want?' Christian asked.

Luis felt the fluttering below his heart subside. He had a sudden, craven impulse to say something grateful, like *Pay me what you think I'm worth*; but he suppressed it. He nodded at Otto. 'Has he passed away in his sleep?'

Otto turned. He was filing his nails.

'I wondered what that noise was,' Luis said. 'I was afraid it might indicate some painful mental process.'

'How much?' Christian asked.

'A thousand pesetas now, five hundred a day expenses, fifteen thousand to get me to England, and thereafter a retainer of five thousand a week,' Luis said.

Christian nodded. 'I see. You want us to pay you a retainer. But you said just now that you wanted to be paid for information supplied, on delivery.'

'My mental processes detect a painful contradiction,' said Otto.

'When I fail to supply the information,' Luis told them, 'you can fail to pay the retainer.'

'Agreed,' Colonel Christian said. 'Now let us turn our attention to the question of your operational efficiency, well-being and survival.'

That was that: Luis was in. It took him a moment to realise, as Otto produced maps and documents, that there would be no handshake, no signature, no welcome-to-the organisation; just this understanding. He had passed their tests; they had accepted his terms.

Starting a few seconds ago, he was a full-time professional German spy, to be paid on results. There must be several hundred British agents whose sole job was to find and kill people like him. How curious; how primitive . . . 'Are you listening?' Christian demanded.

'Yes, yes.'

'No, you're not. Pay attention, for God's sake. I was saying that the *Abwehr*—that's us, you understand, German Intelligence—the *Abwehr* operates three methods of infiltrating agents: landings from U-boats, parachute drops, and travel via neutrals. The same methods work in reverse, except we can't make the parachutes go up so we have to use light aircraft. You will be trained in all three techniques. Now look at this map . . .'

For twenty minutes Christian described the structure of *Abwehr* espionage in Britain. He showed Luis which stretches of coast were approachable by submarine and rubber dinghy, and at what state of tide. He indicated the good areas for parachuting. He spent a lot of time on the rail network, and then explained how the distribution of *Abwehr* agents followed this pattern of railway communications because it was by far the easiest way to travel in time of war. Another map had three transparent overlays on which were plotted all known bases of the British Army, Navy and Air Force. When all the overlays were in position, Christian pointed out those parts of the country which were important to all three

Services. Then he went back to the map of *Abwehr* agents and explained how their location gave the maximum freedom of movement plus the maximum access to these areas of military importance. Finally he unrolled a map of northern Europe and gave Luis a brief account of the system of radio communications between *Abwehr* agents and a chain of receiving stations in France, Belgium and Holland.

'All of this is actually operating now?' Luis asked.

'Well, I'm not making it up as I go along,' Christian said irritably. 'I hope you're taking it seriously.'

'Of course.'

'Good. It's your neck, but what's more important, it's our money. Otto will now explain what steps we take to keep you intact if things go wrong.'

'The most important protection you have,' Otto began, 'is that you will never be entirely on your own. For instance, if you have to disappear temporarily, this network of safe houses is available at any time, day or night . . .' Another map was unrolled. Luis carefully studied the gold stars sprinkled across the counties of Britain; wherever the *Abwehr* sent its spies, it seemed, a haven was not far away. Otto went through the various emergency procedures: how certain innocent-sounding phrases were warnings from one agent to another; how to evade telephone-tapping; rendezvous techniques; recognition signals; communicating via classified advertisements in newspapers; and finally how to get a fresh set of false papers and emergency funds if the situation became really desperate. 'That should never happen,' Otto stressed. 'If it does, you've blundered badly, so get out of there. Get back here.' And he outlined the various routes which the *Abwehr* had prepared and perfected for the extraction of its agents without delay.

'You are very well organised,' Luis said.

Christian rolled up a map and swung it at an imaginary golf ball. He said: 'It suits us that the rest of the world regards all Germans as—what is the English for "dummkopf"?'

'Fathead?'

'As fatheads. Do you know the English joke about the German spy? A fatheaded German spy goes up to a policeman outside an aircraft factory and says "How many people work in there?" and the policeman replies, " Oh, about half of them".'

Luis waited, half-smiling. 'That is all?' he asked at last.

'I told you it was an English joke.' Colonel Christian scrutinised Luis for a few moments, his craggy face heavy with discontent. 'I'd feel a lot happier if you weren't so revoltingly goodlooking,' he said. 'English women lose all self control when they catch sight of a young Spaniard, they hunt him to exhaustion and rape him behind the nearest cricket pavilion. Brutal lot.'

'How awful,' Luis said. 'There doesn't seem much I can do about it.'

'Close your eyes and think of Germany,' Otto advised.

'Anyway, try not to get *involved*,' Christian told him. 'Don't get engaged, and certainly don't get married. You know where to buy contraceptive sheaths in England?'

'Drugstores?' Luis suggested.

'Hairdressers. Peculiar people, the English. Perhaps they wear them on their heads in wet weather. And it's not drugstores in England, it's chemists' shops.'

'Sorry.'

'You'll be more than sorry if you make that kind of mistake . . . What do you want us to do with your money?'

'Pay it,' Luis said, surprised.

'Yes, but where? You'll never spend it all in England. If you're just going to bring it out again, you might as well have it put somewhere handy in the first place.'

'Switzerland,' Otto proposed. 'Central, and safe. Or Sweden, or Portugal, or the United States . . . We can open an account in your name and have the statements sent to any address you specify.' They discussed Luis's financial arrangements in some detail, including which currency he should be paid in; how he might consider investing his funds; his tax status; the advantages and disadvantages of engaging an accountant; what sort of trade or profession to assume; and the possibility of turning oneself into a limited company based on, say, the Bahamas. Luis found it enormously stimulating and gratifying. 'I don't want you worrying about money,' Colonel Christian told him. 'It's in my interests to keep your mind clear so that you can concentrate on your job. Right?'

'Right. And you agreed to pay me a thousand pesetas today.'

Christian whacked Otto on the head with the rolled-up map.

'Fathead!' he cried. Otto pretended to be stunned, and crossed his eyes. 'Pay Mr Cabrillo two thousand pesetas instantly, or I shall have your arms torn off by wild horses.'

Otto emptied his wallet. 'I have only fifteen hundred pesetas,' he said. He gave the notes to Luis.

'In that case only one arm shall be torn off,' Christian ruled.

'The Embassy has no wild horses,' Otto said.

'Then find some tame horses, and enrage the beasts!' Christian shouted, waving his arms. He took Luis by the elbow and steered him out of the room. 'I am surrounded by fatheads,' he murmured loudly.

They walked downstairs, across a courtyard which had a fountain and some shade trees, and into a small ground-floor room. There was a chair, a table, some magazines, a door to the next room, and a view of the street through a barred and dusty window.

'Make yourself comfortable,' Christian said. He went out and closed the door behind him.

Chapter 15

That was 4.25. By five o'clock Luis was bored and becoming slightly irritated.

At first he had been too exhilarated to sit down, and too excited to look at the magazines. He counted and recounted the money, straightening the dog-eared corners and correcting any notes which were upside-down or back-to-front. Fifteen hundred pesetas! And it might so easily have been two thousand! *By God*, he thought, *there is booty to be got out of this war if you have the nerve to go in and claim it* . . . The wad of paper made a fat and reassuring bulge in his hip pocket.

He strolled up and down the room and tried to work out what had happened during the afternoon. Obviously he had been put through a series of tests, and only when he passed those tests had he been accepted into the *Abwehr*. The money had been a symbol of admission; the money, and the fact that

Colonel Christian had shown him so much secret information. That much was clear.

And Colonel Christian: what a character! Who said the Germans had no sense of humour? 'I am surrounded by fat-heads!' Luis murmured happily.

All right, what about fat Franz and the practical joke in the steel room? Luis unbuttoned his shirt. There was a small round mark, not serious enough to be called a bruise, an inch above his breastbone. Franz's pistol fired bullets which bounced off people. How chic! How sophisticated! Civilised warfare at last! Or was it? Would he have felt anything if it had been a real bullet? The serious suffering came *before* Franz pulled the trigger. Expectation was a worse death than perforation. Presumably that episode was just a test, too. Supposing Luis had been a British spy, would he have stayed silent and let Franz fire? No, probably not. In fact definitely not. Luis knew it, conceded it: he would have confessed. It was the blatant absurdity of Franz's action that had forced him to tighten his grip on the truth and refuse to cheat. If Franz was going to be a mad killer then Luis had to die a sane victim: that was the simple logic of the nightmare.

If he *had* confessed, what would they have done? Probably shot him with a real bullet, immediately. And used a real silencer, too. Luis remembered that terrible little bang, the last sound he was going to hear on earth. From a silenced gun. He should have known better. But during those final seconds of horror, the brain had quit and the senses were running riot. One little bang had been enough to pop his over-inflated consciousness; one tiny prod in the chest flattened him. It was death by imagination.

And all that other stuff, in Christian's office? Bleak analyses of the tedium of spying, and of the danger; all leading to an effort to persuade him to accept the security and prestige of a commission in the German army? Just tests. Tests of his determination and self-confidence and driving-power. Naturally they had wanted to know what sort of a man he was, whether or not he was capable of operating alone and under great pressure. Well, now they knew. Luis took out his money again, spread the notes like a deck of cards, and fanned himself. Beautiful winnings! He was eager to start work and make more.

The chair was hard, and the Franco-censored magazines were dull.

The door to the next room was locked.

The view from the dusty window was unexciting. The street was empty except for a cat which sat on a wall and looked at Luis, weighing up his prospects.

After a while it yawned and went away. Now the street was completely vacant.

Luis began to get impatient. Colonel Christian had given no reason for leaving him here, so Luis had assumed it would be for just a few minutes. Already it was half an hour. What the hell did they think they were playing at?

He gave Christian two minutes to return. Otherwise he was going to look for him.

Christian ignored the ultimatum. 'Very well,' Luis said aloud, 'you leave me no choice.' He strode to the door, and it too was locked. 'Ohoh,' he added more softly. 'You really do leave me no choice.'

For a while he paced the room trying to decide whether or not he was justified in feeling so annoyed; and failing. So he sat on the hard chair and flicked through the dull magazines. They were stifling. Stupefying. The table had a drawer. He tugged it open, and a key rattled forward.

'Well, now,' Luis said. He tried the key in the door to the corridor and it did not work. He tried it in the door to the other room and it worked so easily that the door seemed to swing open at his touch.

The room was larger, with two windows (unbarred) and a door (closed). It was more comfortably furnished, but not by much: the main difference was a big settee. On it, a man slept.

Luis tiptoed over and took a good look at him. He was under thirty, cleanshaven, with fair, curly hair and a pleasantly freckled face, boyish now in the ease of sleep. He was wearing a grey polo-neck sweater with buff twill trousers, and he was barefoot.

A smear of mud had dried across his forehead. He was sleeping heavily, with one arm trapped beneath his legs and the other flopping loose.

Luis moved to the door. It was locked. He tried the key but it wouldn't work this lock. Worse, it got stuck, and he had to use his strength to turn it back. The door rattled noisily, and the sleeper awoke. He thrust himself upright, stiff and staring, like a knock-down fairground target swung back into action. *'Hide the set!'* he said in a cracked and furious whisper. All his boyish ease had vanished; he looked thoroughly frightened.

'I'm sorry,' Luis said. 'I'm afraid I disturbed you.' They spoke in English.

The man stared at him, not breathing, grasping the edge of the settee so tightly that Luis could see the raised veins and sinews on the backs of his hands. Then he slowly relaxed, and sucked in a long, shivering lungful of air. 'Oh crikey,' he said, and put his head in his hands. 'It's not Liverpool, is it?'

'You mean this place?' The man nodded. 'This is Madrid,' Luis said.

'I don't care, as long as it's not Liverpool,' the man mumbled. He looked up, his hands still covering half his face. 'I remember now: I got away. Yes . . . Now I remember. My God.' Unexpectedly, he chuckled. 'So did you, eh? Bloody good show . . .'

'I don't know about that,' Luis said. 'Have you the key to this door?'

The eyes narrowed, the voice grated. 'Who the hell are you? How did you get in here? What d'you want?'

'I just want to get out.'

'Why? What's your bloody game?' He was quivering with angry suspicion.

'It's nothing to do with you, I assure you.' Luis attempted a gentle, comforting smile. 'I'm looking for Colonel Christian, that's all.'

The name had a curious effect. The man seemed to withdraw, physically and emotionally. He shifted to the far end of the settee and sat with his feet up, hugging his knees. His face was a blank and his eyes were half-closed. He spoke in a bitter whisper. 'You'd better find him before I do, chummy,' he said, 'because I'm going to kill that bastard.' His head slowly dropped. The tangle of fair curls quivered in an occasional tremor; otherwise he might have been sleeping. Perhaps he was sleeping.

Luis wandered across the room. There were many questions he would have liked to ask, but not at the price of disturbing this man, who seemed disturbed enough already. On the other hand, Luis himself was a lot less happy than he had been half-an-hour ago. It was pretty obvious where this fellow had been, and apparently he hadn't enjoyed it very much. Christian didn't seem to have been a lot of help, either.

A newspaper lay on the floor beside the settee. Luis picked it up. Yesterday's edition of *The Times*, of London, very crumpled and stained. Someone had ringed an item in the personal column: *PONGO: Never say die. See you at the theatre. Rhino.* Luis looked from the newspaper to the silent figure on the settee. A bottle was poking out of a coat pocket; he leaned forward and recognised the label: Johnny Walker. Not a lot left, either.

Time passed. Luis fetched the chair from the other room and tried to keep it from squeaking. The cat walked up the street and yawned at him again. If he held his breath he could just hear, far away, the faintest possible tapping of a typewriter. The old nervous trembling was beginning to come back under his heart.

He glanced across the room and found the barefoot man awake again and watching him. 'Are you, by any chance, Pongo?' Luis inquired. 'Or perhaps Rhino? I only ask because I'm going to England soon, and I'd be grateful for any advice.'

No response.

'My guess is you left in rather a hurry,' Luis said.

More silence.

'Well, I suppose you know best,' Luis said.

That did the trick. The barefoot man stood up, and slowly and methodically searched the room. He found nothing, and returned to the settee, which he prodded cautiously all over. Finally he tipped it onto its back and examined its underside. One corner of the hessian covering had come loose. He seized a handful and ripped more of it away. Luis came closer and watched with interest as he thrust an arm deep into the guts of the settee and dragged out a small microphone on the end of a length of wire. He tossed it to Luis and righted the settee with a contemptuous crash.

'My goodness,' Luis said; but the barefoot man put his finger to his lips. He opened a window and looked out, feeling around the frame and under the sill. Then he beckoned Luis over and together they leaned out.

'There's another mike planted somewhere,' he said softly. 'Yes, I'm Pongo. Or I was until last night. God knows where they find these idiotic codenames. I suppose it's someone's idea of a joke. Their whole bloody operation is a joke.'

'You mentioned Liverpool,' Luis said. They were leaning out, their heads close together, looking down into the basement area. 'Were you in Liverpool?'

'Liverpool, Southampton, Sheffield, Bristol, Glasgow, you name it they sent me there, dozens of times. Always a mad rush, of course. Extreme urgency. Top priority. Take the first train but don't travel first class, we can't afford it, go second class. Christ, the number of hours I've spent flattening my arse in grubby British second-class compartments, you wouldn't believe.'

'But I thought money was no problem,' Luis said. Pongo laughed. 'Well, that was the impression I got, anyway,' Luis added.

'You must be easily impressed. They're tight and they're cheap but you don't discover that until you're over there. I was starving at one point. Can you believe that? Starving. They left me flat broke for weeks on end.'

Luis thought, while Pongo spat his disgust at the battered dustbins below, and missed. 'But . . . how did you survive?'

'Took a job. Had to! Drove a taxi around London and nearly caught my death of cold . . . Every night I signalled Christian: *send money*. Fat lot he cared. Bastard.'

'I used to drive a taxi, once,' Luis said. 'Here.'

'Take my tip, friend. Go back to it. You'll live longer and die richer.'

'Didn't you get sent any money at all?' Luis asked.

Pongo looked up at the sky. Its pure oceanic blue was beginning to fade with the passing of day. Fifty yards to their right, the traffic on Fortuny flicked past this empty backstreet. 'They sent me money,' Pongo said. 'They sent me a hundred guineas, in a leather bag. Great fat clinking golden guineas . . .' He covered his face and rubbed his eyes, and came up blinking at the awful memory.

'Not sovereigns?' Luis said.

'Guineas. As inconspicuous as a three-dollar bill. A bag full of death warrants.'

'It does sound rather . . . ill-advised,' Luis agreed.

Pongo gave him a sharp glance, incredulity touched with anger; hunched his shoulders; looked away. There was a pause.

'You don't mean . . .' Luis failed to find a suitable formula of words.

'What do you think? I wasn't giving them what they asked—hell's teeth, you can't come up with top-grade information every day—so they wrote me off. A bag of bloody guineas . . . They should have sent me a dozen cyanide phials. Jesus Christ . . .' Pongo bunched his fists and gradually relaxed them. 'There were times when I'd have eaten the bloody things, with pleasure.'

'Surely it couldn't have been as bad as all that.'

'I was on the run, chum. Everyone was after me: police, army, Special Branch, Boy Scouts, Home Guard . . . I never slept for ten days. You can't run and sleep. It was bad, believe me.'

'But what about the emergency procedures?' Luis asked. 'Couldn't you find a safe house and lie low?'

'None of that exists,' Pongo said. 'It's all in Christian's head.'

'My God.' Luis stared down at the wet stain left by Pongo's spittle. 'I can't believe it. I mean he's so . . .'

'Friendly? Fatherly? Oh yes, he's a convincing bastard.' Pongo brooded. 'Did he tell you the joke about the German spy and the aircraft factory?'

' "How many people work in there?" That one?'

Pongo nodded. 'And I expect he told you where to buy contraceptives? And that all Englishwomen are nymphos? Christ! When I think that I actually *laughed* at his jokes! But I'll bet he didn't give you any money. No fear. Lots of talk, and the money tomorrow. That's Christian.'

'Actually, he gave me fifteen hundred pesetas,' Luis said.

Pongo stared. The freckles on his white skin were as delicate as speckles on an egg. 'You've actually got it?' he breathed. 'Cash? Not a cheque?' Luis nodded modestly.

Pongo looked down into the basement area. It was a drop of about ten feet. If you hung from the windowsill it would mean a fall of only about three feet. He glanced up the empty street to the bustle of Fortuny, and then back at Luis. 'Then what the hell are you waiting for?' he breathed.

'Nothing,' Luis said. He turned quickly, grabbed Pongo by the bare ankles, and heaved him out of the window. Luis glimpsed a flicker of outspread toes. Then there was a shout, a great crash of dustbins, a metallic clatter as a lid rolled away and fell over, and a certain amount of piteous groaning. But by that time Luis was casually pounding on the door with the chair. Soon someone came and let him out.

*

'You didn't have to do that,' Otto Krafft said. This time he was genuinely angry.

'You didn't have to do it either,' Luis said. They were back in Colonel Christian's exquisite office, where now the atmosphere was much more businesslike. 'Besides, I was right. Wasn't I?'

'A bit less Spanish arrogance, my friend,' Christian growled. 'You could have been wrong.'

'All right.' Luis got up and wandered over to the creamy baby grand. 'Suppose I had been wrong. He was going to kill you, so he said. Isn't that a good enough reason to defenestrate him?' He sat on the piano stool and squinted at the music. 'Jesus: four flats,' he muttered.

'De-what?' Christian said irritably.

'Defenestrate. From the Latin, *fenestra*, window, *de*, chuck out of, *ate*, after lunch.' Luis began picking out the Funeral March with one finger.

'That's awful. That's bloody dreadful,' Christian complained. 'Shut it up, for God's sake. I can see why there aren't any good Spanish composers.' Luis stopped.

The telephone made a single, cautious buzz. Otto answered it, listened, grimaced, muttered his thanks and hung up. 'Broken wrist and ankle, and cracked collarbone,' he said. 'Plus a few lumps on the head.'

'You might have killed him,' Christian told Luis.

'Well, so might you have killed me downstairs with your dummy bullet. Suppose I had a weak heart?' He was feeling lightheaded and a little reckless; this whole day had become so bizarre that there seemed no more point in behaving thoughtfully; instinct ruled. 'Actually I *have* got a weak heart,' he said. 'Look.' His outstretched fingers trembled hideously.

'You've got a weak head,' Christian said. 'He didn't mean

what he said. It was a figure of speech: "I'll kill that fellow one day . . ." If you can't tell the difference between barking and biting, you're no damn use to me.'

'Oh, I know he didn't mean it,' Luis replied. 'He didn't mean *any* of it. He made it all up. The whole stunt was an act, a fairy tale. Pongo's never been to England in his life.'

Otto sniffed. 'What you don't know is he's one of the few decent bridge-players in the embassy and you've gone and bust his arm.'

'I know about bridge,' Luis said. 'Five hearts, two no spades, doubled in diamonds.'

'You don't need me any more, do you?' Otto asked. Christian raised a hand without looking at him. Otto went out. 'Astonish me,' Christian told Luis. He began prowling around the room.

Luis watched him prowl. *Oh Christ*, he thought, *I can't stand that again*. He set off around the room in the other direction, keeping in step with Christian.

'In no particular order,' he said. 'Pongo couldn't have got a job driving a taxi in London. It takes too long to pass the test. Months, years. I read a book about it once.'

'He was a hired-car chauffeur,' Christian announced.

'He *said* taxi-driver.'

'He meant—'

'Listen, colonel,' Luis said forcefully. 'D'you want a debate, or d'you want to be astonished?'

They stopped at opposite sides of the room. Christian jutted his jaw and chewed on one side of his moustache. 'Look here, you arrogant young Spanish buck,' he said. 'D'you really want to work for me, or d'you just want to indulge yourself?'

'I didn't get into your office by saying yes-sir-no-sir, did I?' Luis demanded. 'If all you need is someone to agree with you, then talk to yourself.'

Luis stared and Christian glared. Luis put his hands behind his back to hide the trembling. Christian moodily kicked the furniture. 'Get on with it,' he grunted. They resumed their walks.

'Pongo was never a taxi-driver, and he didn't travel second-class on a British train, because British trains have only first-class and third-class. You didn't pay him in guineas, because there is no such thing as a guinea.'

112

Christian stopped again. This time they were only a few feet apart. He raised his arm and displayed his wristwatch. 'Fifty guineas in Piccadilly,' he stated. 'And worth every guinea.'

'But you didn't pay in guineas,' Luis insisted. 'That coin has been obsolete for years.' They had another little duel of the eyeballs. Luis felt his vision losing its focus. 'Also your watch is three minutes slow,' he lied.

Christian dropped his arm, straightened the sleeve with an impatient shake, and prowled on. Luis watched him and picked up the step again.

'What's more, I don't think microphones work very well in the middle of settees,' he said, 'especially when they're not connected to anything.'

Christian changed step, with a stately little shuffle. 'Anything else?' he asked.

Luis thought back. 'No, that's all.'

'Don't you think he had a very white complexion for a man who's been on the run for ten days?'

'Yes, perhaps.'

'And his feet are remarkably clean and unmarked?'

'That is true.'

'Of course it is. Why do you think we took his shoes and socks off?'

'I assumed it was to make him seem more innocent. Barefoot people always look rather innocent, don't they?'

'You didn't.' Christian dropped into an armchair and hooked a leg over the side.

Luis was briefly baffled. 'Oh,' he said. 'Um . . . Didn't I?'

'We had you stretched out stark naked downstairs while we went through your clothes. When I say "we", I don't mean "me".' He looked at his hands as if he might have forgotten to wash them. 'There was nothing to find, was there? No papers, no money, no wallet, no keys, no cards, no matches, no diary, no driver's licence, no ticket-stubs, no tattered receipts, not even an airmail envelope from Moscow with an incriminating telephone number scribbled on the back. What's wrong with you, Mr Cabrillo? Don't you ever do *anything*?'

'I blow my nose from time to time,' Luis said. He found an armchair facing the colonel and dropped into it, hooking his leg over the side.

'You blow your nose.' Christian unhooked his leg. Luis

unhooked his leg. 'Tell me . . .' Christian cupped his hands behind his head and slumped deeper in the chair. Luis duplicated the action. They half-lay, their heads tugged upright, and examined each other. 'What exactly have you been up to?'

'I've been in prison,' Luis said.

'Your hands are too smooth.'

'They let me wear gloves.'

'Why should they do that?'

'So I could play the violin again.'

Christian moved his hands to the top of his head. Luis did the same. Down on the street, some distant motorist played *La Cucaracha* on his horn, twice. 'I can't play that, though,' Luis said. 'Too many flats.'

Christian sat up and folded his arms; so did Luis. 'This is all nonsense,' the German said. 'I second that!' Luis cried.

He saw the other man dip his head and tighten his lips, and before he could stop himself Luis had mimicked the action. *Sweet Jesus*, he thought, *now you've gone too far, he's going to kick you out into the street* . . . But Christian merely said, in a fed-up voice, 'I don't intend to waste any more time.'

'Well, thank God for that!' Luis exclaimed. He heaved himself out of the chair. 'Because as far as I can see, all you've done since I walked in here is . . . is . . . Do you know the verb "to bugger about"?'

'I can guess what it means.'

'Well, you people have buggered me about all afternoon. And for what? Fifteen hundred pesetas?' Luis astonished and slightly frightened himself by pulling out the banknotes and tossing them into the colonel's lap. 'Now please listen carefully, because I shall never say this again. I am serious when I tell you that I wish to spy for Germany in England. But if you think your grubby little retainer has bought you the right to treat me like an idiot child, then your aims and mine are poles apart.' Luis dusted his hands and headed for the door.

'It's locked,' Christian said.

'Well, I expect the key's hidden somewhere obvious,' Luis said evenly. 'You look in the piano stool and I'll go and throw Otto out of the window.'

'Here, take it back.' Christian came over and stuffed the

money into Luis's pocket. 'I've just made it up to two thousand. You're worth it, d'you know that? And I'll tell you why. You're a games-player, Mr Cabrillo. You take chances. The British are great games-players but we Germans are not. I think maybe you can beat the British at their own game.'

'Which is what?' Luis asked.

'Cheating.'

Christian opened the door. It had not been locked. 'That's dishonest,' Luis pointed out.

'Yes, I try to stay in practice,' Christian said modestly. 'Come back and see me tomorrow morning at nine.'

They actually shook hands, and Colonel Christian actually looked happy.

Chapter 16

Otto escorted Luis down to the lobby. He was delighted to hear that Luis would be returning next morning, and invited him to come earlier and have breakfast. Luis thanked him but declined, saying that he always breakfasted on kippers, a habit he had picked up in England, and he did not wish to put the German embassy to any inconvenience. Otto laughed and promised him excellent kippers. Luis said he was sorry about Pongo, who after all had only been doing his best. His real name was Wolfgang Adler, Otto said, and he was accustomed to breaking his bones: he ski-ed every weekend at the Navacerrada Pass . . .

They were strolling past the official at the reception desk when Luis remembered the woman.

He turned, and looked, and saw her almost at once: still in the same chair, in the same attitude, with the same expression. Still the leopard amongst the gazelle; still able to make his head tingle for no reason that he could have named.

'You forgot something?' Otto enquired.

'That woman over there. In the white sleeveless dress, no hat. Who is she?'

Otto turned aside, murmured to the official, and brought back an embassy form. Luis read: CONROY, *Julia*, followed by something in German plus a date and a time. The date was yesterday's, the time was 9 a.m. 'The lady does not seem to be getting much attention,' Luis said.

'Oh, some of these enquiries are unbelievably complicated,' Otto said. 'When there is a war on—'

'My case was not exactly straightforward, but you dealt with it speedily. Very speedily.'

'Well . . . I'll try and see that she's attended to first thing in the morning, if you feel—'

'Why not now?'

'Now? It may be very complicated.'

'Surely all the more reason to start as soon as possible.'

Otto's smile was growing tired and losing its grip. He took back the embassy form and walked over to the official, snapping his fingers as he went. They talked, and Otto glanced through another, bigger form. 'Frau Conroy,' he called.

She got up from her seat and crossed the room, moving easily, like a good tennis player after three hard sets and a hot shower. Luis ambled nearer. 'Frau Conroy, I regret this delay,' Otto said, still speaking in English. 'A telegram will be sent to Paris tonight. Perhaps if you could return here tomorrow . . .?'

'You're very kind,' she said, but there was a slight twist to her smile which made Otto hunch his shoulders as if in self-defence. For a moment nobody spoke, all three of them caught up in the elegant dishonesty of the situation. Then Otto bowed, and nodded to Luis. 'Until tomorrow,' he said.

'Until kippers,' Luis agreed.

As they came out of the embassy he began: 'Permit me to introduce myself—'

'I know who you are,' she said. 'You're the Count of Zamora and Eggs Benedict.'

'I should explain—'

'No, don't bother.' She signalled a cab. 'Because by a curious coincidence I'm not Eleanor Roosevelt, either. Can I drop you somewhere?'

*

Luis hadn't been in a car since he crawled, head buzzing, out of that wreck in the middle of a forest of softly whispering midday trees five miles outside Guernica, years before. Now

116

all the flashy excitement of motoring came rushing back to him as he smelled old leather upholstery, overworked engine oil and bitter-sweet exhaust fumes. The taxi took off with astonishing acceleration, or so it seemed to him, and manoeuvred quite dashingly; but then so did all the other traffic: it zipped and whirled and stopped itself inches from disaster and leaped away again, brilliantly yet casually. Luis leaned back and admired their driver's slickness, but he also wished that the man would drive a little more slowly. All these flashing streets, all these giddy turns, were making him feel drunk with speed.

But not *Frau* Conroy. She, he noticed, was minding her own business, and a very tranquil job she made of it.

They sat without speaking until Luis suddenly realised that they were getting near her hotel, and therefore near to parting; which would leave him alone in the middle of Madrid, and that prospect scared him. On impulse, he leaned forward and pressed the driver's shoulder. 'Cava Baja,' he said. They turned sharp left.

'Why did you do that?' she asked.

'We are being followed. I have to shake them off.'

Her eyebrows rose and fell. 'Who's following us?'

'German agents. In the third car behind.'

She turned and looked. 'The third car behind is a bus,' she said.

'Make it Cuchilleros instead,' Luis told the driver urgently. 'This way is better,' he explained to her. 'Buses do not use the Calle de Cuchilleros.'

'They don't use the Calle Cava Baja either,' she said, 'especially the one behind us, which is going to the Puerta de Toledo.'

'You would prefer Cava Baja? It is not too late to change.'

'I would prefer my hotel, that's what I would prefer.'

'There are several excellent bars on Cuchilleros.'

She moistened her lips. 'You should have said that first, not last.'

'I do not mean to disparage the bars on Cava Baja, which are also fine bars.'

'Don't louse things up, friend. We can drink to Cava Baja when we get to Cuchilleros.'

'The bus has gone,' Luis observed with satisfaction. 'We have shaken off the bus.'

'Terrific,' she said. 'Nothing worse than a grabby bus.'

They bounced and swung through some of the oldest parts of Old Madrid, all cobblestones and high, balconied houses. The streets never held a straight line for more than a block; they curved and narrowed into sharp turns only to broaden out into odd-shaped little plazas from which three or four equally twisting streets ran away and disappeared. Occasionally a massive church or a hulking citadel caught the eye, but they were rapidly lost as the taxi turned and turned, and turned again. When it stopped Luis had his money ready. He hurried her into the nearest bar and found a table at the back.

'From here we can watch who arrives,' he said.

'Uh-huh.' She took in the walls, curving inwards to form an arched roof, all beige with smoke and scratched with ten thousand names, messages, slogans; the bar, brown and battered; the clusters of garlic and fists of sausage hanging from the ceiling; and the customers, all talking, none listening. 'And what do we do if a couple of gorillas from the Gestapo turn up?' she asked. A man who was thinking of something else brought them two glasses of wine and a saucer of bits of smoked ham, and went away.

'You are safe with me,' Luis said. 'As you saw, I am not without influence at the German embassy.'

'Listen, I was safe *before* I met you.' She ate some ham. 'Who the hell are you, anyway? Since you're not the Count of Thingummy.'

'You seem very sure of that.' Luis stretched his legs, sucked in his cheeks and looked down his nose at the prawn shells littering the floor.

'Sure I'm sure. No Count of Thingummy would walk into a waiting-room, sit down among the peasants, and fill out a form. Right?'

Luis flared his nostrils a little and stored that information away for future use. 'It was an alias,' he agreed. 'My name is Luis Cabrillo. I am a representative of the International Red Cross, and we are trying to trace persons missing as a result of the recent hostilities.'

'Are you, now?' The information impressed her; she studied his face carefully. 'Well, that's certainly a very decent job to be doing. Damn decent.'

He bowed his head in acknowledgement. 'And what brings you to Madrid, Señora Conroy?'

'If you're going to be Luis, I'd better be Julie . . . Me, I work for the movies. Metro-Goldwyn-Mayer. We've got a lot of unfinished business in Europe since Hitler took over. Reels of film lying all over the place, that sort of thing. I'm trying to straighten it out.'

'You are American?'

'From California.'

'Ah . . .' Luis was enormously pleased: far from being a German (even an English-speaking German) she was an American, a genuine Hollywood American. It was the first time he had met anyone from California. Now he understood why she had astonished him at first sight: *this was a Californian who worked for MGM!* There was a gentle glow about her, a cool aura, like those publicity stills where they fogged the background to make the star stand out. He signalled for more wine.

'I still don't see why the Germans should want to have you followed,' she said.

'Oh, they follow everybody, they are very suspicious people. You see, my work for the International Red Cross brings me in contact with other embassies. I dislike people interfering with my private life.'

Cigar smoke was beginning to turn the air a silky blue. It drifted in layers, like the ghosts of ancient banners. 'What do they put in those things?' she asked. 'Apart from bullshit, I mean.'

'Bullshit?' Luis repeated.

'Yes.' He still looked uncertain, so she explained: 'Bullshit. The shit of bulls. Bovine dung. Cattle crap.'

'Ah!' Luis exclaimed. 'Of course, *bull-shit.* Yes, I understand. As in horseshit. And chickenshit. Also dogshit.' He beamed his understanding. 'All good fertiliser,' he said.

'Not bullshit. That does nothing any good. I should know, I've come across enough of it lately.'

'Here? In Madrid?'

'Everywhere. It seems to be Europe's principal industry, since Hitler took over. You don't know what the hell I'm talking about, do you?'

Luis narrowed his eyes, and probed the air with his outstretched fingers. 'The linguistic concept is not unfamiliar,' he said, 'although certain nuances—'

'Bullshit. And that's a good example. The word has a special meaning for Americans, you see, Luis.' She fingered back her hair, dark as wine in the bottle; and when she looked up, her jaw curved to a clean, confident point. 'Bullshit is blowing too hard, coming on too strong. Politicians bullshit at elections, right? Detroit bullshits about cars. Bullshit is ballyhoo. Horseshit, on the other hand, is just bad news.'

'Horseshit on *either* hand has very little to commend it,' Luis observed gravely.

Julie turned her head sharply, almost fooled by his tone, and smiled. 'You said it . . . Horseshit is *lies*, deliberate dirty, greedy, selfish lies. Most religion is horseshit. Chickenshit is different again. Chickenshit is God's way of paying me back for saying religion is horseshit. Burned toast is chickenshit. Soap in your eyes is chickenshit. Menstruation is chickenshit.' She glanced at Luis.

'I know about menstruation,' he said. 'I read about it in a book.'

'Yeah? And what did you think of it?'

Luis considered. 'I thought it was not a very smart idea.'

'Well . . . even God made mistakes.'

Luis held his glass up to the light. The wine glowed like a stormy sunset. 'You are very lovely,' he remarked.

Pause. 'That's horseshit, I think,' she said. 'Or is it bullshit . . .?' She munched some more ham. 'No, I was right first time, it's horseshit. Nice try, though. You said it beautifully.'

Luis furrowed his brow and saddened his eyes in a show of concern which, he knew from experience, older Spanish women found touching. 'Perhaps you are not the best judge of yourself,' he suggested.

'Oh, I think I'm gorgeous. But I also work for MGM, and MGM is in the loveliness business, so I know what I look like. My face rates above the back of a bus and below Rita Hayworth's stand-in. Are you feeling okay?'

'Yes, I'm fine.'

'You're looking kind of haggard there. I thought maybe it was the booze.'

Luis erased the furrows from his brow and squared his shoulders. 'If you don't mind, Julie, I should like to move to another bar. It is still possible that German agents are watching this place. We can leave by a side door and thus evade them.'

She finished her wine, observing him over the rim of the glass. 'Why don't you just go out and chuck 'em through the nearest plate-glass window?' she asked. 'That's what MGM would do.'

'Have you ever seen anyone do it?' He put money on the table, and stood up. 'I have. During our Civil War. I saw some people try to throw a man through a shop window. It was not easy, he kept bouncing off, those windows are tough. It took them a long time and I'm fairly sure that he was not alive when they finally succeeded.'

He led her to the side door.

'Whose side were they on?' she asked.

'I'm damned if I can remember.'

They went through some back-alleys, pungent with garbage-cans and purple with dusk, and into another cave-like bar.

'You never told me the special American meaning of dog-shit,' Luis said.

'Didn't I?' Julie eased behind a table and looked up at the baffled, glassy stare of a bull's-head mounted on the opposite wall. 'Well, war is dogshit, Luis. That is all ye know and all ye need to know. Make sure they understand that in the . . . What did you say? . . . International Red Cross. Or whatever.'

Later, Luis offered to take her to dinner, but she refused. She went back to her hotel, which turned out to be the Bristol, and he went back to his apartment.

It had been a rich, full day and he was tired, yet he had difficulty getting to sleep. He got up and re-read some of the short stories of Ernest Hemingway. They were less satisfying the second time around. Hemingway, he noticed, was not very good at women. He was first-class at bull-fights, prize-fights and big-game-hunting, but he kept women at arm's-length; which seemed to Luis, in his curiously excited and fatigued condition, to be a waste of women. And therefore a waste of Hemingway too. At last he slept.

Chapter 17

After breakfast, Otto Krafft took Luis to Colonel Christian.

'Good kippers?' Christian asked.

'Fair. They were not oak-smoked,' Luis said. 'The best kippers are oak-smoked, you know.'

'I didn't know. What a waste of a noble tree. Dreadful stuff, fish. All those bones. Like booby-trapped chicken. One good thing about Madrid is it's such a long way from the sea. Unlike Denmark, for instance. I once did six months in Copenhagen. Fish, fish, fish; I nearly died. I'm sure that if God meant us to eat fish, he would have made it taste like pork with apple sauce.'

'I like fish,' Luis said. 'Especially oak-smoked kippers.'

'Depraved,' Christian said. 'You must go to Copenhagen one day and indulge yourself. In the meantime, we have this mission to England to arrange.'

'The English like fish,' Krafft observed.

'In that case everyone should be very happy, because one of the things we shall want reports about is the British scale of rations. Do you know the Morse code, Mr Cabrillo?'

'No.'

'Franz will teach you. Can you operate a radio set? Pick a lock? Use firearms? Take microphotographs? Tap a telephone?'

'No, none of those things.'

'Good, I prefer a man with an open mind. We shall stock it with our skills. In two weeks you will be a trained agent. Have you any talents which we should know about?'

Luis thought hard, while Christian riffled through his morning mail and Krafft wound his watch. *Come on, come on,* Luis thought, *there must be some damned thing you can do . . .* The more he searched his memory, the more he realised that his life amounted to fifteen or twenty lost jobs, a bit of snooping in the Civil War, a year wandering around with a donkey, and two years browsing the random pickings of

English literature. Did it have the makings of a spy? Even a trainee spy? 'I don't know whether you'd call it a talent,' he began. Christian and Krafft looked politely interested. 'People seem to like me,' he said.

They examined him for a moment, as if he were about to prove it by, for instance, waggling his ears.

'I don't mean they like me *very much*,' he explained. 'I mean I seem to get on with people quite easily. That can be useful when you want to, you know, make friends.'

'Ah,' Christian said.

'Not that I form any deep attachments as a result. It's not a weakness, you see, it's just a . . . a . . .'

'A facility,' Krafft suggested.

'Right.'

'And very nice too,' Christian said. 'Is that the lot? Very well. You will spend this morning with Franz, forming a deep attachment with the Morse code. Goodbye.'

'Goodbye,' Luis said; but he paused on his way out. 'Nobody around here ever says "Heil Hitler",' he remarked.

Christian looked up at him, peering through shaggy eyebrows. 'That's not a weakness either,' he said. 'It's just a facility.'

For the next three hours Luis sat in a room in a remote corner of the embassy and tapped a Morse buzzer. Franz (whose other name was Werth) was dressed in plus-fours and a fawn cardigan. He still looked pudgy and diffident but he kept Luis working hard. Whenever Luis stretched or yawned, Franz made him run three times around the room. By eleven o'clock he had a rough-and-ready grasp of most of the alphabet, and they paused for coffee.

'You've done this before,' Luis said.

'True.' Franz dipped a biscuit and nibbled the soggy bit.

'And you've taught other agents? People who went to England?'

Franz blinked a good deal and licked a crumb off his lower lip. 'Well, you're not the first, are you?' he said. 'The war's been going on for two years, nearly.'

Luis played with the Morse key until Franz shuddered delicately and took it away from him. 'What sort of luck have the others had?' he asked.

'What do you mean by "luck"?'

'I suppose I mean . . .' Luis cracked a few knuckles. A fly buzzed overhead and he followed its course until his head would turn no more. 'Damn. You know very well what I mean. How many got caught?'

'No idea.' Franz tidied the coffee things away and put the Morse buzzers back in place. 'I'm not told that sort of information, it's not necessary.'

'I suppose it would be foolish to pretend that nobody gets caught.'

'Foolish and dangerous. All wars are much the same, you know. I believe that during the '14–'18 war about half of all spies were captured as soon as they entered the enemy country.'

'About half,' Luis whispered. He sat hunched over the table, fingers gently bound, his smooth, sad face staring at nothing.

'And half were not,' Franz added brightly. He gave the key a brisk, preliminary work-out. 'At least, not immediately. Now then, remember to keep the wrist poised but not stiff . . .'

By midday Luis was sending and receiving very simple messages. His wrist ached and his ears were sick of the probing, peg-legged buzz, but Franz went on and on. Patiently and slowly he tapped out yet another little stream of easy words: *How big is new gun?*

Luis slumped and stared at the writing on his message-pad. His mind refused to suggest an answer. 'It's no good,' he said. 'I'm too bloody hungry.'

'Fine,' Franz told him. 'Send that.'

Grimly, Luis took hold of the buzzer and pecked out his reply.

' "Broody"?' Franz enquired. 'What is this word "broody?" Please repeat.'

Luis clenched his teeth and thumped the buzzer again. Franz scanned what he had written and nodded. 'Ah, *bloody*,' he said, 'I see, you are *bloody hangry*. Is that right? Are you *hangry?*'

'Yes,' Luis said furiously. 'And no.'

'Please repeat.'

Yet again Luis laboriously spelled out his last, desperate signal. Franz studied the message and smiled. 'I expect you are ready for lunch,' he said. Luis grunted.

As they walked along corridors to the embassy diningroom,

124

Franz said: 'There's a lesson to be learned from all that, you know.'

'Yes? What?'

'If an agent wants to eat, he must first send his signals. And not broody hangry signals, either.'

*

After lunch, Otto took charge of Luis. They went to the embassy doctor and Luis was given a long and thorough medical examination. The man weighed and measured him, tested his eye sight and hearing, checked his temperature and the state of his teeth, established that he was free from infectious disease, took samples of blood and urine, X-rayed his lungs and recorded his blood pressure. That much Luis understood. Other tests, involving a lot of cold steel equipment placed against various parts of his body, lasted a further twenty minutes and meant nothing to him. Finally, while he was still naked, a photographer arrived, set up a tripod and took a dozen pictures. 'Hold your chin up and give me a nice smile,' the photographer said.

'I also croon and tap-dance a little,' Luis said.

'You can put your clothes on now,' Otto told him.

'What's the point of all this? I'm not applying for a life-insurance policy. Quite the opposite.'

'We find it helps to know the state of your health.' Otto picked up the doctor's little rubber hammer and began tapping himself, on the knee, the ankle, the shin. 'You could be dying from something incurable, couldn't you? And obviously that would have influenced your motives. It might have affected your performance, too.'

'I've got Quixote's Disease,' Luis said. 'That's usually fatal.'

Otto glanced at the doctor, who shook his head and went on putting away his equipment.

'It's all in your own interest, anyway,' Otto said. 'Suppose you needed spectacles, or a hearing aid? You don't want to go searching for medical treatment in England, do you?' He rapped himself on the skull, first cautiously, then more resolutely.

'One tooth requires a small filling,' the doctor said. 'Dr Graumann will do it tomorrow at three.'

'There you are, you see? We have just saved you from torture at the hands of some brutal British dentist.' Otto located his breastbone and tested it.

'Why the photographs?' Luis asked.

'In case we have to get you some special clothing in an emergency. Military uniform, clerical dress, that sort of thing. The tailor likes to know what you look like.'

'Next time I'll comb my pubic hair.'

'You can wear a spotted bow in it, for all we care. Results are what matter here.' Otto struck himself wristily on the point of his left elbow, and exclaimed loudly. 'By God, that hurts!' he told the doctor.

'Pain is nature's way of telling us to stop hitting ourselves with other people's hammers,' the doctor said. He removed the hammer.

Luis finished tying his laces. 'I take it, then, that I'm not in a state of decay,' he said.

'From the age of twenty-five we are all in a state of irreversible decay,' the doctor said. 'Welcome to the club.'

As Otto walked Luis to another part of the embassy, he said, 'There's no such thing as Quixote's Disease, is there?'

'All Spaniards suffer from it,' Luis told him sombrely.

Otto knew it was a leg-pull but he couldn't leave it alone. 'What are the symptoms?' he asked.

'Hot blood. Steaming hot blood.'

'Ah. That probably explains all the smouldering eyes one sees.'

'Yes. Smouldering eyes and burning lips and blistering tongues and smoking shoulderblades and even, at the height of the summer, occasional warm feet.'

'Sounds uncomfortable.'

'We have an old saying,' Luis said wisely. ' "Scratch a Spaniard, and start a fire".'

Otto found that vastly amusing. He laughed and chuckled all the way to another office. He paused with his hand on the door. 'What happens when you scratch a German?' he asked.

'Start a war?' Luis suggested.

Otto grunted. 'Just don't try that on Colonel Christian.' He took Luis inside.

*

For two hours, a lanky, sandy-haired ex-journalist called
126

Richard Fischer coached Luis in secret writing.

They practised with a variety of invisible inks on a variety of papers. Sometimes Luis wrote on the back of a sheet of notepaper, sometimes between the lines of a typed letter. Fischer showed him how to unseal all the joins of an ordinary envelope so that its inside surface could be used for secret writing, and then how to reseal the envelope, and then how to slit it open without damaging the message. They studied different printed papers—insurance policies, bank statements, furniture catalogues, theatre programmes—while Fischer pointed out advantages and disadvantages: plenty of white space here; glossy surface there, bad for certain inks; this stuff's like blotting-paper, quite useless; that's better but far too small, of course . . . At the end he picked out a British Post Office form, dense with information about revised overseas parcel rates. 'On the whole, I think I'd use this,' he decided.

'Not much space,' Luis said. The margins were cramped, the lines were crowded. 'It would have to be a very short message. "Dear Hitler, Nothing new this end, Love, Luis." That sort of thing.'

'What do you bet that I couldn't get the British Army's Order of Battle on there?' Fischer asked. He was as bland as a bigamist.

Luis found a fifty-peseta note in his back pocket, uncrumpled it and spread it on the table. 'I am sure that I shall soon regret this,' he said.

'Watch.' Fischer took a scent-spray filled with a faintly green liquid and pumped a fine and gentle mist all over the Post Office form. He placed the form in a patch of sunshine. As the mist dried, a message came into being, all over the form. It was clearly readable because it was in red and because the lines of writing ran at right angles to the lines of print. 'British Order of Battle,' he said.

'That's clever.'

'Now watch this.' Fischer took another spray, full of a smoky yellow liquid, and coated the form again. This time, bright green writing appeared between the rows of red words.

'French Order of Battle,' Fischer said.

'Formidable! Is there more?'

'No. Wait a minute: yes.' Fischer turned the form over and held it up to the light. The secret writing showed through, reversed. 'Hebrew Order of Battle,' he announced. Still holding it to the light he turned it upside down. 'Chinese Order of Battle,' he said. He handed the form to Luis.

'That's quite brilliant,' Luis said. 'And the great thing about it is that, once you have defeated the British, French, Hebrew and Chinese armies, you can still find out what it costs to send a parcel to New Zealand.'

Fischer shrugged modestly. 'You know how thorough we Germans are.'

'Mind you, I'm a bit surprised to learn that agents still communicate with invisible ink. This is 1941, after all.'

'Don't underestimate secret writing,' Fischer warned. 'It's survived because it does a good job. Have you any idea how much mail goes between Britain and the neutrals? Tons and tons of it. Spain, Switzerland, Sweden, Ireland, Turkey, Russia, America. The British cannot possibly test every piece of mail. What am I saying? They can't test even one per cent of it! Provided your information isn't red-hot urgent, there's no better way to send it, especially if it's long and complicated.'

Luis nodded, studying the British Order of Battle. 'This would make a long radio signal,' he said.

'Very long. I reckon that by the time you reached *there* . . .' (Fischer's finger snapped against the form) '. . . British counter-intelligence would be closing in with their butterfly-nets at the ready . . . Now then: time for more practice. Let's find you something tough . . . Summary of bomb damage to Coventry: there, that's pretty juicy stuff.'

Luis dipped his pen in the clear liquid and carefully wrote his invisible report. 'How can I be sure I haven't made a mistake?' he asked.

'That's easy,' Fischer told him. 'Each time you make an invisible mistake, we pay you with invisible money.'

'Ah.' Luis copied out a column of casualty figures. 'I think I shall become infallible.'

'Good idea,' Fischer said. 'There's not much future in the alternative, I can tell you that.'

*

At four o'clock Luis was taken to Colonel Christian's office. The colonel had changed his rumpled brown suit for a rumpled blue suit, but he was just as restless as before. He held a steel-shafted putter and he was hunting a golf ball around the room.

Luis sat on the sofa and poured himself a cup of tea.

'Pressure, pressure, pressure,' Christian murmured to himself. 'Think, think, think. Make it happen. *Win.*' He stroked the ball and watched it miss a potted plant. 'Damn.' He strode after it. 'I hear you hate the British almost as much as I do,' he said flatly.

Luis sipped his tea. 'I don't hate the British,' he said.

'Lucky you.' Christian found his ball and hunched over it. 'If you had answered differently, I would have flung you through that large, expensive window and into the street, never to return.' He putted again and tramped on. 'Hatred is about as much use as bile in this job. You'd be amazed at the people I get volunteering to be spies. "Why?" I ask them. "I hate the enemy." Or: "I want to sacrifice myself for the Fatherland." Or: "My father-in-law was a big hero and won several medals." Crash, tinkle-tinkle, straight out the window. Idiots.' He chipped the ball over a foot-rest and watched it ricochet off a small table.

'I wouldn't be amazed at that,' Luis said. 'We had a war too. I remember seeing the Requetés go into action. They were a sort of Basque militia, you know. Fought for Franco. They always wore brilliant scarlet berets and they always stood up to get a better shot, so the Republicans killed them with enormous rapidity.'

Christian grunted. He putted past the fireplace, and walked on.

'I once asked them why they wore such bright red berets, and they said it demonstrated how brave they were. So I asked them why they didn't dig trenches and take cover, and they said they refused to dignify the enemy by hiding from him. Bravery and dignity. More lethal than poison gas.'

'But *you* are brave,' Christian said. He twiddled his putter and frowned at the ball.

'I don't know. I'm not sure that courage really exists. I think it's a necessary myth.'

'Like God.' Christian played his shot. The ball stopped a long way short of its target. He glared at it.

'I thought I met a brave man once,' Luis said. 'Now I think

he was probably just obstinate. I thought *I* was quite brave, once, but now I know I was just showing off.'

'I admire the British, you know.' Christian said. 'We Germans have never really wanted to destroy Britain. You might remember that when you're over there.'

Luis made an acknowledging grunt. Christian found his ball trapped behind an escritoire, and hooked it out. 'The British are remarkably inventive, for one thing. They invented lawn tennis, and several kinds of football, and even golf. Remarkably inventive people. What would you say is their most powerful weapon?'

Luis knew enough of Colonel Christian's fast mental footwork to feel sure that 'inventiveness' was not the right answer. 'Tell you in six months,' he said.

'It's obvious, man. Stark staring obvious.' The ball had rolled onto the carpet and was now perched on a tuft. Christian got into position and waggled the club about while he glanced at his reflection in a large, gilded mirror which covered half of one wall. Luis slumped deeper into the sofa and rested his teacup against his chest. It was a pleasant way to end an industrious day, conversing with one's boss. Christian stopped waggling, brought his bristling eyebrows together, pressed his chin hard down, took one last sideways glance at his reflection, breathed deeply, raised the club until it just missed a chandelier, and whacked the ball as hard as he could. Luis heard the whoosh of the putter-head racing through the air and he ducked behind the arm of the sofa. The thwack was meaty and the ball streaked away, but Christian had hooked his shot. It missed the mirror and smashed into a door, making it shiver. Christian fell to the floor as the ball whizzed furiously about the room, attacking two walls and the fireplace before thudding against an armchair and trickling to a halt.

Very carefully, Luis raised his saucer, which was half-full of spilt tea, and put it on the tray. 'Is that game over now?' he asked. 'And did you win?'

'We nearly had them in 1917, you know.' Christian's voice was soft, a little wistful, almost affectionate. He had rolled onto his back and was lying with his hands linked behind his head. 'It was so close. Another dozen torpedoes in the right place and Germany would have won that war.'

'You mean the submarines? U-boats?'

'We nearly starved them into surrender. They were actually running out of food in 1917. If only we could have sunk a few more ships . . . Just think: none of the shame of 1918 would have happened. No disgrace, no betrayal. No occupation by foreign troops, no mutilated frontiers, no massive reparations, no confiscated industries, no inflation, no economic chaos, no civil disorder . . .' Christian smiled at the ceiling.

'No Hitler?' Luis suggested.

The colonel swivelled his eyes and gave him a hard look.

'Well, it's a logical conclusion,' Luis argued. 'After all, if Germany—'

'To get back to the sea,' Christian said firmly. 'The sea is Britain's greatest weapon. It saved her after the fall of France. The sea is also Britain's greatest weakness. Remember that.'

'All right.'

'Now look in the piano.'

Luis heaved up the top of the baby grand and found, lying on the strings, the maps of Britain which he had been shown the day before. 'Oh yes,' he said. 'I remember this stuff.'

'Well, now you can disremember it.' Christian got up, took the maps, and peeled them off, sheet by sheet. 'Coastal approaches, submarine access, parachute areas: that's all nonsense. Rail network; nonsense. Distribution of *Abwehr* agents: nonsense. Location of British military bases: utter nonsense. *Abwehr* radio network: pure fantasy. Forget them all.' He threw the maps behind the sofa.

'I never took them seriously, anyway,' Luis said. 'You weren't likely to tell me all your big secrets on the first day we met.'

'We're not likely to tell you any big secrets, ever. I just want to be sure you don't depend on any of that rubbish when you get to England. We'll tell you anything you need to know.'

'All right.'

'It wasn't all right yesterday. That railway map showed main lines running up and down mountain ranges like polar bears on heat, and you never even blinked.'

Luis said nothing. The colonel went over to the fireplace with his putter and prodded moodily at the brickwork. 'It's

not going to be like bloody golf over there, you know,'
Christian said with his back to him. 'You don't get given a
handicap, nobody cares about fair play. Just one little stumble
and your neck's broken. I'm told they use a very hairy rope,
too.'

There was a long and unhappy silence. Then Luis said: 'If
you've finished, I'll take my five hundred pesetas and go.'

'What five hundred?' Christian turned; there was something black and fungoid on the end of his putter which he
had prised out of the back of the fireplace. He stared at it
with dislike.

'My daily expenses. Five hundred pesetas. We agreed,
yesterday.'

'What a bore you are about money, Cabrillo.'

You arrogant bastard, Luis thought. *And after all that death-
and-no-glory warning, too!* He said: 'And what a bore you
are about money, colonel.'

For a moment the atmosphere in the room was brittle with
anger. Luis felt that at that moment Christian was capable of
doing almost anything: hurling the putter at him, kicking him
out, perhaps even killing him. 'It galls me,' Christian said, and
his large, muscular face twisted with disgust that was also
self-disgust, 'it galls me to think that we Germans have
achieved a united Europe and yet we are still obliged to depend
on specimens like you.' He tossed the putter behind him and
pressed a button on his telephone.

Otto Krafft came in, smiling pleasantly.

'Pay him his parasitic five hundred pesetas,' Christian ordered.

'Today, and every day,' Luis said. 'I'm not going to keep
asking.'

'You're very touchy, for a whore,' Christian told him.

'And you're very clumsy for a ponce.'

Otto and Luis went out. On the way to the cashier's office,
Luis mentioned the colonel's curious change of mood. Otto
merely smiled and shrugged. Luis described the incident of
the savage golf-ball. Otto nodded. 'But why do a thing like
that?' Luis asked.

'I think there is something about games which annoys him,'
Otto said.

'It was extremely dangerous.'

132

'Yes. Anything which annoys Colonel Christian is always extremely dangerous.'

*

After the cashier's office there was still half-an-hour before the working day ended. As Luis walked in step with Otto to yet another part of the building, he felt weary with so much learning. His brain was heavy with new knowledge. Outside, the air would be fresh and undemanding, and Madrid would be warm and cheerful, hugely inviting; he had his money, he'd surely earned it, now he deserved some rest and re-creation . . .

That was the lingering adolescent in Luis. The adult in him thought differently. Spying was a trade, so you had to acquire the technical skills. Despite Colonel Christian's tantrums—and Luis was not convinced that they were all completely spontaneous—the Germans were professionals: intelligent, experienced and clear-eyed. He was being taught by experts (and getting paid for it). It was a course in lifesaving. The life was his own.

Otto opened a door and waved him in. To Luis's amazement, the man behind the desk was Wolfgang Adler, the blond and barefoot Pongo of yesterday. His head and face were cut and bruised, one wrist was in a sling, and his right leg was propped on a stool, the foot being in plaster.

'Collect you at five,' Otto said, and shut the door.

They looked at each other for perhaps eight seconds.

'I am here to instruct you in how to protect yourself,' Wolfgang said. 'You have my permission to laugh.'

'No, no,' Luis said. 'I wouldn't dream of it.'

'Nevertheless, please make the effort.' Wolfgang's lower lip was split and swollen, making his speech deliberate. 'I think it will make you feel better.'

'But this is not a laughing matter,' Luis said. 'I mean . . .' He gestured at Wolfgang's injuries, and suddenly the situation *was* funny, was overwhelmingly funny, and he laughed until his ribs hurt. Wolfgang sat like a statue and watched, the only movement coming from one slightly blackened eye, which twitched.

'Sorry,' Luis said.

'One day I hope to break both your legs,' Wolfgang said.

133

'But I promise you I shall not laugh. Now . . . Do I have your full attention?'

'Go ahead.'

'When you get to Britain you will face two constant dangers. One from the professional spy-hunters, the men and women of MI5, the other from the great mass of the population. I must tell you that there is very little you can do against the first, except to take every care and to go into hiding as soon as you suspect that you are in danger. Once they decide to arrest you, there is little hope. They have all the advantages. It would be foolish to imagine that even the greatest skill in gunmanship or unarmed combat can save you once you are trapped in a building and surrounded. The spy who shoots his way out of trouble has one enormous advantage: the collaboration of his scriptwriter. Understand?'

'Um,' Luis said. He breathed deeply, looked at the ceiling, exercised his shoulders. 'Let's not be coy. What you're saying is, give up without a fight. I don't see how I can agree to that.'

'Do as you please. I'm here to tell you the facts of life. You will be given a handgun and trained to use it. In my opinion it has only one use for an agent who finds himself cornered.' Wolfgang raised his uninjured arm, poked his index finger in his ear and pulled an imaginary trigger.

'Nothing personal, I hope.'

Wolfgang looked away. 'You flatter yourself, Mr Cabrillo.'

'Sorry. All the same, I don't think I could shoot myself just because . . . I mean, it seems such a waste.'

'It's better than hanging. Being hanged is a very wretched death.' He took a small automatic from a drawer and slid it across the desk. 'Rehearse.'

Luis held the weapon by the fingertips of both hands and made sure that it was empty. He gave the trigger a few practice squeezes. It didn't feel at all lethal. It felt like an office stapler. 'Does it matter which ear?' he inquired. Wolfgang looked at his fingernails. 'No, I don't suppose it does,' Luis murmured. He pressed the muzzle into his right ear, sealing off half the world with a cold and slightly oily plug of steel.

'Wrist up,' Wolfgang ordered. 'Aim for the middle.'

Luis obeyed. 'Just a small technical point,' he said, 'would the bullet go right through and emerge from the other ear? Is that possible?'

Wolfgang hunched his shoulders and twitched his nose. 'If you ever reach this stage,' he said, 'I doubt if you will be concerned with winning extra points for neatness.'

Luis nodded and unplugged the gun. Half the world returned with a rush of sound. 'You recommend the ear, then,' he said. 'I would have thought the forehead was the traditional site.'

'Unreliable. People get the angle wrong, and the bullet bounces off the skull. The ear provides a ready-made opening. You don't want to take any chances.'

'No,' Luis said thoughtfully. 'No, I suppose I don't.'

Wolfgang put the automatic away and produced a small, leather-covered blackjack. 'You will be in greater danger from the amateurs than from the experts. The entire adult population of Britain is on the alert for spies, and the risk is that some idiot civilian will stumble upon some aspect of your operations. A transmission, for instance. You are in your room one evening, sending a radio message, when a stranger, say a middleaged Englishwoman, enters by mistake and sees you.' He allowed a few seconds for that predicament to sink in. 'What do you do?'

'Grab her.'

'Impossible. She's fifteen feet away and you're wearing earphones.'

'Shoot her.'

'You don't shoot her,' Wolfgang said patiently. 'You're in England, remember. Try and fight the enemy with his own weapons. Politeness. Pleasantness. Restraint. The British are extremely reluctant to give offence. They like everyone to be nice, and they like to be nice to everyone. You should exploit that weakness.'

'I see.' Luis gazed at the German's damaged, dogged face. 'No, I don't see,' he said.

'Look . . . Go outside and come in. Pretend to surprise me operating a secret radio transmitter.'

Luis went out and came in again. Wolfgang was tapping a pencil on his desk like a Morse key. 'I say!' Luis exclaimed. 'What the devil d'you think you're up to?'

'Ah, good afternoon . .' Wolfgang, completely at ease, gave

a warm and welcoming smile and waved Luis in, while keeping up a steady stutter with the pencil. 'Do sit down, I shan't keep you a moment . . . I must just finish testing this wretched machine.'

'What d'you mean, "testing"? You're a German spy!'

Wolfgang seemed not to hear that. He smiled amiably and twiddled an imaginary knob. 'I'm sorry if the noise disturbed you. These BBC emergency kits are dreadfully loud, aren't they?'

'BBC *what*?'

'Haven't you been given one? Everybody's supposed to have one, in case of emergency.' Wolfgang tapped away unhurriedly. 'You'd better check whether your name's on this list.' With his spare hand he opened a desk drawer.

Luis came forward and looked into the drawer. Wolfgang flicked him gently on the back of the head with the blackjack. The blow thundered around his skull. He lurched away, legs dissolving, and sat hard on the floor. 'Oh dear,' he mumbled. His voice sounded remote, and climbing up the back of his throat came a hot and angry nausea. He swallowed and swallowed and at last it grudgingly subsided. He breathed deeply and looked up. Wolfgang was watching him, without concern or contempt; he simply watched. 'I hope you know what you're doing with that thing,' Luis muttered. He felt too ill to be angry, but all the same a part of him was getting fed up with the hazards of the German Embassy.

'It doesn't make a noise and it doesn't make a mess,' Wolfgang said. 'You never need to load it or keep it sharp. Used correctly, it produces immediate unconsciousness.'

'And what do you do before he comes round? Flush the body down the toilet?'

Wolfgang gave a little snort of amusement. 'He doesn't come round. He's dead.'

'I thought . . .' Luis heaved himself into a chair. His head buzzed and dots of light wandered across his eyes. 'I mean, surely—'

'You thought that when a man gets hit on the head he merely falls asleep, then wakes up, blinks, and rushes back into battle. As in the cinema.'

Luis sighed, and said nothing.

'The human skull,' said Wolfgang, taking one from his desk,

'has certain weak spots.' He displayed it like a piece of sculpture, aiming his finger down. 'Here . . . and here . . . and especially here. A firm blow at that point will certainly kill.' He put the skull away. 'At another time we shall practise. On a dummy,' he added.

Luis began to resent the man's thoroughness and competence and eternal self-assurance. 'There is still the body to dispose of,' he reminded him.

Wolfgang raised one eyebrow; the other eye was still too bruised to respond. 'I was told that you have read many English detective stories. Yes? Well, then: do as the English do. Leave the body in a trunk in the left-luggage office at the nearest railway station.'

Luis groaned.

'Listen, my friend: what has been good enough for several hundred English killers is good enough for you. But first, start thinking like an Englishman. Remember that they would sooner die than cause an embarrassing scene. Take advantage of that willingness. Be nice. Apologise, smile, reassure, offer to help, and then *whack*!'

'And if it's a lady, should I take my hat off first?' Luis asked sourly.

'Yes, of course,' Wolfgang said. He was quite serious. 'She would suspect something if you didn't, and she would never turn her back on you. Definitely take your hat off.'

*

The corridors were busy with homegoing embassy staff as Otto led Luis towards a side door. 'Starting tomorrow, I shall meet you each morning at a different location and drive you straight into the embassy garage,' he said. 'Otherwise someone might notice that you are spending your days here. Tomorrow's rendezvous will be outside the Prado, main entrance, at nine.'

'All right. Can I bring my bludgeon?'

' "Bludgeon"? What is "bludgeon"?'

'Club for hitting people. Everyone around here has one.'

'I haven't.'

'Get one fast and use it, Otto. You don't want to be left behind. All the best people are doing it, the Colonel, Wolfgang . . .'

137

'Ah. I understand, Wolfgang hit you a little bit. Well, you threw him out of the window.'

'Was that a mistake?'

'Oh no. Quite the opposite.'

'But now he hits me on the head and pretends it's just part of the lesson. Is that fair?'

'Life is not fair. In particular your life—'

Luis had stopped. They were opposite the waiting room, and he was staring past the rows of people at a woman in a red dress. She was doing a crossword puzzle.

'That's Mrs Conroy,' he said. 'You promised to deal with her problem this morning.'

Otto came back and looked. 'We did. We got a telegram from Paris. It answered her question.'

'She is still here.'

'So are many others.'

'I don't care about them.'

Otto seemed slightly put out. He looked at the American woman, at the portrait of Adolf Hitler, at his watch. 'Don't you think you are behaving somewhat presumptuously?' he asked.

'I've changed my mind,' Luis said. 'I'm not going to England after all. The weather there is bad for my chest.' He coughed resonantly. Purple echoes lost themselves in the vaulted corners of the room.

Otto went over to the official on duty, talked, came back. 'It seems she has another problem, in Brussels. We are dealing with that, too.'

'Good, good. My chest is much better now.' Luis coughed again, just as vigorously. 'Hear the difference?'

'You obviously have an interest in this American lady,' Otto said. 'I suggest you consider your position very seriously before . . .' He shrugged. 'Before you involve yourself.'

'She happens to be the daughter of J. Edgar Hoover. A very valuable contact.'

'It's not a joke. Just remember what I said. You have no private life any more; everything about you is the *Abwehr's* business.'

'May I leave now?'

'Yes, you may.' Otto glanced at Julie Conroy, who was on her feet, talking to the official. 'She is very attractive. Do you know much about her?'

138

'Not much, no.'

Otto gave her another long glance. 'I'll bet you ten to one that what little you know is all lies.'

'Oh? What makes you say that?'

Otto took his time before replying, and then he gave Luis a sad smile. 'It's wartime, Spain is neutral, and nine out of ten people you meet are spying for the countries at war.'

'Then she is the tenth.'

'The tenth,' said Otto, 'is spying on the other spies.'

Chapter 18

Madrid in the early evening was magic.

The sky had softened from its earlier remote, ceramic purity to a warm and gentle blue, like a vast and seamless tent. Against this friendly backdrop the richness of palaces and fortresses, churches and statues, looked more theatrical than ever. It was not possible to believe that all these outbreaks of soaring towers and embroidered façades and wedding-cake extravagance had been built for serious purposes by serious, long-dead men. On a mild May evening they added up to the best free stroll in Europe; especially in 1941, when a great deal of Europe was not free to be strolled in unless a German said so. Madrid was different. Madrid had already had its war and now it was happy to be out of this one. The lights came on like an affirmation of peace, big-city jewellery brought out to help celebrate the night's enjoyment. It seemed that one half of Madrid was sauntering through the streets and squares while the other half watched from windows and balconies and café tables.

But not Luis Cabrillo and Julie Conroy. She was temporarily tired of people and he was simply tired. After leaving the embassy she went to her hotel, ordered some ice, took a long bath, made herself a large scotch and ginger ale, and read the airmail edition of the *New York Herald-Tribune*. He went to his apartment, took an aspirin, and slept for two hours. Outside, Madrid was magic, which was nice for Madrid, but it couldn't compare with the wonders worked by a stiff drink or a soft bed.

They met in the lobby of the Hotel Bristol at 9.30. Luis brought a single long-stemmed red rose, and offered it with a slight bow. 'Terrific,' she said. The doorman and the desk clerk smiled at each other in approval: Mrs Conroy was the brightest part of their day. Luis said: 'I thought it would enhance the beauty of your hair.'

'Genius.' She twirled the rose and they stood and looked at it. 'Now what do I do with it?'

Luis had not considered that. 'Behind the ear?' he suggested.

She tried it. 'I feel like I'm wearing one navigation light,' she said, looking sideways.

'Pinned to the bosom?'

'I don't have one. You've got to be forty to have a bosom. The hell with it, I'll just carry the thing and use it to beat off the Gestapo.'

They walked through the old city to a rambling restaurant called the *Dos Amigos*. It rambled over two floors and both floors had several levels. This meant that almost everyone could see almost everyone else, as the upper floor was pierced in the middle with a large, round hole. Underneath this a band played. The place was half-full and noisy, the waiters doing a lot of shouting and customers leaning over the upstairs balcony to call down to friends eating below.

As Luis and Julie walked past the band, the trumpet-player (gaunt-faced and greyhaired, with a jaunty stance and insomniac eyes) followed them around with his trumpet. He played a greasy, sleazy little tune, deliberately cracking some notes and ending on a slow downhill phrase like mockery. It won him laughter and applause from a few customers. He acknowledged this with a chirpy little bugle-call as he turned back into his original melody.

'Friend of yours?' she asked when they got to their table.

'I should have explained about the *Dos Amigos*. It's a little bit unusual. The custom here is to insult everybody. The food is excellent but the waiters, the musicians, even the man who does the washing-up, they all insult the customers. It's a tradition.'

'Uh-huh.'

'The biggest insult is not to be insulted. That means they really don't like you.'

140

'What do they do when they can't stand the sight of you? Throw money?'

'I'll ask him,' Luis said as the waiter arrived. They talked in rapid Spanish and their talk worked up to a hot exchange, with both men waving their arms in her direction. Eventually Luis pulled the menu from under the waiter's arm, ordered a plate of appetisers and a bottle of wine, and dismissed him. The man went away, making a long and contemptuous remark over his shoulder. The people at the next table stamped their feet and grinned in approval.

'What did he say?' Julie asked.

'At first he said that my tie doesn't go with my shirt. Then he alleged that you aren't worth two pesetas. Also he considers that I ordered a totally unsuitable wine.'

'And what did you say?'

'As to the wine and the tie, those are matters of opinion. However, I strongly denied that you are not worth two pesetas.'

'I bet that stopped him cold.'

'No, he continued to express doubts. It became a point of honour. I swore on my mother's grave that you are, indeed, well worth two pesetas.'

'Gee,' she said thoughtfully, 'you Spaniards really go out on a limb for a girl.'

'It is nothing.'

'It's two pesetas.'

'A man's honour is worth more than two pesetas.'

'It is?' She examined his smile for a moment. 'How much more?'

She leaned back and held the rose at full length, hands resting on the table, and twirled it like a tiny red parasol. Luis enjoyed the smooth and supple line of her arms, the cool hollows shaped by her collarbones, the firmness of her neck, the untroubled balance of her features. During the previous two years he had read a lot of descriptions of a lot of women but none had startled and seized his imagination as much as this reality. She had a measurable physical effect on him: he could feel his lungs tightening a little, his heartbeat rising slightly; and all the sights and sounds in the restaurant gained in intensity, like a big scene in a film. A small part of his brain told him that it was all to be expected, simply a necessary biological reaction to ensure that the species reproduced itself, but the rest of his mind was not listening; it was back in the jungle, swinging from tree to tree, delightfully drunk with the prospect of passion . . . Julie stopped twirling the rose. He came to earth. 'A man's honour is beyond price,' he said firmly.

'Yeah? That's the kind of line MGM gives a guy somewhere in the second reel when it knows he's heading for big trouble. Talking of which, here comes the local agent.'

The waiter brought the appetisers and the wine, smiled, and made a short, prepared statement.

'He apologises,' Luis told her. 'He says he spoke in haste, it was not his intention to depreciate you, and after consultation with his colleagues he wishes to make it quite clear that you are not worth four pesetas.'

The waiter spread his hands in a gesture of reconciliation.

'Tell him I accept his apology,' she said, 'and ask him if he always walks like that or did his girl-friend tread on his *cojones*.'

Luis translated. The waiter did not lose his smile but his smile lost its pleasure. He poured the wine, spilling quite a lot, and went away.

'His acting reminds me a lot of Valentino,' she said. 'Stubby Valentino, played shortstop for the Dodgers.'

'That is a baseball team,' Luis said.

'Well, it's never been completely proved . . . What in the name of Chaplin's bootlace is *that*?' She forked up something from the appetisers which looked remarkably like a fat bootlace.

Luis ransacked his memory. 'Eel!' he announced triumphantly. 'Is that right?'

'Eel.' She put it back. 'Why the hell can't you Europeans eat food for food? Ever since I came over here people keep offering me this weird and gruesome junk. What have you got against good honest grub?'

'Eel is good.' He fished it out and ate it.

'Squid, they gave me. And cow's heels. Brains. Tripe. *Larks*, would you believe! How can you do business in a country where they serve hot larks?'

Luis shrugged and munched some radishes. 'A bird is a bird. You Americans are very sentimental, you know. If every

142

chicken could sing like a lark, would you set them all free?'

'Chicken,' she said. 'Now that's genuine food. Do they serve chicken here? Any kind of chicken—bass, baritone, alto, just as long as it's got good legs. I want a chicken. Tell Valentino I'll cancel his contract if I don't get a chicken. I'll cancel his girl-friend's contract. I'll cancel his *cojones*' contract.'

'That reminds me . . . Did you solve your problem in Paris? The missing reel of film.'

Her eyelids flickered as her mind rapidly adjusted. 'Oh. *Gone With The Wind*. Yes, that's all straightened out, thanks.'

'I understand there is now a difficulty in Brussels.'

'Mmm . . .' She drank some wine. 'Second half of *Destry Rides Again* went astray. Jimmy Stewart and Marlene Dietrich are lying lost and forgotten in some bleak, Belgian warehouse. And them so young. Tragic.'

'They will soon be freed. I asked the embassy to do all it can to help you. They are working on it right now.' Luis spoke easily, concentrating on finding a good olive.

'That's very kind of you.' Julie Conroy was briefly silent; Luis chewed cheerfully on his plump olive and enjoyed his success. 'They must think highly of you in the embassy,' she said at last.

'Well, I am not without influence in the Spanish Government, you see. My family has a tradition of public service.' He ducked his head modestly while he reviewed his family's contributions. 'Communications . . . the arts . . . banking . . .'

'Yeah? The Cabrillos are a big deal, then.'

'I can tell you this in all honesty,' Luis said, and paused again while he found something not-too-dishonest. 'Take any train, to any city. A Cabrillo has been there before you and has left his mark. By the way: have you met James Stewart and Marlene Dietrich? What are they like?'

'Just like in the movies. Those legs! Terrific legs, plus that wonderful husky voice. And *she* isn't bad-looking either.'

Luis gave her a crooked, one-eyed grin. 'I think you have never met them,' he said.

'Okay, go ahead and ask me. Ask me anything about anybody in Hollywood. Just ask me.'

For ten minutes she fascinated Luis with the private lives of the stars. Alan Ladd was so short that sometimes the actress he was doing a scene with had to stand in a hole. Paulette Goddard had a mania for cleanliness and scrubbed her floors three times a day. Errol Flynn drank a bottle of vodka for breakfast. Peter Lorre bred goldfish. Judy Garland really wanted to be a tennis-player and was a terrible bore on the subject. Cary Grant had a curious allergy : he couldn't tolerate anyone with flat feet; it was actually written into his contracts. Groucho Marx once tried to grow a moustache for a bet and failed. Betty Grable ate a dozen oranges a day. Last year Abbott and Costello fell in love with the same girl and the studio had to send her to New Zealand . . .

'How lucky you are to have such an interesting job,' Luis said enviously.

'I don't know. People are people, all over the world.' She watched as a new arrival, a fat and ugly woman, was given a sickly-sweet serenade by the trumpet-player. 'Movie-people aren't real, because movies aren't real, but then people don't want reality, do they? People *want* to be deluded. Me, I just take care of the hardware, the cans of celluloid.'

'Have you met Bing Crosby?'

'Millions of times. They have to glue his ears back to stop them flapping in the breeze. Listen, I'm hungry. Tell them to take this junk back to Boris Karloff's laboratory and bring us some real food.'

'I think you would like . . .' Luis studied the menu. '. . . a little fish, perhaps *bacalao a la madrileña*, and then perhaps some veal *al ajo arinero*, that is with a garlic sauce.'

'That's good, is it?'

'Excellent.'

'You have it. I want a steak, a big baked potato, and a huge salad. Order up.'

The waiter openly despised their choice. He wrangled with Luis about the fish and veal, and he sneered at Julie as he wrote down her steak. Then he went off, jerking his thumb at them and calling something to the trumpet-player, who broke into a flattened, dirge-like version of *Yankee Doodle Dandy*.

'I may kill that man,' Julie said.

'It means nothing. Only the tradition of this place.'

'Then I'll start a new tradition : each customer gets one free shot at the trumpet-player. It's what in the United States we call democracy. The fifth freedom: freedom from musicians with lungs of steel and ears of tin.'

'Spain is different,' Luis said soothingly. 'Here we have no politics any more. Only music. It is much easier, much cheaper, and the newspapers can give more space to *futbol*. You see, we have tried politics and we have tried music, and there is no doubt about it: music kills far fewer people. The figures are most impressive. Last year, for instance, in the whole of Spain only one trombonist herniated himself, while rehearsing *The Ride of the Valkyries*. Compare that with our losses during the Civil War! And this year's record will be even better, now that the government has banned the dangerous parts of Wagner. So you see what a marvellously humanitarian country Spain has become.'

'Bullshit.'

'Yes, you are right, but we are all shovelling our bullshit in time to the music, which you must admit is a great step forward.'

'I think all this Red Cross work has scrambled your brains,' she said. 'Have you had a hard day?'

'Oh . . . average.' Luis looked strong and dependable. 'Tracing refugees is a long, slow job. One learns patience.'

'I'm sure. Tell me who you've found lately.'

Luis looked into her alert, grey eyes and briefly considered refusing on the grounds that it was all confidential information. She widened her eyes a fraction. 'Mainly Poles and Czechs,' he said, flicking a bit of fluff from his sleeve. 'They got lost when the Germans overran Europe. For instance, I traced a Polish orchestra to a French prison in Bordeaux; they had been locked up for ten months because they could not pay their hotel bills. Nobody knew they were there.' Luis shrugged. It was easy once you got started.

'That's pretty good going,' Julie said. 'I mean, a whole *orchestra*.'

'They're in Italy now,' Luis said. 'We fixed them up with an opera house.' He drew a little whirlwind on the tablecloth with the blunt end of his fork. 'The Germans are really very helpful,' he said.

'Saved any Jews lately?'

Luis accepted the challenge. 'A few. The Polish orchestra had a Jewish conductor and two Jewish violinists.' For several minutes Luis expanded on the detective-work of the International Red Cross, re-uniting Greek parents with their lost children in Rome, tracking down French prisoners-of-war in Bavaria, rescuing an amnesiac Czech businessman from a mental hospital in Luxembourg. It was good, solid, detailed, humanitarian stuff, and Julie listened intently. 'The Russians are the most difficult,' he told her, now well into his stride, 'and the Cossacks are the most difficult of the Russians. Somewhere in Lithuania an entire brigade—'

'Hokay, hokay!' It was the waiter with their food. 'Gooda morningk, I yam 'appy. 'ow moch is zatin dolleurs, sank you, necks time I peench your hass, hokay?' As he spoke he unloaded the plates from his arm.

'That's a *steak*?' Julie exclaimed.

'Where's the fish?' Luis asked. '*Dónde está mi bacalao?*'

The waiter ignored her, and answered him with scorn. Whether it was scorn for the fish or the chef or Luis, or for all three, she never knew. Meanwhile she had time to look at her *bistec*. It was thin, and it curled like bacon; walnut-brown in colour; lacking any fat; and grained like weathered fencing. She tried to cut a piece off the corner. The knife skidded. 'What the hell is this?' she demanded, pronging it with a bouncing fork, 'Franco's conscience?'

'*No politics!*' Luis hissed angrily. The waiter turned his head slowly and sneered at her down his long and twisted nose. Deliberately, he slid one hand into his pocket and waved his other hand above the steak. '*Está muy bueno,*' he said. '*Está excelente! Está magnífico!*'

'*Está* crap' Julie said, and slapped the meat into his open palm.

He took a short pace backwards and stared at her, his lips working, his brows twitching. Then he reared up on his toes and stretched his arms full length above his head. His fingers curled around the rejected *bistec*, squeezing and crushing until a little stream of bloody gravy spattered the floor. '*Caramba!*' he shouted.

'They really do say that, huh?' Julie said. People all over the restaurant were standing to get a better view. Luis began to feel exposed and vulnerable.

'Let's not have a *big* fight, okay?' he suggested. The head waiter bustled his meaty hips up to their table, rapped out a curt question, and made the mistake of gesturing as he did so. The waiter, now pale with fury, slapped the damaged *bistec* into the widespread hand. The head waiter looked at the tattered meat and without hesitation slapped the waiter's face with it, hard, twice, left and right. *Olés* and handclaps broke out all around. Upstairs, people were leaning over the balcony and whistling through their fingers. The waiter lurched against a chair, toppled it, grabbed, missed, and fell over, landing on his bony backside with a crash that forced up long, thin spurts of dust between the floorboards. The head waiter ripped the *bistec* in half like a dishonoured cheque. Appreciative cheering broke out. 'I think we should perhaps go,' Luis said. The head waiter stooped and murmured in his ear. '*He* think we should perhaps go,' Luis said. Julie picked up her red rose. 'Maybe we'd better not stay,' she said. The waiter was holding his head in his hands and weeping. She succeeded in treading on him twice as she left the table.

The crowd went back to its tables and its interrupted meals, pleased with the brief entertainment. As Luis and Julie walked across the restaurant, the trumpeter played them out with Laurel and Hardy's silly signature-tune: *de-dum, de-dum: de-dum, de-dum* . . . He broke off when he saw a waiter signalling and pointing to the door. Four German officers had arrived, high-ranking, tall-walking men in well-cut uniforms and good tempers. Two wore monocles. At once the trumpeter marshalled the rest of the band and they launched into the opening bars of *Deutschland, Deutschland über Alles*. They played it straight. No jokes, no mockery. Plenty of enthusiasm, but no exaggeration.

Julie stopped, and watched the arrivals basking in the band's attention.

'What happened to tradition, all of a sudden?' she asked.

'The same as happened to the dinosaur,' Luis said. 'Changing circumstances killed it.' He didn't particularly want to meet the Germans. He glanced around for another exit, and saw Julie give the trumpeter a look of loathing. The man was leaning back with his eyes shut and his cheeks as hard as apples. His lungs were full and he was reaching for the climatic high note when she snatched up a bottle of wine and rammed it neck-first into the bell of the trumpet. Like the waiter, the trumpeter lost his balance and fell, wine spraying

147

in a great red curve. Luis glimpsed the startled faces of the officers and saw the head waiter turn from them with a smile that became suddenly savage. The restaurant was silent. 'You're all full of shit!' Julie shouted. 'They serve it, you eat it, he plays it, and those bastards—' She pointed at the Germans. '—they drop it from their airplanes!'

Luis seized her and hustled her away from the onrushing head waiter, back towards the kitchens. They banged through the kitchen doors a few yards ahead of him, but Julie had a message for the chef. 'You call that a steak?' she shouted at him. 'You ought to be ashamed!' The whole kitchen staff paused, expressionless, at the sight of this angry, handsome, incomprehensible woman. Then the doors crashed again and their heads swivelled to the pounding, glaring head waiter. Luis shoved Julie hard towards the back. There was food all around; he grabbed at random and lobbed stuff at the head waiter: half a chicken, a melon, a cucumber, a handful of kidneys; and while the man was catching and dropping and ducking, Luis fled into the back alley. The cooks let him go: they did not fight waiters' battles. 'Run, run!' he bawled at Julie. They sprinted along the alley, Luis knocking over garbage bins and piles of boxes to block any pursuit. The head waiter got one shot at them with the melon, but the light was bad, and the last they heard was his strident cursing above the gloomy thunder of the garbage cans. Then they were around the corner and lost in the crowds.

*

'I guess I'm sorry,' she said.

They were sitting beside a fountain and eating roast chicken, tomatoes and bread, all bought from a grocery store. There was also a flask of wine. The fountain was sending up a changing pattern of spouts and plumes, like a juggler working on a new act. Beyond it the night was a rich, inky black, as definite as a dome. Luis felt at ease and at home: nothing was likely to go wrong here. He pulled some more meat off the chicken and saw the wishbone. 'I'm not sorry,' he said. The wishbone came away and he snapped it into three parts. She pointed at the bits and looked questioning. 'I don't believe in luck,' he said. 'And I don't believe you're really sorry either.'

'No, I'm not. But I've got no right to involve you in my bad temper, have I? I didn't realise quite how much I hate Nazis until I saw those four heelclickers come in.'

'America's neutral.'

'That's Washington, I'm me. Anyway, I was feeling mad long before they turned up. The trouble with me, Luis, is I'm not too crazy about Europe. To tell the truth, the whole damn place annoys me. I'm sick of everything being so goddam foreign all the time. I'm sick of always having to change what *I* want, because you can't get that in Europe, lady. Or *madame* or *señora* or *frau* or what the hell. The food's foreign, the language is foreign, the money's foreign, I spend my whole life adapting and translating and converting, and it's got to stop, because I, Juliet Francis Conroy, am *not* bloody foreign!'

'You are to us,' Luis said.

'I know. I'm being childish. But if I don't stamp and shout and insist on what *I* want every now and then, I'm afraid I'll disappear completely.'

They ate for a while and watched the fountain polishing its act.

'The food was not important,' Luis said. 'That restaurant has got much worse, I shall never go back. But as long as I work for the International Red Cross, I cannot afford to anger the Germans.'

She looked at him very thoughtfully, and nodded. 'You can't, can you?' she said. 'So maybe we'd better not see each other any more.'

Luis ate the last tomato.

'My neutrality is a necessary part of my job, you see,' he said.

'A job is a job.'

Luis had the feeling that they both knew they were talking nonsense, but he decided it would be safer not to say so.

They washed their hands in the fountain and he walked her back to the hotel. She kissed him goodnight. On the cheek. Thoughtfully.

Chapter 19

They worked Luis hard, in the German Embassy.

Each morning Otto picked him up at a different rendezvous and drove him into the embassy garage. For the next seven or eight hours a series of tutors crammed him with knowledge or coached him in skills. He spent at least two hours a day learning Morse from Franz Werth. There were many sessions with Dr Hartmann, a small, bespectacled expert in radio, who was shocked and dismayed to find that Luis was completely ignorant of elementary physics. 'But you must at least comprehend the principles of electricity,' he said urgently. 'It is not possible to grow up in the twentieth century and remain unaware of the basic principles of electricity.' He polished his glasses and squinted fuzzily while Luis dredged up everything he knew about electricity. 'You're not supposed to stick your finger in the light socket,' he told the German. 'That's fairly basic, isn't it?' Hartmann put his glasses on and searched Luis's face for signs of humour. There were none. 'Really, I should have been warned of this,' he said. 'My field is research. High-frequency modulation. I find it difficult to know where to start . . . Presumably you know the difference between positive and negative?' Luis nodded. 'Good,' Hartmann said, relief in his voice. 'But not when it comes to electricity,' Luis warned.

Dr Hartmann went away for ten minutes while he thought himself back into a condition of scientific simplemindedness in which he and Luis could discuss electricity as equals. He succeeded. Within a week Luis had a good grasp of the subject. He could also assemble the *Abwehr's* standard radio transmitter and receiver, operate it, tune it, change frequencies, make small repairs, even take it to bits with his eyes shut. Hartmann was good.

Other men taught other skills. In the embassy gymnasium, the assistant air attaché showed Luis the correct way to fall when landing by parachute. In the embassy swimming pool, a breezy, bearded instructor shouted advice on how to paddle a rubber dinghy, while the boat rocked and lurched to the surging waves made by embassy staff leaping into the water all around him. Luis never mastered the rubber dinghy. 'Never mind,' said the instructor. 'There's a lot of England. Keep thrashing away and you're almost bound to hit some of it sooner or later.'

Otto instructed him in housebreaking, and a series of men in white overalls tried to teach him the use of firearms. He showed promise as a locksmith, but not as a marksman: he could never fire a gun without flinching.

After a few days, Colonel Christian mentioned this to him. 'It can't be the noise, can it?' he said. 'You even flinch when the silencer is on.'

'I know. The trouble is I don't feel that I am in control of the gun. Whenever I fire it, I think that really the gun did that damage, not me. I just held it.'

'But you pull the trigger. You make the decision.'

Luis propped his head on his hand, twisting his face out of shape. 'It's too much power for one man. I have no right to be able to destroy so easily, just by pointing. If I feel strongly about killing someone I should go and do it myself. Actually do it with my own hands.'

Christian stood in front of the fireplace, dead now that summer was near, and rattled the change in his trouser pocket. 'What if the other fellow has a gun?' he asked.

Luis sighed and looked away. 'You're right, of course. But . . . I'm afraid that's just not my kind of war. Too remote. Meaningless, really. I mean, if you never actually meet the man you're trying to kill, you might just as well fight one another by correspondence. It's so petty to stand far away and send a bloody little bullet to do your dirty work for you. What does it prove? The man you kill doesn't even know it was your bullet, does he? Meaningless.'

Christian walked past and patted him on the shoulder. (Now that their financial arrangements were sorted out, the colonel seemed to have forgotten all his contempt. He was friendly, even fatherly. Luis wondered whether this attitude was genuine or calculated; either way, he decided, it was not to be relied on.) 'You're a romantic, Cabrillo,' he said, 'you think everyone is entitled to some sort of fair chance, don't you? That wouldn't appeal to Berlin. The whole point of having a war is to give the other side no kind of chance at all.'

'I can't help that. I'm not going to shoot anybody.'

Christian looked down at him and smiled. 'I admire your honesty,' he said.

'Why shouldn't I be honest?'

'You're a spy. Deception is your trade.'

'Ah, yes, deception. But not deceit. The truth is my business. It's more important to me than anything else. Far more important than shooting bullets into people. Of course,' Luis offered, 'I *can* lie to you, if it makes you feel any better.'

'Well,' Christian looked at his watch. 'Let's say I wouldn't want you to get out of practice . . . Time for your photography lesson, I believe.'

So Luis went off to learn how to make microdots, from Victor, a cheerful young man who had spent two years with Kodak in Rochester, New York, and who said he wanted to go to Hollywood after the war.

'Perhaps you'll be able to go there with the Third Reich,' Luis suggested as he set up the camera.

'How could I? We have no embassy in Los Angeles.'

'But surely Hitler intends to conquer the United States.'

'Who told you that?'

'Colonel Christian.'

Victor whistled. 'Did he tell you when?'

'Oh, you can relax, there's no hurry. According to the colonel, the Fuehrer plans first to overrun Russia, India and China. Have I got this thing in focus?'

Victor squinted into the viewfinder and touched a dial. 'Are you sure you ought to be telling me all this?' he asked.

'What possible harm can the truth do to anybody?' Luis said.

For the next few minutes they got on with the business of reducing a page of aircraft performance specifications to the size of a dot. Then Victor said: 'I wonder how Hollywood will like being part of the Third Reich?' He laughed at the sound of his own words.

'Hollywood will do what it's bloody well told,' Luis assured him, 'and I happen to know that one of the first things it will do is make a new version of "Birth of a

152

Nation". Much bigger and much better, of course.'

'Of course. And . . . um . . . and who do you think will play the part of the Fuehrer?' Victor nearly smiled, but his own daring had made him too nervous.

'Clark Gable,' Luis said at once. 'He was good in *Gone With The Wind*, and he has a moustache. That is an important advantage.'

'Yes . . . You don't think John Wayne could do a better job? More authority, more drive?'

Luis shrugged. 'The decision's been taken, the part has been cast. But in any case I can tell you that the Fuehrer does not approve of John Wayne, politically. He considers him too rightwing. What's more to the point, this re-make of "Birth of a Nation" will be a musical comedy, and Clark Gable has the sort of glamour and charm which Berlin wants the rest of the world to associate with the rise of the Third Reich.'

'*Really* a musical comedy?' Victor said, slitting the seal on a fresh box of negatives.

'Hitler has a gift for this kind of decision,' Luis said. 'He knows what is good for people, he knows it long before they know it themselves. You must admit, there's a touch of genius in the idea.'

'I suppose so. If it works.'

'Of course it'll work. A good song can sell anything. Look what "Happy Days Are Here Again" did for President Roosevelt.'

'Yes. I see what you mean.'

'It'll be the biggest box-office success of all time,' Luis said confidently. 'We're going to get the man who wrote "Yes We Have No Bananas" to do the songs for us. It can't fail.'

After his microdot tuition Luis went to see the embassy doctor. He disliked all medical places—clinics, hospitals, doctors' offices. He felt they threatened him. He had always been healthy, never sick even as a child, and he suspected all doctors because it was their job to seek out illness. You were all right provided you stayed away from doctors. Their interests were the opposite of yours. You wanted to stay healthy, whereas if everybody stayed healthy the doctors would starve. Fundamental conflict of interest there.

'I'm going to give you two immunisations,' the doctor said.

'Anti-tetanus and anti-typhoid. Just a routine precaution against infection when you're in England.' He was preparing the needles.

'I thought fog was the big menace,' Luis said. 'I thought England was full of fog and the fog was full of homicidal maniacs.' He took his shirt off. 'I suppose they can't see the fog for the blackout now,' he said. 'It must make life difficult for the homicidal maniacs, always strangling each other by mistake. It's true what people say about war : the civilians are the ones who suffer most.'

'I'll tell you what England is full of,' the doctor said. 'Dogs. And the dogs evacuate their little bowels all over the streets, all over the paths, all over the parks and squares and public places. Keep still.' Luis shut his eyes and clenched his teeth. 'Suppose, my friend,' the doctor continued as he worked, 'that you are walking down Piccadilly, trying to overhear the conversation of two British generals, when your foot slips on a heap of dog muck. You fall, split your skull, and infect yourself from a second heap. Without my protection, where would you be? In the shit, as the Americans say.' He pressed a couple of sticky plasters onto Luis's arm. 'You can open your eyes,' he said. 'The amputation's finished. Will you take the head now or shall I send it later?' He yawned; the ambassador's wife had had raging neuralgia at four in the morning.

Luis felt his arm cautiously. 'You're probably thinking that all Spaniards are supposed to be brave,' he said. 'Well, I'm not brave. What good does being brave do anyone? The pain hurts just as much, doesn't it?'

'Don't know,' the doctor said. 'Personally I've always been tremendously brave about pain, but then it's never been my pain . . . Except once, when a patient sat up and bit me.'

'Why did he do that?'

'I never discovered. He died soon afterwards. Ungrateful brutes, patients . . . Look, there's another thing I ought to warn you about: air raids. You're more likely to die from English cooking—they make a truly lethal pudding called Spotted Dick which lowers your centre of gravity to somewhere between your knees—but if the Luftwaffe does start dropping bombs anywhere near you, fall on your face as fast as you can. The best thing is to be somewhere else, of course, out in the country or deep down in an underground railway station, but suppose you're caught in a shop or a restaurant . . . Find something to hide behind. Flying glass can chop you up like dogsmeat. Blast can kill you without leaving a mark. Don't worry about making a fool of yourself. Let the plucky British ignore the bombing and have their limbs blown off. You run away and hide. Don't try and prove anything foolish.'

He was being completely serious and unemotional. Luis nodded. He squeezed his biceps and remembered Guernica, the crypt under the bombed church where the bodies were laid in rows, their feet and hands twisted impossibly, as if they had been trying to run in two directions when they died. And that other place had been even worse, that little town where the German bombers kept coming back and missing the arms factory. What had it been called? Luis hunched his shoulders and worried because he couldn't remember the name of the place. He could remember the craters and the blown-up buildings and the smoky air and the flies, and the man with a blood-black bandage on his head and no shoes on his feet and a permanent mad gleam in his eye who had told him that there was no need to take shelter, friend, because the bombers always missed their target, you understand, never once hit their target, so that being the case you were as likely to get killed in one place as in another, you understand me? *Yes I understand you*, Luis had said, worrying about treading on the man's bare toes because he kept coming too close in his eagerness to explain. But the man would not let him go, insisted on asking him where he thought the next lot of bombs would fall. *On the cinema, I expect*, Luis had said, that being one of the few buildings still standing. *Wrong!* the man had shouted in triumph, *Wrong! You are a fool! How can you possibly know? Nobody knows! Not even the bombers themselves know!* And he had hurried off to the cinema to enjoy the pleasure of proving Luis wrong. Perhaps it was the only pleasure left to him. For he was right: the bombers did miss the cinema that day. They blew it to bits the next day, however. Luis sometimes wondered whether the man was still there then, still gambling on Luis's foolishness; whether the high explosive smashed him against a wall like a fly smeared on a windowpane. Funny how they could never hit that damned arms factory. Oh well. All forgotten now. He couldn't even remember the name of the place . . .

'You'd better put your shirt on,' the doctor said. 'You're all goose-bumps.'

'Am I? So I am . . . Wonderful stuff, skin.' Luis buttoned his cuffs. 'Close-fitting, washable, elastic . . .'

'And the holes are all made in exactly the right places,' the doctor said. 'Clever design.'

'Too bad it's not bombproof.'

'A shame, yes. Rips and tears do tend to let the blood out and the weather in.'

Halfway down the corridor, Luis remembered and stopped. 'Durango,' he said aloud.

'*Gesundheit*,' said a passing secretary; but he was not aware of her. He repeated the name: 'Durango.' She walked on, smiling, while he stood and smelled the ghosts of smoky air and reeking craters, and saw the shoeless, bloody-bandaged man vanish in the direction of his lucky cinema. Du-bloody-rango. The poor man's Guernica. Julie Conroy had been right. War was dogshit.

Time to go home.

Chapter 20

After the affair at *Dos Amigos* Luis and Julie had made no arrangement to meet again. She was not to be seen in the embassy waiting room, and he avoided her hotel. This seemed to him a very sensible solution. As an employee of the *Abwehr* he could not afford to go around with an American girl, especially with a bright and alert girl who asked good questions and weighed the answers, and certainly not with a bright and alert anti-Fascist girl who shot from the hip and didn't care who happened to be watching. Julie Conroy was refreshing and exciting and dangerous. At this point in his life, Luis decided, he was obviously moving into a period of great risk. Love affairs were nice but survival came first.

156

So he worked hard at the embassy, ate alone in quiet restaurants and went early to bed. Between dinner and bed, he walked and looked at people. It was still a pleasure for him simply to be out-of-doors; each time he stepped into the freedom and activity of three-dimensional Madrid he felt again the sense of eagerness which a theatre audience feels as the curtain goes up and the scene surprises them. After two years in an apartment filling up with books he felt as if he knew everything and had experienced nothing. Madrid, even under the humourless Franco dictatorship, was a vivid, throbbing experience. There was everywhere a keen awareness of the rewards of living. Spain had punished itself savagely during the Civil War, and now that the rest of Europe seemed determined to have a thoroughly miserable time, the Spaniards recognised when they were well off and they made the most of it. Madrid was all lights and smart uniforms and traffic; no rationing, no sandbags and no air-raid sirens; plenty of food and foreign visitors; and no end of dramatic war news which, *gracias a Dios*, had not the remotest chance of inconveniencing anyone in Madrid.

Whenever Luis strolled through the purple evening he found himself thinking about his brief but vivid relationship with Julie Conroy. Eventually he decided that all this analysis was a healthy corrective. Undeniably she had infatuated him. Why? What was it about her that had thrilled him? It was important to know. Her looks? He pictured her face—alert grey eyes, wide and upturned mouth, simple nose, neatly flared nostrils, strongly curving jawline, all framed in that astonishingly dark yet burning hair. The image was too real; it haunted his mind. He decided it was not the face but the expression that he found so disturbing. Julie Conroy had had her own way of looking at him, interested yet amused too, and something else . . . Provocative, as if she knew very well what he was *not* saying. He remembered it and he felt its impact again : it was her anti-bullshit expression; it meant *Say what you like but don't think you're fooling me.*

One evening he was ambling along the Calle de Alcalá, getting some melancholy, second-hand enjoyment out of the evening crowds, and looking at every beautiful woman in the hope of finding a hint of Julie Conroy's magic. Nobody came close. The more he looked, the less real these people seemed to be. Luis found that he was no longer strolling, he was walking stiffly, woodenly, fists held close to his sides. *This is very interesting*, he thought. *There is a certain type of woman to whom I am unusually susceptible. Clearly this calls for extra precautions.* Quite suddenly he had a strong impression that Julie was nearby, was coming towards him, and he was overcome by an irrational desire to meet her naked: she would be clothed but he must be naked, they would meet and embrace while the crowd passed by and paid no attention. It was not a sexual need, it was . . . What the hell was it? His face grew tense and he wearied his mind with explanation. Was it trust? Or surrender? Why must he be naked? This was dangerous, she could kill him, literally kill him. *You are an idiot*, he told himself, and felt a great anger: no sooner does the fool get well-paid work with the Germans than he falls in love with an American, *an American*, of all the women to choose!

It made no sense, it was totally senseless: a week ago she had not existed so how could she now matter so much? *Shut up shut up shut up*, he shouted silently at himself, *nobody asked me whether I wanted to be in love and if I say I don't, then I don't! So go to hell, all of you!*

A man was selling newspapers. Rather, he was holding a bundle of newspapers for sale and reading one until somebody wanted to buy it. He glanced sideways at Luis and saw a tired young man staring gloomily at the traffic. He went back to his paper.

'Everybody is at war,' he remarked. 'Everybody is fighting everybody.'

Luis looked at him and saw a face that had no purpose in life except to hold a dribbling cigarette. 'Really,' he said.

'It's all here,' the man said comfortably.

'No. That's just a game,' Luis told him. The man didn't look up, shifted his feet, said nothing. 'That's not reality,' Luis said. 'It's unacceptable.'

'Oh yes?' The man turned a page. 'Unacceptable, is it? So what are you going to do about it?'

'I've got my own private war,' Luis said. 'I'm against everybody. That's the only victory worth winning.'

'I'll believe that when I read it on the front page.' Now the man was uncomfortable. Luis was one of those normal-looking lunatics you meet in every big city. Bad for business. Luis sensed the discomfort and turned away. A taxi was stopping, someone got out. For no reason he could name, Luis took the taxi and rode home to his apartment. When they arrived he sat for a moment and looked up at the dark, silent building. 'Oh, this is no damned good to me,' he said miserably.

'Me neither,' the driver said. 'Can't afford the rent.'

'Hotel Bristol,' Luis said.

'You're sure, now.'

'I'm sure. I think.'

*

She was in the hotel bar, talking to an American couple, tourists maybe, middle-fifties. Luis stood by the door and watched, monitoring his feelings. Already the chest-tightening had begun; already his eyes seemed more wide-open, his senses more acute. What in God's name *caused* this? She moved, turning slightly and making a lazy gesture, and the action had such a naturally athletic grace that he instinctively held himself more upright, either in imitation or in envy. She was the leopard amongst the gazelle, all right. Then she turned again and saw him and immediately came over.

His hands were trembling so much that he put them in his pockets. 'Hullo,' he said.

'Hullo.'

He could not look directly at her; his head ducked and dodged and took little glances. 'If it is not too late . . .' he began.

'I thought you'd been run over by a tank.'

'A tank?'

'Yes. I thought probably the Germans hunted you down with a panzer brigade because of that thing at *Dos Amigos*.'

'Oh . . . No. I'm fine.'

'You don't look fine. You look lousy.'

Luis got all his strength together and smiled. 'You don't look lousy,' he said. 'You look fine.'

She took his face in her hands and lightly fingered back his eyelids. 'Been sleeping badly?' she asked.

The shock of her unexpected touch made him start, and

he saw that she noticed this. 'Oh . . . not well, not badly,' he said. 'Many dreams, you know.'

'Let's go over there.' She nodded to an empty table, remote from the American couple. They went and sat down and he told the waiter to bring them two brandies.

'Luis, my friend, you're not going to like this,' she said, 'but please remember you started it, back there in the embassy with your old-fashioned Castilian courtesy—you remember?—so now I'm afraid you're stuck with the appalling consequences.'

'What consequences?' Luis was worried; this was beginning to sound official, governmental.

'I want to make something clear, first.' She rested her arms on the table and edged her forefingers together until they touched. 'When I came to Spain I wanted everything to be simple. I like things to be simple. I'm not a complicated person but the last couple of years have been very complicated for me, what with the war and . . . everything. So. It's best for people if they can have maximum freedom, isn't it? Don't you agree?'

By now Luis was bewildered. What the hell was he being asked to agree to? He gave an unenthusiastic half-smile, half-shrug. The brandies came. He took a good swig.

'Okay.' She smoothed her forehead but almost at once it furrowed again. 'Okay: simplicity, freedom, no entanglements. I'm here in Madrid trying to straighten out my problems. Untie all the knots and chuck out all the junk and start being my own boss again. That's what I'd really like: total independence.'

'Certainly. Your people fought a war about independence.'

'Right. It's worth having, it's very satisfying, very . . . enjoyable. Agreed?'

Luis stared, threw his hands in the air, breathed deeply. 'What has happened?' he demanded. 'Is Spain at war? Have you been arrested? Do you need a lawyer? What the hell is going on?'

'I just want to get the fundamentals straight, Luis, that's all! I just want you to understand, before we both start having a thoroughly miserable time, that it was no part of my plan when I came to Madrid to fall in love with a man like you. No part.'

160

Luis was first astounded, then when he could put words together he was cautious. 'You say . . . forgive me if I misunderstood . . . you said "a man like me". . .'

'Oh, Luis, for Pete's sake! I've fallen in love with *you*, okay? I fell in love with you in that goddam taxi which wasn't being chased by the Gestapo in the bus, and ever since then I think about you all the day and half the night. Is that clear? It's a dumb thing to do and my life would be a million times easier if I hadn't done it but what the hell can I say? It's happened and we're stuck with it.'

'Good. That's very good, that's excellent, because I too have fallen in love with you.' Luis nodded reassuringly.

'Yeah, well, you're a nice guy and all that, Luis, and I don't want to hurt your feelings, but that state of affairs was pretty damn evident a long time ago.'

'Oh.' Luis found reason to blow his nose. 'You knew that I . . .'

'Short of going around with coastguard rockets shooting out of your ears you couldn't have made it much clearer.'

'Ah.' More handkerchief work. 'I see.'

'You're not much good at hiding things, Luis.'

'No? Well . . . obviously not.'

'So we're in love with each other, you and me, both of us. But I've been in love before, and I guess so have you. It's nice while it lasts but it never lasts and then it's a real bitch of a bastard.'

Luis saw with a shock that tears were starting in her eyes. He felt besieged, helpless. He signalled the waiter for more drinks. 'Then I suggest,' he said as lightly as he could, 'that we enjoy it while we can.'

'Okay.'

She was silent until the waiter had come and gone. She picked up her glass. 'Oh well,' she said. 'If it had to happen, it couldn't have happened to two dumber people.'

'Agreed,' Luis said, and they drank to that. They sat back and looked at each other with a fresh, undisguised interest.

'As mature, intelligent, educated adults,' she announced, 'I think we should always treat each other decently, don't you?'

Luis nodded.

'Good,' she said. 'And if I ever find out that you're not as nice as I think you are, I'll kill you. Now I'm starving. Let's go eat.'

Chapter 21

That happened three days after the scuffle at *Dos Amigos* and four days after Luis had begun his training at the embassy. The sudden full flowering of friendship with Julie Conroy perked him up enormously just as the work was beginning to grind him down. Now he slept better, felt fresher, had a greater appetite for Franz Werth's eternal Morse lessons, Richard Fischer's painstaking tuition in secret writing (extended to include codes), Otto Krafft's classes on housebreaking (with special attention to wiretapping and the use of hidden cameras) and much more. Luis had a quick brain; he was brilliant at nothing but he adjusted easily to differing demands and he soaked up knowledge with the thirst of a true convert.

Soon he was spending less time on the groundwork of espionage and more on tactical briefings. These interested him because they revealed a sideways glimpse at the way the war was going—or at least at the way the German High Command thought it was going. A string of military attachés told him what they knew (and also what they would like him to find out) about the British convoy system, about new British aircraft designs, about the pattern of production in British dockyards, about the effect of prolonged bombing on British morale; but not, Luis noticed, much about the British army. The Germans seemed to have decided to defeat the British by sending fleets of bombers to destroy their cities and packs of U-boats to sink their ships while the German army enjoyed a bit of a rest after its whirlwind tour of Europe.

'Commando units,' said one of his briefing officers, a tall, balding major of marines. 'We're always interested in anything you can find out about them. But don't bother us with routine stuff about the British army. So much of that army is already in our prison camps that we know virtually everything we need.'

162

'What about North Africa?' Luis asked.

The officer smiled. 'Regard it as an extension of the naval campaign. Its main advantage is that it obliges the British to send even more ships into the Atlantic, there to be sunk with a loud splash.'

'Oh.' Luis ran his thumbnail along his teeth. 'I never thought of that.'

'Anything *significant* on North Africa you might happen to come across, pop it in the post double-quick. But don't go out of your way to hunt it up.'

'I see.'

'It's all sand, you know. Marvellous training ground but not worth capturing because when you've captured it, what have you got? We wouldn't be there now if Mussolini hadn't failed so miserably in the first place. Too much sand for his chaps, far too much sand. Still, it's a useful place to annoy the British, I suppose.'

'I wonder if they think the same thing about you.'

'Shouldn't be surprised. Shouldn't be at all surprised. The Afrika Korps probably isn't doing much good out there but then again it isn't doing any harm, is it? All just sand, you see. Nothing to worry about.'

Luis was towelling himself after a spell with the rubber dinghy in the embassy pool, when Otto arrived to take him to Colonel Christian. 'Watch out,' Otto warned. 'He's liable to bite you in the leg.'

Christian sent Otto away and told Luis to sit down. He looked a bit strained, not quite rattled but definitely preoccupied. His muscular, shaggy face was shadowed with brooding, and his freshly pressed suit was already rumpled and rucked.

'Getting on all right?' he grunted.

'Yes, I'm getting on all right,' Luis said. He watched the colonel pace over to a window and frown at the clear, careless sunlight. 'Are you getting on all right?' Luis asked politely.

'Listen, you little dago bastard, I ought to have you shot,' Christian growled.

'Oh?' Luis's mouth felt suddenly empty, as his throat drained saliva. He swallowed. 'You already did that once,' he pointed out. 'Let's not get into a rut.'

Christian slowly yawned. He turned and walked towards

163

his desk. As he passed he kicked Luis's chair. It was a revolving chair and Luis spun briskly. He caught glimpses of the German going behind his desk, picking up a piece of paper, coming back towards him. Then Christian booted the chair again, harder. Luis gripped the arms and let the room blur into a pastel haze.

'This is a rocket from our Foreign Ministry in Berlin to my ambassador upstairs.' Christian's words boomed and faded like a bad loudspeaker. 'As a result of this rocket my ambassador upstairs put on his heaviest boots and jumped up and down on my stomach.' Luis's chair slowed, and Christian's words began to come together. 'My ambassador is a large man,' he said. 'with large feet.' The chair drifted to a halt. 'And you were responsible for it all,' Christian accused. Luis blinked, and waited for his brain to catch up with his body. 'You cretinous dago halfwit,' the colonel said, 'I must have been insane to let you in here.' He licked his lips.

Luis stood up, brushed his lapels with his hands, and walked unsteadily away. 'I cannot stand angry people with ill-fitting dentures,' he said as he went. 'They spit so much.'

'I do not wear *dentures*,' Colonel Christian said, hitting the word like a tentpeg.

'That makes it even worse.' Luis reached the end of the room and mopped his tie with his handkerchief. 'I charge extra for working with spitty people. The cleaning bills, you understand.'

'Insolent little sod.'

'There. You see?' Luis dabbed at his sleeve and stared at the result. 'Have you been eating beetroot?' he asked.

Christian leaned against his desk and inhaled slowly, his head nodding slightly with the effort of self-control. 'If you find working here so irresistibly funny,' he said stonily, 'you can just laugh your way to the street, now.'

Luis felt a great desire to do as he was told: just walk out, smiling, into the street, into the mild, cheerful, undemanding Madrid street, go and find Julie Conroy, sit in the sun with her and relax, forget, enjoy. He felt overworked and weary: was all this effort really worth five hundred pesetas a day? And most of that was danger money. Franz said on average one agent in two got caught immediately. Luis thought: *By Christ, they're getting me damned cheap and that doesn't include free insults.* He turned his back on Colonel Christian. 'No, no. Dear me no,' he said. 'That's not the proper form at all. This is your office, you get paid for making the decisions. Don't try and shuffle off your responsibility onto me.'

'Why not?' Christian barked. 'You like responsibility, don't you? Bloody hell, you took it upon yourself to decide that Germany should invade Russia, didn't you?'

'Ah!' Luis turned. 'Is that what all this fuss is about?'

'Your idiot joke went all the way up the line, Cabrillo. First it leaked out of the *Abwehr* and went all around this embassy. Then Spanish Intelligence picked it up. Next thing, their ambassador in Berlin had it. Five minutes later, von Ribbentrop had it from him and nearly choked with gratitude, after all what are friends for, if not to tell you that you're about to invade Russia? Eh? Especially Spanish friends! D'you know what they call the Spanish Intelligence Service, in Berlin?'

'No,' said Luis.

'The Bungalow.'

Luis thought it over and looked blank.

'Nothing upstairs,' Christian explained savagely. 'God help us all . . .'

Luis perched on the huge, wide windowsill and examined his right toecap for scuffs and scratches. He was thinking furiously, driving his brain to guess where Christian was going so that he could get there first and head him off. 'But that doesn't add up,' he said. 'Why should Berlin pay any attention to what Spanish Intelligence says?'

'Because Spanish Intelligence got it from here! And according to them it came from me! So now Berlin wants to know where I got it! What should I tell them? That I got it from a pansy photographer who got it from an amateur comedian?'

'Ah. You found out about Victor, then.'

'Right now young Victor is on his way to the Luftwaffe arctic weather station in northern Norway with my boot up his backside to remind him to keep his mouth shut in future.' Christian glowered at Luis, turned away, and seemed briefly to be overwhelmed by an excess of energy: he seized his desk and manhandled it through a half-circle, spilling papers and dumping it with a crash that made Luis blink. 'Idiot furniture,'

165

he muttered. 'I haven't decided what to do with *you*, Cabrillo. There's no room in the *Abwehr* for comedians. War is not a joke.'

'Who said I was joking?' Luis asked.

There was a silence while the colonel looked at his scattered papers. 'You had better explain,' he said without enthusiasm.

'My information is that Germany intends to attack Russia,' Luis said. 'You must understand that I have friends in other embassies.' He swung his legs up onto the sill and stretched out on his back with his knees up. 'The report originally came from the Japanese embassy in London, but it has since been independently confirmed by the Swedish embassy in Rome and the Swiss embassy in Ankara.'

'Who told you?'

'The American embassy in Lisbon.' Luis scrubbed at the window with the curtain. 'These need cleaning, you know,' he said. 'You can't see across the street.'

Christian sniffed, picked up his papers and worried them into shape. 'I think you're all piss and wind, Cabrillo,' he said.

'If you don't believe me, go and ask them yourself.'

Christian straightened his desk-set.

'You too have contacts inside those embassies, I take it?' Luis asked.

'Listen, Cabrillo.' Christian came over, lips grimly compressed, eyes unblinking, demanding full attention. 'You're in deep trouble. The only way you can save yourself now is by going back to your embassy friends and getting definite proof, written corroboration. Not just your word, that's worth sweet nothing. I want proof, I want it fast, and I want—'

'Wait a minute, wait a minute.' Luis propped himself on his elbows and pushed his head towards the colonel. 'You don't have *any*body inside those embassies, do you? So I'm not in trouble. *You're* in trouble. That means I don't have to do anything. So I'm not *going* to do anything.'

'Oh yes you are. You're not in Spain, Cabrillo. This embassy is German territory and you'll damn well do what we tell you.'

'I'll tell you what,' Luis said amiably, 'why don't *you* do what *I* tell you? Why don't you report to Berlin that you deliberately allowed this information to circulate here in the embassy in order to identify a member of the *Abwehr* who was leaking stuff to Spanish Intelligence? That way, Berlin's cable simply confirms your suspicions, and now you can tell Berlin that you've got rid of the bad apple.'

'Who? Victor?' Christian scoffed, but it was a thoughtful scoff.

'You also put the blame onto Spanish Intelligence for trying to infiltrate the *Abwehr* in the first place.'

'That's too much for anyone to swallow. *We* have already thoroughly infiltrated *them*.' For the first time, Christian's face relaxed. He almost smiled.

'Of course you have. How else could you have known about this leak? So there's nothing to worry about. Especially as you can assure Berlin that you have doublechecked the Russian-invasion story, and it's true.'

The colonel slowly went back to his desk. He pulled up his chair, and slumped in it so that his chin was pressed against his chest. 'Is it true?' he asked.

'For the love of God,' Luis said flatly, 'why should I lie to you?'

Christian sighed, and heaved his feet onto the desk. '*Why* you should lie, I don't know, but you damn well did lie, didn't you? You lied to Victor.'

'But that was your idea!' Luis jumped off the windowsill and flung his arms wide. Christian's eyebrows flickered. 'Don't you remember?' Luis cried. 'You told me! In this very room! You told me you didn't want me to get out of practice! So I went straight off and arranged that little deception.'

'It didn't have to involve *me*,' Christian complained.

Luis let his arms collapse. 'But then you would never have known that I'd done it,' he said.

Christian stared at him for a long time, so long that Luis had to breathe deeply to keep his shoulders from slumping. When at last the German spoke, Luis scarcely heard him. 'Go away,' Christian whispered. 'Go away.'

Luis went away. He shut the door carefully and silently. The long corridor was empty. He tiptoed down it, lengthened his stride, began bounding, running and then let everything go and sprinted flat out. He burst through the revolving doors at the end of the corridor like a boy out of school and fetched up against a wall, sobbing with laughter and gasping for breath.

An office door opened, and a man with a mouth like a geological fault stared his disapproval. Luis slid down the wall, sat on a bucket of sand and stared back, panting. 'No good waiting there,' he said. 'Last bus went by ten minutes ago.' The man sniffed and went inside.

Luis stood up and dusted the seat of his trousers. 'All just sand,' he murmured dreamily. 'Even when you capture it, what have you got? More sand. Bloody silly.'

Chapter 22

The sunset was flame-pink, lightly brushed with streaks of white which bore softly feathered edges, as if fanned by the dying heat of the sun. The white streaks became tinged with blue as they spread up into the arc of the sky, and the blue darkened to an indigo hugeness above the opposite horizon. It was a moment when you could turn your head from the assembling of night to the disintegration of day and back again, and find a new star pin-pricking the darkness. Julie Conroy turned her head once again and watched the flickering of swallows under and around the wide eaves of the courtyard where she and Luis were sitting. The birds were nesting up there, and their sharp wings and pointed tails came and went like sudden scratches on cine-film, along with a constant conversation of squeaks and squeals.

'You know, this sherry isn't bad,' she said. 'It's not as good as booze but it isn't as bad as for instance kerosene.'

'I hope you're not becoming kind-hearted,' Luis warned. He took her hand, and they linked fingers. 'I don't think I could stand that. If you start being kind-hearted, I shall start being gentlemanly.'

'You already did. Back in the hotel bedroom, you were a perfectly gentle man. Surely you haven't forgotten?'

Luis adjusted his tie and cleared his throat. 'Was I?' he asked. 'How humiliating. That was supposed to be a flood of ungovernable desire, savage and insatiable.'

'What?' She squeezed his fingers until he looked at her.

'Did you just make that up?'

'No. I saw it outside a cinema.'

'Ah . . . Well, you were all that, too, of course.'

'Good.'

'Yes, I thought so.'

She smiled at him with such open pleasure that he smiled back. 'Well, that's all right then,' he said.

'Yes indeed.' She squeezed his fingers. 'I told you it was worth waiting for.'

Luis had gone to her hotel straight from the embassy. On the way there he bought a very large bunch of flowers, tulips, and the hotel receptionist, flustered by a sudden flurry of business, had mistaken him for a florist's deliveryman and sent him up to Mrs Conroy's room. 'Hullo,' she said when he arrived. 'Are those for me?' She kissed him. 'I've been thinking about you . . .' She kept her arms around his neck and looked at his mouth. 'I couldn't remember what your teeth look like, it's been driving me mad, show me.' He showed her his teeth. 'Yes, of course,' she murmured. 'Absolutely perfect. Have you been swimming? I smell chlorine.'

'You haven't changed a bit since yesterday,' Luis said. 'Not a bit.'

'There's something we ought to decide,' she told him. 'It's been worrying me all day.' She chewed her lip.

'What is it?'

She swung her head up and looked him full in the eyes. 'Sex,' she said.

'Oh. Yes, I see.' He nodded thoughtfully. For the last two years he had got along without a sexual companion. This announcement was something of a shock. Like discovering a forgotten bank account with a healthy balance. 'I suppose we ought perhaps to do something about that, some day.'

'That's the point. If we're in love, then we can't avoid making decisions. I mean, if we don't ever go to bed, that's a decision too.'

'Of course.' The more Luis thought about that sort of decision, the less he liked it. His interest swung strongly in the opposite direction; then, with instinctive caution, it swung back again. 'Naturally, one does not wish to rush into a hasty commitment, either,' he said.

'Damn right,' she agreed. 'I make it a strict rule never

to jump into the sack without thinking first.'

'After all, we have our whole lives ahead of us.'

'Exactly.' She gave him a swift kiss. 'So what I suggest is we wait five minutes and then, provided we both still feel the same . . . Okay?'

'Excellent solution,' Luis said. 'It combines moderation with initiative. Excellent.'

So it turned out. They shared the hotel's enormous bed for some considerable time, and later they shared its vast bath. Now, as the day died splendidly in the west, they drank *palo cortado* sherry, dark yet dry, in the courtyard of a restaurant which was so hard to find that Luis was confident no Germans would arrive.

'I know very little about you, Mrs Conroy,' he said. 'Tell me something. How about Mr Conroy, for instance?'

'Yes, how about old Harry?' She made a face. 'What a pain he turned out to be. Harry Conroy sold more aspirin than the Great War and the common cold put together . . . You want to know about my family? I'll tell you the story of great-uncle Eli, the famous American guide and explorer. He got snowed-up leading three men through the Alleghany mountains during the winter of 1874, ran out of food, had to eat the customers. Celebrated case. Old Eli nearly got himself hanged over that.'

'Indeed? For murder or for cannibalism?'

'Neither. Election-tampering, that was the charge. All three men were Ohio Democrats, and the Democrats were pretty thin in Ohio that year.'

'Your great-uncle was a Republican?'

'Hell, no. My people always voted Democrat. Old Eli said himself, when he gave evidence, he said he could never have eaten a Republican, not even to save his life. Said he simply couldn't stomach the taste, it made him sick just to think about it. Powerful speech. Won him a lot of support from the jury. Not enough, but a lot.'

'They found him guilty, then.'

'Sure. Convicted, sentenced, reprieved by the Governor.'

'Who was also a Democrat.'

'No, he was a Republican. Said he couldn't find it in his conscience to hang a man who had set such a fine example to his fellow-Americans.'

'I don't believe a word of all that.'

'Well, that's where you make a big mistake, Luis, because some of it's true. The bit about old Eli never eating Republicans, that's true. Anyway . . . what do I know about you? Come on, tell me something about the Cabrillos.'

Luis stretched his legs and rested his neck against the cool wicker chair. The effect of the sherry was mingling with the pleasant fatigue left by love-making, and gently dissolving it. 'I shall tell you how the Cabrillo family came to be elevated to a position of power and influence by the Spanish monarchy,' he decided.

'Bullshit. I looked you up in *Who's Who in Spain*, Luis, and you're not there.'

He turned his head slightly and glanced at her through confident, half-lidded eyes. 'Nobody who is anybody in Spain is listed in *Who's Who*, Julie. One does not seek to . . .' He frowned slightly as he found the word and expelled it. '. . . advertise.'

'Hey, that's good. That's terrific,' she said.

'It was in the year . . . Well, never mind the year, it was long ago and the armies of the Moors were attacking Madrid. In fact they were drawn up behind the Palacio Real. The park is still known as the Campo del Moro.'

'I've seen it. Very pretty fountains.'

'A recent addition. The Moors were led by a brilliant general, the Emir Ali ben Yusuf ben Texfin.'

'Flare your nostrils again.'

'Pay attention. And the king of Spain placed the command of his crack troops, the Guardia Civil, in the hands of an unknown lieutenant, Juan Eduardo Joaquin Cabrillo.'

'Lovely flaring. Real arrogance.'

'So young Cabrillo assembled the Guardia Civil. "Forty thousand fanatical Moors threaten Madrid," he said to them, "and only you can save it." '

'MGM could use that line.'

'Then he told them to take off their hats and turn up the brims at the back. "Now that we have our backs to the wall," he said, "our hats must not get in the way." And that is why, to this very day, the Guardia Civil wear those peculiar, varnished hats which they call "dust-shovels", turned up at the back.'

'Who won?' she asked.

Luis sighed. 'You Americans . . . Obsessed with results. Never thinking of style, of manners . . .'

'I guess your guys must've won. Otherwise nowadays Madrid would look like an audition for *The Desert Song*.' She ran her finger along Luis's jawline and tipped his head back so that he looked hawklike and haughty. 'Maybe not, though. Maybe it was a stand-off. You have a touch of the Arab in you, Luis.'

'Well, there is a family tradition that the beautiful daughter of Ali ben Yusuf one day saw Juan Eduardo Joaquin through a telescope and fell in love and got into his tent that night, and they lived happily ever after until shortly before dawn, when she had to go home for breakfast.'

Julie moistened her lips. 'All this talk of food . . . Do they sell any grub here?'

'They serve an excellent *gazpacho*.'

'That doesn't scare me. I'll take it on my forehand, and you can cut off the volleys at the net.'

They went inside and ate a long, leisurely dinner of *gazpacho*, herb omelettes and green salad, fruit, and a keen, firm cheese from Navarre. They drank Chacoli, a brisk and bubbly wine from the Basque country, and topped it all with Benedictine and black coffee. As he paid the bill, Luis knew that he could afford to do this sort of thing every night and still save half his income from the embassy. He felt enormously accomplished: he was regularly employed, the work was challenging, the rewards could only get better, and here beside him, touching his hand, was the most exciting woman in Madrid. The future looked golden. He drained his Benedictine, and as the last drops trickled down his throat he realised, with a slight jolt, that he was a little drunk: the glass in his fingers was blurred, the colours of the room were too soft. He blinked hard, and the golden future came into sharp focus. In a week and a bit, his training would be over. Soon the Germans would send him out to spy for them. Then he would be alone, hunted, always in danger. This, now, was just a holiday.

They took a taxi back to the hotel.

On the way, she said: 'Thank you for dinner. It wasn't like genuine American food, but it tasted good.'

'I'm glad.'

172

The taxi slowed for a corner, and Luis leaned in front of her to look out of the window. He grunted with surprise.

'What is it?' she asked.

'Nothing, just an office block. It used to be a warehouse until a shell hit it. I was inside that shop when it happened. Nearly got killed. If those gunners had fired their shell ten seconds later I would have been crossing the street when it exploded. Makes you think.'

'I had a narrow escape at breakfast,' she said. 'I poured a whole cup of milky coffee straight down my throat. Just three inches to the left and I would have drowned an ear.'

'You wouldn't be making fun of it if you had been back there in 1937. What high explosive does to people is not funny.'

'My dear Luis, I have seen what high explosive does to people.' She put her head close to his and gently nipped him on the ear. 'It re-arranges their bodies in a violent and painful way. I was in London during the blitz last October and I saw it happen night after night.'

'Well, then.'

'Well phooey. More Londoners got run over by cars in the blackout than were blown up by German bombs. I mean, life is dangerous.'

Luis thought about that. 'What were you doing in London?' he asked.

She swished her hair from side to side. 'Enjoying the bombing,' she said. 'This is about the time of night that it gets really serious, usually about midnight. I bet they're flying over London right now, blowing up an orphanage here, a hospital there, an old-folks'-home somewhere else.'

'I don't believe you really enjoyed it.'

'Oh, I enjoyed the excitement. A lot of Londoners did, too. But not the mines. They drop huge mines by parachute, you know, big black bastards, if you're unlucky you can actually watch them floating down. Then there's a blinding flash and a deafening crump and suddenly everything for half a mile around is a heap of ruins. I could have done without the mines.' She twisted her head to look out of the rear window. 'Big fat moon up there tonight. They like that. Yes, I bet the krauts are bombing the bejesus out of London right this very minute.'

By now they were in central Madrid, cruising along an avenue. The traffic thickened, and the taxi gradually lost speed until it eased to a crawl and stopped. The line of vehicles on their left gained a few yards, and another taxi slid beside them. Clearly visible in the back was a quartet of German officers. They looked as if they had spent an enjoyable evening.

When Luis noticed them he was too late to distract her attention; already she was winding down the window. 'Fascist faggots!' she cried, and her twang cut sharply through the mumble of idling engines. The officers looked at her, attracted, interested, smiling. One of them opened a window. 'You fornicating fascist finks,' she told them. Luis watched their faces change, saw them look from her to him, studying, remembering. Then the traffic moved, and she sat back.

'Sorry,' she said. 'I was thinking about what they did to London. And other places.' Luis shrugged. 'Why not?' he said. But he noticed that the other taxi followed them all the way to her hotel and waited while they got out, before it drove away.

Chapter 23

Next morning at ten o'clock Luis was again summoned to see Colonel Christian. He trudged upstairs, glumly convinced that he was in for another squabble and not feeling up to it. But Christian was calm and considerate: he offered Luis coffee and he did not kick, hit or throw any piece of furniture.

'I have had a signal from Berlin,' he said. 'They would like to know if you would be willing to change your area of operations and go to Russia instead.'

Luis sat back and stared. His first reaction was a rush of pleasure: he'd guessed right, Germany *was* getting ready to attack Russia. Marvellous! Now Berlin would respect Christian and Christian would respect Luis Cabrillo . . . Then the greater implications struck him: Hitler had given up the idea of invading Britain. Hitler was going to fight this war on two fronts at once. Hitler was following Napoleon eastwards. The whole world was about to change . . . 'No,' he said, 'I'm not going to go to Russia.'

'Why ever not? The work is the same, and Berlin says that you would be paid many times more than you can expect to earn in Britain.'

'In that case it can't be the same work.'

'Same *sort* of work.'

'What? I don't speak Russian. How many Russians speak Spanish? The idea's insane. There's no Spanish embassy in Moscow, and Stalin hates Franco. I'd never get in. If I did get in I'd never get out.'

'Berlin can arrange to have you infiltrated through Scandinavia as a Spanish Communist refugee. There are plenty of those in Russia.'

'And none of them has ever heard of me, so they'll ask a lot of questions which I can't answer, and inside ten minutes I'll be looking down the barrel of a gun.'

'No fear of that,' Christian said reassuringly. 'The Russians shoot people in the back of the head.'

'Not me.'

'No, of course not. As you say, the idea's insane, but Berlin instructed me to put it to you. Evidently your discovery impressed them.'

'I see.' Luis put his hands in his pockets and waited calmly for Christian to say something more. He sensed that their relationship had shifted slightly, away from master-and-servant and towards tutor-and-student. Maybe even tutor-and-gifted-student.

'Anyway . . .' Christian buffed up his moustache. 'Next time you get hold of something like that, come and see me straight away.' He set off on a little walk, carefully following a seam in the carpet, each foot sliding along the line. 'You know, Cabrillo . . . the *Abwehr* can be a curious organisation at times. Berlin doesn't really understand how we work in Madrid. They can be remarkably crass, as you've just seen. We have to spell things out for them. Never give them a choice, they'll choose the wrong thing every time. Understand?'

'Yes, of course.' Luis noted a new tone in the colonel's voice, a suggestion of wariness, perhaps even of defensiveness.

'We're not in competition, you and I, Cabrillo.'

'I certainly hope not.'

'We need each other, to succeed.'

'Indeed we do.'

'And after what you've told them concerning the Russian situation, Berlin will be expecting great things from you in England.' Christian's seam had led him to the baby grand. He raised the top and raked his fingers across the strings, making a dry, anxious noise. 'We mustn't disappoint them, must we?'

'I certainly intend to earn as much money as I possibly can.'

'Good. Good. A great deal depends on it. Now there is someone I want you to meet.'

Christian thumbed his desktop buzzer, and Otto came in with a man who brought a fresh charge of life to the room.

He was introduced as Frederick Ryan. As soon as Luis shook hands he felt encouraged and stimulated, like an actor meeting a star who is going to revitalise a play. Ryan was middleaged, medium height, and looked very fit. He was dressed in a dark suit which, for discretion, taste and cost, was better than a letter of introduction from a banker. He was cleanshaven and his face had a keen, alert expression. Soft brown hair was brushed back from a wide and tranquil forehead, and he knew how to stand without fidgeting his fingers or twitching his feet. His voice was interesting and sounded genuinely English. Luis looked at Frederick Ryan and was more than impressed: he was utterly charmed. By a man who had done nothing but walk ten paces and shake hands! *Watch out, dummy*, he warned himself.

'I have decided that it is time for you two to get to know each other,' Christian said. Otto smiled and rubbed his hands.

'*You* seem very happy,' Luis remarked.

'I believe this could be a great combination,' Otto said. 'The Rolls-Royce of German espionage.'

'That makes me Henry Royce,' Ryan said, 'because you, Luis, must obviously be the young Lord Rolls, who died at the sadly early age of thirty-three.'

Everybody laughed. Ryan spoke so easily and unaffectedly that he was irresistible.

'Let's make it Mercedes and Benz,' Luis said.

'Make it Donner and Blitzen, Castor and Pollux, or cheese and pickles,' said Christian, 'but just make it work. You'll both be going to England at the same time. I want you to co-operate and help each other. From now on you'll train together.'

'Splendid,' Ryan said. 'At last I have someone to talk cricket with.'

'I said training,' Christian told him sharply, 'not gossip.'

'My poor fish, understanding the gossip is part of the training,' Ryan replied, and Luis saw how confidently the Englishman countered. 'It's no good tapping a British general's line if you don't know what he means when you hear him say he's going to open his shoulders.' Ryan blinked three times. 'For instance.'

Christian looked at the dots of dust eternally wandering through the bars of sunlight. Otto breathed deeply and held his breath as if waiting for orders. 'What does it mean?' Christian grunted.

'Oh, it means he's going to try to collar the bowling and biff it for six,' Ryan said, smiling gently. Otto exhaled. Christian frowned at him. 'You might say it means he's thinking of stepping down the wicket and using the long handle,' Ryan added. 'Wouldn't you say?' he asked Luis.

'Possibly,' Luis said. 'An awful lot depends on what school the chap went to.'

'That's enough of that,' Christian said. 'Now go and work.' He looked stiff and uncomfortable.

'Damned huns have absolutely no sense of humour,' Ryan remarked as they walked down the corridor. 'Isn't that right, Otto?'

'I expect so.' Krafft was checking through some typewritten papers. 'If all goes well, you will finish your training at the end of next week and leave for England as soon as possible.' He folded the papers and put them away. 'Until then, you are not to meet outside the embassy.'

'What rubbish,' Ryan said.

'Colonel Christian's orders.'

'Christian's an ass. Of course we shall meet outside. Come and have a game of tennis at my club, Luis.'

'A pleasure, Frederick.'

They looked at Otto. 'I shall have to report this to Colonel Christian,' he muttered.

'Well, tell him he can come too: we'll need a ball-boy. This

177

place is quite extraordinary,' Ryan said to Luis. 'I haven't met so many buffoons under one roof since I was cashiered from the Royal Horse Artillery.'

*

Luis enjoyed the next few days enormously. They were busy, funny, well paid, and laced with sex. He had never slept so soundly nor woken with such an appetite. Everything gave him pleasure, because it involved being with either Freddy Ryan or Julie Conroy, and they were delightful companions. Different, but delightful.

With Freddy the work was always fun. He treated the embassy tutors with a kind of cheerful contempt, as if they were tradesmen of low intelligence, or distant relatives who had to be discouraged from trying to borrow money. Franz Werth in particular did not know what to make of him. Freddy usually took charge of their Morse-buzzer lessons after the first two minutes: just long enough for Franz to start sounding authoritative, for instance on the subject of consistency:

'This cannot be overemphasised. Never rush your transmission, no matter how long the message, no matter what pressures you may feel. The first essential—'

'What have you got there?' Freddy asked.

Franz looked at the sheaf of papers with which he was gesturing. 'Today's test messages. They—'

'Don't be a complete idiot, Franz, we did that lot last week.'

'No, these are new. I—'

'Chuck 'em over.' Freddy stretched out a hand.

'You cannot have seen them before.' Franz tapped the papers nervously against his palm. 'It is impossible.'

'Soon tell you that. Come on, let's see the evidence.' Freddy's critical tone, steady gaze and outstretched hand were too much for Franz. He surrendered the papers.

'Hmm . . .' Freddy gave half to Luis. They glanced through them in silence.

Franz began: 'I assure you—'

'Hush!' Freddy collected the papers again. 'What do you think, old chap?' he said. 'Deadly dull, isn't it?'

'I never thought much of it the first time,' Luis replied.

Freddy got up, dumped the papers in a waste basket and

178

dusted his hands. 'Now then!' he said briskly, 'let's see what else you have in stock.'

'Why . . . nothing.' Franz headed for the waste basket but Freddy stepped into it and began trampling the papers. 'Those were new messages,' Franz insisted, 'I chose them myself—'

'Don't try and deceive us, you dreadful hun. We're professionals at the game, remember? Fortunately for you . . .' Freddy, still casually trampling, pulled a book from his pocket: *Lady Chatterley's Lover.* '. . . I have a humorous novel which should fill the gap nicely. Will you wash or dry?' he asked Luis.

'Dry,' Luis said. He opened the message-pad. Freddy sat down at the buzzer. 'Chapter 17 is pretty fruity,' Luis suggested.

'I shall make a real effort to stop my hand trembling.' Freddy began transmitting. 'You're too immature for this stuff, Franz,' he said without looking up. 'Go and get some coffee.'

Franz's chubby features sagged with guilt and worry.

'And doughnuts,' said Luis, scribbling *and dough* before he caught himself and crossed it out and got back to the transmission.

'This cannot—'

'For God's sake stop interrupting.' Freddy paused, and pounded the book flat with a sudden angry thunder. 'What do you want? Money?'

'No, no—'

'I should bloody well think not. Luis, you haven't been lending him money, have you?'

Luis sucked his breath in and shook his head.

'Damn right, old chap.' Freddy rapped out an indignant stutter of Morse. '*Damn* right.' Franz walked away and looked out of the window while they got on with the lesson. After a while he went out and came back with coffee. 'The thing you have to understand about the English,' Freddy was saying, 'is they're all snobs. Even the meanest, sorriest, most wretched of them.' They looked up. 'No doughnuts,' Franz said. They looked at each other, eyebrows raised in silent disapproval. 'And that is the last time I ever bring you coffee!' Franz shouted. He put the tray down so violently that he spilled the stuff.

'If that's your attitude, my good fellow,' Freddy said quietly,

'I don't care to have any. Take it away, it's interfering with our work. And I warn you: if you ever ask me for money, I shall report you to Colonel Christian.'

'I have never asked for money!'

'I should think not. You don't get people in British intelligence,' Freddy told Luis, 'borrowing money from the agents. They wouldn't dream of it.'

Franz Werth was relatively easy meat: he was just a signals technician, blinkered by his work, nervous of straying outside it. But Freddy manipulated all their tutors, varying his approach according to each man's character and interests. Otto's weakness, Luis discovered, was humour. He could not resist jokes. Freddy knew dozens. In the middle of a lecture on the *Abwehr*'s safe-house system in southern England, Otto mentioned a building called 'Abbey Gates' near Swindon. Freddy raised a finger. 'Extraordinary coincidence. Last time I was in Swindon—which, incidentally, is often described as the arsehole of England, and frankly, having visited Swindon several times, I think that remark is an insult to the British rectum—anyway . . . What was I saying?'

'Extraordinary coincidence,' Otto said, already hooked.

'Yes. This man Delahaye, Major Delahaye, they say he introduced the head-on attack when he was in the Royal Flying Corps. He flew head-on at the stinking enemy—that was your chaps, Otto—and the first man to give way presented an easy target.'

'Evidently Delahaye never gave way,' Luis said. He swung his feet onto Otto's desk.

'Never. "De-constipate or bust", that was Delahaye's motto. According to his adjutant Delahaye never knew the meaning of fear. I doubt if he knew the meaning of many other words, either, but that's not the point.'

'This has something to do with Swindon?' Otto inquired, as a gesture to responsibility.

'Patience, Otto, *patience*. The trouble with these Prussians,' Freddy said to Luis, 'no self-control. Headstrong, impetuous fellows. Awfully good at hacking each other about the face with sabres, but I sometimes ask myself: is that the way to get on in the world? Is it, Luis?'

'It's a beginning, I suppose,' Luis said. 'Unless one of them hacks too hard, in which case it could be an end.'

180

'Could indeed. That sort of thing wouldn't have appealed to Delahaye, especially when they put him in charge of security at the Spitfire factory . . . Otto, you're looking rather pale. Isn't he looking rather pale, Luis?'

'I think it's all this unarmed-combat training.' Luis was rapidly learning how to pick up Freddy's clues. 'You've been overdoing it, Otto.'

'Why don't you send for some nice cold beer?' Freddy suggested. 'My God, you've certainly earned it.'

Together they stared with concern at Otto's paleness.

'You stay there, old chap,' Freddy said, half-rising, 'I'll get them to—'

'Please!' Reluctantly Otto picked up the telephone and ordered three cold beers.

'I don't think he's been getting enough sleep,' Luis said to Freddy.

'I'm *sure* he hasn't. How much sleep have you been getting, Otto?'

'*Please*. I feel fine. You were talking about the Spitfire factory in Swindon.'

'The beer will do him good,' Freddy murmured. 'Anyway,' he went on, 'Stubby Delahaye—he was only five-foot-four, you know—Stubby bought me a drink one day and told me a remarkable story about the wife of his managing director. While the chap was at work building lots of lovely Spitfires to play havoc with the poor bloody *Luftwaffe*—that's your crowd, Otto—she was being unfaithful. Committing rather a lot of adultery, which is the sort of thing you get stoned to death for in Arabia, but not in Swindon. The soil's all wrong, very little stone, lots of rather sticky clay which clings to the fingers, you can't chuck it more than about seven feet and even then it has very little impact.' Freddy made feeble throwing gestures.

'Extraordinary the way geography shapes people's manners,' Luis remarked.

'She was unfaithful, you say,' Otto prompted.

'With any man who would lie still for five minutes. The lady was rabid, absolutely rabid with lust. It's not an uncommon thing in certain sectors of the British middle class, Luis. Chaps like us have to be damned careful. You get invited round for sherry and the next thing you know the bank manager's wife whips your bags off and seizes you warmly by the origin of species. Terrifying.'

'Good God . . .' Luis whistled. 'Still, I expect they do things differently in Prussia, don't they, Otto? More formality?'

Otto said: 'We seem to be losing the point.'

'Exactly what the bank manager's wife told me on more than one occasion,' Freddy said. 'An extremely impatient lady.'

'You know, for the risks we run,' Luis remarked. 'I really think the *Abwehr* ought to pay us more, don't you, Freddy? I mean, dash it all . . .'

'Swindon,' Otto insisted. 'Spitfires, adultery.'

'Oh yes.' Freddy shook his head sadly. 'Tragedy, really. Shows just how corrupt and degenerate the British have become. Even the Catholics, and this was a Catholic family. What happened was their little boy, a precocious brat, noticed what was going on, and after each infidelity he pedalled off on his tricycle to pay a call on the lucky man, looked him straight in the eye, and offered to sell him his teddy-bear for five pounds.'

'A lot of money,' Luis said. 'That's a week's pay.'

'It's incredible,' Otto said.

'Government statistics,' Luis protested.

'Five pounds,' Freddy repeated firmly. 'Every time his mum wandered off the straight and narrow path, sonny followed through and sold the man his teddy-bear for a fiver. Well, dad was fully occupied at the Spitfire factory, mum was keeping herself amused, and sonny was getting rich quick selling teddy-bears—so much so that his mother began to suspect. She noticed all the banknotes stuffed inside his rompers.' Freddy stopped and looked away.

'Well, go on,' Otto demanded. 'What happened?'

Freddy sighed. 'I had a very unhappy childhood, you know,' he said. 'People were rotten to me. I'd rather not be reminded of it, if you don't mind.'

'But I do mind. I want to know what happened.' Otto was half-pleading, half-threatening.

'All right. All right, if you insist. It's very tragic, it really is. The kid wouldn't tell his mother how he got the money so she packed him off to confession. The priest said 'What d'you want?' And the kid said, 'I've come to confess.' 'Thank God for that,' the priest said, 'I thought you were going to sell me another bloody teddy-bear.'

Otto stared for a moment, and then burst out laughing. 'Very good!' he cried. 'Excellent! I must remember . . .'

'And today,' Freddy added firmly, tapping his forefinger on the desk, 'that boy is Governor of the Bank of England *and* plays inside-right for Tottenham Hotspur.'

Otto, by now well alight, went off into further fits of laughter. 'He hasn't the vaguest idea what Tottenham Hotspur is,' Freddy said. 'Tottenham Hotspur is in fact a first-class football team.'

'Well, that's never been completely proved,' Luis said.

Otto got his lungs under control. 'And now, to get back to the *Abwehr*'s safe-house system,' he began.

'I haven't finished yet,' Freddy said. The beer came, the picaresque adventures of the Swindon Spitfire factory's managing director's wife continued to grip Otto; and Luis marvelled at Freddy's fluent, effortless dominance.

He seemed to know something about everything. He could talk about aircraft with Wolfgang/Pongo (who, Luis discovered, was an ex-pilot), about journalism with Richard Fischer, about short-wave radio with Dr Hartmann. Luis was fairly sure that Freddy made up half of everything he told them, but he was never sure which half it was. 'Funny thing,' Freddy told Wolfgang, 'seven out of nine murderers in the state of Michigan have brown eyes. And sixty per cent of them are lefthanded. *And* threequarters are unemployed.'

'That is quite remarkable,' Wolfgang agreed.

'When I was over there, the Michigan police did an experiment. They rounded up all the lefthanded brown-eyed unemployed they could lay their hands on. The murder rate fell almost to zero.'

'What happened when they set them free?' Luis asked.

'Total carnage,' Freddy said. 'Look here, Wolfgang: can't you get hold of some better detonators than this? The Mexican guerillas stopped using this rubbish twenty years ago.'

Wolfgang, who was supposed to be coaching them in sabotage techniques, began defending the quality of his detonators.

'They're junk,' Freddy scoffed cheerfully. 'I remember we used to use them as firelighters in Manchuria in '34. They're

183

not bad firelighters provided you soak them in paraffin overnight . . . Still, if this is the best the Third Reich can do, I
suppose . . .'

'Give me a chance, Freddy, for heaven's sake,' Wolfgang
said. 'I'll try to get something better. What were you doing
in Manchuria in '34?'

Freddy was equally brisk with Fischer's secret inks and Dr
Hartmann's radios. 'It's gnat's-piss, old boy,' he said to
Fischer. 'And what's more I'm pretty sure the gnat was glad
to be rid of it.' Dr Hartmann was halfway through his talk
on the repair and maintenance of *Abwehr* transmitters when
Freddy exclaimed: 'Dundonald!' and slapped his thigh. Hartmann and Luis stared. 'Jock Dundonald at Cambridge!' Freddy
explained eagerly. 'I've been trying to remember his name all
day. Now *he* could get one for me.'

'One what?' Hartmann asked.

'A Shoebox. The American miniature version of the
Russians' Obolensky ultra-long-range transmitter. Jock works
for GPO research, they're bound to have a few going spare, and
Jock owes me a favour or two . . . Yes, of course. The very
man.'

'I am not familiar with anything by anyone called
Obolensky,' Hartmann said warily.

'Oh, old Obo's dead,' Freddy said. 'In any case he pinched
the idea from Beiderbecke.'

'Ah.' Hartmann polished his glasses. 'Beiderbecke. Now his
name is familiar to me, but I cannot quite place his work.'

'Not surprising. Bix Beiderbecke, bit of a recluse, not the
sort of chap to blow his own trumpet.'

Luis's brow cleared. 'Of course!' he said.

Freddy hurried on. 'They call it the Shoebox because that's
about the size of it. Nice and compact.'

Hartmann replaced his glasses. '*Ultra*-long-range, you said?'

'Fairly ultra. They used to experience slight distortion above
ten thousand miles, but Jock Dundonald was working on that,
he's probably got the answer by now . . . Sorry, doctor. Didn't
mean to interrupt your lesson.'

'It's not possible, a shoebox.' Hartmann looked unhappily
at the standard *Abwehr* equipment. It filled a large suitcase.
'How can it be possible?'

'Jock explained it to me once, but I'm afraid I wasn't paying much attention.' Hartmann threw up his hands in shocked dismay. 'The crucial thing, I seem to remember,' Freddy went on, 'is the way the Shoebox sort of kidnaps the local electricity network and converts it into an enormous free antenna for transmitting signals and things.'

'I say, that's clever!' Luis said, not understanding a word of it. Hartmann's head swung and stared at him, heavy with anxiety.

'It cannot be done,' he said, in the voice of a non-swimmer trapped on a raft. 'It is a scientific impossibility.'

'Well, all I know is I saw Jock unplug his Hoover, plug in his Shoebox, and start talking to some bloke in British Columbia,' Freddy said.

'I must inform Berlin of this.'

'Not that they had much to say to each other,' Freddy added. 'What's-the-weather-like-with-you, that sort of thing.'

'Yes, Berlin must know at once.' Hartmann reached his decision and stood. 'I must report everything.'

'He said it was raining over there at the time, if that's any help,' Freddy called as he bustled out.

They sat and listened to his eager heels attacking the tiled corridor with diminishing zeal.

'Bix Beiderbecke,' Luis said. 'You know, they'll catch you out one of these days.'

Ryan stretched easily and looked at the tiny, shivering dapples of sunlight reflected onto the ceiling from the highly polished floor. 'Why can't the weather be like this in England?' he asked. 'It'll soon be coming up to Wimbledon fortnight, which is usually hot, but of course there won't be any Wimbledon this year so I expect it'll pee down.'

'I don't see why you take such risks,' Luis said.

'It's safer than not taking any risks at all.' Ryan slowly closed his eyes. 'You've got to give them what they want, old chap. They *expect* agents to be colourful characters, a touch of the rogue-and-vagabond, a bit of a buccaneer, adventurer, gentleman-crook. Damn it all, Luis, anybody who was completely straight wouldn't do the job. Would he?'

'No,' Luis said, grudgingly. *Admit it, you're not completely straight*, he told himself, *you tell lies, you pinch bank money, you used to twist news-stories right left and centre* . . . 'Still,'

185

he said, 'I don't see why you tell them such enormous lies. They're bound to find out, eventually.'

'And by that time we shall be in England. Meanwhile they want mystery, glamour, intrigue . . . Not too much, but enough to flatter them that their boring, dusty little lives are worthwhile.'

'I thought Germans were more efficient than that. More . . . coldblooded.'

'They try to be. Deep down they're all sentimental romantics, great soft sentimental romantics.' Ryan yawned. 'D'you really think they want us just to sit quietly, pay attention, work hard, get good marks? Pishtosh. We're *spies*, Luis, a special breed of men, full of guile and flair and swagger and a fantastic eel-like ability to wriggle in and out of dangers that would leave the bravest soldier pissing down his left leg.'

'Guile and flair,' Luis said. 'I don't think I've got a lot of guile and flair.'

'Well then, pretend. Put on an act. That's what I do, and that's what they pay me for.' Ryan opened his eyes and let his head turn towards Luis. 'More than they pay you, I shouldn't be surprised. I get a thousand pesetas a day.'

Envy stuck its bony fingers into Luis's bowels. 'I get less,' he mumbled.

Ryan climbed onto his chair and took a pencil and wrote on the ceiling in huge letters THIS WAY UP. He climbed down. 'Come on, you poor undervalued Spanish eavesdropper,' he said, 'I'll buy you lunch.'

'It's too early,' Luis began, but then he saw Ryan's expression. 'Sorry, Freddy,' he said. He raised a thumb at the ceiling. 'What does that mean?' he asked.

'I haven't the faintest idea,' Ryan said, 'but whatever it means, I challenge the Gestapo to deny it.'

Halfway down the corridor they met Dr Hartmann coming back. His brow was knitted like spaghetti. He opened his mouth but Ryan spoke first. 'Berlin on the phone for you, Herr Doktor,' he announced cheerfully. Hartmann broke into a run. They went to lunch.

Chapter 24

Luis wanted to tell Julie about Freddy Ryan, to share some of the pleasure of his company with her, but he decided that it would be too dangerous. However, he told Freddy Ryan about Julie.

'She sounds delightful,' Freddy said. 'Not a bit like the typical American woman.'

'Really? This is the first one I've met.'

'You've been lucky, old chap. The typical American woman devours her mate immediately after the act of sex. She doesn't eat all of him; that would be bad manners. Spits out the watch and leaves it on the side of the bed. You're not thinking of marrying Julie, I hope?'

Luis wondered. They were down in the embassy basement, practising on the small-arms range. As usual, Freddy was faultlessly dressed and creating an impression of calm strength, like an athlete whose training has peaked at just the right time for a big contest. Freddy encouraged confidence and trust; it was one of the things you took for granted about him; presumably it was what made him such a worthwhile agent. That, and his all-round competence. Despite the fun and games they enjoyed with their tutors, Luis saw again and again that Freddy knew his stuff. He handled all the equipment, from the Morse buzzer to the micro-photography gear to the picklocks, with experienced skill. Now Luis watched him raise and level a silenced automatic and squeeze off a full clip. The shots made a series of little fluffs of sound, neatly and regularly spaced: a man's hand could have covered all the sudden holes in the target. Freddy lowered his arm. 'Isn't that odd,' he said. 'I have a sudden craving for a real American hamburger.'

'You might get a good frankfurter upstairs,' Luis suggested. 'And Frankfurt is close to Hamburg, isn't it?'

'No, no,' said an assistant military attaché. 'Hamburg is at least 350 kilometres from Frankfurt.' He went off to change the targets.

'Still, it always seems a lot shorter when you're coming back,' Freddy called after him.

'I'm not thinking of marrying her,' Luis said. 'But I'm also not thinking of *not* marrying her.'

'An agent should never be married,' Freddy stated flatly. 'Never. It spoils his rest. He's afraid that he'll talk in his sleep. Besides, women always want to help, and that becomes downright embarrassing. I mean to say, good spelling is so important in intelligence.'

'She works for MGM. I think you'd like her.'

'Well, no harm in meeting. How about that spot of tennis we talked about? You could bring her along, and meet my girlfriend too. Angela; she's Italian. Tomorrow evening suit you?'

The Madrid Sporting Club occupied a large estate on the fashionable flank of the city. Its high walls guarded a golf course, a pigeon-shooting range, a swimming pool, two polo fields, and more tennis courts than Luis could count as Freddy drove past them. There was also a palatial clubhouse—truly palatial, since it had been the palace of a minor duke until he gambled it away—which was where they parted, Julie and Angela going off to the Ladies' Side while Freddy took Luis into the Gentlemen's Changing Rooms.

'You know, I've never played tennis in my life,' Luis said. He thrust a leg into his brand-new shorts. They felt very crisp and looked startlingly white.

'It's easy. Just hit the ball over the net. The important thing is not to make the women look silly. They don't like that, so they burst into tears and accuse us of cheating. Which I suppose we are, really.'

'Are we? I don't even know the rules, Freddy.'

'Well . . .' Freddy pulled on a sweater which bore the colours and monogram of a distinguished rowing club. 'There are really two sets of rules, Luis: ours and theirs. Theirs are more imaginative than ours. First they have a rule which says they are entitled to win because they're women. Then they have a second rule, which says that if they look like losing, they're allowed to change all the other rules, until they start winning again.'

'Good heavens.'

'Watch Angela, she's an expert.' They went into the sun

and sat on a bench in the rose-garden overlooking the courts. 'What does Julie think I do for a living?' Freddy asked.

'Same as me. International Red Cross.'

'Fine, fine.' He aimed a stern forefinger at a bee which was hovering in front of him. 'Go away, bee.' The bee went away.

'Freddy . . . Do you mind if I ask you a highly personal professional question?'

'My power over the insect world? I can't explain it.'

'Not that. I keep wondering how you feel about doing this sort of job for the Germans while you're still a British citizen.' Freddy nodded gently, and looked away. 'Forget it,' Luis said, 'it's absolutely none of my business.'

'On the contrary, it's very much your business, if we're going to work together in England.' Freddy got up and played a few easy backhand shots, the air singing softly past the strings. 'It's treason, of course, if you go by what the lawyers say. On the other hand I can claim to have been somewhat betrayed myself. For a start, I was very thoroughly swindled by the crooks in command of one of the most illustrious regiments in His Majesty's Brigade of Guards. You've heard of the Brigade of Guards?'

'Haven't they won a lot of battles?'

'Yes, but that was incidental. The real purpose of the Guards is to lend a spot of tone to what would otherwise be little more than a vulgar brawl. At least, that's what the family always told me. The Ryans have been in the Guards for generations.'

'I suppose you were an officer.'

'Yes. It was expensive, but I could just about afford it. Unfortunately somebody else couldn't and he raided the regimental funds. I got the blame. They cooked up a great stew of evidence against me and I had to resign. End of act one. *Go away,*' he said sternly to the bee, which was back again. 'It thinks I'm a rose, I suppose. Dim creature. Bloody miracle it ever manages to get itself airborne.'

The bee wandered off. 'I didn't think that sort of thing went on in England,' Luis said. 'Did you lose much money?'

'Oh, they cleaned me out. There were about a dozen officers involved, some of them because they'd borrowed money from the man who'd done the embezzling, and some because they'd lent him money in return for favours of a fairly squalid nature.

Either way, it was much more convenient for everyone if I could be proved guilty.'

'You were framed.'

'I'm not sure whether I was framed, or stuffed and mounted. What was made clear to me was that if I replaced the money I was supposed to have stolen and quietly resigned my commission, I wouldn't go to jail. It was a very great deal of money, but that just meant that I should go to jail for a very long time, so I sold everything, and behold: the honour of the regiment was saved.'

The evening breeze changed direction and washed a scent of roses over them, so sweet and so strong that both men lifted their heads for a moment. In the distance there was a pleasant plunking of tennis balls. Everything from the sky down to the gravel paths looked clean and healthy and well-behaved. Luis looked around at what money could buy and he approved.

'You don't sound bitter,' he said.

'It was a long time ago.'

'What did you do?'

Freddy gnawed a tennis ball. 'Ugh,' he said, and picked something off his tongue. 'Well, the only trade I knew was soldiering, so I wandered from war to war, South America, Palestine, Manchuria, Ethiopia, wherever they needed a freelance, and ended up in Spain. Here come the girls. I say, what splendid legs! If only their brains were in their bottoms, like dinosaurs.'

Luis and Freddy stood up. 'Now I understand,' Luis said. 'I can see that you have no cause to love your country.'

'Don't misunderstand me. I wouldn't do anything to harm Britain.'

'But surely—'

'No. Surely nothing. Spies have absolutely no effect on wars, Luis. All through the last war both sides spied on each other furiously, and then went ahead and did exactly what they were going to do anyway. This war will be just the same.'

'Good God. So . . . if that's right, our trip to England won't make any difference.'

'It'll make a certain significant difference to one man,' Freddy said softly. 'I'm going to blow that stinking embezzler's head off . . . *Look, I'm tired of telling you,*' he said to the bee,

190

and gently swept it into the roses with a stylish forehand.

The girls reached them smiling, skipping, sidestepping. 'Okay, you Red Cross dummies!' Julie announced. 'This means war! We're gonna pound you two into spaghetti sauce! Isn't that right, Angela?'

'No sheet,' Angela said.

Freddy raised his eyebrows.

'Is what they say all-a-time in MGM,' Angela explained. 'Means yes, big yes! No sheet! Julie says.'

'It wouldn't have done for the Brigade of Guards,' Freddy said. 'Up to the ears in sheet, they were.'

Chapter 25

The tennis was an education.

Luis began fearfully and played hopelessly, crashing and thrashing about the court until he was so bad that he could only improve, and then he started watching the others in order to try and find out what he should copy. Julie was his partner. She really didn't need him. Her splendid legs flitted effortlessly and carried her to almost all the shots. Whenever something utterly harmless came over the net, a ball so leisurely and innocent that even Luis could take it, she left it for him. Focussing fiercely, Luis struck it as if he were trying to fell a tree with one blow, and hit it ten feet past the baseline.

'Out!' shouted Angela happily.

'There you are, Luis, I told you she would cheat,' Freddy called.

'It was damn out!' Angela protested.

'I didn't say it wasn't, darling. I just said you would cheat, and so you will.' They began to argue in Italian.

'Relax, Luis.' Julie patted him on the backside with her racket. 'Save your lovely muscles. Just knock it over the net, that's all.'

'I tried to win the point,' he explained.

She wrinkled her nose. 'That's overrated. We ought to

keep the rally going, not kill it off too soon.'

'Oh. I don't know the rules, you see.'

'I never paid them much attention myself. Have fun, that's the main rule.'

After that he noticed how skilfully Julie and Freddy kept the rallies going. Angela, like Luis, was slim and strong; and like Luis she could hit the ball if she were given good warning that it was coming. Their partners nursed them tactfully so that everybody got a chance to play, and the rallies often went on and on until at last someone fell down laughing. If Angela cheated, Luis couldn't tell the difference. But after half-a-dozen games, when they were beginning to get to know each other, he noticed flashes of true ability from Freddy and Julie: occasionally one of them would lose patience and power a long, low drive that dipped over the net and raced down the sidelines; and the other would cover what seemed an impossible distance to punch back a return which had venom in it. Then a genial lob would allow Luis or Angela back into the game again and the flicker of excitement would be over.

They stopped for a rest, and lay on a lawn so green and smooth it looked as if it had been shampooed and shaved every morning for six hundred years.

'Now Freddy, you play Julie,' Angela said.

'Sure, go ahead,' Luis said. 'Let's see some blood.'

'Good evening, ladies and gentlemen,' boomed a confident voice. They all turned. Colonel Christian, dressed in pale blue seersucker and a straw hat, strolled across the lawn to them, as genial as a dreadnought on a goodwill visit.

Freddy did the introductions, smoothly. He made no mention of the German embassy.

'You have played already?' Christian asked.

'We knocked a few balls back and forth,' Julie said.

'And who won?'

Freddy laughed. 'Let's say nobody lost.'

Luis felt it was time he said something. 'Are you thinking of becoming a member here?' he asked.

'I *am* a member,' Christian said.

'Oh.' Luis felt foolish.

'As a matter of fact,' Freddy said, expertly taking the strain off Luis, 'the colonel and I first met here, in the clubhouse.'

'Ah.' Luis nodded, as if that explained everything.

'Well, I'm sorry I missed all the action,' Christian said.

Luis hoped that remark meant Christian was about to go. He was afraid of what Julie might do if she found that he was a German. His English gave her no clue. He might be Scandinavian, or Swiss, or . . . Luis looked away from the sky and saw a group of tennis players coming through the rose garden. That man on the left looked like Otto Krafft. By God, it *was* Otto. And Richard Fischer next to him, and that new cipher expert and . . . Luis turned to get Freddy's attention but Freddy had already seen them. 'Your party, colonel?' he asked.

'My party, yes. We work hard at the embassy, but we play hard too.'

Luis saw Julie's head come up at the word 'embassy', and then he knew that she had recognised Otto. As the group arrived, she aimed her racket at Otto. 'We met,' she said.

Otto smiled and bowed. 'And a pleasure it is to meet again, Mrs Conroy.'

'Are you all from the same embassy?'

'All.'

'Ah. I see.' She lay back and smiled at Luis. It was an extraordinary smile, perfectly innocent to any bystander but, to Luis, as menacing as a whiff of cyanide from a cup of cream. He tried to frown and smile at her simultaneously, and regretted it. 'Wouldn't you like to go for a swim?' he asked.

'I'd like to play some tennis.' She stood up. 'How about it, Freddy? You and me against the pick of the embassy.'

'Not sure, old girl.' He got up and limped in a circle, his left leg rigid. 'I've been carrying six pounds of rusty shrapnel in that knee ever since Passchendaele, you know.'

'No matter,' Richard Fischer remarked. 'I myself lost this arm on the Somme.' He waved his right arm.

'What bad luck,' Freddy said. 'If I'd been there I'd have helped you look for it.'

'Shall we begin?' Christian suggested. They all went over to the courts.

After a certain amount of deferring to each other, the Germans decided that Otto Krafft and Richard Fischer should play Julie and Freddy. Christian offered to umpire.

Everyone else wandered over to the seats behind the umpire's perch and made themselves comfortable while the players knocked-up. Luis smiled and chatted. It was a scene straight out of a magazine illustration: lustrous turf, each blade of grass sharp in the golden light of evening; the sidelines as sharp as tape; the young men dapper in their snowy flannels, the young women bright and brisk; and all around, the trees and flowers and cultured slopes of an ancient estate. It symbolised the triumph of style over savagery. It was a reminder that even in the Europe of 1941, civilised encounters were possible. Luis noticed Christian's shadow stretching huge and long across the grass. The silhouette of his arm swung up enormously, brushed his elongated head, and fell away. Luis felt his stomach muscles trembling. He wondered how good the Germans were at tennis. Somebody was going to lose. Luis wished he could simply disappear and take Julie with him. That being impossible, he made the most out of watching her move around the court, as lithe and definite as a gymnast. *What a creature*, he thought, *what a lovely animal, what a body, what the hell are we doing here with this gang when we could be in bed together?* Lust romped through him and left him weak with unsatisfied desire. *This is your last week in Madrid*, he told himself angrily. *Your last bloody week, for God's sake. Is this how you want to remember it?*

'Play,' Christian said.

The first game proceeded quietly. The Germans were no more than competent. Freddy and Julie played down to their level, carried the score to deuce, and discreetly lost.

'Game to the embassy,' Christian announced.

Midway through the second game, Freddy hit a forehand shot deep to Otto's backhand and made him stretch. The best Otto could do was to dredge up the tamest sort of lob. Julie was at the net, waiting. Her overhead smash was perfectly timed, a full-blooded winner all the way, even if it hadn't hit Fischer on the head. The two sounds almost merged: *whang-blonk*! The ball rebounded high over the net and Freddy volleyed it neatly past Fischer's collapsing body.

Julie walked back to the baseline and waited for Fischer to recover. It was two minutes before he got helped back to his feet and another two minutes before his vision cleared.

'Sorry,' Julie called.

She hit Otto powerfully in the stomach during the next

rally. He pretended that he was not hurt, but it was obvious that his breathing was difficult.

'Sorry,' she said.

Fischer very nearly got out of the way of her next short-range blast. It clipped him on the elbow and made him drop his racket. A little later Otto was obliged to charge forward to retrieve a shot which Freddy had chipped over the net. As Julie pounced on the return, Otto swung sideways and covered his face, and stopped a cannonball in the kidneys.

'Sorry,' she said. 'Is that game to us?'

'Game to the visitors,' Christian said stonily.

She hit Fischer three times during the next game, including a scorching sweep, with every ounce of her body and every inch of her swing in it, which scored the tender flesh inside his thigh. Otto was struck again on the stomach (and winded), on the ear, and in the ribs. The Germans tried to play a safe, long-range game but Freddy's chipped returns kept drawing them to the net where there was no escape from Julie's bruising blows. She no longer apologised. The spectators were silent. Christian kept score in a voice like tarnished brass.

The Germans lost the third game. As they changed ends, Julie called out to Christian in a clear, cold voice: 'Please ask your players to make some effort to get out of the way of the ball.'

Christian leaned forward, and forced his shaggy eyebrows into an angry overhang. 'I beg your pardon,' he growled.

'God damn it, they're deliberately running into the ball,' she complained. 'It's obviously an attempt to put me off my game.'

Christian said nothing. His body remained hunched in the umpire's chair, his fingers squeezing the woodwork.

There were no injuries in the next game. Christian awarded every point to Krafft and Fischer long before they could be lured to the net. None of the points was good; Christian simply called all of Freddy's or Julie's shots out, the instant they touched the ground, wherever they landed. It was a very quick game.

Fischer got ready to serve the fifth. He was not in the best shape to play tennis but he knew now that all he had to do was get the ball over the net and the colonel would take care of the rest. He took a deep breath and served. The ball wandered over the net and bounced generously. Julie took a pace back and walloped her return wide down the sidelines: too wide. It biffed Christian just behind the ear and sent the umpire's chair rocking madly. The non-playing embassy staff rushed forward to steady it. All the players stood motionless. Luis felt Angela's fingers squeezing his arm. He suddenly felt very sleepy. It was a sensation he remembered from the Civil War, from occasions when he had watched the smoke drift away after a bombing raid or an artillery attack, and he had registered the dead flat silence and had not wanted to find out any more about it. He yawned enormously, uncontrollably.

'Did I hurt you?' Julie asked.

Christian climbed down. His head was still twitching from the blow. 'That was an insult,' he said thickly.

'So was the bombing of Warsaw and Rotterdam and London.'

'You stupid American bitch,' he snapped.

'Arrogant Nazi bastard,' she snapped back.

Luis heard voices behind him, and turned to see a passing group of tennis-players, all Spaniards, who had paused to watch. '*Qué pasa?*' someone called. One of the Germans went over, smiling excessively. '*Es ist alles in Ordnung,*' he assured, but they kept coming forward. '*Es ist alles in Ordnung!*' he said again.

'Colonel, you owe Mrs Conroy an apology,' Freddy Ryan said.

'I shall report you both to the club committee.' Rage or shock, or both, made Christian's voice tremble.

'Will you? Why?' Freddy walked towards him, whanging his racket against his leg. 'You huns have never given a two-penny damn for other people's laws, so why start now? You didn't report Warsaw to the club committee, did you? Or Rotterdam.'

The Spanish spectators repeated the cities to each other, seeking a hint about the nature of the argument.

'You will regret your insolence, Ryan,' Christian barked. Luis could see the beginning of a circular red weal on his neck.

Freddy hooted with laughter. 'What are you going to do? Seize my bank account in London? You'll have to conquer England first, you beastly boche.'

196

'England? That irrelevance? England is no longer an obstacle to the Thi_d Reich.'

'And the Third Reich is the biggest joke in Europe. Call yourself the master race?' Freddy scoffed. 'You'd lose a talent contest with the hole in the elephant's bottom.'

'And you have a mouth like a toilet seat, Ryan, with a brain to match.' Christian was making a huge effort to get his anger under control. He held himself very stiff and upright, and his mouth was set in scorn, but a yearning for revenge narrowed and sickened his eyes. 'You need to be taught manners, Ryan.' He began to walk away. His men followed.

'Listen, you squalid hun!' Freddy called. 'I'm British, you hear? British! That makes me worth fifty of your square-headed Teutonic robots!'

Christian paused. 'I promise you an early opportunity to put that to the test,' he said, and went on. More onlookers had been attracted by the noise. They stood aside to let the Germans through.

'We smashed you in 1918,' Freddy shouted, 'and we'll bloody well pulverise you again!'

The embassy party trailed away, across the lawns. The spectators stood staring for a while and then drifted off, discussing the melodrama. Luis and Angela went over to Freddy and Julie. She was sitting on the grass, watching a small, hairy caterpillar crawl up her finger.

'What on earth was all that for?' Luis asked.

'Well, he started it,' Freddy said. 'Foulmouthed sod.'

'No, you start it,' Angela said. 'Remember?'

They looked down at Julie. She raised her finger. The caterpillar had reached the tip and was standing, waving, looking. 'Imagine what a hell of a view that must be,' she said. She swung her hand around so that the caterpillar could see the others. 'Get a load of them hideous monsters. Did you ever see three such hulking fiends?'

'Come on, Julie,' Luis said. 'Be serious.'

'And they're on *our* side,' Julie told the caterpillar. 'Imagine what the baddies must look like!'

Freddy turned away and performed a graceful handstand. 'Anyway, who cares?' he said, upside-down. 'It's all over now.' He toppled gently and cartwheeled onto his feet.

'Are you sure?' Luis asked, but Freddy looked the other way.

The caterpillar turned and crawled down the finger. 'Okay,' Julie said, 'time to hit the hay, friend.' She placed it gently on a daisy, and stood up. 'What now? A little alligator-wrestling before dinner?'

'I thought you were going to kill those two men,' Luis said.

'What nonsense,' Freddy remarked. 'They were never in danger of anything worse than severe maiming.'

'Where 'ave you learn to 'it so 'ard?' Angela asked.

'I was California ladies singles champion,' Julie said. 'In fact I went to the University of California on a tennis scholarship.'

Luis was amazed. 'American universities give scholarships for playing *tennis*?'

'Sure. Damn tough to get, too. First you have to hit a tennis ball clean through a sheet of corrugated iron, and then you have to spell "corrugated iron".'

'Which you accomplished?' Freddy asked.

'Well,' Julie said, picking up her racket, 'I got fifty per cent, which was considered good enough. I'm hungry. Let's go eat.'

They went eat. Luis tried to relax, but he found it hard to enjoy his food with tomorrow morning getting closer every minute. As it turned out, he was even wrong about that.

Chapter 26

The fish were ugly, angry and dangerous. Luis kept catching them and he kept nearly getting bitten when he took them off the hook. The river was big and dirty and cold, but he had to keep fishing until he caught the one he was looking for. He caught another, still not the one he wanted. It was thrashing about with anger. It bit him on the hand. Enraged, he bit the fish back, and was astonished to see it smiling up at him. They were biting each other yet the fish was his friend. *You're dreaming again*, he told himself, *and a bloody silly dream it is too.* He made himself wake up, and while his consciousness was dragging itself through the murky surf between sleep and waking he held onto the important details in case they tried to slip away from him. Fishing in dirty waters . . . *Jesus Christ*, he complained to his subconscious, *is that the best you can do? Where's your imagination?*

All the lights were on.

Luis struggled up, feeling afraid because he had escaped from a dream to an unreality. The all-white dazzle gradually faded. He was looking at the old man, the caretaker from downstairs. Nightshirt, nightcap, eyes like inkstains.

'Man downstairs wants you,' the caretaker said, and worked his jaws to persuade his dentures to fit.

'Man? What man? What's the time?' Luis found a clock. It was five minutes past two. He wasn't fully awake; the murky river was still running. 'Who is it?'

The old man had a card, already bent and dog-eared by his heavy fingers. He held it close to his eyes and pulled his head back to focus. 'Otto something,' he said.

There had been a shower of rain, which made Madrid seem even darker and emptier. Otto drove fast and said nothing. They reached the embassy in a matter of minutes. Otto put the car in the underground car park and they went up in the lift. Freddy Ryan was waiting in Colonel Christian's ante-room. He was dressed in blue duck trousers and a white polo-neck sweater, and he was beginning to need a shave. 'Get us some coffee, Otto, there's a good chap,' he said. Otto went out without looking at him. Freddy sighed. 'They're such damn bad losers. Not like the Italians. If this had been the Italian embassy we'd be surrounded by coffee and three different flavours of ice cream and a bucket of Chianti per person, but your typical Jerry can't see the funny side of getting pounded with tennis-balls. He goes all bitter and sulky. It's true: they really have no sense of humour. I remember—'

'What's up?' Luis asked. 'What's going on?'

'Good question,' Freddy said. 'My guess is that the colonel is having trouble with *The Times* crossword, but I could be wrong.'

Ten minutes later Christian strode in, trailed by Otto Krafft and Richard Fischer. His face was brick-hard and his eyes were not looking at anyone. The three men went straight into his room. There was a dark rumble of talk, then silence. Luis looked anxiously at Freddy, but Freddy was occupied with balancing a pencil on his fingertip.

The inner door opened. Otto nodded to them. Luis wiped his palms on his thighs. Freddy flicked the pencil high in the air and caught it behind his back. 'Good Lord!' he said, genuinely surprised. 'I've never been able to do that before.' They went in.

Christian was sitting behind his desk. He glanced sideways at them, groaned his disgust, got up and took off his blue seer-sucker jacket. He threw it in the corner, the gesture of a man forced to soil his hands on someone else's mess. Luis got a whiff of dried sweat. Christian's shirt was ringed at the arm-pits. 'You maniacs,' Christian said.

Ryan aimed his thumb at Krafft and Fischer, who were standing by the door. 'Them or us?' he asked.

'You maniacs have endangered the existence of my entire section of the *Abwehr*,' Christian said. 'Can you begin to realise the significance of that? Do you know what happens to *your* future when *my* future is in doubt?'

Freddy found himself a chair and pulled forward another for Luis. 'This may take a little time,' he said.

'Stand up!' Christian ordered. 'You have not been given permission to—'

'For heaven's sake, colonel, just get on with it,' Freddy said. 'Whether we sit or stand is irrelevant. If we're in the soup, standing won't save us; and if we're not in the soup why should you give a damn whether we sit, stand or blow bubbles in the bath?'

Christian glared. 'Has it ever occurred to you that your behaviour might offend someone in this organisation *other than myself*?'

'The ambassador,' Luis said.

'No, no,' Freddy said, 'not that kindly old gentleman, in theory he doesn't even know the *Abwehr* is under his roof. No, I think the colonel's talking about his boss.'

'His boss?' It had never occurred to Luis that Christian might not be in complete command of the *Abwehr* in Madrid. 'The colonel's boss?'

'Shut up!' Christian barked.

'Captain Mullen,' Freddy said. 'A sailor.'

For a moment Luis thought that Colonel Christian was going to attack someone. Then all the rage seemed to drain out of him. He took off his tie, picking clumsily at the knot. He walked over to his jacket, let the tie run through his fingers, and watched it coil on the floor. 'You know so bloody much, Ryan,' he said. 'You tell us why you're here now.'

'Easy,' Freddy said. 'Mullen heard about the argy-bargy out at the Country Club, he didn't like it, sent for you and sank his dentures into your bottom, and *you* didn't like *that*, so you decided to unload the pain and you sent for us.'

There was a silence, while Krafft and Fischer breathed quietly, Luis tried to think of something helpful to say, and Christian scratched his armpits.

'Well, if that's all that's troubling you,' Freddy said, getting up, 'just keep taking the tablets and—'

Christian waved him to sit, without looking at him. 'You two can go,' he said.

'Go out or go to bed?' Fischer asked.

'Go to bed.' He waited until the door had closed and then waited as long again. 'Let me tell you about Captain Mullen,' he said. He sat on the floor, going down slowly and straightening his legs as if they had rheumatism. 'Captain Mullen is not like me,' he said. 'I believe in taking risks. For me, espionage cannot be safe. It is essentially a business in which one gambles in search of big winnings. If one is in no danger of great loss then one is not likely to be rewarded with great success either.'

'But Captain Mullen is not like you,' Luis said.

Christian leaned against his desk. 'Unlike the British, our sailors have never been adventurers. For Captain Mullen the secret of success is to eliminate all mistakes.'

'Some truth in that,' Freddy said.

'So Captain Mullen is a great believer in counter-intelligence. He thinks we should let the enemy make his mistakes, and then we should exploit them.'

'Are you trying to say,' Luis asked, 'that Captain Mullen doesn't approve of sending agents to England?' He experienced a twinge of anger.

'I am not trying to say anything, Cabrillo. I am telling you what happens to people in this department who make mistakes: Captain Mullen eliminates them.'

'Would he eliminate you, for instance?'

'If I am not successful I shall certainly be sacked.'

'Just sacked?' Freddy said. 'I don't mind being sacked. I've been sacked from all the best armies. And some of the worst.'

'Oh, for God's sake, Ryan.' Christian began taking off his shoes. 'Put your cricket-bat away and listen to me. If Mullen thinks either you or Cabrillo have gone wrong he won't just sack you and leave you lying around for the British to sweep up. He'll have you killed, double-quick.'

'Oh Christ,' Luis said. He stared as Christian exercised his toes. They moved stiffly in his socks, as if they too had just been woken up. 'You mean to say, even when we're in England . . .'

'*Especially* when you're in England.' Christian tossed his shoes over his desk and stretched out on his back.

Luis was holding his head in his hands. 'Colonel, why are you telling us all this?' he asked. 'It seems very strange.'

'Two reasons,' Christian said. 'First, because I want you to succeed and that cannot happen if you blunder and end up getting strangled by your replacement in some filthy London back-alley. And second, because you have already blundered, especially tonight, and I have spent the past hour trying to persuade Captain Mullen that you should not be strangled immediately in some filthy Madrid back-alley.'

'Or, indeed, in some quite clean Madrid back-alley,' Freddy murmured.

'How did you get on?' Luis asked.

'Badly,' Christian began, when the doorhandle rattled. They all looked at it, and it rattled again. Luis stared. He was helpless with fright.

'Open it,' Christian said.

The door was not locked. Freddy opened it to reveal a black tomcat standing on its hind legs. The animal dropped through the gap and padded inside, its tail as erect as a sabre. 'What a cheap trick,' Freddy said.

'That unpleasant beast has very little brain,' Christian said. 'It thinks that it is clever when in fact it is merely annoying.' The cat sniffed his toes and looked thoughtful. 'Just like you two,' Christian said.

'Whose doorknobs have we been rattling?' Freddy asked.

'Your association with Mrs Conroy,' Christian said wearily. 'Stupid, ostentatious and damagingly offensive. She has insulted German officers all over Madrid, in your company. Tonight's episode was only the worst. We don't pay foreigners to piss on us.'

'You see what you've done?' Freddy said to the cat. 'You've gone and upset Colonel Christian.'

'Mullen told me that any agent who behaves like you is by definition incompetent and unreliable. He wants you dead.'

'You said yourself that Mullen's a dummy,' Freddy observed. 'I think somebody must have screwed his head on the wrong way round. Does he want Luis and me to go around Madrid in *lederhosen*, singing the Horst Wessel song and giving flowers to German officers?' Christian sighed and closed his eyes. 'Well, why not?' Freddy demanded. 'That would show everyone whose side we were on, wouldn't it?'

Christian heaved himself up. 'This is a secret service,' he said. 'Captain Mullen won't stand for publicity of any kind.'

'I can't stop her shouting at Germans,' Luis said.

'You should never have allowed the situation to arise in the first place,' Christian told him sharply. 'How the devil can I run this department when you turn a simple tennis-match into a brawl?'

'We didn't approach you tonight, colonel,' Freddy pointed out. 'You made the first move.'

'You could have stopped her.'

'Bosh! Look: once you'd insulted her I had to defend her. Right? In any case, what's the panic about? Personally, I think that little dust-up was the best thing that could have happened for everyone.'

'Fischer may have concussion.'

'Excellent,' Luis said. 'The British will never suspect us now.

They argued the point for another ten minutes, while the cat walked amongst them and rubbed itself on their legs. In the end Christian seemed suddenly to get bored. He told them they could go.

'Perhaps the cat is not so stupid,' Luis said as they went out. 'After all, it does succeed in entering the room.'

Christian yawned. 'One day' he said, 'it will rattle that

doorknob and I shall open the door and boot it straight through the window.'

Luis and Freddy shared a taxi back to their apartments. 'What d'you think all that was about?' Freddy asked.

'Wasn't it about Julie and the tennis?' Luis was surprised at his question.

'Christian isn't that stupid. And neither is Mullen. It's all rather odd.'

'Oh sweet Jesus,' Luis said miserably. 'Why did you have to tell me that? I was just beginning to relax.'

'Oh, never relax,' Freddy told him seriously. 'It rots your socks.'

Chapter 27

Next morning they continued training as if nothing had happened. The first lesson was in converting British weights, measures and currency to metric and German units. Luis felt tired; he missed the couple of hours sleep he had lost. Freddy, looking as refreshed as ever, helped Richard Fischer to coach him.

'All right, Luis: you pay for a threepenny bar of Cadbury's milk chocolate with a ten-bob note. How much change d'you get?'

'A bob is a shilling,' Fischer reminded.

'Ten bob . . . Three pence . . .' Luis yawned. 'Sixteen pence equal one shilling, so . . .'

'No, no,' Fischer said. 'You're thinking of ounces. Sixteen ounces make one pound.'

'I thought that was twenty shillings,' Luis said.

'One pound *weight*,' Fischer explained.

'Oh yes. Pound weight.' Luis wrote 16 = 1, and stared at it hard. 'That's right, I remember now. And a hundred of them is called . . . a hundredweight.'

'Actually, a hundred and twelve, Luis,' said Freddy. 'One hundredweight equals a hundred and twelve pounds.'

'That doesn't make any sense.'

'Well, it does if you remember that fourteen pounds equal one stone and two stone make one quarter,' Fischer told him. 'The sequence is sixteen, fourteen, twenty-eight, one hundred and twelve.'

Luis wrote it all down. 'Bloody hell,' he said.

'No, you're thinking of liquid measure,' Freddy said. '*That's* bloody hell. Four gills one pint, two pints one quart, four quarts one gallon, except in America, where their measures are ever so slightly smaller.'

'Why?'

Freddy shrugged. 'So they can imagine they drink more, I suppose.'

'I shall forget about America,' Luis decided.

'Oh no.' Fischer winced: he still had a dull headache and a slight singing in the ears. 'That could lead to serious inaccuracy, for instance in fuel-consumption figures—'

'All right, all right . . . Now I've forgotten what I was buying.'

'Tell you what,' Freddy said. 'Let's make it a yard and a half of pork sausage, at two-pence-farthing a foot.'

'A foot.' Luis looked at his own feet. 'A foot is what?'

'Twelve inches,' said Fischer automatically.

'Or think of it this way,' Freddy suggested. 'Three-and-a-bit feet give you one metre.'

'What would I want with such a great length of pork sausage?' Luis asked.

'Listen, chum, if you can get a yard and a half of genuine pork bangers, you grab 'em,' Freddy advised. 'I'll scoff 'em, if you don't. Britain's gift to western civilisation, the noble banger.'

When they left Fischer and went to the restaurant for a coffee break, Luis felt as tired as if he had worked a full day. The steady buzz of conversation seemed to wrap him in a seamless cloak. He propped his head on his fist and let his eyes watch Freddy writing a letter. That too was soothing: the pen danced smoothly across the page, trailing line after line of neatly manufactured words. Freddy wrote well; he did everything well; he was a brilliant all-rounder. That was what made him such a reassuring person to have on one's side. Luis found it impossible to imagine anything very unpleasant happening to him as long as Freddy was around . . .

'How would you pass a secret note to an accomplice in a crowded restaurant?' Freddy asked.

Luis came awake with a start. 'Make it look like the bill?' he suggested.

'A *long* note,' Freddy said. 'And please don't suggest eating a long meal.'

'Give up.'

Freddy leaned back and linked his hands behind his head. 'Move your chair forward and slouch a bit. Now let your hands hang between your knees, under the tablecloth.'

Luis did as he was told. Freddy's foot nudged one hand. He felt around the foot and found an envelope tucked down the side of the shoe. 'Got it,' he said.

'Good. Now this is the difficult bit. Can you eat it, without moving your hands?'

Luis stiffened, and stared.

'Never mind, we'll practise that next week. For now, just fold it and stuff it up your sleeve, as far as it'll go. Successful?' Freddy stood up. 'Keep it hidden. Shall we go?'

They set off for Dr Hartmann and a refresher lesson in radio maintenance. 'Who taught you that trick?' Luis asked.

'W. C. Fields. Only he did it with the ace of diamonds.'

Dr Hartmann was eager to start work. He had rigged up a gadget which made the electric light flash off and on at brief but irregular intervals; this, he said, would simulate difficult conditions in the field and thus make today's exercise in emergency repairs as realistic as possible.

'Tell you what,' Freddy suggested. 'I'll stand in the corridor and toss hand-grenades through the fanlight, while Luis hides all the screwdrivers. That should be even more realistic.'

Dr Hartmann conceded a short and wintry smile, and closed the curtains. The training exercise began.

After five minutes the telephone rang. Dr Hartmann answered it, his face changing expression jerkily as the light found him and lost him and found him again.

'A change in the schedule,' he announced. 'You are to report to the sub-basement immediately.'

For a moment Freddy remained bent over the dismantled transmitter, his hands full of parts. Carefully he put them down. 'What a bore,' he said. 'Just as I was expanding the frontiers of science.'

Otto Krafft met them when the lift opened at the sub-basement level. 'Follow me,' he said. They walked along a corridor. Luis was puzzled: he couldn't remember having come this way before, yet it looked oddly familiar. The oddness was that he had no idea where it led. They turned a corner, and Otto opened a steel door. He held it while Luis and Freddy went inside. Franz Werth, in freshly laundered white overalls, was sitting in a steel chair behind a steel table. The whole room was steel. Suddenly Luis understood the strange familiarity of the corridor. The only other time he had used it, he had walked in the opposite direction, away from this room. It seemed a very long time ago.

Freddy breathed on a wall and watched his misted breath fade to nothing. 'I suppose it makes for easy dusting,' he remarked.

'This is the Joke Department,' Luis said. 'Nothing is what it seems.'

'Please do not talk,' Otto announced.

He stood by the door and stared at the opposite wall. Franz sat at the table and maintained a plump and gentle smile. A minute passed. Luis stopped walking up and down, and stood with his arms crossed, watching Freddy do little tricks with a coin: tossing it and catching it on the back of his hand. Another minute passed. Luis began to get bored, and he entertained himself with thoughts of Julie Conroy, her satisfying face, her splendid body, her altogether admirable relish for lovemaking . . . He was almost too successful: the prospect made him inhale sharply, and Otto glanced at him. But then the door opened and Colonel Christian came in, followed by Richard Fischer and Wolfgang Adler, who was still using a stick. Otto swung the door shut. The firm, well-made *chunk* echoed briefly off the walls. Christian walked over to the desk, while the other men stood beside Otto.

Luis and Freddy waited and watched. Christian seemed to be considering something; he rippled his fingertips on the table-top, then breathed in deeply through his nose, and cleared his throat. 'This man Ryan,' he said to Franz, 'is a British spy. Shoot him.'

Luis half-suppressed a snort of amusement. Franz brought his right hand from under the table. It held the same black pistol with the same fat silencer. His arm extended. He shut one eye. The gun made a feathery *phphutt* and the impact made a thud like a rubber stamp. Freddy Ryan collapsed to his knees as if seized with a compulsion to pray, and at once fell forward, his arms flopping, his face skidding on the steel floor.

'You know, somebody's going to get hurt if you keep on doing that,' Luis said.

Nobody moved.

'Two things,' Christian said. 'One: this was *not* done at Captain Mullen's command, this was *my* decision entirely. Two: your mission to England will take place as planned. Make sure,' he said to Otto.

Luis felt a stoniness begin to settle on his guts. He moved aside to let Otto kneel and heave Freddy Ryan onto his back. There were odd drops and dribbles of blood on the floor. The centre of the shirt wore a rich red splash, like a winespill, which kept soaking outwards. Using only the tips of his thumb and index finger, Otto lifted the tie so that he could see the bullet-hole. He nodded and dropped the tie. Only then did Luis move to see Freddy Ryan's face. The eyes were halfshut and the mouth was gaping; he looked outwitted. That was unacceptable, it was insulting, it was obscene; Freddy never looked like that, not the real Freddy, never in his life; he was incapable of . . . Luis straightened, and stared at Colonel Christian. 'You have really killed him,' he said. He was shaking with rage.

'Of course we have,' Christian said sharply. 'He was a British spy, he had to be killed.'

'But for God's sake!' The room seemed frozen, while Luis was in turmoil. 'You didn't even let him speak!'

'Why should I let him speak? He was spying on us for the British. We found evidence last night when we searched his apartment. I myself doublechecked the evidence this morning. The only thing left to do was to kill him. Which I decided you ought to see. Now please get back to your training with . . .'

'Dr Hartmann,' Otto said.

'No,' said Luis, 'I don't believe it.' Part of him wanted to cry, and part of him wanted to fight someone; anyone. 'Somebody's made a mistake, this is all wrong.'

'Ryan made a mistake,' Christian said flatly, 'and now everything is all right. Get back to your training.'

'After this?' Luis cried. 'After *this*?'

'After this . . .' Christian snapped his fingers at Ryan's body. '. . . it is twice as important to make sure that you succeed. You must try harder than he did, or one day you will look as foolish as he does now.'

'You sonofabitch,' Luis said weakly.

'I'm glad you realise it,' Christian told him. 'That considerably improves your chances of survival.'

Chapter 28

Midway through the buffet luncheon in Colonel Christian's room, Luis knew why he felt so good. At first, when he had gone back to Dr Hartmann to finish the lesson in emergency radio repairs, he had felt nothing; it was as if the shock had swept him clean of all emotion, left him scoured and purified; nothing could touch him. That feeling lasted while he methodically reassembled the *Abwehr* transmitter, comforted by routine. Then, when he tested the set and it worked perfectly, he was startled by a little surge of pleasure. Otto came in at 12.30 and told him to wash his hands : the Colonel was giving a little luncheon party to discuss Luis's mission.

All the tutors were present; there was wine, and an atmosphere as of a graduation ceremony. Luis was treated with friendly respect. He found himself being gently circulated so that everybody chatted to him but nobody monopolised him. They discussed his progress (which they found encouraging) and his prospects (which they regarded as favourable).

From time to time the embassy waiters attended to his glass or to his plate; once every ten or fifteen minutes Christian drifted across and mentioned some interesting snippet of war news : the triumph of the Luftwaffe in Crete, the amusing likelihood that Vichy France would declare war on Britain if Churchill tried to occupy Syria, the way the German navy was sinking Atlantic convoys faster than Admiral Raeder could count them, which admittedly was not very fast; indeed, said Christian, Raeder's mental arithmetic was probably the biggest obstacle the U-boat captains faced . . . He crowded his shaggy eyebrows together with mock-intensity; people chuckled; Luis found himself smiling. He felt good, and he knew why. Death was intolerable, unthinkable, and so he had turned his back on it; rather than weep, he chose to smile. Christian drifted away again. Wolfgang Adler limped over, said something nice about Luis's aptitude for codes and ciphers, and asked his opinion on current British writers of humorous fiction: Waugh or Wodehouse, for instance, which was better?

It was all very comfortable, very reassuring, slightly flattering, and completely unreal. Luis felt part of his mind clamouring to scream obscenities at them all, to smash chairs and rip down loaded tablecloths and erupt into a whirling, flailing frenzy of attack: anything, as long as it shattered this gentle, well-mannered burble which was pressing him down like a great, soft, padded lid. But after a minute Otto wandered by and mentioned that they shared a common interest in the cinema; what did Luis think of the director Alfred Hitchcock . . .?

Lunch ended at two o'clock, and Franz Werth took Luis away for an hour's Morse-code practice.

Ten minutes into the lesson, a man walked briskly along the corridor outside Franz's room. Luis stopped transmitting. As the footsteps came to the door, his heart panicked and tried to outrace itself. He looked at Franz: but Franz just smiled, questioningly. He turned and stared at the door. The footsteps went on, fading. Luis was hunched like a question-mark; there was sweat on his face and in his armpits.

'You have nothing to be afraid of,' said Franz.

'It sounded like him,' Luis whispered. 'I thought . . . I thought it was Freddy.' His voice was stretched thin.

'Your technique is now quite excellent,' Franz said, 'so I think we can concentrate on improving the speed.'

Luis shoved the Morse key aside. 'What did you do with him?'

'Let us try a fresh—'

'Where is he? I want to see him. Freddy was . . . *Jesus Christ Almighty!*' Luis hammered both fists on the table as grief and fury swept away his flimsy defences. 'He was my friend!

Don't you understand? You killed my friend!'

'Please, please . . .' Franz hurried around the table, chubby face unhappy, neat little hands reaching out to restrain. As soon as the fingers touched him, Luis felt a jolt of revulsion. He struggled to stand but one foot was hooked behind the chair leg. Franz gripped him. He kept making soothing sounds in a curiously fluted voice: 'Sit back now . . . rest . . . please, please . . . do rest . . .' There was something wrong with Luis's lungs, he couldn't get enough air, his face felt waxy, his legs were enormously heavy and remote. Then he was uncontrollably sick.

Franz got the wastepaper bin underneath him in time to catch the worst of it, but Luis and the table and the floor were still a mess. Franz sat him in a corner and gave him the bin to hold, while he telephoned somebody. A nurse came with towels and warm water. A doctor came, with strong fingers and a stethoscope which slid over and around Luis's naked chest as if tracking some sly enemy who kept trying to hide in a new place. A porter came, with mops and buckets. Franz had opened a window; now he stood beside it, looking concerned. Finally, Otto Krafft came and, as soon as Luis could walk, led him away to a very quiet bedroom.

Luis lay down and watched the dim dapples of reflected sunlight tremble on the ceiling. He felt gutted.

'You never cease to surprise me, Mr Cabrillo,' Otto said. 'During your Civil War you must have seen many executions, and some a lot less efficient than today's.'

Luis thought about that for a while. Undeniably, clubs, bayonets and garrottes were less efficient than Franz's big black pistol. *Phphutt-thud.* Instant destruction. Probably quite painless. But that was what made it so wrong; it was unacceptable that Freddy Ryan, a splendid man, a gifted, handsome, funny, clever, lively person, could be wiped out so easily. A man with so much to give to life deserved to be able to fight against death, not just be switched off like an electric light. It was all grotesquely lopsided. 'You didn't even give him a chance to say anything,' he said.

'Come; you know what he would have said. He had to be killed; you must see that.'

Otto waited. Luis searched for an escape. Nothing offered itself, but he could not tell Otto that he was right. 'I don't believe Freddy was a British spy,' he muttered.

'The evidence we have absolutely damns him. The humane, as well as the efficient, thing was to kill him at once. He knew that.'

'I don't suppose you will show me the evidence.'

'No.'

'It was such a lousy, rotten way to die.' Luis heard the catch in his own voice, and swallowed a couple of times. 'It was such a piece of shit,' he said.

'Again, I am surprised at you,' Otto told him calmly. 'Surely it must be obvious that, if you had gone to England with Ryan, he would have betrayed you to the British.'

Luis turned his head away. He did not want even to see Otto talking.

'When the British arrested you,' Otto went on, 'they would not have been as humane as we were, today. They would have locked you in their Tower of London for a week and then hung you by the neck.' He went on over to the door and opened it. 'I'll leave you to rest,' he said, 'and also, perhaps, to think how lucky you are.'

Luis rested and thought for about five minutes. He did not think how lucky he was. He thought how unhappy he was, and how the person he wanted more than anybody in the world was Julie Conroy. So he got up and went out. Nobody stopped him. It was half-past three when he stepped into the street.

Chapter 29

The café baked in a midafternoon fug of sunlight and stale food. Sawdust coated the floor like sediment on a seabed. Behind the bar, a radio with tired valves talked to itself through a continuous crackle and buzz. The only other people in the place were the proprietor, squat and gloomy, and a scrawny youth. They sat on either side of the counter and watched Luis use the telephone.

He got halfway through dialling the number of the Hotel

Bristol and stopped. It was midafternoon. She wouldn't be at the hotel, she would be at work. He hung up.

The proprietor found him a copy of the Madrid phone book.

They watched him search for Metro-Goldwyn-Mayer. It wasn't listed. He looked for MGM. Nothing there either. He shut the book and tried to think of any other possible way the studio might have chosen to be listed. He gave the book back.

There were two possibilities. Either Julie Conroy's office had no telephone, or Julie Conroy had no office. Both seemed highly improbable.

Luis asked for the book again. They watched him thumb through it, looking for an entry for Warner Brothers, or Columbia, or Twentieth Century-Fox, or RKO, or Universal. Nothing. No American film studio had an office in Madrid. He gave the book back.

Something else was missing, something besides the MGM office number. Luis leaned on the counter and hid his face in his hands while he thought. His stomach rumbled restlessly; it was empty but he was not hungry. The scrawny youth tittered. Luis had an idea and asked for the book. The squat proprietor looked at him for several seconds before he handed it across.

Somebody in Madrid had to be in the business of distributing films, Luis told himself, and the chances were that the business was called Film Distribution, or something like that. He failed to find anything under F for Film, under C for Cinema, under K for Kine, under M for Motion Pictures, but he scored with I for International. There was a company called *Inter-Cine Distribución S.A.*, at 65 Avenida de José Antonio.

Luis carried the book over to the phone and began dialling the number. Halfway through he had a better idea. He hung up, and returned the book. 'Thanks,' he said.

The squat proprietor looked from the book to the telephone to Luis. 'Next time, bring your friends and have a real party,' he said. 'If you have any friends,' he added.

'You are very kind,' Luis said, and walked to the door. 'Your establishment deserves its enormous popularity. Forty thousand flies cannot be wrong.' He stepped into the street.

Inter-Cine Distribución was five minutes' walk away. Luis found the manager in his office. He was holding a length of film up to the light and studying it through a magnifying glass. 'I can't release *that*, for God's sake,' he muttered. 'This girl commits all the deadly sins at once, except sloth . . . I don't know what the hell they think they're up to in Hollywood. They don't seem to give a damn what the Generalisimo thinks.'

'What does he think?' Luis asked.

'He's against sex, for a start.'

'What other start is there?'

'I don't know.' The manager rewound the film. 'What can I do for you?'

'I'm trying to trace an American woman called Conroy. She represents MGM in Madrid.'

'I remember the lady. Only you have the wrong name. Hoffman, Mrs Betty Hoffman. She went back to America about a year ago.'

Luis smiled his thanks, turned to go, then paused. 'Did anyone replace her? I mean, who takes care of MGM's business in Europe now?'

'That's easy. We do.'

Back on the street, Luis took refuge in irrelevance: he bought a newspaper and had a shoe-shine. It was a waste of time. There was no escape in the paper, which was concerned with desert battles in North Africa and road accidents in Barcelona. The only fact that mattered was that Julie Conroy was a fake, a liar, a cheat. And he knew also that he had suspected this for a long time. What a filthy, evil day: Freddy killed, put down like a diseased animal, and now Julie soiled with the same stain that touched everyone else he knew. What a bloody, lousy day . . . He thrust money at the shoeshine boy and swung down from the chair, one shoe still dull with polish.

He walked to the hotel on legs that were stiff with sternness, and sucking in a belly that was beginning to ache with emptiness. He felt helplessly angry, like an agnostic who has been robbed by God. He reached the hotel full of hate which was simply rancid love.

The clerk at reception scrapped his smile in the face of such grimness and merely said that Señora Conroy was usually at the hotel swimming pool at that hour of the afternoon.

She was sitting on the springboard, curled up with her head resting between her knees, so that her face was hidden. There

214

was nobody else around except some children splashing in the shallow end.

Luis stood and stared. She seemed to be drying off in the sun. Her legs and arms had a gauzy, golden haziness which showed off their slim and supple strength. The white bathing suit was stretched and creased like skin.

'Hullo, you,' she said. Her face was still hidden; he realised that she could see his reflection in the water. 'Why aren't you at work?'

'Same to you.' He was talking to her reflection.

'I asked first.'

He waited for a moment, and then said: 'Maybe I am at work.'

There was another pause while she flexed her toes. 'Well, that's good,' she said. She stood up, leaned forward and gripped the end of the springboard. In one easy, liquid motion she raised herself into a handstand. 'You look as if you're wearing three suits and four ties,' she said, and dived in.

She swam the length of the pool underwater, turning around one of the children (which made them shriek with delight), and headed back, still skimming the bottom. Luis walked to the diving platform and watched her slide towards him, as flat as cardboard. When she touched the end she looked up at him, and her face was made elastic by the wandering surface. Then she popped up and sucked in a great gasp of breath.

'You lied to me,' Luis said.

'Well, you lied to me too.' She began a leisurely backstroke down the pool.

'Why did you say you were working for MGM?' he demanded.

'Same reason you said you worked for International Red Cross,' she called.

'And so I do.'

'Balls!' She rolled over, surface-dived with a neat flurry of shining buttock, and emerged on her back, going in the opposite direction. 'I phoned,' she shouted. 'They never heard of you.'

She swam two more lengths of the pool and climbed out. 'So who cares?' she said.

'I care. Since you are not working for MGM, what *are* you doing in Madrid?'

'I sometimes wonder.' She towelled her face. 'Swimming, a little tennis, the odd picnic in the woods.'

'And who pays for these pleasures?'

She dried her hands and threw the towel around her shoulders. 'Well, you sure as hell don't,' she said evenly. 'So what goddam business is it of yours?'

Luis rubbed his knuckles across his forehead, scrubbing at the worry-lines as if he could erase the problem. 'All right,' he said. 'My International Red Cross work is camouflage.'

'What for?'

'I can't tell you.'

'That's what I thought.'

He glared at the glittering water. 'Listen, there's a war on, Mrs Conroy. You Americans don't understand war. You think it's simple, like fighting your Indians—'

'Oh, shut up,' she said.

'Certainly. It's a waste of time trying to explain.'

'Then why do it?'

There was an answer, but Luis couldn't find the words. He walked away.

•

It was still too early for dinner but Luis was so hungry that he found it difficult to think straight. He walked to the railway station and had a big bowl of soup in the buffet. Then he walked home. He felt very sleepy as he trudged up the stairs to his apartment. The bed looked enormously inviting. He had just enough self-discipline left to take off his clothes. Something fell out of his sleeve: an envelope, folded in half and bent. Freddy Ryan's letter. Luis straightened it out. The envelope was addressed to Angela. Luis ripped it open. Inside was another envelope, addressed to P.D.Q. at the British Embassy, Madrid. It contained a sheet of paper covered with writing in a language he did not recognise. It looked Oriental or Indian. Christian was right. Freddy Ryan had been spying for the British all along. What's more, he had known that Christian suspected him.

Luis burnt the lot and went to bed.

Chapter 30

He awoke at six. The first thing he remembered was the shooting. That entire sequence was as clear in his mind as a clip of film. He sat on the side of his bed and played it back several times, killing Freddy Ryan over and over again in his head until he was so dead that he could be killed no more. It was like holding a wake, he thought. There was some brandy in the bathroom. He drank a mouthful in Freddy's memory and whacked the cork into the bottle with great decisiveness. He was ready for the day.

There was mist everywhere, a smoky whiteness which clung to the streets and made the city unusually quiet. Luis walked to the vegetable market and ate a big breakfast in one of the cafés that opened early for the porters: eggs, ham, black sausage, fried potatoes, strong coffee. He read a newspaper and strolled to the rendezvous point for that morning: the eastern corner of the Plaza España, near the Cervantes monument. Otto arrived on time, and leaned across to open the passenger door. 'What happened to you yesterday?' he asked. 'We were worried.'

'I needed some fresh air,' Luis said. 'I'm not coming to the embassy today, either.'

'Why not?' Otto squirmed across the front seats to get a better look at Luis. 'Aren't you feeling well?'

'I don't *like* the embassy, that's all. It's a dump.'

'I see.' Otto laughed in a bewildered sort of way. 'A dump . . . Well, I must say I've worked in worse dumps.'

Luis straightened up and looked around. The mist had cleared; there were soft white ribs of cloud, very high in the sky; it was going to be another crisp, bright day.

Otto said: 'The thing is, Colonel Christian wants very much to speak to you. He's waiting now, in fact.'

'Tell him to meet me . . .' Luis squeezed his eyes shut, and thought hard. 'Yes. Place called Purgatorio. It's just a village, about fifteen kilometres outside Madrid, off the road to Corunna.'

'Purgatorio?' Otto looked at Luis as if he were joking.

'That's right.' The name had stuck in his mind from one evening when he and Julie had driven into the countryside. 'One hour from now.' Luis walked away.

He took a taxi to Purgatorio. It turned out to be an appropriately depressing place. A dozen houses, all lopsided and flaking, struggled to make up a single street. The church had collapsed, and from somewhere nearby came the acrid tang of pig manure in large quantities. There was a one-room shop which doubled as a bar, run by a shuffling widow who was heavily moustached; her fingernails were long and yellow and she scratched herself a good deal. Luis found a bench and settled down to wait.

Colonel Christian was ten minutes late. He stood in the doorway and stared at Luis. 'What the hell's all this about?' he asked. He sounded more puzzled than angry.

'Mother wants to meet you.' Luis nodded at the shuffling widow. 'She's heard so much about you, and she's such a keen tennis-player.'

'I have a meeting with the ambassador at noon,' Christian said. He came in. Otto followed him. They sat on the bench, one on either side of Luis.

'She's terribly independent,' Luis said. 'You know what old people are like. I think we'd better order something, don't you?'

Christian sighed, and nodded. Luis asked the old woman to make them three cups of hot chocolate. She grunted and went away, scratching.

'Now,' Luis said. 'I'm ready to go to England.'

Christian leaned back and looked at him. 'What's your hurry?'

'No hurry. It's simply that I have nothing to keep me here so I want to go there.'

An extremely muddy dog trotted in, pissed briefly on a sack of potatoes, looked at the three men, and trotted out again.

'You can't go to England yet,' Christian said.

'I don't see why not.'

'Originally we were going to parachute you in with Ryan. Now we have to find somebody else to go with you. Experi-

218

ence shows that two men have more than double the chance of success.'

'I can go on my own,' Luis said. 'I can go by passenger boat. I told you before: I'm a Spanish neutral, travelling on business. It's the obvious way to get there.'

'Obvious to the British too,' Otto said.

'That's my problem. I've done enough training. I want to get to work.'

'No you don't,' Christian said. 'You want to run away from Freddy Ryan and Mrs Julie Conroy.'

The old woman shuffled in with their cups of hot chocolate, and went away, leaving a faint smell of mildew.

'I'm not drinking that,' Christian said.

'Look: two weeks ago I'd never met either of them,' Luis said, 'and two weeks from now I'll have forgotten them both. Provided I'm in England and working, that is.'

'Is he technically competent?' Christian asked Otto.

'Yes. His Morse transmission is a little slow.'

'I shan't be using Morse,' Luis declared. 'In fact I shan't be using radio.'

'What then?' Christian was getting restless.

'All my reports will come to you via the Spanish diplomatic bag. I have a friend in the London embassy.'

'What?' Christian was more than startled; he was disturbed. 'Who is he? Do we know him?'

'I sincerely hope not. I'm certainly not going to tell you.'

'How did you arrange this?' Otto asked.

'That's my business.'

'No,' Christian decided. 'No, no, no. Too many areas of risk. Your whole mission would be out of our control. Far too hazardous.'

'You would prefer me to paddle ashore one dark night with a large suitcase full of temperamental radio gear and an invisible fountain-pen?'

'That's what you've been trained for,' Otto said.

'You are a fathead,' Luis told him.

'I can't agree to it.' Christian got up and stamped about the shop, exercising the stiffness from his legs. 'You would be totally isolated. Damn it all, we must be able to get instructions to you.'

'The diplomatic bag travels both ways.'

'How do you know it isn't a trap?' Christian found a bunch of bananas on a hook from the ceiling, and snapped one off. 'How do you know British Intelligence haven't planted this obliging chap in the Spanish Embassy? Huh?' He stripped off the skin and took a challenging bite. The old woman came back in and looked at them. 'How do you know *she* isn't with British Intelligence?' Luis said.

Christian munched the rest of his banana. 'Where is the lavatory?' he asked.

'Outside.' Luis made a circular gesture. 'Anywhere. Everywhere.'

As Christian moved to the door, the woman made a harsh cry. 'The banana,' Luis said. Christian gave her the skin and the first banknote he found in his pocket. She glared, flung the skin on the floor, spat on it, crumpled the money and shook her fist. 'You gave her far too much,' Luis said wearily. 'Now she's insulted.'

Christian grunted. 'If you want me, I shall be in the shit,' he said. He went out.

Luis leaned back and inhaled the simple, strong aromas of peasant food: beans, bread, goatsmilk cheese, spiced sausage. 'What is the matter with him?' he asked.

Otto spooned up chocolate-grounds from the bottom of his cup. 'It would be improper for me to comment,' he said.

'All right, you can go to hell too.'

Otto tugged at his ear and looked at the empty doorway. 'If Colonel Christian doesn't get a big success soon, he will be removed. Colonel Christian was depending very heavily on Freddy Ryan. He desperately wants you to succeed, and quickly. But he doesn't want to let you go until he is sure that you are fully trained and able to survive.'

'I don't care,' Luis said. 'I'm going to England, and I'm going my way, not his.'

'I know that. So does he. Just give him a little time to accept it.'

Christian came back, looking more relaxed. 'We'll talk about it in the car,' he said. Luis paid for the hot chocolates and received from the shuffling widow the sullen gift of half-a-dozen bananas, wrapped in newspaper. He thanked her, briefly but elegantly, and she stopped scratching to watch them go.

'Why did she do that?' Christian asked.

'It's a matter of style. Of breeding, perhaps. I can't explain. One is born to it.'

Otto drove them back to Madrid. As they were entering the suburbs Christian said: 'All right: go to England on your own. But when you arrive I want you to link up with one of our agents in London, a man we call "Mercury".'

'For God's sake . . .' Luis looked thoroughly disgusted. 'What's the good of that? I don't *like* working with other people. I *know* what to do. And after that awful mess over Ryan, the less I see of your other agents, the happier I shall be.'

'Ah, but Mercury can help you. There will be all sorts of problems: ration cards, travel restrictions, even finding somewhere to live can be difficult. Mercury knows his way around London.'

'So you say.' Luis's fingers worried a seam in the car upholstery. 'I wonder how many people know their way around Mercury.'

'Mercury is one of our most established agents,' Otto said. 'A translator in the British Ministry of Information. They trust him completely.'

'Which just goes to show that nobody should trust anybody completely,' Luis said. 'All right, tell me where he is and if I need him, I'll find him. But—'

'No, no, no.' Christian's hand cut through the air like an underscore. 'I can't wait while you find your feet, d'you understand? I want results. You and Mercury together should be worth more than double.'

'I'll think about it.'

'You'll damn well do it.' Colonel Christian insisted on the point. Eventually Luis gave in. 'But if the bastard betrays me,' he said, 'I shall expect a written apology.'

Chapter 31

Luis spent the rest of the day getting ready for his journey. He bought clothes, luggage, a soft leather toilet case, a portable typewriter, a travelling clock, a set of hair-brushes, and the smallest camera he could find. He collected a new passport and a new driver's licence, from government departments which treated him with wary respect: the effect of a discreet request from the German Embassy that he be given maximum priority. He changed most of his money into traveller's cheques, and found out from the bank what were the currency-exchange regulations between Spain and Britain. He had a haircut.

After that there was nothing to do but wait.

He killed the evening at a restaurant and a cinema. Although he could stop himself thinking of Julie Conroy, he was aware that she would not therefore leave him. The ghost in his mind was wearying but unarguable. He was glad when the film ended so that he could go home to bed and, for a while, stop having to forget.

*

Next morning Otto and Luis were waiting in the anteroom, while Colonel Christian was on the phone.

They had allocated Luis a codename: *Eldorado*. No special significance, Otto said; it was the next on the list, that's all. In communications between them, Madrid would be code-named *Tomcat*.

They had covered the procedure for contacting Mercury: Luis had memorised his address, telephone number, and several codewords; these varied according to the day of the week. The information was now stored in his head. Otto had de-scribed Mercury: a grave, middleaged, bookish man, no sense of humour, set in his ways, extremely cautious; he always thought three times before he did anything, even before he put salt on his egg. Luis nodded, and stored that away too.

There was nothing else to be said about Mercury.

When Colonel Christian opened his door and waved them in, he was chuckling with jubilation. 'By God, you were absolutely right, Cabrillo,' he said, punching him amiably on the shoulder. 'We've just invaded Russia. It's curtain-up on the last act. Berlin say they expect to finish Russia in six weeks.'

'Good Lord. That's faster than France,' Otto said.

'It had to come,' Luis remarked.

'Let's hope it's an omen for your mission.' Christian was

222

so pleased that he could not keep still. 'Naturally, it's put your stock up several points.'

'I hope that means I shall get paid more,' Luis said.

'It means that Britain is isolated. Just concentrate on that, help us to bring the British to their knees, and your reward will follow.'

Luis waited for a moment, and watched Christian pace the carpet. 'I still hope that means I shall get paid more,' he said.

'Don't worry,' Christian chuckled.

'I'm not worrying. I just want to be damned sure that what you mean by reward is the same as what I mean by reward.'

'Money, for God's sake! Money, money.' Christian dropped into a chair with such a crash that it jolted backwards, its castors furrowing the carpet. 'Money! Does that satisfy you? What arrangements have we made to get all these cartloads of cash to Mr Cabrillo?' he asked Otto.

'He has two new bank accounts, one in Zurich and one in Lisbon. We set them up yesterday.'

'And you've made a will?' Christian asked. Luis nodded. 'Good, good. Well, you might as well push off, mightn't you? Have a good trip, and give my best wishes to Mercury. And to your invaluable friend in the Spanish Embassy, of course. If I knew his name I'd write him a nice letter.'

'If he thought I might tell you his name,' Luis said, 'he'd never speak to me again.'

They shook hands, and Luis went out. Otto escorted him down to the street and walked a short way with him. 'It's a pity about this Russian thing, in a way,' Otto said. 'Now the Colonel will expect even more from you.'

'What's wrong with that?' Luis asked.

Otto's eyes flickered. 'Well, supposing you can't satisfy him. Supposing you hit a bad patch. He may feel cheated and become very angry.'

'He'll just have to be patient.'

'He wasn't patient with Ryan.'

'That was completely different. Besides, I shall be in England.'

Otto merely looked at him, as expressionless as a man could be. 'Yes, of course,' he said. They strolled to the corner. 'You've worked very hard, Luis. You certainly deserve to succeed.' It was the first time Otto had called him Luis. 'I hope your luck is good. I very much hope we meet again.'

'Well, thank you.'

They shook hands, and for a moment Luis sensed that Otto had something else to say. But he merely twitched his mouth in a wry smile, and said goodbye.

Luis got home to find a message from the caretaker asking him to contact Mrs Conroy. He went out and used a telephone in a café. As he dialled the Hotel Bristol he found himself wondering about Otto, not Julie. Otto's remarks had been odd. Perhaps Christian had told Otto to say what he did in order to stimulate him to work harder, take bigger risks. If so it was a crude device. But then sometimes Christian was remarkably crude—

Julie answered.

'I had a message to call you,' he said.

'Yes. Thanks. Something's kind of . . . weird.' She sounded tense. 'Can we meet? Not here. Outdoors, somewhere.'

Luis named a place, a small park behind a church. She was waiting at the gate when he got there.

'Angela came to see me last night,' she said, and most of his secret pleasure at seeing Julie was immediately wiped out. 'She's very worried about Freddy. Do you know where he is?'

'No, I don't know where he is.' That was true. Not honest, but true.

'He was supposed to meet her but he didn't turn up. No message, no nothing.'

Luis took her arm and they walked along the flagstoned path. 'Maybe he had to make a sudden trip.'

'I doubt it. We went around to his apartment and got the building manager to open it up. Somebody had packed all his bags! They were standing in the middle of the room, lined up like dominoes.'

'What d'you mean, "somebody"?' Luis kicked a piece of pebble ahead in order to give himself something to look at. 'Why couldn't Freddy have packed his own bags? Maybe he decided to move.'

'Without telling the building manager? His rent's paid three months in advance.'

'It's curious, I agree.'

'Angela thinks he's dead.'

Luis missed the pebble, and had to stop and kick it again.

'That probably says more about Angela than about Freddy,' he said.

'I don't think so. We opened a couple of the suitcases. Everything had been packed, absolutely *everything*: books, letters, dirty laundry, medicines, and even some things that belonged to Angela. Souvenirs and photographs and stuff. Why the hell would Freddy pack all that?'

Luis said nothing. They reached the end of the path, and stopped. A high brick wall made a long, easy curve which trapped the sun and harboured magnolias and flowering vines. He wondered whether the German Embassy or the British Embassy had done Freddy's packing. There was nothing to be said, but he had to say something. 'Did Angela take her things?' he asked.

'No, she didn't want to. She's very upset.'

'There's no actual evidence—'

'You're damn right there's no evidence. I went back to the apartment this morning. The bags are gone. Somebody came in the night and took them.'

They discussed it for another ten minutes, until Luis began to feel slightly sick with the guilt of dishonesty, and he changed the subject abruptly. 'I have to go to England,' he said. 'A business trip, probably for quite a long time.'

'When d'you leave?'

'This afternoon.'

That shocked her a little; more than a little, as the realisation sank in. 'Madrid's getting kind of empty,' she said.

'Yes. I suppose it's all come to an end sooner than we thought.'

'Will you come back?'

'There's no way of knowing. Would you still be here if I did?'

She gave a small, lopsided grin. 'You're right. One dumb question deserves another.'

Three very young children came racing up the path, shouting out long, happy screams just for the pleasure of doing it. They reached the end, found nothing to do there, and raced away, still shouting.

'How can they shout and run at the same time?' Luis asked.

'They can't. It's impossible. But they don't know that yet, so they go right out and do it.'

225

'We could always write,' he said. 'If we thought we wanted to.'

'How would we know if we wanted to?'

'We could write and ask.'

'Oh, Luis . . .' She gave a gentle, defeated sigh. 'You may be a crook but at least you're a friendly crook. Okay: you know my address. How do I reach you?'

'Care of my Lisbon bank. Banco Espirito Santo.' He wrote the address on a card and gave it to her. 'I have an arrangement. The bank forwards everything, airmail.'

They shook hands, their grip tightening. 'I miss Freddy,' she said. 'I only met him once but I miss him a lot. Don't get killed in England, Luis. Promise?'

'I promise.' He very much wanted to kiss her but he was afraid that it would be unfair. She released his hand and he walked away, quickly, while he still had control of himself.

Two hours later he was in the smoky, clamorous bustle of the *Estación del Norte*, watching a porter stack his luggage in a first-class compartment of the Lisbon train. He felt great excitement and great sadness at the same time, and he wished that Julie Conroy were there to share his emotions. In fact she was sitting by the grimy window of the station buffet, nursing a fizzy drink and studying him in his new clothes, in his last few minutes in Madrid. Something stopped her going over to him. Perhaps she had seen too many movies. Smoke, steam, locomotive noises. Whistle blows, flag waves, door slams. Final embrace. Train moves, the big bad world separates yet another pair of doomed lovers, crescendo the soundtrack. Pass the popcorn.

A whistle blew, a flag waved. Luis glanced around, stepped up into the train and slammed the door. He knew that she had done the correct and sensible thing by staying away. She was an intelligent, sensible woman; it was part of her great attraction. The train moved.

Julie Conroy watched it go. It left a great gap in the station and a great gap in her heart. *Bum script*, she told herself. *Corny corny corny.*

＊

'All right, what are we going to do if Eldorado lets us down?' Christian asked.

226

Wolfgang, Franz, Otto and Richard considered the question seriously and waited for each other to answer.

'You must agree he has a record as a loser,' Christian said. He flicked through Luis Cabrillo's file. 'If he goes on losing, what then? Huh? Do I just go to my good friend Mullen with a light laugh and say awfully sorry sir, we did our best sir, and please sir can I have another great big sackful of money?'

Nobody had an answer to that.

'I can tell you now, there are no more great big sackfuls of money,' Christian said. 'Until we get some good, solid return, the bank is shut.'

'He did do rather well over this Russian business,' Franz said cautiously.

'All picked up through neutrals.'

'I honestly can't see Eldorado sending us anything really solid for at least three months,' Richard Fischer said. 'It'll take him a month just to get settled and as long again—'

'I can't wait three months,' Christian said. He looked for other answers. Wolfgang cleared his throat. Christian stared at him.

'If Eldorado doesn't find his feet,' Wolfgang said, 'you could always stand him on his head and see what falls out of his pockets.'

Christian rotated his little finger inside his ear and examined the tip. 'Explain,' he said.

'Eldorado fails. You signal Mercury. Mercury turns Eldorado over to British Intelligence. Anonymously. They find his transmitter and codebook. Immediately British Intelligence start sending us false intelligence, posing as Eldorado.'

There was a pause while they reviewed the idea.

'Misinformation is better than no information,' Richard Fischer remarked.

'Sometimes you can reverse it,' Franz said, 'and see what the enemy is trying to hide.'

'Of course Eldorado would deny everything,' Otto pointed out.

'They'd hang him all the faster,' Wolfgang said. Christian softly drummed his fingers on the desk and thought.

The meeting ended. As he walked along the corridor, adjusting his pace to Wolfgang's limp, Otto said: 'The way I see it, young Cabrillo either acquires for us a great number of valuable secrets by taking insane risks at enormous speed, and therefore inevitably gets himself caught, or we betray him. Is that the way you see it?'

'A fair summary,' Wolfgang said.

'There's not a lot of hope for him, then.'

'My dear Otto,' Wolfgang said, 'there's never any hope for idiots like Cabrillo from the moment they step eagerly out of the womb and trip over the umbilical cord. That doesn't mean we should feel sorry for them. Cabrillo's a very necessary part of the system. Without losers like him, there couldn't be winners like us.'

'You're a great comfort, Wolfgang,' Otto said.

'What are friends for,' asked Wolfgang, 'if not to fill you up with lies?'

Part Three

Part Three

Chapter 32

The telegram arrived at 11 a.m. while Julie Conroy was in the hotel pool. She swam a lot these days. For one thing it helped to give her an appetite, and for another thing it helped her to sleep. A further advantage was that it made it difficult for people to talk to her.

Difficult but not impossible. The youth who carried messages for the hotel receptionist kept walking around the pool and calling her name until the sound penetrated the bubbling rush of water. She let her backstroke fade to nothing and looked at him. He held up the silver tray.

She swam across, rested her elbows on the side, and took the envelope. It held a telegram. The paper got wet and sticky as she unfolded it, so she pasted it on the smooth tiles like a tiny poster. At once the ink began running, and this gave the words a crude irony, like a film-director straining for effect. FLYING MADRID TOMORROW FOR BARBER BEANO HANG ONTO YOUR HAT LOVE HARRY.

She sucked in a deep breath and looked up. The youth had chestnut-brown eyes and a neck like a stick of celery. He was very happy to have delivered the telegram. Now he polished the tray with the sleeve of his hotel-uniform jacket.

'Thanks for nothing, buster,' she said.

'*Por nada, señora.*'

'I said it first.'

She left the thing pasted onto the tiles and swam slowly away. The wrong man had sent the wrong telegram. For months she had been trying to trace Harry so that she could straighten out their future, begin the divorce, start to free herself. Now he was on his way back to her and she didn't want to see him. He wouldn't want to face reality. Harry wasn't much good at being serious. He always evaded bad news, unless it was the other kind of news, newspaper-news. Harry would light up and sparkle at the first hint of an international disaster but he wouldn't face a serious talk with his wife.

Julie floated in the middle of the pool, arms and legs outstretched in a star-shape. She wondered where he had been when he sent the telegram. Also when. Yesterday, perhaps? Did 'tomorrow' mean today? A couple of strokes took her to the side, but the ink had bled until all its meaning was lost in a soft, fading blur. The telegram tore when she tried to peel it off. *Barber Beano*, she thought; *what the hell was that supposed to mean? Trust a newspaperman to confuse you. They can do almost anything with words except make them sit up and talk.*

She was in her room, wondering whether lunch was worth the effort of going somewhere, when the phone rang.

'Langham at the American Embassy, Mrs Conroy.' A New Yorker's voice, calm, confident, vastly reassuring. 'My apologies for this late notice, but the Ambassador hopes very much that you'll be able to attend our reception this afternoon. It's in honour of Senator Barber. Four o'clock.'

'Senator Barber? What's that dinosaur doing here?'

'A fact-finding tour. He's chairman of a Senate Committee which—'

'Forget it. That guy makes my skin crawl.'

'The senator has a very individual political style, to be sure, Mrs Conroy.' The warmth and strength of Langham's voice impressed her. It was as firm and friendly as the clasp of old leather.

Barber Beano, she thought. 'I guess Harry's going to be there,' she said.

'You are right, Mrs Conroy.'

'Has he arrived?'

'Not yet. He's expected soon. Is there any message, in case I see him first?'

'Yes, tell him . . . No, never mind, I'll tell him myself.'

She had something very specific to tell Harry: her money hadn't arrived. Normally, the New York agency for which he worked sent her a cheque every month. This month, no cheque. That angered her. Harry was going to get hell over that.

An angry monologue went on in her head all the way to the embassy. All Americans weren't jokers, so how come she'd picked this comedian? Why couldn't she have married a guy like Langham, a man you could at least talk to without a lot of wisecracks? Langham's voice had reminded her of all that was good and strong about America; none of this fluty, European gabbling; he said what he meant and what he said was sturdy and yet sympathetic too. All of a sudden she felt a great yearning, not so much for Americans as for American-ism: things like real icecream and big cars, and singing com-mercials on radio, and freight trains as long as you could see, and kids so freckled they looked as if they'd been stencilled. At that moment Julie wanted to be back in America so utterly that she had to pause and take a deep breath before she could go up the embassy steps.

A U.S. Marine sergeant was checking the arrivals. He directed her across the lobby to a small, fidgety man who seemed to be all potbelly and no chin.

'I'm Mrs Conroy,' she told him.

He smiled in a way that left the corners of his mouth wet. 'Welcome,' he said. 'I'm George Langham.' She gave him a sharp stare. 'Something's wrong?' he asked.

'No. It's just . . .' She felt more than cheated: betrayed. 'You looked different over the phone,' she said.

'Yes? I was probably wearing my glasses.' He put them on. Now he looked even more like a frog. Her prince had turned into a frog. Fairy tales really do come true.

They went into the reception. Neither Senator Barber nor Harry had arrived yet, the frog said, but there was a large and hardworking bar. The frog got her a martini and in-troduced her to a tall, goodlooking Frenchman, who turned out to be a representative of the Vichy Government, doing some kind of liaison work with the Spanish Ministry of War. 'I attend every reception at the American embassy,' he told her. 'It is the sole place where one is given decent gin now-adays.'

'I thought all Frenchmen drank wine.'

He let his mouth droop. 'Since 1940, for me, wine is not enough.'

'Were you in the fighting?'

'Yes and no. I commanded a regiment, but the Germans were too quick for us. They advanced at great speed and went be-tween my regiment and the next formation. We pursued them but we could never catch them. Meanwhile the *Luftwaffe* damaged us every day. When the Armistice came my regiment had travelled nearly eight hundred kilometres without firing a single shot, except at enemy airplanes.' He sniffed his drink and widened his eyes in appreciation. 'One cannot fight an enemy one cannot catch. The German army is extremely fast.'

It was a neat summary. Julie had the feeling he had delivered it many times before. They stood and looked at the crowd for a while. 'How do you get along with the Germans now?' she asked.

'Reasonably well.'

'No goosestepping jackboots?'

'They leave us alone in Vichy. Up in the north of France it is different because England is so close, but once that situation comes to an end I think most of the German army will go home. Perhaps next year.'

Julie began to feel annoyed. This Frenchman was so enormously detached and objective, it was like talking to an insurance assessor. 'What makes you so sure the British will give in?' she asked.

'Because they are very good historians and they know from past experience that they must have a powerful ally if they are to defeat Germany. There is only one possibility: Russia. But Germany will beat Russia. Then Hitler will turn back and confront Britain with the first truly united Europe since Charlemagne.'

'Churchill said they'll never surrender.'

'Ah! That fatal word, "never". The first rule of politics is: "Never say never".'

Julie was fed up with this professional survivor, but she was reluctant to leave him unmarked. 'Listen, what about your Napoleon?' she demanded. 'He ended up on his ass in the snow. So much for history.'

'Napoleon had no tanks, no trucks, no trains, no air force, no radio.' The Frenchman counted them off on his fingers and ended with his thumb raised. 'Yet he reached Moscow. *This* German army overran France when the French army was by far the strongest in Europe. Much stronger than the Russian army is now. Do you see that man with the red hair?'

'You mean the guy talking to the crewcut in tweeds?'

'Yes. Swiss military attaché. The other man is with your

embassy. According to that Swiss, it will take Germany a maximum of eight weeks, and a minimum of four, to bring Russia to her knees. The American estimates nine weeks and five.'

'What do you think?'

'Six weeks maximum.'

'Shit,' Julie said gloomily.

'Hitler will reap the wheat which Stalin has sowed,' the Frenchman said smoothly. 'England will accept the inevitable, and life will return to normal once more. May I get you another drink?'

'You can go to hell.'

She walked away and left him unperturbed, sniffing his gin, and she got another drink by herself. The frog came over, looking depressed.

'Barber's plane's got engine trouble. He's still in the Azores.'

'And Harry?'

He shrugged. 'No news, I'm afraid.'

'Excuse me,' Julie said. 'I think I see a friend.'

She took her drink to the ladies' room and slumped in a chair. After a while she eased her shoes off. The wallpaper carried a repeating pattern of fat red roses. Everywhere she looked, roses. They climbed until they hit the ceiling and they dived until they hit the floor. Then they rebounded and climbed for the ceiling again. It was like being divebombed by florists. 'Roses stink,' she said.

A toilet flushed, a cubicle opened, and a dumpy, middle-aged woman came out, smoothing her dress. 'You talking about the wallpaper?' she said. 'My husband chose it.' She began washing her hands.

'Then he stinks too.'

'That's what I keep telling him. "Harry, you stink", I tell him. He never listens. Too busy choosing wallpaper, I guess.'

'My husband's name is Harry, too.'

'Yeah? Does he stink?'

'Oh, he's out in front. Harry stank for America in the Olympics.'

The other woman took a Scotch-and-water from a shelf. 'Sounds like he trains real hard,' she said.

'He would've won,' Julie said, 'only it was held in Berlin, and the krauts can out-stink the whole damn world when they try.'

'Yeah. I feel sorry for those poor bastards in Russia. We were in Warsaw when it got bombed, and friends of ours were in Rotterdam.'

'I saw what they did to Rotterdam. And to London.' They traded war stories for a couple of minutes. 'You know, everybody out there seems to think Hitler's going to smash Russia without even breaking sweat,' Julie said. 'The only thing they're arguing about is whether he'll be in Moscow by Tuesday or Friday.'

'Right. I say to Harry: "When is someone going to stand up to the sonofabitch?", and Harry just smiles like daddy-knows-best and feeds me some dumb line about giving Hitler enough rope so he'll hang himself.'

'That's crap,' Julie said. 'If we give him any more rope he'll hang everyone he doesn't like the look of.'

'You should tell Harry that.'

'Okay, I will,' Julie announced. 'Lead me to him.' She put on her shoes.

'Okay.'

By now the reception was more crowded and much louder. They found her husband in the middle, a blue-suited, bun-faced man with hornrim glasses and a permanent smile. He was talking with two people: a man in U.S. naval uniform, and a middle-aged woman in a light oatmeal-tweed suit.

'Can it, Harry,' his wife interrupted. 'You're boring the pants off these folk and besides, my friend here has a question.'

He tightened his smile. 'If it's about Senator Barber, I'm afraid he's been unavoidably delayed.'

'The hell with Senator Barber and his delays,' Julie said, 'I want to know what's holding up the rest of the U.S.A. When is America going to wake up and start fighting?'

'Well, the State Department keeps the entire European situation under constant review,' he replied with every appearance of sincerity, 'and, given any significant shift of circumstances, the President will be advised accordingly *without the slightest delay.*'

'That's a bullshit answer,' Julie snapped.

'It's not even that,' the middle-aged woman said. 'It's no answer at all.'

'With respect—' Harry began.

236

'Oh, forget respect,' she said. 'I write for *Life* magazine,' she told Julie, 'and the people who read my stuff don't want to fight another war. They're just out of the Depression, they want to make some money, buy a new car, pay for their kids' teeth to be fixed. So *there's* your answer.'

'Well . . . it's just not good enough,' Julie said.

'Sweety, we give the Hitler war as much play as the traffic will bear,' said the woman from *Life*. 'You can't talk to folk who don't want to listen.'

Julie stabbed the air with her finger. 'But how in God's name—'

'I think we should keep this thing in some kind of overall military perspective,' the naval officer broke in. 'First off, our strategic response is very limited. We can hardly send a battleship to bombard Berlin.' Harry chuckled warmly. Julie glared. 'Secondly,' the officer said, 'this latest development vis-à-vis Russia is not necessarily entirely to our disadvantage. The Soviets have been meddling all over the world lately.'

'So you think the best solution is to let Hitler wipe them out?' Julie asked. The officer shrugged. 'You callous bastard,' she said.

Nobody in the group spoke for a few seconds. They stood in stiff discomfort, while the abortive reception chattered and swigged all around them. Harry broke the silence with his easy, practised chuckle. 'These are mighty complex issues, folks,' he said. 'I don't think we should blame ourselves for not reaching total accord in the space of a few minutes. Furthermore, I'm sure that better men than us have got a pretty damn good grip on affairs. So . . . can I freshen up anyone's drink?'

Julie walked away and found a marble pillar at the end of the bar to lean against. She felt angry and defeated. After a while the frog saw her and hurried over. 'I was afraid you'd gone, Mrs Conroy. We've just had a message from your husband. Unfortunately he's not coming to Madrid. When his office heard about Senator Barber's delay they sent him to Vienna instead.'

'Whoopee,' she said bleakly.

'Is there any kind of message you'd like me to send?'

'No. Yes. You could ask the barman to make me a double martini.'

She was working her way through the drink when the woman from *Life* came over. 'I just discovered you're Harry Conroy's wife,' she said.

Julie nodded. 'It's an honorary position.'

'I met him on a plane, about a month ago . . . Listen, I didn't mean to be so hardnosed with you just now, but you've got to remember we don't create the goddam news, we just cover it.'

'Sure, sure. It just makes me burn to think that Britain . . . Oh, I don't know.'

The woman from *Life* took a handful of peanuts and began eating them one at a time. 'Maybe it's none of my business, honey, but you seem to be fighting everybody all on your own, too.'

Julie gave that a lot of thought. She took a drink and looked over the rim. The other woman was on the wrong side of forty. Her face looked as if it had seen a lot of human wreckage. And maybe some salvage too.

'Okay, since it's so obvious,' Julie said. 'This has been an especially bad day, and maybe I've had too much sauce, and Christ knows I didn't actually want to meet my Harry, but still . . .' Her hand suddenly trembled; she put the glass down.

'Toss me a clean napkin,' the woman called to a barman, raising her open hand. She caught it, shook it open, gave it to Julie. 'Ladies' handkerchiefs are no dumb use to anyone,' she said. Julie used both hands to press the crisp white linen against her face. She pressed hard. It was as if all her self-control were disintegrating. She kept pressing, and braced her body against the pillar. Eventually the threat passed. She folded the napkin and sniffed hard. 'Jesus,' she whispered. 'Where the hell did that come from?'

'Out of the past, where they all come from.' The woman ate another peanut, slowly. 'How long since you saw Harry?'

'Six months.' Julie picked up her glass, not to drink but to have something to hold. 'Madrid was where I finally gave up on him, if you want the whole godawful story.'

'I'll listen if you'll talk.'

'Well . . . First of all, when we got married, I used to live somewhere central, Paris, Berlin, London, and wait for Harry to come home. Trouble was he didn't come home very often.

238

I'd see him once, maybe twice, in a month, then the phone would ring and . . . zip.'

'He's a good newspaperman. Great reputation.'

'Oh, sure. Meanwhile I was living with the reputation and not the guy. So one day I got mad and decided we were going to live together if it meant hotels and suitcases for the rest of time. I called New York, they told me he was in Istanbul. Right, I flew to Istanbul. He'd gone to Budapest. I went to Budapest, he'd gone to Rome. I chased Harry to Rome, to Zurich, to Paris.'

'You could've cabled him to wait for you somewhere.'

'No, I had to catch him all by myself. I had to find him and grab him and say, "Okay, buster, from now on where you go, I go". It was crazy. Like a crusade.'

'What happened in Paris?'

'He wasn't there. Nobody knew where he was. I called New York. They'd sent him to Madrid. The airline schedules were all fouled up by the war. It took me three days to get to Madrid. As I flew in, so Harry flew out.'

'To Paris?'

'Helsinki. I sat down and cried. End of story, close quotes. You asked for it, you got it. Just another crumpled page torn from life's diary.'

'Why don't you go back to the States?'

Julie bundled up the napkin and lobbed it over the bar. 'My family didn't approve of Harry. They said it would end in disaster.'

'Still, you might *have* to go back, sooner or later.'

'I can survive here. The agency sends me money.' Sometimes.

'I didn't mean that. I meant suppose Hitler beats Russia, and Britain has to quit? Life in Europe could become very rough for someone with your opinions, even in Spain. Maybe *especially* in Spain.'

Julie hunched her shoulders and looked away. The crowd was thinning; people were glancing at watches, shaking hands, waving goodbye. There was an atmosphere of anticlimax : the Barber Beano had been a non-starter. 'Maybe I should go to Russia and fight while there's still time,' she said.

'From what I hear, Moscow's in such a state of panic they wouldn't know what to do if you turned up leading an

239

armoured brigade.' The last peanut had got eaten. She dusted her hands.

'Okay,' Julie said briskly, 'then I'll go to *England* and fight.'

'Have a good meal before you leave. They're down to a ration of two ounces of butter, two ounces of cheese, 25-cents'-worth of meat. That's per week. Just enough to make a light lunch for a Tennessee farmhand.'

'I don't care. I'm sick of Madrid and I'm sick of waiting. Waiting for Harry, waiting for America, waiting for something worth waiting for.'

'Sweety,' said the woman from *Life*, 'with what you've got, it's a *crime* to wait. Don't waste it on a war, for God's sake. There's always going to be wars. Go fall in love. It's more laughs than getting bombed.'

'I just did,' Julie said.

'And?'

'He went to England.'

'What for?'

'Business.' Julie finished her drink. It tasted oily and unexciting. 'That's what he said, anyway. Business.'

'And what do you think?' They began to walk across the room.

'I think I ought to forget him.'

They reached the door before the other woman spoke. 'You know, sometimes it's a great relief to be old and leathery and past all that jazz.' She smiled: a brief gift of great sympathy. 'You're in a spot, aren't you? I wish you all the luck. I think you may need it.'

'Me and the British both,' Julie said. 'Who knows? If we pool our luck, maybe we'll both win.'

Chapter 33

George Clark sat with his back to the window, looking like the man who inspired the bowler hat. His whole build, stocky and strong, led up to a head which was as round as a football and so powerfully muscled that his face, at rest, looked grim.

That build, clothed in a very dark suit and a very white shirt with a club tie of almost stifling restraint, demanded to be completed by a bowler hat.

Julie sat on a straightbacked chair and tried not to watch him reading her application form. She looked around the room: an official photograph of King George and Queen Elizabeth; two small potted shrubs (one not doing very well); a tiny model locomotive in a glass case; and a much-engraved silver cup, in need of polishing. Also, hanging behind the door, a bowler hat. He cleared his throat, and she leaned forward, eager to help. Her mouth still tasted of spearmint gum. She hoped she was now quite sober but she wasn't absolutely sure of it.

Clark cleared his throat again. 'Mrs Conroy,' he said, 'may I ask: why do you want to go to the United Kingdom?'

'To help you guys win the war.' The words came out promptly and confidently and they sounded exactly right.

'I see.' He scratched his left eyebrow while he looked again at her application form. 'Yes. Mrs Conroy . . . May I ask: how?'

Julie spread her hands. 'Any way you like,' she said. 'Just lead me to the action.'

'I see. You do realise, of course, that there's actually not an awful lot of action *in* the United Kingdom at the moment.' He opened his eyes very wide.

'Sure. I mean, I wasn't counting on becoming a Commando, exactly.'

'May I ask, Mrs Conroy: what *were* you counting on becoming?'

'Like I said, whatever you need. I just want to—'

'Yes, indeed: to help. Please understand that your willingness and sincerity are not in doubt. Could you, for instance, be a nurse?'

'Sure. If necessary.' Julie forced a smile. She didn't want to be a nurse.

'And have you any nursing qualifications?'

'No, but . . .' She cast around for a good, strong counterargument and found nothing. 'I can learn,' she said.

'As it happens we have no shortage of nursing volunteers,' Clark said. 'What we need rather urgently is more trained people.'

241

'I can drive a car,' Julie said doggedly. 'In fact I drive damn well.'

'Splendid.' Clark rewarded her with a smile but immediately his face lapsed into muscular gloom. 'The fact remains that you do it on what we insular British persist in calling the wrong side of the road, so even that skill would require some retraining . . . How are your typing and shorthand?'

Julie shook her head. Clark grunted softly and pursed his lips. In the mild, late-afternoon silence there came the faint sound of distant, rhythmic chanting. It reminded Julie of going to college football games. Clark appeared not to hear anything. He was thinking.

'Look, Mr Clark,' she said. 'You British need all the friends you can get. Okay, here's one friend. I'm young, healthy, not too stupid, and I hate the Germans. Now surely to God, if there's something I can do to make life difficult for Nazis, that's got to be good for your side.'

'Oh, undoubtedly,' Clark agreed. 'I wonder . . . Were you thinking perhaps of taking them on at tennis?'

Julie sat back and stared. Outside, the chanting was growing more distinct and more jubilant. 'You heard about that game, huh?' she said.

'Word soon gets around. I must say it bucked us up no end, Mrs Conroy.'

'I'm glad.'

'We'd been losing rather a lot of convoys, and it was a relief to have something to smile at. However trifling.'

'If I had my way the U.S. Navy would be out there now, blasting those U-boats out of the Atlantic.'

Clark nodded his appreciation. Now the noise had reached the street outside; they could hear the hurrying beat of feet like a muffled drumroll beneath the eager chant. He got up and closed the windows. 'Do you understand Spanish?' he asked.

'Not much. Not enough to understand that stuff. What's going on out there?'

'I can't really tell.' Clark's room was on the second floor. 'We often get this sort of thing; there are embassies all around here. One doesn't mind the noise, but they do drop such a lot of litter in the street.' He came back to his desk. 'I'll be frank, Mrs Conroy. There is nothing you could do to

242

assist the British war effort. On the contrary, His Majesty's Government would find itself with another mouth to feed at a time when food is already extremely scarce and likely to become more so. Therefore . . .' Clark paused and glanced sideways as the noise in the street gained a new level. 'I regret I cannot recommend your application for approval.'

Julie had seen it coming and was ready to counter-attack. 'Listen, this is *my* war too, you know! If Britain goes under, how the hell is the United States ever going to stop Hitler? You think I want that kind of future? You just get me to London, Mr Clark. I'll soon find some way to help beat those bastards, if it's only by giving blood to the Red Cross three times a week.'

'As I've already explained—'

'Okay, I lied, I'm a trained nurse and fighter pilot and I can type three thousand words a minute.' Julie was leaning forward, gazing hard at George Clark's sombre face when a brick shattered the window and, still spinning end-over-end, rushed at her head. Her hands were gripping the arms of the chair and she thrust herself sideways, twisting her neck and contorting her face. The last thing she saw was Clark's solid torso surrounded by glittering fragments; the brick battered her shoulder and the chair crashed over backwards in a wild somersault of pain and shock and confusion. She lay for a long moment, stunned, and heard clearly the tinkle of glass on polished floorboards, followed by a raucous, exultant roar gushing through the hole. Then she dimly saw the extraordinary sight of George Clark vaulting over his desk, landing nimbly beside her, and kicking the chair away. She felt herself being dragged rapidly across the room, her shoes coming off, sunlight suddenly giving way to deep shadow, a hard, cool corner propping her up. The racket in the street swelled and faded and swelled again like waves on a beach. Clark was gone, then he was back. Cushions slid behind her. For a while she felt sick and she closed her eyes. Elsewhere, more windows were being broken. When her eyes opened, Clark was sitting cross-legged in front of her. One ear was brilliantly red. It was all very strange.

'As soon as you can,' he said, 'I think you should try to raise that arm.'

Julie thought about that. Clark, she decided, seemed to

243

know best. Another brick smashed through their window and they saw it whizz across the room, a long way off. Glass fragments tumbled harmlessly over the desk. She sat up and slowly raised her arm. Her shoulder felt like a sack of cement.

'Good,' he said. 'That means your collarbone isn't broken.'

'How did you jump over that desk?' she asked weakly.

'I used to play scrum-half for Blackheath.'

She looked at him. He was serious. 'I don't know what that means,' she said.

'It means you learn to move bloody fast unless you want your head kicked in.'

Julie gave up on that. 'Who threw that goddam rock at me?'

'Probably the Falange. The Spanish government wouldn't let such a demonstration happen unless they approved, so it must be the Falange. Do you hear those slogans?' They listened to the pounding chant of the mob. 'They're expressing support for Germany's invasion of Russia.'

'By chucking rocks?'

'Well, this *is* the British embassy.'

Julie began a gesture of disgust which sent a streak of pain flaring through her shoulder. 'Who the hell do those bums think they are?' she demanded. 'I'm a neutral! And Spain's neutral! Tell 'em to go chuck their rocks at the Russians!'

'No doubt some of them will,' Clark said. 'The Falange is already recruiting volunteers to fight on the Russian front. As to your neutral status . . .' He found a piece of glass in a fold of his sleeve and delicately removed it. 'I wonder if anyone is really neutral any more.'

'What are you talking about?'

'Well, take the Irish Republic. They say they're neutral, but that didn't do Dublin any good last month when the Germans bombed it by mistake.'

'Just shows how crazy they are,' Julie grumbled.

'Of course. Then there's Sweden. Is Sweden neutral? She's just allowed a division of German troops to cross her territory, *en route* from Norway to Finland. Finland, of course, is stuffed quite full of German troops. One could argue that the Russians are quite entitled to, as you put it, chuck rocks at neutral Finland.'

'I don't care,' Julie said. 'America's certainly neutral, and *I'm* American, and my *shoulder's* American, and as far as I'm

244

concerned that rock counts as a declaration of war. Your ear's bleeding.'

'I know. The blood congeals more readily if one doesn't touch it.'

'You sound like this sort of thing happens all the time.'

'Oh, occasionally. Stoning the embassy is an irregular event in the diplomatic calendar. This is my sixth or seventh, I suppose.'

Outside, there was a short lull.

'Egypt too is technically neutral,' Clark said. 'We, of course, have even more troops in Egypt than Hitler has in Finland. As for Turkey—'

'I don't care,' Julie said. 'How much longer are we going to be stuck here?'

Clark checked his watch. 'The Spanish police usually allow them fifteen minutes. We can expect relief before long.'

He was right. Soon the wail of approaching sirens cleared the demonstrators from the street. Clark fetched Julie's shoes and helped her up. 'I expect you could do with a cup of tea,' he said.

'Tell me something,' Julie said. 'Why have you been going on and on about neutrals?'

'To show you that this war is a confused and confusing affair,' he told her. 'One cannot always join in on one's own terms.'

'Or stay out, either,' she said, touching her shoulder gingerly.

'Quite so.' Clark took his bowler hat and opened the door for her.

Chapter 34

Colonel Christian came back from the lavatory as Otto Krafft was opening the afternoon mail in the anteroom. It was the colonel's fourth visit that day; Otto could tell where he'd been by the smell of soap on his hands. It was Spanish soap and it smelled of lemons. A great number of lemons.

'Whose idea was that silliness outside the British embassy?'
Christian asked.

'Don't know, sir.'

'Childish self-indulgence. Just the sort of idiotic provocation
that gives us a bad name in the diplomatic corps.'

'Yes sir.' Otto slit a few more envelopes. 'I heard a rumour
that Captain Mullen has set up a new team to encourage anti-
British agitators,' he said. 'Perhaps they were behind it.'

'Mullen set up a new team?' Christian squared his shoulders
and stared. 'That's the first I heard of it. I was with him
yesterday and he said nothing. I don't think he would create
a new unit without at least consulting me.'

'You know what these rumours are like, sir,' Otto said.
shuffling the correspondence into a pile. 'Probably nothing to it.'

Christian sucked his teeth. 'Mullen's so damn short-sighted
he can't see beyond tomorrow. Quick results: that's all he
can think of. Whether they might not be the *right* results is
something that doesn't seem to occur to him.'

Christian wandered away into his room, and Otto saw him
lunging about, swatting flies with a rolled-up copy of *Deutsche
Allgemeine Zeitung*. After a while he came back, looking more
restless than ever. 'You know what he'll say, don't you?' he
said. 'He'll want to know why we can't show any results.'

'Eldorado's only been gone just over a week, sir.'

'Listen: von Bock has advanced a quarter of the way to
Moscow in just over a week! Raeder's U-boats have sunk two
dozen ships in just over a week!' Christian threw his newspaper into a waste bin. 'I can't afford to wait while Eldorado
learns his trade. Let's face it, the lad's a lousy spy, he looks
like Rudolph Valentino playing the Duke of Windsor, I mean
who's going to trust him? Anyway I don't suppose he can
tell the difference between a bomb-aimer and a boy scout.
No, he's a waste of time. I think I'll switch him to sabotage.'

'Well now . . .' Otto risked a smile. 'That's a bold decision,
sir.'

'Hit their morale, that's what we've got to do. Mercury
can put Eldorado in touch with those I.R.A. fanatics from
Ireland. I don't care what they blow up, it doesn't matter, in
fact it's better if the sabotage is utterly random. Senseless,
sporadic destruction: even Eldorado should be capable of that,
shouldn't he?'

246

Otto didn't answer. He was looking at the first page of a six-page letter, closely typed. He leaned back and held it at arm's length, then, with a little snort of surprise, riffled through the other pages. He got up, stapled the corners together, and handed the document to Christian. 'Eldorado's first report, sir,' he said. 'He seems to be thoroughly enjoying himself in London.'

Christian took it and fanned himself with it. 'Fancy that,' he said. 'Bang goes my bright idea.'

*

Next morning Christian called a breakfast meeting to consider the Eldorado report. All those attending—the men who had played a major part in Luis's training—had been given copies to read the night before.

Christian tapped salt into his boiled egg, and called for comments.

The others looked at each other, politely deferring. Richard Fischer paused, then raised one cautious finger. Christian waved him on.

'In my opinion this is undoubtedly Cabrillo's work, sir,' he said. 'The style, the syntax, the overall format: it couldn't be anyone else. I believe it's authentic.'

'Did anyone suggest otherwise?' Christian asked.

'No sir, but since the channel of communication used is, I believe, new and different, I thought it best to . . .' Fischer let the sentence die while he buttered some toast.

'So he didn't use radio,' Franz Werth said. 'I suspected not, with a message of such length.'

'Eldorado has his own private channel,' Christian said. 'An official in the Spanish embassy in London puts Eldorado's report in their diplomatic bag. The bag travels airmail to Lisbon and another kind gentleman in their Lisbon embassy extracts it and mails it to us.'

'Presumably those are the two men he refers to in Appendix "A",' Dr Hartmann said. There was a flapping of pages. ' "Financial remuneration of communications assistants",' he read out. ' "I have agreed a rate of twenty English pounds per week for BLUEBIRD (in London) and twenty-five U.S. Dollars per week for STORK (in Lisbon). This is best paid direct to them by me. Please credit my Lisbon account accordingly".'

247

'Steep,' said Wolfgang Adler.

'Surely not.' Franz swallowed hastily and licked crumbs from his lips. 'Not if the system works as well as this.'

'I like it,' Fischer said. 'It's as rapid and painless as any method I've come across.'

'Agreed,' Christian grunted. 'Pay him, Otto.'

'Yes sir. This stuff on page three about their new tank is very interesting,' Otto said. 'In many ways it parallels what our own people are working on. Greater speed, heavier armour-plating, automatic gun-sight . . .'

During the next twenty minutes, each man picked his own plums out of the report. Dr Hartmann was impressed by Luis's summary of new bomber airfields in eastern England. Fischer endorsed what Luis had to say about the effect of rationing on morale, based on Fischer's own experience in other wars. Franz got quite excited over Luis's analysis of British convoy strategy and how it might be turned to advantage by the U-boat packs. Even Wolfgang Adler conceded that Luis was probably not far wrong in his brief review of British, Russian and Axis prospects as seen by officials of the major neutral embassies in London. It became quite a cheerful and optimistic meal.

'Thank you, gentlemen,' Christian said. 'It seems that we are all pleased with Eldorado.'

'After only a week at work,' Franz pointed out, 'this is a remarkable achievement.'

Christian wiped his mouth, and stood up. The others stood too. 'Nobody has overlooked anything?' he inquired.

Dangerous question. No takers.

'I operate on the basis that all agents are fools and villains until proved otherwise,' Christian declared. He rapped the report with his knuckles. 'For all we know, Eldorado wrote this while sitting in a pub in Piccadilly, gathering worthless gossip.' He stabbed Otto in the chest with a hard finger and made him wince. 'Get all this in code and have it transmitted to Mercury as soon as you can. Tell him I want it checked, and I want the answers on my desk in forty-eight hours. *All* the answers.'

'Yes sir.' Otto hurried away.

'I suppose it's not impossible,' Wolfgang suggested, 'that Mercury himself is sitting alongside Cabrillo in the very same pub.'

248

'Mercury doesn't drink,' Christian said. 'It gives him heart-burn.'

Wolfgang grunted. The meeting broke up.

Chapter 35

When Julie left the British embassy, Spanish workmen were sweeping up the last of the broken glass and carpenters were nailing boards over the ground-floor windows. She wondered if the Falange organisers had had them standing by during the demonstration. That would be very Spanish, she decided gloomily. Everything here was such a damn ritual. Even when they bust you with a rock, there was nothing personal about it. It was just a formal rock.

She felt restless and dissatisfied, and decided to visit Angela, maybe see if she could call up some friends and all go out for dinner. But Angela, when she opened the door, was obviously in the middle of packing.

'Oh, Christ . . . You're not leaving too, are you?' Julie stepped over open suitcases and between heaps of coat-hangers. 'Madrid's going to be like the tomb, at this rate.'

'Tomb?' Angela didn't know the word.

'You know: dead, buried, cemetery . . .'

'Ah, yes.' She went on wrapping shoes in tissue paper. 'Well, for me, Madrid is a cemetery.'

Julie sat on the arm of a sofa and watched. It was not a happy line of conversation to follow, but what else was there? 'You still reckon Freddy's finished, then.'

'Oh, I know he is dead.' Without pausing in her packing, Angela very lightly touched the middle of her forehead. 'Here, I know it.'

Julie thought: *She seems very tough about it.* She said, 'You can never be sure until there's a body.'

Angela just looked at her: a cool, Mediterranean, Catholic look which said Death is death so don't give me that fuzzy Protestant optimism.

249

'Supposing the worst,' Julie said. 'Any ideas about what might have happened?'

'It was the war. Freddy was doing something.'

'Spying?'

'Maybe. Or maybe catching spies.' Angela began sorting through a pile of books, keeping some, dropping others into a waste basket. 'Often they are the same, I think.' The basket shuddered to the thud of books. 'Ask your Luis.'

'I can't. He went away, to England. That's what he said, anyway . . .'

'I go to Brazil,' Angela said. 'Away from the war, away from stupid fools like Freddy and Luis. I am glad Luis went away. If he had stayed I think I would have tried to kill him too.'

'You would?' Julie studied her intently and saw nothing but porcelain calm. 'What did Luis ever do to you?'

'I think he killed Freddy.'

Julie felt slightly sick. The effect of so much alcohol, pain and medication seemed to have weakened her body until with this last shock it suffered a thousand tiny cracks. She got up and walked to the window. There was a man in the apartment opposite doing bar-bell exercises. She took a couple of deep breaths. 'You don't know that,' she said.

'I know that Freddy was thinking of killing Luis. So I think Luis acted first.'

The man doing the bar-bell exercises saw her watching and moved out of sight. 'That's crazy,' she said.

'Crazy to kill someone before he kills you?'

Julie turned away from the window, massaging her face to drive away the weary, grubby feeling. 'It's all guesswork,' she said. 'You don't know—'

'I knew Freddy. For years I have known Freddy, and sometimes he had to kill people, I don't know why but I could tell when he was thinking of it. And at that tennis game I caught him looking at Luis, very serious and sad, and I knew straight away, because I have seen that look before.'

'Oh . . .' Julie let out a long cry of despair. 'Why can't they all just sell goddam insurance, like any normal idiot?' She pounded the wall with her fists.

'If you want to break something,' Angela said, 'I have no use for those ornaments.'

250

Julie kicked a suitcase instead.

'A long time ago I discovered that everything is a game for men like that,' Angela said. 'Look at this.' She showed Julie a cartoon sketched on the flyleaf of a book. It showed Angela playing cricket, naked except for the huge pads strapped to her slim legs and a cap with a peak like an eagle's beak. She looked funny and happy and exciting. 'Freddy drew that,' she said. 'He was very clever at some things.' She threw the book into the basket.

Later they went out for dinner. It was pleasant, but they had nothing left to say. They parted without emotion and without promises. When Julie got back to the Hotel Bristol the night clerk had a letter for her. She recognised Luis's writing, and all the wretchedness she had carefully pushed away during dinner came sweeping back. She gave the letter back to the man. 'I'll pick it up in the morning,' she said.

*

In Spain breakfast is not so much a meal as a gesture, something to acknowledge the passage of night. Julie woke up with a shoulder so stiff and sore that she had to eat her breakfast one-handed, and this gave her an excuse for making it last. Nevertheless the time came when she had finished all the rolls and drunk all the coffee and it seemed there was nothing for it but to go and get Luis's letter.

She used the back of her knife to rake all the crumbs and flakes of bread into a line. She shaped the line into a square, and turned the square into a triangle. The whole situation was so damn obvious that unless she was going to be utterly dishonest, there was only one decision. Angela believed that Luis had killed Freddy, and Angela knew a lot about that sort of thing. Luis had ducked and dodged so many questions that he was obviously up to the neck in some kind of dirty work. He was very cosy with the German embassy; almost certainly they were paying him; and now he was in England. Put all that together, and Luis came out at best a mercenary and at worst a hired assassin. *Okay*, she told herself, *so he's got a nice face, so he's hot stuff in the sack, so what? Do you seriously imagine you have any future with a man like that?*

She went to the front desk and asked for her letter, crumpled it in her fist, and took it up to her room. She got some matches. The letter was squeezed into a hard ball. That would never burn. She opened it out. The handwriting was bold and fluent. Did that reveal the man, or conceal him? Luis had seemed childishly honest at times. So what? Absolutely honest children could also be the most sadistic, fascist little bastards . . . 'Oh, the hell with everything!' she said angrily, and ripped open the envelope. There was a single sheet of paper inside.

Dear Mrs Conroy:

All week I have been looking forward to writing this letter, and now that I find some spare time at last, there is almost nothing I can tell you which is new. This is because the British censorship is very strict, so I cannot even mention the weather here, or describe London, or tell you about my business dealings, in case the censor decides that it might give the Axis powers some useful information.

So I shall merely say that I am well and working hard. I don't see how those facts can make any difference to anyone, except perhaps to you!

I miss Madrid very much, and I miss you a very great deal. It is hard for me to make friends here. In any case, I am not sure that I want to. This is a poor letter. There is so much that I should be able to say, and cannot.

Yours sincerely,
Luis Cabrillo.

Julie read it quickly, twice, and put it away. She was relieved and disappointed. *It is hard for me to make friends here . . .* Tough shit, Luis; you should've thought of that before you took the lousy job. She imagined him tramping around Westminster and Whitehall and Leicester Square, snooping on everyone, trusting no one, going home to a lonely bed, with a headful of crappy secrets and a gutful of lousy rations. Half a gutful, more likely. *You dumb joker, Luis,* she thought. *You sold out, didn't you? How in God's name could anyone so smart be so stupid?*

*

The rest of the day was a waste of time. Her shoulder throbbed. She couldn't sit or lie comfortably. Her monthly

cheque still hadn't arrived. The skies clouded over in the afternoon and kept a grey padded lid on the city. She wandered
around her room, sometimes fiddling with the dials of a radio
in search of the BBC; but the dry static of the Spanish plateau
crackled endlessly, and all she could find was meaningless
European gabble, or shrunken accordion-music. When dusk
came she gave up, took a long hot bath, and stunned the
ache in her shoulder with a litre of wine. Even so, sleep came
slowly. Luis's letter had been no help to her. He'd gone away;
he should have stayed away.

Next morning her shoulder moved a little more easily. In
a burst of decisiveness, she telephoned the U.S. Embassy and
made an appointment to see George Langham.

She met him at noon. By twelve-twenty she was out in the
street again, angry and depressed. Langham had been blunt:
the embassy would not attempt to persuade the British authorities to let her enter that country. 'We don't let them pressure us about our imigration procedures,' he said, 'and they
feel the same way about theirs. Those people are fighting for
their lives, you know. Shiploads of food are getting torpedoed
in the Atlantic every day. Everything's rationed over there.
Everything.'

'I don't care, I can live on fresh air, I'll do without my
rations, I just want to *be* there.'

'Look, Mrs Conroy, the last thing the British need right now
is tourists.' Langham compressed his lips while he looked at
her. 'Take my advice and find yourself another boyfriend.'

Julie reddened. 'What the hell is that supposed to mean?'

He made a sour face. 'We're not complete stuffed shirts here
in the embassy, Mrs Conroy. We know all about Mr Cabrillo.'
Flabby, wet-lipped little George Langham was revealing a
surprising toughness; even a hint of hostility. 'As far as this
embassy is concerned, Mr Cabrillo was no joke when he was
here in Madrid. In Britain, he can only be very bad news to
anyone who contacts him.'

'I don't want to go to Britain to contact him.'

Langham looked away. He didn't believe her, but he wasn't
going to argue about it.

'You're saying: go home and play with your dolls, little
girl,' Julie said angrily. 'Leave the fighting to the grown-ups.
What the hell are the grown-ups of America doing right now?'

253

'Be your age, Mrs Conroy. Everything's changed since Hitler went into Russia.' Langham stood. The meeting was over. 'Didn't you read what Senator Truman just said? He said we should stand aside and let the Russians and Germans cut each other's throats. Now why does he say that? Because he knows a hundred million Americans already think it, that's why.'

'Then they're all crazy.'

'Don't sit here and tell me that, Mrs Conroy. Go back home and tell *them*. You're itching for a fight, aren't you? Well, they'll give you one.'

She killed the rest of the day, just walking about Madrid. Langham's final suggestion kept annoying her, largely because she knew he was right. The obvious, sensible thing to do was to go back to her family in Indiana. Back to her father, who operated a Coca-Cola distributorship; his idea of war began and ended with Pepsi-Cola, Dr Pepper and 7-Up. Back to her mother, who was secretary of the Republican Ladies' Circle; whenever Julie argued politics, her mother kept a fixed smile until she could play her ace: 'You can't change human nature, deary.' There was an elder sister, married to a real-estate agent, and a younger brother, studying to be an optician. There was also a gang of aunts and uncles and cousins, all lifetime subscribers to Readers Digest and dedicated opponents of divorce, gambling and Socialism, which (as everyone knew) came out of places like New York City. Harry Conroy had come out of New York City: he didn't wear a tie, he never went to church, he said Readers Digest was pre-shrunk junk for happy hicks, and when Julie announced they were going to get married, everyone just knew it was bound to end in disaster and unhappiness all round. And as it happened, everyone was damn right. Which was why Julie, wandering along the Alcalá and the Gran Via and then getting hopelessly lost in the Old City and just walking and walking with her shadow always in front of her until she ended up looking across an avenue at the hulking mass of the Prado, her feet aching and her mind dazed—Julie Conroy knew that, above all, she didn't want to go back to bloody Indiana. On the other hand, what the hell else was there?

*

Mercury normally transmitted messages, from his house on

Clapham Common in South London to the *Abwehr* monitoring station in Holland, at 3 a.m. Otto Krafft set his alarm clock for 3.30 a.m. and by the time he had shaved and dressed, Mercury's report was waiting for him in the teleprinter room. Otto Krafft decoded it in less than five minutes. The transcript was on Colonel Christian's desk when he came in from breakfast at 8 a.m., lying alongside Eldorado's report. Christian read it at a glance. In two dozen words, Mercury had confirmed everything.

Christian felt a surge of excitement. He smiled, and stretched his strong arms and legs until their muscles would give no more. It was time now to share the good news. He lifted the phone and asked for Captain Mullen.

When Otto mentioned Mercury's signal to the others, Richard Fischer said he was not surprised. 'I've been checking Eldorado's information about bomber airfields in eastern England.' Fischer said. 'It fits the pattern of British raids on northern Europe.'

'Airfields are hard to hide,' Wolfgang Adler said.

'Could *you* plot every Spanish airfield within two hundred miles of Madrid, in less than a week?' Fischer asked. 'And without a car?'

But Wolfgang refused to be enthusiastic.

'I don't rate Mercury highly,' he said. 'He's a frightened little bureaucratic asslicker, working for his pension. He hates responsibility and he's got no more initiative than the janitor's cat.'

'How's your ankle, Wolfgang?' Otto asked.

'It's got nothing to do with my ankle. I don't like Eldorado and I never did, but that doesn't influence my judgement. In my opinion, Eldorado's unreliable and Mercury's a featherweight.'

'So what do you suggest?' Dr Hartmann asked. 'That we ignore their reports?'

Wolfgang was silent.

'You know your trouble,' Richard Fischer told him. 'You think everybody cheats.'

'Well, spies are professional cheats,' Wolfgang replied, 'and some of them don't know when to stop.'

'Perhaps that explains Eldorado's amazing output,' Otto said. 'We've just received another report from him. Twelve pages, this time. The colonel's reading it now.'

'Good heavens!' Fischer exclaimed. 'Twelve pages?'

'And not a single spelling mistake,' Otto said.

Wolfgang sniffed.

'You might as well face it, friend,' Fischer told him. 'We're stuck with a success.'

*

Wolfgang Adler was not telling the truth when he said that his attitude towards Eldorado had nothing to do with his ankle.

The truth was that his ankle was mending slowly and painfully. The doctors suspected permanent damage to the joint, and they had warned him that he might never be able to ski again. The injury to his wrist was also giving him trouble: numbness in the fingers, and a nagging ache that often refused to let him sleep. He hid his pain from the others, and as a result it more and more occupied his mind: the pain, and his sense of grievance against the man who had caused it. Wolfgang Adler had always suspected that life would cheat him. It had happened once already. He was bitter about that. He was a man who found it easy to be bitter.

As long as he could remember, Wolfgang had resented his circumstances. His parents had been a dull couple—father an architect, mother a teacher—and growing up in the suburbs of Cologne never satisfied him. School was boring. He was a clever boy and he didn't try to hide his contempt for less clever children, so they soon left him alone. That suited Wolfgang: he found all their games slow and irksome. Girls had much the same effect. By the age of seventeen he was a gloomy little prig.

Then he discovered flying. It happened because, at the time, he believed that mathematics was the only thing worth his attention, and the University of Vienna the only place worth studying it. When the University required an interview, his father astonished everyone. He sent Wolfgang to Vienna by air.

The experience shattered all Wolfgang's armourplated adolescent disdain. The pilot was a showman who entertained his passengers by banking steeply soon after take-off, and by skimming like a skier along the hills and valleys of the clouds.

256

Wolfgang got permission to sit beside him in the cockpit. As he watched the lucky genius in command of this astonishing machine, alone and untroubled, high in the vastness of the sky, he surrendered to a strange, new feeling. It was envy. He wanted to be a pilot so much that it hurt.

Next year he went to London University and studied engineering, simply and solely in order to help him get into the *Luftwaffe*. He graduated, and the *Luftwaffe* accepted him for training. He was happy at last. He was flying and he was good at it. He was the first on his course to go solo, and he was flying solo when he got the terrible pain in his ear.

It hurt so much that he made a bad landing, and he pretended to be slightly airsick so that he could go away and hide. The pain faded after an hour, leaving him tired and afraid. Next day it happened again and he thought he knew the cause : change of pressure caused by sudden loss of height. He went up and tried it once more, just to be sure. This time it hurt so much that he screamed.

The medical officer explained everything, but Wolfgang was too depressed and disgusted to listen or even to speak. His stupid, shitty ear had betrayed him : nothing else mattered. What was the point of having a damn ear if it didn't work? He felt like cutting the idiot thing off. He felt like cutting his throat while he was at it.

In this frame of mind he got an order to see the station commander. He went expecting polite sympathy and a firm goodbye. The station commander said nothing about his ear; instead, he invited him to apply for the *Abwehr*. He made the work sound challenging, unpredictable and risky. Glad of any distraction, Wolfgang agreed. The *Abwehr* was quite pleased to have him; nevertheless there was always something missing, a lack which left him emotionally lopsided. His natural enthusiasm had burned itself out. He was still ambitious, but his ambition was scarred by resentment. He had been cheated out of flying and he would always be dissatisfied with second-best. And now, thanks to Luis Cabrillo, it looked as if he would even be cheated out of second-best. The rank unfairness hurt him more than the pain. He carried his grudge with every step he limped.

Chapter 36

The next week passed slowly for Julie. Her shoulder improved enough to let her go swimming again, and she trudged up and down the pool. She bought a bigger radio and received much louder static. Either the BBC was jammed or she was looking in the wrong place. She bought a Spanish newspaper and, pocket-dictionary in hand, began doggedly translating the lead story, a speech by Foreign Minister Suñer: *'The Falange now takes up arms in the European crusade against Asiatic barbarism . . .'* There was a map showing the latest German advances. *The Spanish contingent had better hurry,* Julie thought, *or there won't be any Asiatic barbarism left to conquer.* Suñer went on: *'Victory by the axis over Russia will convince the USA that her entry into the war would be useless. Britain will then accept peace as her only salvation . . .'* She skipped to the next story. The French Vichy Government had broken off relations with Russia. Hungary had declared war on Russia. So had Rumania, Slovakia and Finland. *Jesus!* she thought, *any more join in and they'll have to take turns to fight.*

An American journalist called Evans took her out to dinner. He was a friend of Harry's, in Madrid to try for an interview with Franco. 'It wouldn't surprise anyone if he joined the Axis,' Evans said.

'I still can't believe those sons-of-bitches are really going to win,' Julie said.

'Well, it certainly looks like the end of the war,' Evans remarked. 'If I were you, I'd get the hell out of Europe while I could.'

She told him about wanting to go to Britain. He thought about the problem. 'I came across a guy in Lisbon who might be able to help,' he said. 'I was going to do a story around him, but . . . Seems he has a line in passports, visas, entry papers, that sort of thing. I mean, it's all strictly illegal.'

Julie shrugged.

'Okay. The only address I have is a hospital.' He wrote it out for her and added the name: Antonio da Silva. 'Whatever he sells you, don't give him more than fifty dollars, tops.'

Julie got fairly drunk that night. Evans had offered to call New York and find out where her cheque was; stubbornly, stupidly, she told him that was Harry's problem. Evans could tell her nothing of Harry's whereabouts. She felt lost: she had no liking for Spain; Britain didn't need her; and she didn't want America. It was half-past three in the morning when she awoke, alone and crying. For several long and wretched seconds she did not know where she was. Then the dim, familiar outlines of her room gradually took shape. She got up, still crying, washed her face, and cried some more into the hotel's bulky towel, until the fit had exhausted itself. She dragged a blanket off the bed, wrapped herself in it and wrote to Luis Cabrillo.

It was a long letter, full of self-pity and anger and tenderness and self-mocking. She wrote without pause, almost without thought: the words were waiting piled up inside her. When she had stuffed the pages into an envelope and addressed it care of Banco Espirito Santo, Lisbon, she went back to bed and fell asleep at once.

*

They were clearing away the breakfast things when she came down, feeling stretched and wary because of her hangover. It created an over-inflated, insecure sensation, like going down in a fast lift. She had an irrational conviction that she was going to drop Luis's letter unless she constantly remembered to hold it.

The assistant manager hurried towards her. 'Señora Conroy! Something for you!' His smile made his moustache bristle with pride. 'From New York, Señora!'

'Hey, that's great.' Julie took the letter and sat in the nearest chair. The letter was from Harry's agency; their return address was on the envelope. She slit the flap. There was no cheque inside, only a short letter. It informed her, as a matter of courtesy, that Mr Conroy was no longer employed by them.

Julie got Evans on the phone. 'My guess is he's gone freelance,' Evans said. 'Harry often talked about doing that, you know.'

'And what about me?'

'Well, I can lend you a few bucks if—'

'No, no, no. I've *got* a few bucks. But he's supposed to support me, for Christ's sake! What the hell does he think he's doing?'

Pause. Evans sighed. 'You know old Harry,' he said.

'Yeah. That was where I made my big mistake.'

She drank a cup of coffee and went back upstairs. She took the lift; it went like a rocket and made her feel like a melting snowman. In her room, she did some rough reckoning and let out a groan. What she'd told Evans was right: she had a few bucks. Enough to pay the hotel, get to Lisbon, and buy an airline ticket, one-way, to New York. She glared at the magnificent Madrid sunshine, flooding through her window. The entire goddam world was ganging up to drive her back to goddam Indiana, led by Harry goddam Conroy!

Luis's letter was on the bed. No point in sending that now. She tore it up and began packing.

Chapter 37

Only one thing spoiled Colonel Christian's general happiness in July of 1941, and that was Wolfgang Adler's coldness.

The war was going extremely well and Eldorado was doing even better: twice a week, sometimes three times a week, Otto Krafft opened new reports which were stuffed with valuable information about British military abilities and intentions. The Madrid weather was sunny and invigorating. Captain Mullen had stopped nagging him for action, Berlin was congratulatory, and Christian's bowels had resumed normal service. Everyone was cheerful and enthusiastic except Wolfgang Adler. He was not antagonistic; he was just silent. He limped into meetings, sat with his damaged hand tucked inside his jacket and said nothing. But his stony expression plainly disapproved of what he heard.

Christian said nothing and hoped that the mood would pass. The contrary happened: Wolfgang's grimness became more obvious. Eventually, Christian decided that he must do something about it. The decision reached him during a meeting he had called to discuss an exciting development in Eldorado's affairs. The Spaniard had recruited two sub-agents.

'Eldorado has given them suitable codenames,' Christian informed the meeting. ' "Seagull" ' is a foreman working in the Liverpool docks, and "Knickers" is a travelling salesman operating in south-east England. Eldorado has sent us their first reports, together with his own comments. Richard has read the lot, I hope.'

'With great interest, sir. Seagull's effort is written on wrapping-paper—' Fischer held up a brown sheet, covered with pencil scribblings. '—but no less valuable for that. He gives us a lot of good stuff about shipping movements, especially British aid to Russia. Eldorado's note says that Seagull is fanatically anti-Comminist. He's not well educated, by the way. Mis-spellings everywhere.'

'Could be Irish,' Dr Hartmann suggested. 'Lots of Irish in Liverpool.'

'That would explain the anti-Communist element too,' said Otto Krafft. 'He's probably a rabid Catholic.'

'Quite possibly,' Richard Fischer said. 'The other sub-agent, Knickers, is very different. His job as a soft-drinks salesman takes him into Royal Air Force bases where, according to Eldorado, he also visits the officers' messes in order to sell black-market nylon stockings.' Everyone chuckled except Wolfgang, who winced. 'This enables him to pick up useful information,' Fischer went on. 'I may say his first report is very promising indeed . . .'

When the meeting broke up, Christian asked Wolfgang to stay behind for a minute.

Wolfgang leaned on his stick and said nothing. Christian closed the door, walked back to his desk and perched on a corner of it. 'You're not enjoying your work, are you?'

Wolfgang looked down and then up. His expression remained blank.

'Is it because of your injuries?' Christian asked. 'Would you like a few weeks' leave to help you recuperate?'

Wolfgang gave a single shake of the head.

'Well, *something's* obviously wrong, isn't it?' Christian said briskly. 'What is it: a woman, money, trouble at home?'

261

'None of those.'

'Look, Adler, you're intelligent, you're perceptive, and most of the time you're well-balanced. You've got a mind of your own. Good. Now I don't go to the trouble of recruiting lively minds in order to shut them up whenever they speak out. I believe in poking people in the ribs but not in beating them over the head. Right? So if you have something on your mind, for God's sake unload it. That's what you're paid for.'

Wolfgang breathed in deeply. His eyes showed the strain of fatigue: his aching hand had kept him awake most of the night. 'All right,' he said. 'Since you ask me, I'll tell you. This whole Eldorado operation leaves me cold. I don't trust it.'

Christian looked at Wolfgang's stick. 'Perhaps you have a special reason.'

'That's what everyone thinks, and that's why I keep my mouth shut in these meetings. Nobody's prepared to look beyond the obvious.'

'What is there to see?'

'It's what there *isn't* to see that's important. There's a total lack of proof, of corroboration. Eldorado is operating in isolation. That means we never check his reliability.'

'There's Mercury.'

'Mercury can't even check his own laundry-list. He's not a voice, he's an echo.'

'Well, let's not argue about Mercury. But can you point to anything that suggests Eldorado's unreliability?'

'Yes. In last week's report he located Waterloo station on the wrong side of London.'

'True. But surely that's just a detail. All agents make minor mistakes. After all, the man's under great stress.'

'Then he shouldn't be left operating on his own.'

'Oh.' Christian took out his handkerchief and tromboned a lengthy snort into it. 'Do you mean we should send another agent to work alongside him?'

'Why not send several?'

'There are plenty of reasons why not. Every additional agent increases the risk, the cost, the administrative complications. And the encouraging aspect of the Seagull-Knickers development is that if Eldorado can find his own sub-agents, we shan't *need* to send anyone else.'

Wolfgang made a sour face. 'It's all happening too easily.

Eldorado's in England as a Spanish businessman. How can he recruit a soft-drinks salesman and a foreman docker, just like that? Especially as one of them's a rabid Catholic? Eldorado's an atheist.'

'So what? You're a cultural attaché, according to the embassy. That proves nothing.'

Wolfgang was silent for a moment. 'Nothing proves anything, does it?' he said. He glanced at the door.

'You're still not convinced, Adler, are you?' Christian tried to give him a sympathetic smile. 'Well, I admire your consistency. And your courage. I'm glad you're not prepared to change your tune just because its unpopular. That could be quite useful. After all, Eldorado's only human. He has weak areas, he makes mistakes. I depend on you to spot them.' Christian thought of adding *Only try not to be so bloody miserable about it*, but he gave an encouraging nod instead.

'That won't be difficult,' Wolfgang said. He went out, the end of his stick leaving a trail of indentations in Christian's carpet.

Chapter 38

The Lusitania Express steamed into Lisbon's Santa Apolonia station some time between 9.25 a.m. and 10.12 a.m., depending on which of the two station clocks you didn't believe. To Julie it didn't matter a lot. Her sleeper from Madrid had been comfortable. Since she awoke she had been looking at mile after mile of olive trees, cork woods and rice fields, until the track met the Tagus and she watched the Tagus grow from a river to an estuary to a bay, and they were trundling past the Lisbon suburbs. She counted a dozen big freighters anchored out there, plus another dozen warships flying a variety of flags. She knew that the open Atlantic was only a few miles away but somehow Lisbon didn't feel like a big, tough, deep-water port. The air was soft and mild. Nobody hurried. If the time really was 9.25 the express was a little early. If it was actually 10.12, the train was a bit late. What difference did it make?

She checked her bags at the station and walked along the waterfront until the streets opened onto a big square calling itself the Praça do Comercio. It had a blackened statue of a man on a horse in the middle and it was flanked by colonnaded government offices. This seemed to be where everything began; the city rose behind it in a great, shallow bowl, with the old castle perched on the right-hand side. There were odd echoes of London: doubledecker buses, red pillar-boxes, even businessmen with rolled umbrellas and regimental-looking ties. But where were the Pan Am offices? She found a phone box and looked them up, found a taxi and showed him the address: Avenida da Liberdade.

It turned out to be Lisbon's Park Avenue, only wider and pleasanter. The Pan Am people turned out to be friendly and helpful, but the weather in the Atlantic was not. The Clipper route to New York went via Portuguese Guinea, Trinidad and Puerto Rico. Somewhere in that seven and a half thousand miles the incoming Clipper had run into a storm and been delayed. As a result, the Lisbon schedules were disrupted. Pan Am hoped, with luck, to get Julie's flight away on Thursday. Today was Monday. 'Please don't be late,' the ticket clerk told her. 'If anyone doesn't check-in on time, that seat automatically goes to a stand-by. And believe me, there are always stand-bys.'

Julie paid him and counted her change. There was not a lot to count. If she found a cheap *pensão* and lived on beans she might reach New York with enough to make a collect call to Indiana. So, no more taxis. She walked back down the *Avenida*, enjoying the sunshine, the scenery, the smells and the *Liberdade*: all, thank God, free.

Chapter 39

There may have been a cheaper *pensão* in Lisbon, but not much. The *Pensão São Vicente* was in a courtyard off a small square in the heart of the Alfama. The inside smelt strongly of cooked cabbage and the outside, when she opened a window, smelt more strongly of live chickens. The bed groaned when she sat on it, and the only picture on the walls—a startlingly realistic lithograph of the Sacred Heart—bled in sympathy for her sufferings to come. But the place was fairly clean, the owner had a friendly smile, and above all she was bone-weary of tramping around Lisbon, looking rich and sounding poor; so Julie took the room for three nights. It cost her the equivalent of two and a half dollars.

The Alfama was ancient Lisbon. It staggered up the hillside below the castle of São Jorge in a confusion of twisted alleys, staircases and dead-ends. It had plenty of atmosphere, aside from cooked cabbage and chickens: a Moorish look in the faces, a gypsy look in the clothes. The Alfama felt like an independent village within the city. Julie liked it. The kids peed in the gutters. The cats chased the pigeons. People stared, and when she stared back they said *Boa tarde*, which had to mean either good afternoon or get lost, so she *boa-tarded* them right back in her godawful Middle-Western Portuguese, and they grinned; so that was all right. No bullshit about the Alfama.

By eight o'clock she was ravenous. She walked into a crowded café where nobody had shaved for a week and everybody was having a good time. Her arrival created a small hub-bub of surprise, which brought out the cook, who was also the waiter. She guessed at what he said: sorry, no tables. 'Can't I sit there?' she asked, pointing to a place at a table which had three pairs of hairy elbows on it. Pan Am gave its passengers a free phrase-book, and she'd memorised a little Portuguese. '*Com licença?*' she enquired. The hairy elbows were vastly impressed. She sat down. The menu, chalked on the

265

wall, was beyond translation. What the hairy elbows were eating smelled good. She looked up 'same' in her little book, and said to the cook, very clearly: '*Mesmo.*' The word was repeated, approvingly, all over the café. She was in. *Mesmo* turned out to be beans with chunks of spiced sausage and hunks of pork. It was called *feijoada*: this she learned from the hairy elbows. They adopted her, gave her red wine, taught her words: glass, *copo*; enough, *basta*; so long, *T'amanha!* They were building labourers. Her choice of their table made them proud and pleased; it was like being visited by a film star. They escorted her home, and they all shook hands in the moonlit courtyard. *T'amanha!*

Julie slept deeply, despite the groaning bed, and was woken by a cock-crow. She stretched and relaxed, and could hear half-a-dozen other cocks crowing. Right in the middle of Lisbon! Delightful.

She felt lighthearted, for a good and simple reason. She had nothing left to worry about: not money, not men, not the problem of what to do about Harry or Hitler or the survival of Soviet Russia. All her decisions were made. Her past was now irrelevant, and her future was still seven and a half thousand miles away. For the first time in many months she was free to be happy, happy to be free.

She got up and enjoyed her day, exploring Lisbon in the sun, coming back to eat in her café, sleeping well and getting up next day to enjoy it all over again. By Thursday morning she felt better than ever: calm and optimistic, looking forward to her noon flight.

Noon check-in, or noon take-off?

She fished the ticket out of her bag. Along with it came a piece of paper, ragged-edged, torn from a notebook. HOSPITAL DE XABREGAS, she read. ANTONIO DA SILVA. and scribbled underneath: *$50 max, remember!*

Evans's pal. The Portuguese who ran the black market in travel documents.

Oh well. That was all history now. She had a perfectly good American passport, and in any case what she didn't have was $50, either max or min. Always supposing she still wanted to go to Britain, which everyone she knew had told her was an extremely lousy idea. She screwed up the paper and threw it away.

266

Ten minutes later she found it and unscrewed it. There were three hours to kill before her flight—check-in time was noon—and why turn up a chance to meet a genuine Portuguese black-marketeer? They'd be thin on the ground in Indiana. And not having fifty bucks just meant she had nothing to lose.

There was a pawn shop she'd noticed, below the Alfama, near the waterfront. She got there just as they were taking down the shutters, and she got two hundred escudos for her watch. That financed a taxi; Xabregas was just a name to her and this was no time to get lost. The driver took water-front streets for a mile or two, then turned inland and drove through semi-suburbs, where houses met country. The hospital was up a dead-end. It was smallish but newish, just a three-storey concrete block with a lot of flowers growing up the side.

Julie let the taxi drive away while she thought about tactics. Antonio da Silva sounded like a smooth crook. What would be the best approach? Her imagination revived a string of scenes from 'B' movies. They all involved a lot of leg and a lot of cigar smoke and a lot of saxophone on the soundtrack. Not much use in this sunny, healthy setting. She gave up and went in.

Everything the nurse behind the reception desk had on was starched, including her expression. She creaked when she looked up.

'Doctor da Silva?' Julie said. 'Antonio da Silva, that is.'

'*Senhor da Silva*,' the nurse corrected. 'Your name?' Her accent was good.

Julie gave her name. The nurse made a telephone call and had a short, rapid conversation in Portuguese. 'Please sit,' she said.

Julie sat.

Nothing happened for fifteen minutes.

The reception area was small and bare. The nurse had some kind of work to do: sorting file cards. Otherwise, only the clock moved.

'Did Senhor da Silva say how long?' Julie asked.

The nurse gave a small, stiff smile.

Another ten minutes of nothing happened. Julie began to worry about the time: nearly ten o'clock, and her bags were still at the *pensão*. This was crazy. The sane thing to do was to get up and walk out. Forget Britain. Go home, while you still can. The guy's not worth crossing the street for. He's a bum, a mercenary bum. Get up now and walk out.

The clock reached ten, and it was the nurse that got up and walked out. She took her handbag and gave Julie a starched half-glance. Off to the ladies' room.

Julie gave her ten seconds' lead and followed. Short corridor, empty. First door on the right revealed a broom cupboard. Second door was a laundry store. Julie moved on, then went back to the store and took a white coat. The sleeves crackled as her arms thrust into them.

Next was a set of double-doors. She pushed them open, walked past some nurses chattering in Portuguese, and went through more double-doors into a broad corridor. The air had the aromatic, disciplined smell of all hospital wards.

The first three rooms were closed. In the fourth she saw a man sitting in a wheelchair. His hands, feet and head were bandaged. She stopped, and he smiled.

'*Faz favor*,' she said. '*Senhor da Silva?*'

'Funny you should say that.' He brightened up even more. 'I mean, I was one of the lucky ones, right?' He was English, from somewhere north, like Yorkshire.

'I'm looking for a man named da Silva,' she said.

'Take poor old George,' he went on happily. 'Silly bugger couldn't swim. Didn't stand a chance, did he? Yours truly knew how to swim, though.' He chuckled warmly.

'Da Silva,' she said. 'He's not a doctor.'

'No, you got to look on the bright side, haven't you? Look on the bright side, I always say.'

He gave a most intense grin. Julie realised that he was blind. His eyes were milkily opaque, unfocusing. She felt helplessly sorry. For some seconds there was silence, while he kept up his strenuous grin.

'Goodbye,' she said; stupidly.

'Funny you should say that,' he answered.

She left, quickly and quietly, walked to the end of the corridor, and took the staircase to the next floor. This was an open ward, and busy. Julie hesitated, looked around for an alternative, and saw the name *A. da Silva* on a door. What luck! She knocked, tried the handle, and had to use her weight to make the door move. A sigh of cold air slid past her, followed by the tang of chemicals. Inside, a man was bending over a marble slab; she saw a pair of naked feet with a label tied to a big toe.

'Senhor da Silva?' she said.

'*Sim.*' He paused with his hands resting on the corpse. He didn't look like a smooth crook. He looked like Julie's headmaster in high school: stocky, middle-aged, with a square, intelligent face and a permanent expression of slightly amused surprise. '*Feche a porta, senhora, faz favor.*'

'I'm sorry?' She began to have serious misgivings about the whole damn thing.

'Close the door. Please.'

'Oh, sure.' Of course: to keep the cold in. 'I'm Mrs Conroy. Douglas Evans gave me your name. The journalist . . .' Julie moved forward and caught a glimpse of the body. At once she looked away. *Oh Christ*, she prayed, *don't let me faint.*

'Ah yes, Senhor Evans.' Da Silva nodded cheerfully. 'A most interesting man. For what publication do you write?'

'Chicago Tribune,' she said, without thinking.

He looked impressed. 'The hospital is much busier now than when Senhor Evans came here. This of course reflects the increased warfare in the Atlantic. You see here a typical victim.'

It was the last thing she wanted to see. 'Your English is extremely good,' she said.

'Thank you. Most of our patients are British. This young man was . . .' He straightened the label on the big toe. 'Yes, English. About twenty-three years of age. Merchant seaman, almost certainly from a tanker. His injuries are immediately recognisable. You see this phenomenon?'

Now there was no escape. Julie made her head turn and her eyes look. At once her stomach kicked in rebellion, but she swallowed hard, over and over, and kept everything down.

'The skin on the legs has ballooned out as a result of being trapped in intense heat,' Da Silva said. He picked up a double-handful from the thigh. 'We call it the "plus-fours effect". You understand? Like the golfing trousers?' Julie nodded. The mortuary was chilly but she felt like stone. Da Silva said: 'Sometimes men arrive here with their skin hanging below their ankles in big folds. Of course the exposed parts of the body suffer much more severely.' He lifted the left arm. The hand had been burned to the bone; the fingers were black talons. Julie glanced quickly at the rest. The torso was only slightly damaged but the face looked as if it had been blow-torched. She looked away.

'I don't suppose he wanted to live anyway,' she said huskily.

'On the contrary, he put up a good fight,' da Silva replied. 'He was in the sea first, and then in a lifeboat for some days, and finally for a week here. Yes, quite a good fight.'

He took her through the ward. All the beds were occupied by badly burned seamen. Da Silva was responsible only for the morgue, but he explained that he took an interest in all the patients. Julie nodded. She felt numbed by so much suffering. 'Can we get some fresh air?' she asked.

They went outside. The sunshine was gentle, the flowers were innocent, the birds went about doing nobody any harm. Julie felt a huge need to go right away from this terrible place and to be with normal, healthy people again. Da Silva was watching. 'Mrs Conroy,' he said gently, 'are you really a journalist?'

She shook her head.

'Then why did you come to see me?'

She looked at the soft blue sky and decided she'd had much more than enough for one day. 'It doesn't matter any more,' she said.

'As you wish. May I take your coat?'

The starched receptionist telephoned for a taxi. Julie was back at the *pensão* before eleven o'clock. It was one way to kill a morning.

Chapter 40

'Did you remember to warm the pot first?' Colonel Christian asked.

Otto Krafft nodded, and added teaspoons to the cups and saucers.

'The British always warm the pot first,' Christian told the

others. 'They say it's the secret of successful tea-making.'

Wolfgang Adler tried another position in his chair. Nothing made his leg comfortable.

'You're not impressed, Wolfgang,' Christian said. 'Why is that?'

'I think Eldorado could find better things to put in the Spanish diplomatic bag than his week's tea ration, that's all.'

'I don't agree,' Fischer said. 'You keep asking for proof. Well, this is proof that our blockade is damn well *working*.'

'And there is also some evidence,' Wolfgang said, rubbing his fingers, 'that whatever the R.A.F. is dropping on Germany, it is not tea-leaves.'

'What does that matter?' Dr Hartmann asked. 'Their accuracy is pathetic.'

'And of course they don't know that,' Wolfgang said. 'So they're not doing anything about it. I see.'

'The fact is,' Franz Werth said firmly, 'we're getting a tremendous amount of good stuff from Eldorado on other areas, particularly convoys. This man Seagull in Liverpool is a goldmine.'

'Time for the tea, I think,' Christian said. He put milk in the cups. Otto poured. 'Franz is right, you know,' Christian told Wolfgang. 'Our U-boat kill-rate in the Atlantic is quite phenomenal.'

'Drowning sailors is an inefficient way to win a war,' Wolfgang said.

'What an impatient chap you are,' Christian murmured. He sipped his tea. 'You're not drinking?'

'Tea with the milk put in first is undrinkable,' Wolfgang said. 'In Britain only the lower classes drink it that way. The upper classes add milk afterwards.'

'Oh dear. Eldorado didn't tell us that.'

Wolfgang grunted. 'It just shows how careless it is to swallow everything he sends.'

Christian hid his smile in his tea-cup, but the others laughed without restraint. Wolfgang sat and watched the steam curling out of the teapot spout as if he were a thousand miles away.

Chapter 41

For the first time since she left Madrid, Julie Conroy desperately needed someone to talk to.

She sat on her bed and stared at the grotesquely bleeding multicoloured Sacred Heart. It was shapely and plump, like an air cushion. The dead seaman with the claw for a hand didn't have that kind of heart. His was just a bunch of exhausted muscles. They had worked too hard and too long, until they quit.

Julie had thought she knew all about war. After all : foreign correspondent's wife, all over Europe, first-hand experience, you couldn't beat that. Now she realised that she had seen it all through Harry's eyes; a newspaper war. Sure, some got killed, but they were sprawled uniforms at the roadside, or blanket-covered stretchers being carried away. Victims, casualties, losses. Not people. Not suffering. Not young men having their legs boiled and their heads charred, out in the middle of a heaving ocean, so that Nazi Germany could starve Britain into defeat. *That* was war. Forget all the crap about dashing tank-battles and thrilling dog-fights. War wasn't just conflict, for Christ's sake. War was hurting people. You didn't spend bullets, you spent pain, other people's pain, screaming, roasting, agonising pain. So that greed and arrogance could conquer half the world.

What made it even worse was the thought that any halfway decent person would help them do it, just for money. That was evil living off evil.

She got notepaper and an envelope from her bag and wrote *Dear Luis*, and looked at it for ten minutes, until a church clock sounded the quarter-hour, and she nearly panicked. There was too much to say, and all unsayable. In an impulsive, uneven scrawl she wrote :

> *I am sure you don't know what you are doing. Or, if you do know, then I hate you for it.*

It looked feeble and childish but she despaired of adding

anything worthwhile, quickly signed it, *Julie*, and addressed the envelope, *Sr L. Cabrillo, Banco Espirito Santo, Rua do Comercio*, marked: *Please forward*. That was that. Another door closed.

The man who ran the *pensão* helped with her bags and found a taxi. Twenty-five minutes to check-in. No sweat.

She watched Lisbon drift past, as sunny and amiable as ever. Unreal.

'*A senhora vai para América?*'

'Yeah.'

'*Estados Unidos?*'

'Yeah.' She wished he'd shut up.

'*Ah . . .*' The driver nodded, enviously. They rippled over flattened cobbles. '*Nova York?*' he asked, saving the best for last.

'*Nova York*,' she agreed and saw a red pillar-box. 'Wait a minute,' she called, before she remembered the envelope wasn't stamped; but he was already pulling over. 'I have to mail this.' She showed him the letter.

'*Rua do Comercio, sim*.' He pulled out again.

'I didn't mean—'

'*Compreendo, compreendo. Está bem!*' Horns complained as he bluffed his way across the stream. Julie gave up.

Rua do Comercio turned out to be just off *Praça do Comercio*, naturally, and therefore not two minutes away. The bank was like all Portuguese banks: marble and mahogany and three-piece suits. She found a counter with a sign saying *Secçao Estrangeira* and rang its little bell. A three-piece suit came out, frowning. Not frowning at her, just frowning in general. '*Bom dia, senhora.*'

She gave him the letter, and said: 'I understand you have an arrangement with Senhor Cabrillo.'

He nodded at once. '*Sim, senhora.* I shall take care of it. *Obrigado, senhora.*' The frown lifted a fraction.

Julie hesitated. This was a lousy way to say goodbye: by proxy, standing in a damn bank. 'When will he get it, d'you think?' she asked.

The three-piece suit glanced at a wall calendar. 'Probably this afternoon.'

Julie experienced a tiny shiver of astonishment. She tried to hide it by nodding, slowly, and pursing her lips. 'This afternoon, huh?' she said. 'As soon as that?'

'Oh yes. Tomorrow possibly, but today is usual.'

He waited in case she needed more information, such as what time the bank closed. She stood, still nodding like a donkey. The rest of Lisbon, the rest of the world, seemed suddenly remote and unimportant. Only this spot mattered. She smiled her gratitude. He allowed a little warmth to creep into his frown. They parted.

Her pro-American driver held the door open. She looked around for a clock. Thirteen minutes to twelve. 'Damn, damn, damn,' she muttered.

'Pan Am. *Doze horas.* Okay.' He smiled reassuringly.

'No, it's not okay. Not any more.' She was still struggling to catch up with the decision she had made back there inside the bank; almost certainly a bad decision and one she'd regret, but all that was irrelevant now. 'Forget New York,' she told him. 'Take the stuff, the *bagagem*, back to the *pensão*. Okay? *Pensão São Vicente.* How much? *Quanto custa?'*

It took a little while before he was convinced that she was serious, but eventually he left, looking disapproving. She began strolling up and down the street, watching the bank. Noon struck at various times from various churches, as if to make a point of repeating what a blunder she'd made. At that moment somebody on stand-by for the Pan Am Clipper to New York was about to be made very happy. Now that the sun was overhead, the *Rua do Comercio* was getting very hot. *Possibly tomorrow*, the man had said. She began to feel hungry. It was going to be a long time until the bank closed. What a way to kill an afternoon.

*

By two-thirty the air in the street was sultry and dead. The only time it moved was when a car or a truck displaced it. The bowl of Lisbon trapped the steamy heat, and people stewed in it.

Julie's legs ached from standing. Her skin was sticky, and she felt as if she'd been wearing the same underwear since Christmas. Every few minutes she moved on and looked in the window of a different shop. She had become expert at watching the bank in the reflection. She had also developed a tremendous respect for cops' feet: they walked their beat for twice or three times as long as this, without complaining. But not without eating. She had a vision of a half-pound hamburger, medium-rare with onions, hot off the grill, so real she could taste it. She'd give a hundred bucks for that hamburger, and another hundred for a cold beer. Sweat briefly stuck her thighs together. She'd give a cool thousand for a cold shower.

Three o'clock struck and struck and struck. The shops which had closed for lunch began to reopen. Julie propped herself in front of a display of men's shoes and wondered gloomily how much Pan Am would give her back on her ticket. She watched a man in uniform who was standing outside the bank, and realised that he was a cop, and then realised that he was watching her. *What's on your mind, buster?* she thought; and the answer presented itself quite obviously. Hang around a city bank for two or three hours and the law takes an interest in you. At once she turned and strolled away. The cop strolled with her, stopped when she stopped. She did some more double-window-shopping until he made a move to cross the street, so she went inside the damn shop.

It was a bookshop. There was one spot near the front which gave her a good view of the bank. She opened a fat cookbook, frowned over the recipes, glanced up, and found the cop on the other side of the glass. He was young and intelligent-looking. *Oh Christ*, she thought, *do they arrest you for this sort of thing in Portugal?* She changed the cookbook for a dictionary. The cop watched, and chewed his lip, and Luis Cabrillo came out of the bank.

She must have twitched, because the cop turned to look too. Despite a big hat and a small moustache there was no doubt; Luis's walk, his build, the way he held his head—she recognised them all. He was walking away. She dumped the dictionary and darted out.

She followed him and the cop followed her.

Luis turned the corner and headed north, away from the river. If traffic clogged an intersection he turned west for a block, then north again. He walked unhurriedly and un-worriedly, never looking back.

Julie felt shaky with a blend of tension, hunger and anxiety. She was out of her depth, worried about the policeman, afraid of what she might get led into, yet driven by the simple excitement of it all. As they crossed the big square called the Rossio, it flashed through her mind that perhaps he knew she was there, and knew the policeman was following her; perhaps he meant to keep on walking until they both gave up; Lisbon was big enough, and he had that sort of determination. But no: halfway along a side street, he went into an oldfashioned, severe-looking office building. She noted the number, 23, as she hurried past, pretending she was heading elsewhere. The street was quiet and the cop's footsteps sounded crisply. Her mouth felt dry but her body was sweating and one ear was singing as if from a change in altitude. She pounded on, too scared to stop but without the slightest idea where she was going; turned a corner, pounded some more, turned again, saw a taxi cruising by, waved, shouted, and got it. Small sensation of triumph.

'Alfama,' she said, the only place she could think of. He took off. She counted to ten, and looked out of the rear window. The cop was standing on one leg while he scratched the other and watched them go. He looked lonely and tired.

Her driver took a bewilderingly zig-zag route. After a couple of minutes she reckoned she was safe, so she stopped him, paid him, began walking back, and soon discovered that she was lost. This was obviously a moment for reason and commonsense. She knew Alfama was to the east. The sun, still glaringly hot, should by now be moving to the west. It was towards the north that she wanted to go. She re-oriented herself and set off again. But the streets kept curving and cheating, and ten minutes' hard walking left her looking at a dusty neighbourhood of grey, prison-like warehouses.

She plodded on and caught a bus. The idea that it might go anywhere near the Rossio vastly amused the conductor. He showed her where to get the right tram. She got the wrong tram and had to change again. When eventually she reached the Rossio it was 4.30 and her skull was throbbing to a headache. She headed for the side-street in a thoroughly foul temper. Nothing much had gone right this day. If anybody got in her way now she was in a mood to punch his teeth in.

Number 23 had been built to last, and that was a mistake. Everything about it was too big: hulking doorways, remote ceilings, a high-stepped staircase which climbed around a lift-shaft the size of a lion's cage. The lift was out of order.

The hallway was empty and patrolled by three flies. Julie slashed at them and made them scatter. She looked for a list of tenants: nothing. The ground-floor offices had *Nogueira-Ricardo Lda.* painted on the door. Whatever business they did in there, they did it silently. As she went up the oversized steps, the three flies were back on patrol.

Next floor: *João Arouca, Antiguidades*. Above him: *Instito Folclórico*. Julie trudged on. *Vasco da Gama Ferreira, Engenheiro* and *P. G. Melo, dentista*. Another flight. *Lopes e Coelho Lda.* faced *Arte Rústica de Madeira Lda.* She paused for breath. Somewhere far below, a man coughed, once, as if in his sleep. With each floor the smell of dust and defeat grew stronger. The sixth floor was the last. It was also the only office with no name on the door.

She held her breath and listened. Nothing except a certain pounding in her ears. She thought: *What if he is in there? What do I say?* and then: *What if someone else answers? Some total stranger? What if . . .* She released her breath and rapped smartly on the glass before things got worse.

Nobody answered.

There was a letterslot. She crouched and peered through it. A big room, gaunt-looking, with an office table and a type-writer. 'Hey, you in there!' she called through the slot.

One half of her had very cold feet and wanted to beat it right now, urging sensibly that everything possible had been done. 'Just shut up!' she snarled, and delivered another angry rap on the glass. It cracked. They were small panes, set in lead, and this one had cracked from edge to edge. The half of her with cold feet felt slightly sick.

She squinted through the slot again and saw a letter on the table. She stood up and thought about that.

The cracked pane resisted the pressure of her thumbs, but eventually the lead channelling around it stretched and split. The glass fell inside and smashed.

Nobody heard. Nobody came. Her hand was trembling as she reached through and turned the handle.

It was her letter. Torn open and quickly read, by the look of it: the single sheet of notepaper hastily stuffed back in the envelope.

Right all along.

She felt some relief and a great amount of bitterness. He

277

never told the truth. A cheat and a swindler. He used everyone for his own gain, without having the balls and the bravado to admit it. He lied and then he ran away. Here was proof.

It was a bleak sort of room, just a few thin books on a shelf, two scruffy filing cabinets, the table, the chair, the typewriter. It made her feel empty just to look at it: her determined hunting had brought her to this dusty nothingness. The typewriter had paper in it. She sat and read, and became steadily enraged.

To: TOMCAT
From: ELDORADO
Subject: Allied Convoy Routes, North Atlantic
I have today returned from further discussions in Liverpool with SEAGULL (whom I paid according to the rates agreed with you; he asked me to express his satisfaction) and also with a colleague of SEAGULL's employed in the Liverpool oil-storage depot. They informed me that the British Admiralty is now so concerned about the sinkings of ships by U-boats that it plans to introduce a new convoy system.

The essence of this is the separation of fast and slow merchant ships into different convoys, so that the fast convoy may stand a better chance of getting through, while the slow convoy is to be more heavily defended.

SEAGULL's colleague has information that slow convoys will include a very high proportion of oil tankers, thus making them an unusually attractive target for U-boat attack. SEAGULL himself has gathered details of planned convoy sailings in the next 4—6 weeks and I include these in his report, attached.

Morale among seamen, especially those who have experi

The ink faded as the ribbon ran out. Julie re-read the page, not because the meaning was unclear but because it was too clear. She got up and searched the filing cabinets. There were files marked Convoy, Troop Movements, Airfields, Naval Strength, Rationing, Civilian Morale; each holding carbon copies of typed reports which were dense with facts and figures. She heaved the cabinets shut and leaned on them. She would have liked to cry but crying would be an act of self-pity at a time when millions of others needed far more pity than she could ever create. Pity couldn't help them but maybe

278

action would: destroying all his lousy stinking files, for a start. She tugged open a drawer and something rattled in the back. She opened the drawer completely. It was a gun. A large revolver. It had a lanyard-ring on the base of the butt and its cylinder looked as fat as a pineapple. She picked it up. Her hands were strong but her fingers barely reached the trigger. Out on the end of the barrel the foresight stuck up like a thumbnail.

She carried it over to the desk. It was very heavy, like carrying a mason's hammer. There were patches of rust, scratches, dents. Was it loaded? She shook it: nothing rattled. She despised her stupidity: bullets don't *rattle*, for God's sake. With enormous caution she broke it open. Six bullets filled six holes. She was holding a goddam six-shooter. She closed the gun and spun the cylinder, not knowing why but if Hollywood always did it there must be a reason; found the safety and thumbed it back.

She knew what to do. She found herself staring at the unfinished report in the typewriter, not seeing the words clearly because her eyes were filling with tears. The tears were for the unknown seaman and his tortured face. Her eyes were blurred but her mind was very clear. Nobody could be allowed to go on doing that sort of thing. Nobody.

Probably because of her tears she didn't hear the footsteps until they reached the last flight of stairs, but that was plenty of time. As the door handle turned she finished wiping her eyes and got a good grip of the revolver. When Luis Cabrillo came in she only had to pull the trigger and the gun went off with a roar like a quarry-blast. He fell as if his legs had been hooked. Julie didn't see him drop. She was on her back, and her wrist hurt like fire.

Chapter 42

Otto Krafft met Wolfgang Adler on the way to the weekly review meeting. 'How's the old foot coming along?' he asked.

'They remove the plaster next week.'

'Oh, good.'

The two men covered half the length of the corridor without saying any more. Otto strolled while Wolfgang trudged.

'Look, Wolfgang: I know you've had rotten luck with your leg and so on,' Otto said, 'but can I give you some advice? Try and forget you ever met Eldorado, and for heaven's sake drop this one-man vendetta against him. You can't win.'

'It's not a matter of winning. It's a matter of the truth.'

'So you say, and that's all very noble, but you'll never persuade Christian to drop Eldorado, will you? He's doing too well out of him. I happen to know there's a promotion on the way, and the section budget's already gone up forty per cent.'

'I don't care.'

'Then you ought to. And please don't push your luck today. The old man's feeling a bit liverish. We can all do without your dyspeptic help, thanks very much.'

For most of the meeting, Wolfgang sat silent while the others went over the activities of what was now known as the Eldorado Network. Occasionally he cleared his throat and suggested a possible weakness or an omission, but these were few and nobody else considered them important. Christian cut the discussion short. 'That's all,' he said. 'Eldorado continues to show every sign of becoming one of the *Abwehr's* most successful operatives.'

Wolfgang sucked his teeth in a way that made the others look.

Christian said: 'An important factor in Eldorado's success is his adaptability. In this business it's dangerous to let yourself become inflexible. If an attitude gets you nowhere— change it. That completes everything for today.' He stood, and the others gathered their papers.

'Nothing about America,' Wolfgang said.

Christian ignored him. When the lack of response became uncomfortably obvious, Otto said: 'What do you want about America?'

'How do I know? I'm not in England. But there must be something. The U.S.A. has given Britain fifty destroyers.'

'Not given,' Fischer said. 'Exchanged. Lend-Lease.'

'Which means America is in the war.'

'Rubbish,' Christian said. 'And furthermore Roosevelt has said—'

280

'Yes, I read it in the papers.'

'Well then.' Christian was annoyed at being interrupted.

'I read the papers in 1938 too,' Wolfgang said, 'when some-one announced that he had no further territorial demands in Europe.'

That brought a considerable silence.

'Make your point,' Christian snapped. 'I haven't got all day.'

'My point is that Eldorado has failed to report any American intelligence of—'

'Yes, all right, put it in a memo.' Christian started banging open his desk drawers, noisily searching for something. Wolf-gang sat stiffly for a moment, and then just as stiffly walked out.

The others followed, except Otto Krafft. Christian gave up his search and thumped the last drawer shut with his knee. 'Yes?' he barked.

'It may be nothing, sir,' Otto said, 'but I thought you ought to know I've had a rather unusual offer from someone in the Swiss embassy.'

'*You?* Why you?'

Otto shrugged modestly. 'Don't know, sir. Perhaps he met me somewhere and remembered my name.'

'Who is he?'

'Oh, nobody you'd recognise, sir. A very junior attaché. That's what makes it all so unusual.'

Christian dropped into his chair and heaved both feet onto his desk. 'Then you'd better get it off your chest, hadn't you?' he said.

'Well, sir,' Otto began.

*

The ambulance doubled as a hearse. It was a glossy black with a lot of chromium trim and the driver kept a wreath under his seat which, when necessary, covered the red light on the roof. There was nothing he could do to alter the inside, which had ample room for a coffin or a stretcher but only cramped space for anyone sitting alongside. Luis Cabrillo lay on the stretcher. Julie Conroy braced herself in her seat and tried to keep her right arm absolutely still in its sling.

'Well, you can't say you didn't have it coming to you,' she said. 'You asked for it and you got it. Right?'

The ambulance took a corner and Luis Cabrillo rolled slightly, then rolled back again.

'Until the doctors have made their examination,' he said, 'I suggest you talk as little as possible. You may be concussed.'

She thought about that for a while.

'Who were all those people?' she asked.

'From the other offices. They heard the noise. I told them you fell off the table while changing the light bulb.' He sounded terse and formal. Like his new moustache.

'Oh yes. Bits of glass everywhere.'

'I did that.'

'Terrific. You're a terrific liar, aren't you? Let me tell you one thing. You had it coming to you, mac. You and your terrific lies.'

She felt suddenly dizzy. She shut her eyes, and time began doing its accordion-trick again, stretching itself out very slowly for a spell and then squeezing itself together very fast. It was hard to keep track of what was happening.

When the accordion-trick stopped, they were sitting in a hospital room and her wrist was in plaster. She was sipping a glass of blue liquid. It tasted red. She examined his face and was pleased to notice that it was extremely pale and tired.

'I see you bled to death, then,' she said. 'That's good. I'm very very glad. You had it coming and I'm glad I gave it to you. Glad.'

There was a tiny graze on his chin. He touched it with the tip of one finger.

'Have you ever fired a revolver before?' he asked.

That was very funny, asking an American if she'd ever fired a revolver before, hell of a joke, made her laugh out loud. 'Never,' she said.

'You were holding it like this.' He crooked his arm as if his hand held an imaginary teacup. 'All wrong.'

'They do it like that in the movies.'

'You hit the picture-rail.'

A doctor came in, shone a light in each of her eyes, said something in Portuguese, and went out.

'Listen, you Spanish shit,' she said. 'As soon as this plaster gets good and hard I'm going to beat your goddam head in. Okay?'

'Okay,' he said. Anger sent blood pounding into her head,

282

and that triggered off the accordion-trick again, stretching and squeezing time for the best part of a good bit.

The next clear scene happened in a restaurant. There was a lot of bustle and she was not eating an omelette.

'You wanted it so much,' he said. 'Eat the bloody thing.'

'It tastes green. Looks yellow but that doesn't fool me. Definite greeny taste.' She stuck her fork in it like a flagpole. Slowly it toppled. 'See?' she said. 'Not ripe.'

'Well . . . have something else.' He sawed at his steak. 'The hospital said your blood-sugar level is low. Understand? You need to eat.'

She watched the bustle until it hurt her eyes, so she looked instead at his steak.

'Ever seen a sailor with a face like that?' she demanded. 'I have. And it's *your goddam fault*!' She threw a punch at him with her overloaded arm, and fell off her chair. After that the bustle intensified considerably.

There was a car, which looked deep red but smelled light brown. There was an elevator which sang to itself and was definitely the happiest thing she had met all day. There was a bedroom, with Luis Cabrillo handing her a pair of his pyjamas. She handed them back. 'Stripes keep me awake,' she accused, stiffly.

'Jesus Christ Almighty,' he said. He sat on the bed and rubbed his face. 'This is just what I don't need. There is so much work I—'

'Yeah, sure, I know, I saw. Convoys, oil tankers. All that spying shit. I know, chum. It's a hell of a hard life. Not as hard as getting torpedoed and drowned, but nearly. Why don't—'

'If you're so damn sure I'm spying for the Germans,' he said harshly, 'then what am I doing living in Lisbon?'

She couldn't answer that, so she glared instead.

'Listen.' He stood up. 'Tonight I must work. Tomorrow I shall explain. Now go to bed.'

This time she was ready for him. 'If you're *not* spying for the Germans,' she said, 'why are you writing to them about convoys?'

'I really don't think you are in a condition to understand.'

'No? It seems pretty clear to me. You're working for the bastards.'

'Yes, I am. But I'm not *spying* for them. I'm not spying for anyone, anywhere.'

'But they're paying you.'

'Yes.'

'For nothing?'

'No, for information which they think I get from Britain. But I don't.'

'Then where do you get it?'

'I make it up.'

Julie sneered as hard as she could. 'I don't believe you!' she shouted. Her head reverberated painfully.

'Good,' Luis said. 'The more incredible you find the truth, the less likely the *Abwehr* is to suspect it.'

'All you ever gave me was lies,' she said. Her eyes were getting very tired. She had difficulty focusing on him. 'You're a shitty German spy and I'm going to kill you,' she insisted. 'I'm going to kill both of you.'

'Fine. Do it tomorrow. Now I'm going to work.' He switched off the light and went out.

She took off all her clothes, dragging the sleeves over the plaster cast, and got into bed. Immediately she had an idea. If Luis really wasn't a genuine German spy, she could inform Colonel Christian of that fact and Christian would therefore arrange to have him killed. There was something wrong with this idea, but she fell asleep before she could work it out.

Chapter 43

There was a note on the kitchen table. It read : *5.30 a.m. Gone to bed. Please wake me at 10.30. Coffee in big blue and white jar. Beware hot water very hot.*

Julie, wearing a red towelling robe she had found hanging behind the door, padded around the apartment. It was spacious : four rooms, kitchen and bathroom. One room was shut. Presumably he was asleep in there.

She stood and looked at the door and tried to make sense of her scrambled memories of yesterday. A corpse, a cop, several

284

taxis, a revolver as big as a starting cannon, pain, anger, steamy heat, bustle, bad temper, night, lies, exhaustion. They made no sense. Nothing made sense at that moment except her stomach. It sent a loud, clear message. She went back to the kitchen, found coffee, bread and eggs, and cooked breakfast, slowly because the plaster cast made her virtually one-handed.

Sunlight flooded the room. There was a balcony with scarlet geraniums and a view over Lisbon so huge that it made her breathe deeply just to look at it: a flood of angled, red-tiled roofs falling away to the glittering Tagus. The coffee was good, too. She remembered that it was all bought with German money, asked herself whether she should be enjoying it, and got the answer: *Why not?*

Just after ten he appeared in pyjamas, looking stiff and tired, and raised a hand in greeting. She said nothing. He put water on to boil, went into the bathroom, came out shaved and awake, made coffee.

'You had breakfast?' he asked, looking at the dishes in the sink.

She rapped her cast with her knuckles. 'Can't wash up with this,' she said.

He ate a rapid breakfast of bread rolls and black coffee.

'Can you dress yourself?' he asked.

'Are we going somewhere?'

'We're going to the office.'

'Suppose I don't want to go to the office.'

'Suppose you shut up and get dressed.'

They took a taxi. When they arrived, the lift still wasn't working and the three flies on patrol had been joined by two friends. Because the staircase climbed to the right she could not hold on to the banister. The climb left her with leaden feet and gasping lungs. Luis Cabrillo said nothing until they were in the office.

'Let's get one thing clear from the start,' he told her. 'I didn't ask you to find me, and life would have been a lot easier for me if you had stayed away.'

'You and Hitler both, maybe.'

'Please shut up and listen. I have a great deal of work to do today. The only reason I'm taking the time to explain my situation to you is because otherwise you might go to the

German embassy with a story of your own, and I can't afford that risk.'

'I don't collaborate with krauts,' she muttered.

'Alternatively you might go to the British embassy, and I can't risk that either.'

'Sure. You don't want the truth to get around.'

'I certainly don't. As long as the Germans think I'm spying on the British for them, they're happy. As long as the British don't know what the Germans think, they're happy too. So let's not upset people with the facts.'

There was a muscular discipline about Luis Cabrillo that surprised her. 'I'm not people,' she said. 'Go ahead and upset the hell out of me.'

'The simplest way is to start at the beginning. The German embassy in Madrid trained me as a spy and—'

'Whose idea was that?'

He waved the question away. 'Irrelevant. They believe I'm now operating in England and communicating with them via the Spanish embassy in London. In theory I give my reports to a man in the London embassy who sends them in the diplomatic bag to Lisbon where someone else forwards them to Madrid. In fact when I left Spain I never went further than Lisbon. The reality is that I write all my reports here in this office and then mail them to the *Abwehr* in Madrid. That's what I was doing all last night. I produced four thousand words of secret information about Great Britain and her allies, which is on its way to Madrid right now. Colonel Christian, whom you met, should be reading it first thing tomorrow.'

'No,' she said. 'That doesn't work. There must be things *they* want to say to *you*. Instructions, messages. *Payment*, for God's sake. According to you it's all one-way traffic. I don't believe the spy business works that way.'

'They communicate,' he said. 'In theory the system works in reverse. The *Abwehr* writes to an address in Lisbon. My friend in the Spanish embassy here collects the letter, off it goes to London in the bag. I get it from my contact there. In fact what happens is I simply pick up the letters myself.'

'From the bank?'

'Correct.'

'And money? You expect me to believe they pay you through the mail, too?'

286

'I have bank accounts here and in Switzerland. My earnings are automatically credited to one of them.'

'Meanwhile in England you live off wholesome fattening English air.'

'Not at all. As a Spanish citizen, a neutral, who is doing business in England, I can easily transfer funds from Lisbon.'

'You can, sure. But you don't.'

Luis rubbed his chin. 'You have a point. Perhaps I should open an account in London, for the sake of appearances.' He scribbled a note.

'Meanwhile,' she said, 'all those highpowered experts in German military intelligence are dumb enough to keep on buying the fairy-tales you're supposed to have been sending them.'

Luis shrugged. 'It is true. What else can I say?'

'You've never been to England. You don't know any British people. But you come up here every day and just sit down and invent their secrets.'

'Not quite. I have some reference books which help me.' He took them off a shelf and showed her.

'This explains everything,' she said. '*1923 Michelin Guide to Great Britain*. Gee whiz. Great Western Railway's *Holiday Haunts*, price sixpence, the rare 1937 edition. *Plus* would you believe this evergreen of the schoolroom, *Exploring the British Isles* by Jasper H. Stembridge, Book 4!' She opened it at random. '*Spring in the Fen-lands,*' she read out, '*and the farmers are busy ploughing the huge, flat fields.*' She shut it. 'Gee, I bet Colonel Christian never knew *that* until you told him. I bet he leaped to the telephone and called Berlin in a white-hot frenzy and—'

'That page,' Luis said, 'gave me all the basic information I needed for a big report on R.A.F. airfields in eastern England.' He took the books back. 'And I shall be very surprised if some of what I wrote isn't actually true. If it isn't true, the R.A.F. is making a big mistake, that's all I can say.'

Julie looked around the bare, dingy room, and sniffed. 'I don't believe you, Luis,' she said. A sliver of broken lightbulb glinted on the floor. She picked it up and dropped it on the desk. 'I don't believe they'd send you off on your own like that. I don't believe they'd trust your crazy diplomatic-bag system. I don't believe you're brilliant enough to invent phony reports, and I don't believe they'd be so damn-fool gullible as to swallow an endless stream of crap.'

'I see,' he said.

She felt very tired. She sat at his desk and rested her plaster cast on the scratched and dented surface.

'What *do* you believe?' he asked.

She looked at him. He was thinner than he had been in Madrid, and he seemed constantly to be thinking about something else. 'I believe there's a simple answer to everything,' she said. 'You've been spying like hell in Britain, you're back here on a flying visit, and you made up all that stuff to keep me quiet.'

They thought about that, in silence. He picked gently at the graze on his chin until he made it bleed. He inspected the blood on his fingertip and carefully licked it off.

'In that case there's only one thing to do,' he said. 'You'll just have to stay here and see for yourself.'

'Well, that's better than what I expected,' she said. 'I thought you were going to take out your howitzer and blow my head off.'

'I fight a non-violent war,' he said. 'You'd better find something to read. This report I'm doing is all about Commando training in north Wales, and it'll take at least two hours.'

She picked up Jasper H. Stembridge. 'Which are the juicy bits?' she asked.

'Try chapter nine: "The Busy Midlands",' Luis said. 'A veritable goldmine.'

*

'Read this,' said Meredith. 'Then you'll know as much as I do.'

While Squadron Leader Blake read it, Meredith poured tea for them both. He chose a digestive biscuit and dunked it in his tea. 'Frightful habit,' he murmured.

Blake looked at the back of the paper, which was blank. 'Not much to go on, is there, sir? Just the name, when you boil it all down.'

'Eldorado. Mean anything?'

'Only ice-cream. Stop-me-and-buy-one, the Eldorado man on a tricycle. Haven't we got an agent codenamed Tricycle?'

'Yes.'

288

'No connection, though, I shouldn't think.'

'No.'

They sipped their tea. 'Perhaps London's asking us because it's Spanish, sir,' Blake suggested. 'Eldorado: something to do with gold, isn't it?'

'Mmm. Means "the gilded one" or "the golden one". That could signify anything from bullion-smuggling to blondes.'

'London seem sure it was an *Abwehr* signal they intercepted. I suppose that's something. On the other hand the transmitter was in *Hamburg*, sir. Miles from here.'

Meredith glanced at the decoded message again. '*Context suggests Eldorado involves high-grade operation*,' he read. 'That means London is worried and guessing furiously. I bet this signal's gone to every office from Stockholm to Kabul. Still . . . Keep your ears open, Teddy. Chat up the neutral embassies, you never know your luck. Madrid's a very chatty place.'

'Yes sir. Of course, if Eldorado's a German agent, he won't actually be in Madrid, will he? He'll be in England.'

'Perhaps that's what's worrying London.'

'Perhaps.' Blake stared at the dregs of his tea, and sighed. 'It really was awfully good ice-cream,' he said.

*

Julie read the last page of the report and handed it back. 'Impressive,' she said.

'I chose the north part of Wales because of the mountains.' Luis opened Jasper H. Stembridge at chapter seven and showed her a photograph of Mount Snowdon. 'Stembridge says: "Here and there ranges and peaks, rising above the surrounding uplands, add more rugged charm to the wild wind-swept moors". Doesn't that sound to you like ideal country for training British Commandos?'

'Oh, perfectly spiffing,' she said.

'And if you check it against the section for North Wales in the GWR Holiday Haunts . . .' He thumbed through that book. 'Yes: "a scattered rural population . . . towns are neither numerous nor large . . . happy hunting ground for those in search of perfect peace and seclusion", and so on. I bet it's stiff with Commandos.'

'No question. I liked that bit about using live ammunition and the casualty rate.'

'Yes. You see, it works two ways at once. The Germans are impressed by the *toughness* of Commando training, but they're also pleased to know that so many British soldiers get hurt by it. You don't think I went too far with the casualty statistics? Four point seven three per cent: maybe it sounds *too* precise.'

'Well, you got it straight from that medical corporal you met in the bar at wherever-it-was.'

'The Royal Victoria Hotel, Llanberis.' Luis opened the 1923 Michelin Guide at a page marked with a ribbon. 'Five miles north of Snowdon. Lunch three shillings and sixpence, dinner five shillings, parking for forty cars. I don't think he was staying at the hotel, not on his pay. He just popped in for a drink.'

'The angry chicken-farmer was good too.'

'It's just a matter of identification. I said to myself, "Imagine you live in a remote and tranquil area. Suddenly troops arrive and begin firing sten guns and bren guns and shooting off mortars and throwing grenades, at all hours of the day and night. What is the effect?" Obvious: the farmers complain. They say the noise alarms their chickens, which stop laying, and they demand compensation.'

'And you actually saw all this training.'

'It's not a prohibited area. I make that clear in paragraph one.'

'So what are they training *for?*'

Luis shrugged. 'Not even they know that. But as I point out, those Welsh mountains are very steep, like cliffs.'

'Uh-huh. More Commando raids on the coast of Europe.'

'I leave that for the *Abwehr*'s experts to decide.'

'The human touch. Neat.'

'Well . . .' Luis stretched enormously. 'Now you've seen for yourself. That's how it's done.' He put the books back on the shelf.

'No, I don't think so,' Julie said.

'Come with me to the post office, if you like.'

'Oh, I'm sure you'll mail it. This stuff is too good to waste.'

'Then what more do you want?' Luis slapped a carbon copy into a file and slammed the file cabinet shut. 'Short of getting

Colonel Christian on the telephone and—'

'Hell, no, I'm sure he loves your stuff too. So he should. It's all true.'

'You just saw me—'

'I just saw you do another snow job. You were in north Wales last week, or whenever, and you personally saw all that Commando training, which is why it sounds so convincing. Nice try, Luis. A little *too* nice, maybe. About four point seven three per cent too nice.'

He sat on his desk and rubbed his eyes. When he took his hands away, his fingers were trembling slightly.

'Incidentally, Angela sends her love,' she said.

'Angela?' He sounded flat and tired.

'You wouldn't remember Angela. You wouldn't even remember Freddy. And Freddy wouldn't remember you, that's for sure.'

Luis gave her a long, speculative look. She stared back, unblinking. He looked away.

'I don't blame you,' she said. 'I wouldn't want to talk about it either. Not even for a snow job.'

He stood up. 'It's time for lunch.'

'Just give me an aspirin. This wrist hurts.'

'Aspirin. I see. There is a *farmácia* around the corner.' He frowned. 'What is that in English?'

'Who the hell cares?' she said. Her anger had the raw edge of bitterness. They went downstairs in silence. At the *farmácia* Luis bought aspirin and asked for a glass of water. While she was swallowing the tablets he asked: 'Will you come with me to the bank, later?' She nodded. If she had shaken her head she might have choked.

They ate a silent lunch in a noisy restaurant overlooking the Rossio, and walked down to the Rua do Comercio. It was hot again, and the streets were quiet. The Banco Espirito Santo received them into its cool and spacious gloom, and when Luis tapped the bell on the *Secçao Estrangeira* counter, the same sombre three-piece-suit came forward.

'*Boa tarde, senhor Cabrillo.*' He registered Julie's presence with a minimal flicker of the eyes.

'Good afternoon,' Luis said, a fraction more clearly than was necessary; and Julie knew he was speaking English for her benefit. 'Are there any letters for me?'

'I shall see.'

He came back with a stiff brown envelope, heavily sealed. Luis had to sign for it. He showed her the form: it carried a longish column of his signatures, at least ten of them. 'Three or four times each week I come here,' he said.

'Or someone with your signature.'

The three-piece-suit pretended not to hear that.

'What days did I come in last week?'

'Monday, Wednesday and Friday, *senhor*. As usual.'

'Yes. I'd like to see a statement of my account, please.'

'Of course, *senhor*.'

Julie studied it. There were regular weekly credits during the previous month. The sums increased towards the end. There were a few extra credits, each rounded off to the nearest thousand escudos. Luis pointed at those. 'Bonus payments,' he said. She looked at the last figure and did a quick conversion in her head. Luis had something over twelve hundred dollars in the bank. 'So they pay you,' she said. 'So what?'

Luis returned the statement and they went out into the street.

'I don't exactly know what to do now,' he said. 'I hoped you would believe the man in the bank.'

'Bankers are finks. We're all finks, according to you. The Germans are idiots, because they buy your junk, I'm an idiot, because I *don't* buy your junk. You probably think the British are idiots, too. And the Russians.'

'Well, the British *are* idiots,' Luis said, remembering his visit to the embassy in Madrid. 'Sometimes.'

'And you're the lonely genius who's making a killing out of this war. Terrific.'

'I wish—'

'You wish you could pack me off to America with a pat on the head, so that you could get back to Britain and make your pile before peace breaks out and spoils everything.'

'I have never been to Britain,' Luis insisted. 'I have no wish to go to Britain. Why should I?'

'No reason at all. Who wants to live with an idiot?'

'This is becoming silly. Look: I can show you my passport, it hasn't a single—'

'Oh, passports, passports, I can show you a guy here in Lisbon who sells 'em by the yard, he gets them off dead

292

British seamen. Want to see what those guys look like? Not like their passport pictures, I can tell you. Give yourself a break, Luis, take the afternoon off, go browse through the British seamen's morgue. After all, who deserves it more? You helped put the poor bastards there.'

'You are determined to hate me.'

'I hate what you're doing.'

Luis sucked his teeth. They were walking slowly, and he was stepping between the cracks in the pavingstones.

'What's in that?' she demanded, pointing at the stiff brown envelope. 'Is it from them?'

'Yes. Probably a new briefing.'

'Show me.'

The letter contained two sheets of typewritten instructions. She scanned them quickly. 'Are you going to answer this?'

'In due course.'

'No.' She folded the pages and stuffed them down the front of her dress. 'You're going to answer it today, right now. They want a report on the new British paratroop school near Oxford, and they want your opinion of the chances of an Allied attack on Norway this year.'

He stopped and stared at her.

'What's the matter: can't you do it?' she asked crisply.

'I worked all bloody yesterday,' he said. 'Then you came and ruined my evening, so I had to work all bloody night. Then I got four hours bad sleep and went back and hammered out all that bloody Commando stuff. And now you want me to do *what*?'

'Do what you say you can do.'

Luis's shoulders slumped. He squinted wearily into the glare. 'Tomorrow,' he said.

'Piss, or get off the pot,' she told him. 'I'll be waiting for you in the Rossio in . . . let's see . . . three hours.'

'I can't work that fast,' he pleaded.

'Tough luck. I'll be knocking on the front door of the British embassy in three hours and five minutes.'

Luis groaned.

'And while I remember,' she said, 'that's a really lousy moustache.'

She watched him trudge away.

Chapter 44

'In short, Eldorado continues to live up to his name,' said Richard Fischer. He had just finished his analysis of the latest reports from Knickers, the soft-drinks salesman. Franz had already dealt with the information supplied by Seagull, the Liverpool docker.

It was all good, worthwhile stuff. As Dr Hartmann pointed out, the great thing about Eldorado was that, when he forwarded material from his sub-agents, he distinguished clearly between observed fact, reported fact, and rumour. It made evaluation and deduction so much easier. One always knew where one stood. Everyone nodded except Wolfgang Adler; he sat in the same attitude he had held since the meeting began : legs crossed at the ankle, thumbs hooked into his belt-loops, eyes staring at nothing in particular.

'The last item today,' Colonel Christian announced, 'is also good news. It seems that we may have recruited a second Eldorado.'

Wolfgang's eyes came up at that, but not for long.

'The other day, Otto Krafft came to me and asked permission to follow up a contact initially made through a member of the Swiss embassy. This has now led to an American businessman of German origin, Mr Francis X. Tanenbaum of Oklahoma.' Christian suddenly frowned, and cocked his head. 'Oklahoma?'

'Arizona,' Otto said. There was a gentle ripple of amusement, except for Wolfgang, who closed his eyes.

'An understandable mistake,' Christian defended blandly, 'both states being populated entirely by cattle and film producers.'

'Which are themselves easily confused,' Franz Werth added.

'Not at all,' Fischer said. 'The ones you see stampeding in a cloud of dust are the producers.'

'Arizona,' Christian went on. 'Otto has established that Tanenbaum regularly trades with and visits Britain *and* Spain.

Now, however, he has indicated his willingness to trade with the *Abwehr*.'

'If he's any good,' Dr Hartmann said, 'that could be very good.'

'Well, he's certainly fairly shrewd,' Christian remarked, 'because we know that Tanenbaum is not his real name, he doesn't come from Oklahoma or Arizona, and he will do business with only one representative of the *Abwehr*, and that's the man he first met.' Christian indicated Otto. Otto looked mildly pleased.

'What *do* we know about him?' Fischer asked.

'He's a successful, middle-aged American businessman, with extreme right-wing and ultra-Catholic beliefs,' Otto said. 'His father and uncle were killed in the last war. On the eastern front,' he added.

'Explains a lot,' Franz commented.

'We need a codename,' Christian said. 'Any suggestions?'

'How about "Cowboy"?' Fischer suggested, and immediately shook his head. 'Too obvious.'

'Bathtub,' said Franz. They looked at him. 'It just popped into my head,' he explained.

'Eagle?' Dr Hartmann proposed.

'Eagle . . .' Richard Fischer mused.

'Eagle it is,' Christian decided. He peered over his glasses at Otto. 'Open a file, start an account and pay Eagle some money. I have great faith in the boundless greed of businessmen.'

The meeting ended. As they went out, Christian raised a finger in Wolfgang's direction. 'Are you feeling better, Adler?' he asked.

Wolfgang shrugged. 'Somewhat,' he said.

'I'm very happy to hear it.' But Christian didn't look very happy. Wolfgang left.

*

The air in the Rossio was as warm as fresh milk. The buildings framed an astonishingly amiable sky where a few soft strips of high cloud lay motionless, like rippled sand under clear blue water. Julie Conroy rested on a bench, watching the clouds do nothing, and doing nothing in return. It was a deal she had made with them. A non-aggression pact. So far both sides had honoured it fully.

A package landed in her lap and jolted her awake. Luis was ten minutes early. She opened the big envelope and began reading the contents. He went across to a fountain and took a long time over washing his face. Then he sat on the rim of the fountain and watched a few pigeons. Occasionally he flicked some water and made them jump. His shirt had stuck to his back, but now the cool air around the fountain was beginning to release it.

Julie read the papers, twice. She slid them back into the envelope and tucked the flap in. She waited while he put his hand in the fountain and ran it through his hair. She waited while he wiped his hand on his shirt. She even waited while he leaned back and enjoyed looking at the sky, before she realised that he might sit there for the rest of the evening, so she got up and went over.

'Okay,' she said. 'I believe you.'

He didn't take the envelope. He didn't speak.

'You'd better have this back,' she said. 'And this.' She held out the letter from the *Abwehr* in Madrid.

He examined the middle finger of his right hand, calloused from the pressure of a pen, and he sucked the callous. 'Do you think my answers will satisfy them?' he enquired.

'No. I'm sorry, Luis. I invented different questions. You see, I had to make sure you're as good as you said.'

He turned his head, slowly, and looked at the envelope. 'So that's all wasted.' His eyelids were heavy with fatigue, but his eyes had a curious glitter. 'Keep it,' he said. 'Go away. I have seen enough of you.'

She went away, turned north, walked halfway up the Avenida da Liberdade, found the Pan Am office. She changed her ticket for cash, and checked into the nearest hotel. 'One night,' she told the desk clerk. '*Uma noite.*' Luis Cabrillo had seen enough of her, and she could understand that; but she was far from finished with him. The man was a genius, and she was still in love with him.

Part Four

Chapter 45

As July became August of 1941, Europe was remarkably peaceful. True, in certain parts of Germany at night there was some risk of being hurt by a bomb; but it was a very slight risk. Usually the R.A.F. bombers completely missed their targets. The people most in danger were the aircrew: in 1941 the British bomber offensive killed more R.A.F. personnel than German civilians.

The real war was taking place far away, and Germany was doing very well. More U-boats than ever were prowling the Atlantic, and the British had had to cut their scale of rations. Rommel had just made mincemeat of a British counter-attack and was now poised to gobble up Egypt. In Russia, three German army-groups had smashed clean through the frontier defences. In the north and south these armies were reaching for Leningrad and Kiev; in the centre they had taken Smolensk. In midsummer 1941, the Third Reich thrived like a booming multinational corporation, and its off-shoots in Lisbon and Madrid were correspondingly busy.

Luis Cabrillo worked an eight-hour day: from nine until one; then a long lunch and a short nap; and from three until seven. On the day after they parted at the fountain he had already written over two thousand words when Julie came into his office at noon to return the *Abwehr* briefing letter. Creativity gripped him like a mild drug. Even when he stood up, brought her a chair, politely thanked her, she could see that his mind was elsewhere.

'Don't you think you ought to read it?' she asked.

'Plenty of time. According to the system, it won't reach me in London until tomorrow.' He tossed the letter into a wire tray, and squared his shoulders. 'I apologise for my churlish behaviour,' he said.

'Hell, no, forget it. I was the one who was wrong.'

'That does not excuse my ill manners.'

'I gave you a very hard time.'

'Surely that is exactly when courtesy and consideration are most needed.'

'Look, if anybody loused things up, I did. For Pete's sake, I might have killed you.'

He dismissed the idea with a brisk gesture. 'You were in much greater danger. It was criminally careless of me to leave such a stupid weapon lying around.'

'It went off with one almighty hell of a bang.'

They looked at the ragged hole in the picture-rail. 'I don't think the other tenants were altogether convinced that it was an exploding lightbulb,' Luis said. 'There was a strong smell of gunpowder, and several of them wanted to know why you were changing the lightbulb in the middle of the afternoon.'

'Good question.'

'Not at all. I pointed out the great difficulty of changing a lightbulb after dark. But a good deal of curious sniffing took place, all the same.'

'Gee, I'm sorry.'

'It was my fault.'

That seemed to complete the exchange of apologies. Luis went back to his desk. They sat in silence. A breath of wind crept through the open window and curled a sheet of paper, until he put a bottle of ink on it. 'When do you go to America?' he asked.

She stiffened. 'Who says I'm going to America?'

'The ticket was in your bag. I searched your bag, you see,' Luis said. 'It seemed an obvious thing to do, in the circumstances. If you remember.'

Julie remembered. 'I guess you're right . . . Anyway, I'm not going to America. Things are different today. I don't even have a ticket any more.'

'Oh,' Luis said. 'I see.' He squared-off his papers and put them to one side. After a moment he placed the ink-bottle on top of them. 'Well,' he said.

'Listen, you great Spanish dummy, is that all you can say?' Julie cried.

'What's wrong?' He looked slightly alarmed.

'*Everything's* wrong! Why the hell are we sitting here talking about *airline* tickets, for Chrissake?'

He thought hard. 'As distinct from what?'

She got up and kicked a filing cabinet. It made a gloomy

boom. 'I can remember, and it wasn't so long ago, when you came crashing into my hotel and let it be known that you loved me.'

'Yes, that's true.' He shuffled in his chair. 'In Madrid, it was a luxury we could both afford. What's more, in those days we had a lot in common.'

'Sure. Still do.'

'I believe there were even occasions when you said that *you* loved *me*.'

'Thank God for that. I thought you'd forgotten.'

He opened a drawer and took out her letter. 'This isn't exactly an expression of warmest affection,' he said.

'What d'you expect, after all your lying and cheating? Monogrammed condoms?'

'I didn't expect anything.'

'Okay, I love you, goddam it. Is that good enough?'

Luis cleared his throat. 'I'm not sure. Yesterday you tried to kill me.'

She gasped. 'You just said that didn't matter.'

'Oh no. It was the *danger* that didn't matter. Life itself has little value. But your gesture was insulting. To murder someone is the supreme act of contempt. That's what makes it such a cheap act. There's absolutely no respect involved.'

'But all that was yesterday! Things are different today. Anyway, I wouldn't ever have wanted to kill you unless you once mattered to me so damn much. Can't you see that?'

'I'm not sure.' He stroked his young moustache. 'To be absolutely honest, I'm not really sure of anything any more. I mean, I'm *fairly* sure I told you all those lies in Madrid because you were important at the time, but since then I've been doing a tremendous amount of lying to just about everyone, so maybe I've started lying to myself as well. It gets to be a habit, you see, and you can't stop. I mean, I could probably get up now and say, "I love you, Julie", and I might really mean it. Or I might quite possibly be lying.'

'Try it,' she said.

'For example, when you came in just now I was writing about a new British tank called the "crusher", and I really meant every word.'

'Try it, Luis,' she said.

'But it doesn't exist,' he added.

'I don't care.'

'As far as I know, that is. Perhaps it *does* exist.'

'For God's sake, Luis!'

'All right, I love you,' he said fast.

'Oh, forget it, I don't care any more. It doesn't matter. God, my wrist hurts.'

'How did it sound?' he asked. 'Did it sound right?' He got out the aspirin.

'It sounded lousy.' She salivated hard and swallowed an aspirin. It went down painfully slowly.

'Then maybe I don't love you. How does *that* sound?'

'Go to hell.'

He shook the aspirin bottle. 'Another?'

She glared. 'You'd like me to take an overdose?'

He wandered away and looked out of the window. It was a short view of about six feet, onto a blank wall. 'What are we going to do?' he asked.

'Well . . . I can't go home. No money. And Harry's disappeared.' It was beginning to sound like a very negative answer. 'I suggest I stay here. You've got money, and you look like you need some help.'

Luis thoroughly scrutinised the wall. 'Can you type?' he asked.

'I can learn.' As soon as the words were out, she recognised them, and uttered an amused snort which made him turn. 'Last time I said that, I was in the British embassy in Madrid,' she explained. 'Just as well they didn't believe me then.'

'Why?'

'I was trying to get into England.'

That made him blink. 'Good heavens above,' he said. 'What on earth for?' And then his brain caught up. 'Oh, oh, oh,' he said.

'Don't take it personally, Luis. It's just a passing madness. Like yours.'

He heaved in a deep breath, stretching his chest, flooding his lungs. 'What a lot of terrible rubbish you talk,' he said. They came together, cautiously, avoiding her broken wrist and his grazed jaw, and briefly kissed. 'Maybe you should give me lessons,' she mumbled. 'At least your brand of rubbish makes money.'

'There is that to be said for it,' he agreed.

302

*

Julie collected her bags from the *pensão* and moved into Luis's apartment. For the next week she spent every day with him in the office. While he wrote his reports, she read his files; and when he took a break, she asked questions: about Seagull, about Knickers, about the *Abwehr's* scale of payment for sub-agents, about his controllers in Madrid. Eventually she had a grasp of the entire operation.

'One thing worries me,' she said. They were at lunch, eating baked stuffed crab and drinking *vinho verde* in a rooftop restaurant with a view of all the hills of Lisbon. Her wrist was mending; now she could manage a knife and fork. 'They must have other agents. What if one of them doublechecks some of your information? And finds that it's all baloney?'

'All right. Let's examine that.' Luis ate a little salad while he organised his thoughts. 'As far as I know, Christian has only one other agent in England. He's called Mercury, which is a joke, because he's really very slow. He never takes risks, never argues, never contradicts, just sits tight and plays safe, which probably explains how he's survived so long. Nobody in Madrid has much faith in him. If Christian asked Mercury for a second opinion, my guess is Mercury would just leave it for a couple of days, and then radio back a confirmation.'

'On the other hand, he might actually do what he's told and drop you in the sewage.'

'Then they have to choose who to believe.'

'He's got seniority.'

'I'm getting paid more.'

The waiter came by and topped up their glasses. Luis held a fingertip in the sparkling fizz, and licked it. 'Anyway,' he said, 'the Germans are very painstaking people. Christian would probably ask me to explain the discrepancies.'

'Which you can't do.'

'Who says? I simply point out the time-lapse between my report and Mercury's—a couple of weeks, at least. For instance, suppose I find a Commando training school in north Wales but Mercury doesn't. So what? The Commandos moved elsewhere.'

'Are Commandos really that mobile?'

'My Commandos are.'

They strolled through the botanical gardens on the way back to the office, taking wide detours to avoid the sprinklers which hissed and pattered in glittering sweeps, cooling the air and sharpening the scent of the flowers. She said: 'It's not going to last, though, is it?'

'Of course it's going to last.'

'Come on, be your age, Luis. What are you doing? You're flying a kite, that's all, and it's a great big kite but one day the wind's going to drop and then what'll you do?'

He stopped. 'Look,' he said. 'I'm not a suicide. I'm a businessman. I do just what Ford Motors does, and Coca-Cola, and MGM. I give the customer what he wants. When I sit down to write, I ask myself two questions. What would the *Abwehr* like to know next? And what is Britain probably doing now? Then I put the two answers together. I tell you, it works.'

'And I tell you it's crazy.'

'Okay, good, fine, it's crazy.' They began walking again. 'If it makes me the richest maniac in Lisbon, I can stand a little insanity.'

*

Later that afternoon, Luis stopped writing and sat with his fist propping his head.

Julie put aside a rather boring report about the dispersal of fuel dumps. 'There *must* be other agents, though,' she said.

He lifted his head, revealing a red mark from the pressure of his fist. 'Sorry,' he said. 'I was in Yorkshire. Problems with a new aircraft factory. I think it may be the climate.'

'Oh.' She waited, but he was back in Yorkshire. 'What does climate have to do with making aircraft?'

He sighed heavily, and slumped in his chair. 'Damp. Jasper Stembridge says it's awfully damp in the north of England. That's why they make so much textiles up there. Now I have a feeling the damp is getting into the radio valves in these new aircraft.'

She scratched her plaster cast. 'Sounds pretty unlikely to me.'

'You think it could be sabotage?'

'I think they're just bum valves.'

'Well, that's possible, but I don't think we should rule out sabotage. The *Abwehr* like sabotage. They were very keen for me to be a saboteur, once. And a couple of weeks ago I located a refugee camp in Yorkshire, just outside Huddersfield. Now what if . . .' He made a few notes and began to look more cheerful. 'No, I don't think it's the damp,' he said.

'What about all the other agents, Luis?'

He got up, lit a gas-ring and put on a kettle of water. 'It's a funny thing about the *Abwehr*,' he said. 'It operates in separate units, all over Europe. Every big city has its little *Abwehr*: Paris, Amsterdam, Brussels. I'm sure there's one here in Lisbon.'

'And they've each got spies in England.'

'Certainly. But each section is terribly independent and jealous of the others. When I was there, Madrid *Abwehr* wouldn't even speak to Paris *Abwehr*.'

'Ah. So they're not likely to compare reports.'

'Not much.'

'But somebody might. I mean, who gets all the reports in the end?'

'Berlin, I suppose.'

'I have to pee,' she said.

When she came back he had made a pot of tea, and he was browsing through the 1937 GWR *Holiday Haunts*. 'Budleigh Salterton, bracing climate, pebbly beach,' he said. ' "Its tranquillity soothes those who have become wearied of the bustle of modern life." I think I might give them a couple of batteries of heavy anti-aircraft guns.'

'To protect the tranquillity?'

He sipped his tea. 'Don't know. Something important must be going on there.'

'Well, forget it for a minute. I've been thinking about your *Abwehr* set-up. Look: suppose there are ten sections operating from ten cities. That means they're running a total of maybe two dozen German agents inside Britain right now.'

'Yes, at least that number.'

'Well, hell . . .' She took her cup in her left hand and rested it on her cast. 'You're outnumbered, Luis! Those guys are all selling the genuine article. When they dig up some dirt it's real dirt, the stuff you can grow things in. Sooner or later some smart-ass at *Abwehr* headquarters is going to start noticing that one guy is always out of step. Those square heads are full of square brains, remember.'

'Perhaps.'

'It doesn't worry you.'

'There's lots of room in Britain for two dozen spies without treading on each other's toes. Besides . . . the others are making mistakes, too. Spies always get things wrong. The *Abwehr* expects it. I myself stumble from time to time, just to be more convincing. C.L.B., for instance.'

'C.L.B.' She drank some tea. 'Wasn't there something about C.L.B. in a report you made last week? Canadian something. Canadian Lowflying Bombardiers. Isn't that right?'

Luis finished his tea and examined the pattern of leaves in the bottom. 'Looks like a dead camel,' he said. 'That's very significant.'

'Come on, tell me. What does it really mean?'

Luis went back to his desk. 'Don't miss next week's gripping instalment,' he said; and began writing.

Chapter 46

Julie practised on Luis's typewriter until she had a degree of two-fingered competence. Luis then agreed to pay her the equivalent in escudos of twenty-five dollars a week. After pounding the machine for two days she struck for fifty dollars a week. He refused, and threatened to finish the job himself. She pointed out that, if he did, the difference in typing styles would be obvious to the Madrid *Abwehr*. A moody silence fell.

It was the end of a particularly sultry afternoon. He had worked until two in the morning for three days in a row, he wanted the report to be mailed as soon as possible, and he was obsessively worried about Seagull's travelling expenses. To provide an extra touch of authenticity, he itemised these in pounds, shillings and pence; but every time he totalled them he got a different result. It was infuriating. Already he had given it far more time than it justified. Bloody British currency!

'Anyway, I reckon I'm worth more than fifty bucks,' Julie said, picking at a hangnail.

'It's out of the question.'

'I mean, look at the hours.'

Luis flung down his pencil. 'Have you any idea how much it costs me to run this business? Look at this. Just bringing Seagull down from Liverpool to London for a lousy meeting at the Strand Palace Hotel comes to . . .' He glanced at his crossed-out sums. 'Comes to a hell of a lot,' he mumbled.

'Why put him up at the Strand Palace, for God's sake?' she asked.

'I like the name,' Luis said curtly.

'Well, it won't impress the Germans. Go somewhere that has a bit of style. Go to the Connaught.'

'How much is that for a single room?'

'With bath? Call it five pounds.'

'*Five pounds*? What are you trying to do, bankrupt me?'

'Luis,' Julie said. 'For Christ's sake. It's not your money. *You* don't pay these expenses; the Germans do. Who cares what it costs? Give the guy the Ritz bridal suite for a week and send the bill to Hitler.'

Luis stood in the middle of the room, shoulders slumped, toes turned in, face as tired as a wrung-out rag. 'What's wrong with me?' he muttered. He heaved a great, shuddering sigh. 'I keep getting a strange feeling inside my head. It's as if a glass shutter comes down. I can see the next thought, but I can't reach it.'

'You've been working too hard,' she said. 'You've got to learn to take it easy, Luis.'

'Yes. Yes.' He nodded, frowning. His eyes kept drifting sideways, seeking something which was always escaping. 'You're right. I've got to stop worrying.'

'Now.'

'I'll tell you what.' He braced his shoulders and rotated his head, loosening the weary neck muscles. 'Seagull can stay at the Connaught. Yes.'

'Good decision,' Julie said. 'If you ask me, the fellow deserves it, the way he's been working his ass off.'

Luis smiled, and the smile triggered off a chuckle. 'He has, hasn't he? I'm very proud of Seagull. D'you know, I think I'll get him a raise.'

'Okay.' Julie came over and took his hands. 'Now let's get something else straight. Seagull doesn't exist. He doesn't get his pay and he doesn't run up his expenses. All the money comes to you and stays with you.'

Luis nodded.

'And if you want to know what makes me worth fifty bucks a week,' she said, 'it's not just my brilliant typing, it's also the way I keep you out of the funny-farm.'

Luis nodded again.

'Fine.' She kissed him and slapped him on the backside. 'Now let's go and get thoroughly smashed.'

*

They got moderately smashed in a succession of bars, and eventually found themselves in a stately establishment with much engraved glass and dark wood. They were about to leave when the head waiter appeared, benign as a bishop. Julie explained that they were looking for the Connaught Hotel. He smiled at her, delightedly, and said he had a brother in Phoenix, Arizona. Luis told him that Julie herself came from Indiana which was in California and therefore virtually indistinguishable from Phoenix. They shook hands and stayed for dinner: partridge soaked in port, extremely rich. As soon as the plates had been cleared away, Luis fell asleep. A waiter fetched a taxi. Luis fell asleep again in the taxi, and again as soon as they got home. She took off most of his clothes and steered him into bed. He looked as if he had been sandbagged.

But next morning he was as good as new again: fresh, full of energy, his face clear and his eyes alert. Julie, who was feeling slightly rusty, marvelled, and asked him how the hell he did it. 'Simple,' he said. 'It's my royal blood. You see, at birth I was exchanged by gypsies. By rights, I should now be king of Albania.'

'Oh yeah? I've seen the king of Albania. He wasn't so fast on his feet.'

'Exactly. The wrong man grew up to get the job.' Luis stepped into his shoes and picked up his jacket. 'If you're coming with me—'

'Sit down a minute and listen. I've been thinking some more about your crazy Eldorado operation.'

'It's not crazy as long as it works.'

308

'Well, that's what bothers me. Have you ever stopped to think that you might some day give the krauts a piece of secret information which is not only valuable but true? I mean, *really* true?'

Luis sat down. 'By mistake,' he said.

'Sure, accidentally. A coincidence.'

'I invent something which actually happens.' He shrugged. 'Does it matter if there really is a Commando school in north Wales? The Luftwaffe can't bomb north Wales, it's too big. In fact the British would sooner they bombed north Wales than—'

'How about convoys?' Julie asked.

Luis got up and poured himself more coffee. 'Oh dear, oh dear, oh dear,' he muttered.

'You invent a convoy. Size, route, sailing-date, the lot. When the U-boats turn up, there *is* a convoy, smack in their sights.'

'It couldn't happen.'

'Maybe it's happened already. *You* don't know.'

'All right, it's not impossible. But on balance—'

'Luis, stop kidding yourself. On balance you're likely to get steadily better at guessing what the British are doing, so on balance you're going to become more and more—'

'All right! Yes, fine, I understand, you make it very clear.' He scowled into his cup. 'So now you want me to stop. You want me to abandon the business.'

'Not necessarily. But I certainly think you should go to the British and tell them what you're doing.'

'I went to the British once, in Madrid.'

'And?'

Luis brooded over the memory. 'They kept giving me tea. I had to pee in the bath.' He wandered out to the balcony and emptied his coffee into a pot of geraniums. 'I'll tell you the truth,' he said, 'but I don't care if you don't believe it. Sometimes when I was with Freddy Ryan I wasn't sure if I believed it myself. After a while Freddy could make you believe that down was up, and sometimes now I think maybe he was right, that down *is* up, and the law of gravity is just a regulation invented by all those dull, heavy people who can't fly and want to make it illegal for everyone else to get up off the ground, the way Freddy Ryan could.'

'What really happened to him, anyway?'

'He got shot down,' Luis said. 'They invoked the law of gravity. No appeal against that, is there?'

She joined him on the balcony. 'Hey, let's keep it simple,' she said. 'Tell me what it is you don't care if I don't believe.'

Far below them, a chunky woman dressed in black wool from her shawl to her ankle-length skirt was tramping up the steep and narrow street. She carried a basket of fish on her head. 'That's what they call a *varina*,' he said. 'She sells fish.'

'You don't say. Looks more like the king of Albania in drag.' She nudged him in the ribs. 'Come on.'

'Okay, I'll tell you. When the British embassy kicked me out I decided there was only one way to make them change their minds, and that was to get myself recruited by the Germans. You understand? Once I was working for the *Abwehr* I'd be much more useful to the British. That was the whole damn idea.'

'Gee whiz.' She was genuinely impressed. 'I would never have thought of that. I'd never have *dared* think of that.'

'It seemed like a good idea at the time. I mean, I didn't know I was going to meet you and Freddy.'

'But why didn't you go to England?'

'Because to make it work, I must send information to the *Abwehr*. I must be able to prove to the British that the *Abwehr* really trusts me.'

'Well, you could do that from England. You'd be far less likely to get found out by the *Abwehr*. I mean, what you're doing here is pretty dangerous, Luis.'

He gave her a sharp, sideways glance. 'And if the British caught me in England, transmitting secret information,' he said, 'would they believe it was all for their good in the long run?'

'Um. Well,' she said. 'Yes. I see what you mean.'

'They hang people by the neck for doing that sort of thing.'

A tiny money-spider sailed across the balcony on its shining thread and crash-landed on her arm. She let it scramble over the downy slopes to her hand, and gently blew it away. 'What a brutal bloody business,' she said.

'Of course it is,' Luis told her. 'That's why it pays so well.'

They went inside. 'I still think you should go to the British,' she said.

'Yes.' He made a face. 'It's a great pity to interfere with

an enterprise which is working so smoothly and earning so much money, but . . . If it has to be done . . .'

'Would you like me to arrange it?'

'Yes. Thank you.'

*

Colonel Christian didn't boot Wolfgang Adler off the Eldorado team; he let him drop, slowly, day by day and bit by bit. He gave him all the routine paperwork to do: filing, cross-referencing, summarising. Meanwhile the other *Abwehr* personnel got the exciting jobs as controllers of Eldorado and his sub-agents, and by the time their information reached Wolfgang it was stale. He was being sidetracked, and he knew it, and the knowledge fed his sense of grievance, of being cheated. What made this worse was Otto's sudden perkiness. Eagle had filed his first report. Compared with Eldorado's material it was no better than worthy: Eagle analysed the isolationist mood of American big business and did a short round-up of British rearmament in the year since Dunkirk. But Otto was delighted. 'He's making an effort, that's the main thing,' Otto told Wolfgang over breakfast. 'It's a start. You wait till he earns his first bonus. Then you'll see Eagle lay some golden eggs.' Wolfgang chewed his toast and looked away.

As it happened, the next delivery came from Eldorado; and as usual Wolfgang was not invited to share its contents.

It was a lengthy report, and it arrived only twenty minutes before Christian had to leave for Madrid's Barajas Airport. He rounded up Fischer, Werth, Krafft and Hartmann, packed them into the biggest Mercedes the embassy could provide, and farmed out pages for them to read on the way.

By the time they tramped onto the bright and breezy runway, every word had been read by at least two men. Otto Krafft had his notebook open for their comments. 'Richard?' Christian said.

'Well, sir, Knickers has been hanging around the pubs near the R.A.F. bases again,' Fischer reported. 'I suggest you draw especial attention to his information about a new four-engined bomber; about an improved Spitfire with extra fuel-tanks; and about some special kind of radar codenamed "Jam Tart". That's all he knows about it but he's digging. Also he says there's a serious shortage of aluminium because of the U-boat sink-ings, and use of alternative materials in aircraft has led to several crashes. Nothing absolutely startling, sir, but I'd rate it all valuable and reliable stuff.'

Christian nodded. 'Franz?'

'Seagull also provides evidence that the U-boat war is really hurting the enemy, sir,' Werth announced. 'When the last convoy reached Liverpool, the port was sealed off in order to keep all news about the losses from the civilian population; crews were not allowed ashore; and when the authorities or-dered them to sail again, many mutinies broke out. That seems to me of major importance, sir. The only other item worth studying is a remarkable plan which Seagull has heard about. It involves towing a huge iceberg to mid-Atlantic and keeping it there as an R.A.F. airstrip, so that convoys can be given air cover throughout their voyage.'

'Good heavens,' Christian said. 'Can that be done?'

'It's technically possible, yes.'

'You amaze me. Dr Hartmann? What do you make of Eldorado's own discoveries?'

'As usual, sir, the sheer quantity is impressive.' Hartmann riffled the pages with his thumb. 'I recommend three topics which should repay especial examination. The first is the marked increase in Commando training, with clear implica-tions for coastal security throughout northern Europe. The second is the secret arrival in London of a purchasing com-mission from Soviet Russia; Eldorado has some interesting in-formation on that. The third is an outbreak of sabotage in certain aircraft factories in Yorkshire; Eldorado links this with the employment of French refugees from a nearby camp. There is obvious propaganda potential there. Of course it goes without saying that Eldorado's entire report is a pleasure to read, sir, but those are the three main points.'

'Good.' Christian took the pages, and Otto's notes, and stuffed them all into his briefcase. 'Did they miss anything, Otto?' he asked.

'Nothing important, sir. There's just one small point worth noting.'

'Cough it up, then.'

'I don't know whether you remember the Canadian Low-flying Bombardiers, sir?' The aircraft was ready for boarding;

they strolled toward the steps. 'Eldorado sent us a few lines on them, two weeks ago.'

'Yes . . . Didn't he meet an officer, in Oxford? In a bar, wasn't it?'

'The Randolph Hotel, yes. Eldorado got into conversation about his shoulder-badge, which bore the initials C.L.B. It seems that the man must have been joking. Eldorado has discovered that he is in fact a major in the Church Lads' Brigade. That's an organisation rather like the Boy Scouts, only godlier.'

Colonel Christian laughed so much that he stumbled on the aircraft steps and banged his shin. 'That's the cherry on the cake!' he called down, rubbing his leg vigorously. 'Give that man a bonus!'

He disappeared into the cabin. Ten minutes later he was in the sky, heading for Germany, a conference with the head of the *Abwehr*, Admiral Canaris, and a deserved promotion to brigadier.

Chapter 47

Walter Witteridge looked as if he should have been the headmaster of some minor cathedral school. His build was angular, his face suggested skin uncomfortably stretched over a thrusting skull, and his large teeth flashed frequently in an apprehensive smile. Even in the heat of a Lisbon summer, he wore a tweed suit. Luis Cabrillo had never been inside a school commonroom but he had read enough English novels to know how people were supposed to sound in them; and as soon as he heard Walter Witteridge speak, he recognised those tortured vowels: sometimes stretched thin as if to see if the words would snap; sometimes overinflated, as if the statements were trial balloons, sent up only to be shot down. Luis found it difficult not to twitch and grimace in imitation of the man.

'May I tell you what I find most frightfully intriguing?' Walter Witteridge said, hunching and twisting his body as if his underwear chafed. 'It's this. How, Mr Cabrillo, did you come to ask for an appointment with me? That is to say, with me specifically?' He suddenly scratched the very top of his head, fluffing up the sandy hair. 'How impertinent that sounds! You are fully entitled to ignore it. Let it be stricken from the records. Stricken? Struck?' He glanced longingly at his bookshelf. 'I am an idle fellow, Mr Cabrillo. Pray forgive me.'

'My secretary did it,' Luis said.

'Ah.' Witteridge widened his eyes. 'But then how—'

'She called a friend in the American embassy in Madrid. He called a colleague in Lisbon, who suggested we should approach you.'

'Fascinating. When one is nominally a member of the Secret Service, you see, these little glimpses have a certain piquancy . . . It is as if one were a *voyeur* upon oneself.'

'I think he met you at a cocktail party.'

'I'm sure he's absolutely correct. Americans are so blindingly efficient, aren't they? One suspects that their efficiency is a byproduct of their constantly-repeated faith in a Divine Providence. D'you know, before all this unpleasantness broke out I was tempted to write a book called *When God Dies, Will He Go To America?*'

'How interesting,' Luis said.

Witteridge coiled his arms around his head and peered at Luis from behind his splayed fingers. 'My dear fellow,' he said, 'I have been boring you.'

'Not at all.' Luis sat back. 'You must be *that* Walter Witteridge, the journalist and writer and so on.'

Witteridge nodded glumly. 'Currently I seem to be in my so-on phase. Have you read my book, *There's No Future In Progress*?'

Luis nodded.

'How awfully gratifying.' But Walter Witteridge seemed saddened.

'I have read all your books,' Luis said.

Witteridge slowly looked up. 'Have you really?' he said. 'Really all?' Now he seemed thoroughly depressed. There was a long pause while he stared past Luis's left ear. Then he braced himself, and engineered a brave, tormented smile. 'I expect you'd like some tea,' he suggested.

'No,' said Luis, firmly. 'I want to tell you why I'm here.'

314

Witteridge opened his arms wide, and appealed to an invisible audience. 'Why not?' he asked.

Luis told him.

'How fascinating,' Witteridge said, 'And how totally admirable.'

'Well . . . thank you.'

'Not only have you duped the *Abwehr* in a commendably skilful manner, but you have contrived to make a comfortable living out of it.'

'I suppose so.'

'Then I must congratulate you.' Witteridge came around the desk and shook his hand. 'I *do* congratulate you.' He completed the circuit and got back into his chair.

'You're very kind,' Luis said. 'I was rather hoping that you would give me some help.'

'My dear chap, I doubt if the British Secret Service could negotiate better terms with the *Abwehr* on your behalf. My advice is to carry on.'

Luis explained his concern about the risk of inventing information which might accidentally benefit the German war effort.

'Oh . . .' Walter Witteridge squeezed and squashed his face into an expression of intense thought. 'Frightfully remote possibility, don't you think? I mean, you would have to be jolly good, wouldn't you? I know you *are* jolly good. What I'm saying, I suppose, is you'd have to be jolly *jolly* good, quite phenomenally jolly good.'

'It could happen, all the same.'

Witteridge entwined his legs, and hooked an arm over and under the arm of his chair. 'If it did ever happen,' he suggested, 'you could always pop round and tell us about it.'

'How could I? I've no way of knowing whether it's happened or not. That's why I thought it was time I started working with your people.'

'My dear boy,' Witteridge said, 'if you think our chaps are going to supply you with dummy information so that you can stay in business with the enemy—'

'No, no. I'm proposing to come and join you, work for you.'

'While continuing to take money from the Germans?'

Luis gestured helplessly. 'There's no alternative to that. They've got to pay me, otherwise—'

Witteridge was shaking his head. 'I don't think the British Secret Service goes in for that sort of thing, old chap. I mean, we're still very oldfashioned about loyalties: if you come to work for us, then you really ought to resign from the competition. Frightfully stuffy and Victorian, I agree, and frankly I very much question the value of it, but there you are.'

'But if I leave the *Abwehr*,' Luis said, 'what use will I be to the British Secret Service?'

Walter Witteridge sucked his lips while he considered the question. He slid open a drawer and took out a typewritten paper. 'How willing are you,' he asked, 'to be parachuted into Occupied Europe?'

'Not at all.'

'Then I'm afraid that settles the matter.' Witteridge put the paper back. 'At the moment, so I'm told, we're only looking for chaps who don't mind leaping into the night over France. I wouldn't do it, either; not in a million years.'

Luis stared at him. Witteridge grinned reassuringly. 'So you don't need me at all, then,' Luis said.

'Isn't it more a case of your not needing us? Let me be wildly indiscreet, Mr Cabrillo. I honestly don't believe you would benefit terribly from contact with the people here. Most of them, I've found, are rather dense.'

'Dense?'

'Unimaginative. I may say I was disappointed. I certainly expected better things when they recruited me. *Brighter* things.'

Luis stood. 'All the same,' he said, 'I wish there were some way of eliminating that risk.'

'Put it out of your mind, dear boy,' Witteridge assured him. 'Your little business will obviously go bust within six months, so your anxiety is redundant.'

'Six months, you reckon?' Luis said.

'At the absolute extreme. Nothing lasts in wartime, old chap; nothing. Come back in six months and I doubt very much if even *I* shall be here.'

Luis returned to the office. Julie stopped typing. 'What did they say?' she asked.

'Buzz off,' Luis said.

She waited. 'Was that all?'

'All that mattered. By the way, I called at the bank afterwards.' He showed her the bank statement. 'See? Another fat bonus. Somebody appreciates us.'

Chapter 48

Eagle, at his third attempt, laid a golden egg. It made Otto Krafft, his controller, quite proud.

'*Operation Bandstand*,' Christian (now a brigadier) read aloud. '*The invasion of Norway by an Allied force of not less than six divisions including airborne troops, supported by major elements of the British Home Fleet and . . .*' He fell silent, and raced through the rest of the report with only an occasional muttered comment: '*. . . massive minelaying in the Skagerrak . . . co-ordinated civilian uprising . . . decoy attack on Stavanger . . . main bridgehead south of Bergen . . .*' At the end he sat for a moment, staring at the final words while his fingers made a little ripple of sound on the paper. He looked up. 'Good for Eagle,' he said.

'I think he deserves an extra bag of birdseed, sir,' said Otto.

'Yes indeed. Send the man buckets of birdseed. I told you Canaris approved my budget proposals? Well, that's what money is for: to keep people like Eagle happy and productive. Chuck the stuff at him with both hands. This is excellent, isn't it? A lot better than his other efforts.'

'I don't think he quite got the hang of it at first, sir,' Otto said. 'But now that he's in London on a long visit, I expect we'll hear a lot from him.'

Christian glanced at the date on the front. 'Only four days old,' he said. 'That's fast.'

'Airmail via Oporto. Eagle's branch office.'

'Yes, of course. Every eagle needs a branch.' Christian flipped through the pages again. 'Norway is a very attractive target for the British, you know. Not far from Scotland, lots of sea for their great big navy to play in, and a chance to cut off supplies of whatever-it-is we get from Scandinavia.'

'Iron ore, sir.'

'Yes. You know, I might prepare a few deft observations on the subject, for Berlin.'

'Don't forget the Russian aspect, sir. I mean to say, with Leningrad about to fall, Stalin must be screaming at the British to do something to relieve the pressure. Operation Bandstand could well be it.'

'Very good, Otto!' Christian bounced to his feet and thrust Eagle's report into his hands. 'By the time you've got that coded I'll have the covering signal ready. *Schnell, schnell!*' He sent Otto trotting happily from the room.

*

It was early evening, and the light was as soft as honey. Luis Cabrillo was paging through the 1923 Michelin Guide, looking for Derby, because he thought Rolls-Royce had a factory there, when *Stalactite Caverns* caught his eye. According to Michelin they were something to see in Cheddar (Somerset), population 1,975, market day Wednesday. How interesting.

He left Derby and looked up Somerset in Jasper Stembridge. Jasper knew all about Cheddar and its limestone. He said the rain ran into cracks, dissolved the limestone, and hollowed out caves. There was even a photograph of one, looking very cold. Luis turned to the GWR *Holiday Haunts*. It went on at some length about the famous Cheddar caverns that run for more than 600 yards, and included a smart backhander at unthinking people who condemned their exploitation without appreciating how much it cost to install the electric lighting.

'Damn right,' Luis said, making a note of the page. Julie looked up from the latest *Abwehr* briefing letter. 'Caves,' he explained. 'I can use caves.'

'Oh yes,' she said. 'I remember the picture. They look kind of like railroad tunnels, don't they?'

Luis went back to the photograph. The cave interior looked more like a heap of coal, and there was definitely only one of it. 'Railroad tunnels?' he said. 'This?'

She took the book from him and thumbed through it until she found a picture of a rugged hillside with two big, black, circular holes in it. 'You want caves,' she said, 'we got the best.'

'Dovedale . . . Hey, that's near Derby!' Luis scanned the text. ' "These beautiful dales",' he read, ' "through whose narrow troughs the glistening streams are ever eating their way

318

deeper and deeper into the porous limestone". I say, that's excellent.'

'Sounds kind of purple, if you ask me.' Julie stared at the Dovedale photograph. 'Luis, how long since we made love?'

'Wait a minute, wait a minute . . . Here we are, it's under Ashbourne: "Thor's Cave (prehistoric) . . . Derby 13 miles".' He flourished the Michelin. 'That's the answer!'

'No, I don't think it was 1923,' she said.

'A vast underground arms depot! A whole new secret communications centre! Perfect!'

'Didn't we do it once during the Thirties? Late '34 or maybe early '35?'

Luis was scribbling notes. 'Rolls-Royce. They put their factory down in the cave. Bombproof. Obvious!'

'I think I've forgotten how,' she said. 'Is it like the foxtrot or the tango? Which leg do you put forward first? Where do you hold your handbag?'

'Caves,' Luis exulted. 'I'm going to fill up every damn cave in Britain, you watch.'

'We led such sheltered lives at the mission school,' she said, fondling his lapels. 'Please be gentle, or I'll break your arms.'

'I don't know what's the matter with you, Julie,' he said. 'We made love last night. Twice.'

'As long ago as that?' She put the big black hat on his head. 'Come on, let's get out of here. You've done enough for one day.'

As they went downstairs, she said: 'By the way: Madrid wants you to go to Glasgow.'

'How can I? I've got all this work to do in Cheddar and Derby.'

'So don't go. Send someone else.'

He thought about it all the way to the street. 'I need more help,' he said. 'The business is getting too big for me. It's time I had more sub-agents.'

She took his arm. 'Damn right. You can't be expected to do everything, can you? Learn to delegate, that's the secret of success.'

'Exactly.' He waved at a taxi. 'On the other hand, if I take on a new sub-agent I shall have to do all his work.'

'But you'll get all his pay.'

'I know, I know.' They climbed into the taxi. 'Glasgow,'

Luis said gloomily, and it was several seconds before he realised why the driver was looking at him like that.

Chapter 49

Wolfgang Adler put all the blame for his decline on Luis Cabrillo. The Spaniard had wilfuly and irresponsibly caused him permanent physical suffering, and as a direct result of that, nobody in the *Abwehr* now took him seriously when he tried to expose the man's frauds and failures.

Whenever his clerical duties allowed, Wolfgang read and re-read the Eldorado reports, searching for one fatal flaw, just one clear and unarguable blunder which he could take to Christian as proof of what he knew to be true: that Eldorado's success was totally undeserved. Just one. It had to be there, sooner or later. Otherwise what was the point of going on?

A week after his visit to Berlin, Christian sent for Wolfgang. When he got to the brigadier's room the four controllers were already there, drinking coffee.

'Maniacs,' Christian said flatly. 'Fools, mules and gibbering idiots.' He had been reading a long teleprinter signal; now he concertina-ed it flat and impaled it on a spike. 'Despite all my urgent recommendations to Canaris, Berlin has ordered that Krafft, Fischer, Werth and Hartmann be promoted forthwith.'

Gasps of surprise and small whoops of pleasure.

'You are all equally unworthy, so at least Berlin is consistent,' Christian said, spinning the signal on its spike like a propeller. 'Nevertheless I can explain this disastrous decision only as the evil fruits of infiltration at the highest level by the British Secret Service.'

General amusement and scattered applause.

'As an act of sabotage,' Christian added, 'it makes the burning of the Reichstag look like an infringement of the blackout regulations.'

More all-round laughter, except from Wolfgang. Nobody looked at him.

'And now to work,' Christian said.

They spent an hour reviewing the recent output of Eldorado, Seagull, Knickers and Eagle. Discussion centred mainly on Seagull's report that Britain was suddenly expanding and improving her meteorological stations in Iceland and Greenland and was planning to instal a clandestine station on the Azores; the implication was that transatlantic convoys might take a far more northerly route when the weather allowed, in order to avoid U-boats. There was also a lot of interest in Eagle's news that a Cabinet Minister, an Air Vice Marshal and a bishop's wife were involved in a financial and sexual scandal which the Government had hushed up by invoking the Official Secrets Act.

Wolfgang took no part in the discussion.

'One small thought,' Christian said at the end. 'Canaris told me that the various *Abwehr* sections in Europe are, at present, running a total of twenty-seven active agents in Britain and Ireland. He rates Eldorado as one of the two most valuable; somebody controlled by Brussels *Abwehr* is the other. Eagle ranks fourth or fifth and is rising steadily.'

Everyone except Wolfgang looked pleased.

'My small thought is this,' Christian went on. 'Here we have Eldorado and Eagle, both working the same territory and both getting remarkably good results. Suppose we were to bring them back to Madrid for a very brief, very high-level conference or seminar? A chance for the top men in the *Abwehr* to find out how the experts operate. Does that excite anybody?'

He reorganised the papers on his desk, while the idea sank in.

Richard Fischer was first. '*I'm* excited,' he said.

'It could provide the basis of a whole new training programme,' Dr Hartmann suggested.

'Just a very brief gathering,' Christian said. 'Only the very top men.'

'Eagle won't come,' Otto said.

They all looked at him.

'In my opinion it would be dangerous even to suggest it to him,' Otto said. 'Eagle made it very clear to me at the start that he wanted no personal contact with anyone, ever.'

'But surely this is different,' Fischer protested. 'I mean, Admiral Canaris himself might—'

'It's not different for Eagle,' Otto insisted. 'He won't come, I tell you. He just won't.' Otto folded his arms and tightened his lips. There had been an impressive note of conviction in his voice.

'Do we really need two speakers?' Franz Werth asked. 'What's wrong with . . .' He gave up when he saw the brigadier twitch his nostrils.

'It wouldn't be the same without Eagle,' Christian said. 'The whole point is to demonstrate a contrast in styles, a difference in approach. And by the way: Otto Krafft is absolutely right to protect Eagle in that way. A good controller identifies himself with his agent utterly and completely.'

Otto ducked his head modestly.

'One last piece of business,' Christian said. 'Eldorado has recruited another new sub-agent.'

'What a man!' Fischer exclaimed. 'If he keeps this up, we shan't need to invade.'

'He's a Venezuelan studying medicine at Glasgow University,' Christian told them. 'His codename is "Garlic". I've given some considerable thought to the choice of a controller for Garlic.' Wolfgang held his breath. 'As you know, I believe that a selfless dedication to routine work deserves to be rewarded.' He shot his cuffs, and glanced at a piece of paper, as if to remind himself of something. 'That being so, the man for the job is Dr Hartmann.'

Wolfgang let his breath out and looked away. He felt as if he had swallowed a gutful of lead shot. Christian was telling Hartmann something about Garlic's scale of payment but Wolfgang scarcely heard.

He stood up when the others stood, moved to the door when they moved. The meeting was over and not one person had spoken to him.

'Oh, Adler,' Christian said. 'Did you want to see me about something?'

They all paused, politely interested.

'You sent for me,' Wolfgang said.

'Did I? Why?'

Wolfgang stood and looked at him.

'There must have been a reason, surely,' Christian said.

Wolfgang shifted his weight from his bad leg.

'Well, if you think of it, come back and let me know,'

Christian said. The others laughed, and Wolfgang felt a drum-roll of hatred building inside him. This injustice could not go on. He felt sick to death with bitterness. It would kill him if he didn't destroy it first, and that meant destroying its cause. Christian was watching him carefully, studying him. Wolfgang turned and went out.

Chapter 50

At the beginning of the eighteenth century, Huguenot refugees settled in Derby, Macclesfield and Leek and established the silk industry in these towns.

Luis Cabrillo put Jasper Stembridge aside and made a note: *Derby/Macclesfield/Leek—silk. Parachutes? Knickers? He* thought for a moment, and added: *Black-market stockings?*

He looked up Macclesfield in the 1923 Michelin. It was 41 miles from Liverpool. There was a reference to the Cat and Fiddle public house, reputed to be the highest licensed inn in England.

He made a note of that. *Seagull visits pub-owning relatives at weekend,* he wrote. *Landmark? Radio station? Robot bomber?*

The afternoon sun had reached the edge of his paper. He scribbled with his pen in the sunny strip, just for the pleasure of watching the ink dry, and he thought of holidays. It was summer; vacation-time. Why keep Garlic stuck in Glasgow?

Holiday Haunts had a map of the Great Western Railway routes which showed an island far out in the Irish Sea, the Isle of Man. He looked it up. *In the comparatively small compass of this island are great cliffs, delightful bathing beaches, fertile valleys, lush meadows . . . heart-warming hospitality . . . exhilarating air . . . abundance of amusements . . .* Just the place for an overworked overseas medical student. Just the place to put a German prisoner-of-war camp, too. Garlic might as well bring back news of all those Luftwaffe pilots shot down and captured and now—

Somebody knocked on the door.

It startled him so much that every muscle jumped. Julie put down the report she had been proofreading. They looked at each other, looked at the door, listened intently. They were listening to someone else's listening. Nobody had ever visited the office before. It was unnecessary. Nobody had any business to call here. So maybe this was a mistake.

Somebody knocked again. Confidently, *rap ta-ta rap rap.*

Luis tiptoed over to the filing cabinet where he kept the rusted Colt revolver. The drawer groaned and squealed like an angry pig. Julie vibrated with suppressed laughter, but he gave her such a savage scowl that the comedy abruptly evaporated and left an even greater tension. He abandoned the gun, slammed home the drawer, stamped to the door and swung it open.

The man looked baggy. His ageing brown suit was baggy, his sallow face was baggy, even his leather bag was baggy. He looked at Luis with his baggy eyes as if Luis were the electricity meter and he had come to read it. He was a man who knocked on a lot of doors.

'*Senhor* Cabrillo?' he said. Luis moved his head in what might have been a nod. '*Boa tarde, senhor.*' He took a very creased business-card from his top pocket and offered it.

'*Ministério da Fazenda e . . .*' Luis's head recoiled. The baggy man patiently switched his bag to the other hand. Evidently he was familiar with this sort of reaction. Luis said: '*Desculpe-me, mas . . . Não compreendo. O que . . . ?*'

'*Com licença?*' The baggy man made a small and economical gesture of entry. Luis waved him in. '*Obrigado, senhor. O gerente, lá em baixo . . .*' the baggy man began, and they were off into a fast exchange of sibilant, switchbacking Portuguese which meant nothing to Julie except that Luis didn't seem to be winning. After ten minutes he was left moodily holding a long, printed form while the baggy man raised his baggy hat to each of them in turn and went away.

His footsteps ticked and tocked down the big stone staircase until they merged with their own echoes.

'Who was he?' she asked.

'Tax inspector.' Luis sat heavily and stared at the form. 'Portuguese government. Ministry of Taxation. Bloody hell.'

'They can't be serious. How can they expect you to pay taxes? You're not a real businessman or anything.'

'The manager of this building gave him a list of tenants. What am I doing renting this office if I'm not running a business?'

Julie came over and looked at the form. It was enormously complicated. 'What did you tell him?' she asked.

'Oh . . . rubbish, nonsense. I said I was only an agent, I was looking for products to sell, nothing doing yet, no income to speak of. He didn't actually *say* he didn't believe me, but he's coming back next week.'

'Then we'd better get out, fast. You can keep your files in the apartment.'

He got up, hands in pockets, and shouldered the door shut. 'I hate working at home,' he said. 'It doesn't feel right. This is a business, it belongs in an office. So do I.'

'You'll belong in jail if you don't pay your taxes.'

He reached up and hung by his fingers from the coat-hook on the back of the door. 'Then . . . I shall have to pay taxes.'

'Oh, sure.' She wandered across and put her arms around his neck. 'And you're going to register with the Portuguese Government as a foreign spy,' she said into his right ear.

'That tickles.'

'Yeah, it's hilarious.' She chewed gently on a lobe. 'They probably have a special rate for foreign spies. After all, Lisbon's full of them.'

'Let's go back to the beginning.' Luis gently rubbed the point of his chin against her neck. 'The Portuguese want to tax me because they believe I am doing business. Therefore the answer is to do business so that the Portuguese can tax me. Then they will be satisfied and go away.'

'What sort of business, Luis?'

His neck muscles tensed. 'You have no idea how much that *tickles*,' he said. 'I don't know, any sort. Buying things, selling things. Business business.'

'But Luis, my sweet,' she whispered insistently, 'you've got no *experience* in selling—'

His right ear rebelled, his head jerked sideways, the coat-hook wrenched free under the strain, and they both fell to the floor.

'I *told* you that tickled,' he complained. They lay in a heap and looked at the ceiling. 'It's a pretty lousy office where a chap can't even hang himself behind the door.' He threw the coat-hook at the wall.

'What it comes down to is this,' Julie said. She made her head comfortable on his chest. 'Can you afford to pay real taxes on an imaginary business? How much money are you making now?'

'Not much. Including Garlic's pay, about seven or eight hundred dollars a week, I suppose.'

'Good God.'

'But it won't *be* an imaginary business, Julie. I'll deal in something genuine, so that if anyone wants to know what I do, there it is. Coal, or olive oil, or plywood, or—'

'Eight hundred bucks a week? And we're pigging it in this crappy walk-up on the four hundred and twenty-sixth floor of the most boring office block in town?' She banged her head against his chest until he gasped. 'You're going to move, you tight bastard!'

'All *right*,' he wheezed. 'All right! We'll move tomorrow. Jesus, I think you've broken a rib.'

They got up, and Julie beat the dust out of her clothes. 'It really is a hell of a thing,' she complained, 'when a spy has to actually go out of his way to pay his lousy taxes.'

Luis wasn't listening. 'Business expenses,' he said. 'We'll need to keep records of them. Receipts, invoices. Postal charges.'

'It's not so much the disgrace as the disillusion. Damn it all, doesn't tradition mean anything anymore?'

Luis polished his right shoe on his left trouser-leg while he looked at her, seriously. 'An accountant,' he said. 'Where can I get a good accountant?'

*

It took them a week to find and move into new offices. They began the search together, but after a couple of hours Luis began worrying about a report from Knickers (on R.A.F. experiments with a new high-altitude anti-aircraft shell made out of plastic) which would soon be overdue; so he went back to his desk while Julie kept looking. Eventually she found a place in the *Bairro Alto*, the high ground just to the west of the Rossio. It was the third floor of a newish building; it had a lift and a telephone; it was clean, quiet, carpeted, and decently removed from any embassies, consulates or legations. There were good bars and restaurants within walking distance. Luis signed a twelve-month lease and they shifted their files into the new premises that same night.

Julie had bought a bottle of wine, to christen the place. They touched glasses, and Luis said: 'Well, here's to . . . uh . . . Here's to . . .'

'Yeah, sure, I'll drink to that.'

They toasted whatever it was they were toasting. He strolled around, opening doors; glancing at the view across the centre of Lisbon to the great, hunched bulk of the castle; testing the pile of the carpet with his feet. 'I suppose a business as prosperous as this should really have a name,' he said.

'Cabrillo and Conroy,' she suggested. 'Or Cabroy, for short.'

'Cabroy is awful.'

'Okay, call it Universal Enterprises.'

Luis liked that but he didn't buy it. He found the 1923 Michelin Guide and searched through it. 'Here we are,' he said. 'Bradburn & Wedge. That has the right sound.'

'Bradburn & Wedge sound like a couple of carpenters who double as undertakers. Where did you dig them up?'

'Wolverhampton. That's in Staffordshire. They run a garage. Or they did in 1923. They were agents for Morris, Sunbeam, Austin, Fiat, Bianchi, De Dion Bouton, and Rolls-Royce. Not bad.'

'I see.' She waited, but Luis had moved off and was testing a light switch. 'You wouldn't rather call it General Motors?'

'No, no. It has to sound English. The Portuguese are very impressed by anything English. Don't you think Bradburn & Wedge sound thoroughly English?'

'I guess so. They remind me of cricket, which is like eternity, only not so exciting.'

'Well, that's perfect, isn't it? We want to appear solid and unexciting. Bradburn & Wedge are a firm you can trust.'

'Trust to do what?'

'Well . . . Look, why don't you handle that aspect, Julie? I'll be too busy with all the Eldorado stuff.'

'Yes, but . . .' She poured herself more wine. 'I don't know where to start. What are Bradburn & Wedge going to *do*?'

The previous tenant had left them a Lisbon trade directory, published by the Portuguese Chamber of Commerce. Luis

327

opened it at random. 'Lemonade crystals,' he said. 'Highly desirable. Go out and buy lemonade crystals.'

'And what do I do with them when I've bought them?'

'You sell them, I suppose.' He smiled encouragingly. 'What else is there to do? Buying and selling, that's what business is all about.'

Chapter 51

As the summer of 1941 drifted into autumn, and the German offensives in Russia and the Atlantic continued to register steady success, people in beleaguered Britain snatched a quick holiday as and when they could. Garlic, luckier than most, managed a week on the Isle of Man. Seagull visited his pub-owning relatives near Macclesfield: very quiet, after the Liverpool docks, if only those strange planes hadn't kept roaring around, day and night. Knickers enjoyed a dirty weekend with an old flame in Leicester, where she worked in a parachute factory and told him all sorts of amusing stories about the stealing and corruption that went on there. Even Eldorado took a break and had a day in Cambridge, wandering around the ancient colleges, punting on the placid river, and sampling the local ale at a friendly tavern, where several R.A.F. pilots in civilian clothing were to be heard speaking occasional phrases of elementary Russian.

There was no holiday for Luis Cabrillo in Lisbon. He rarely left his office, except to take his bulky envelopes to the big post office in the Avenida da Liberdade, or to collect the *Abwehr*'s slimmer letters from the Banco Espirito Santo in the Rua do Comercio.

Nevertheless, there was more time for him to think and to plan, now that Julie—her wrist mended, the cast removed—took care of the office routine.

His first reports to Madrid had required two or three drafts, sometimes more; now, with the confidence of experience, he usually got it right first time. The files were growing fatter, and he made a practice of re-reading them regularly so as to make sure that his sub-agents behaved consistently : if Seagull made friends with an American seaman at the beginning of the month, for instance, they should not meet again until the end of the month, to allow time for two crossings of the Atlantic. Madrid knew that Knickers had escaped military service because of his poor eyesight; this made it unwise for him to report in too much detail about aircraft or equipment he might have seen. And so on.

Meanwhile Julie found someone in the commercial department of the American embassy who knew about lemonade crystals, as a result of which she bought a thousand dollars' worth, that being close to the limit of the credit which Luis had arranged for her with the Banco Espirito Santo.

'Who the hell uses this stuff?' she asked. She had brought back a sample to show Luis. He was munching a few crystals.

'Who drinks lemonade?' he asked in return.

'I'll ask Bradburn & Wedge . . . You look different, Luis. Has something happened?'

'How different?'

'I don't know.' She put her head on one side. 'Chirpier. More buoyant.'

'Ah, that's because of Knickers. Knickers has fallen in love.'

'Wow. And the sheets in Leicester are barely cool. What a man! Who is it this time?'

'I'm not sure,' Luis said, bouncing on his heels, 'but I think her father's a rear-admiral or something.'

'Hey, that's *class*,' Julie exclaimed. 'That should be worth a few bucks.'

'I'm told she looks like the back of a bus,' Luis said, 'but Knickers can't tell the difference even with his glasses on, so who cares?'

'Sure. As long as they're happy.' She put the lemonade crystals away. 'They are happy, aren't they?'

Luis sucked in his breath. 'I'll be honest with you, Julie,' he said. 'The real trouble is, she drinks.'

'Like a fish?'

'Like a barracuda,' he said happily. 'The family is very worried.'

*

Wolfgang turned the pages with his left hand. The numbness in his right fingers made them clumsy and unreliable. He sat with his hand tucked inside his shirt, where the body-warmth to some extent countered the numbness, and he painstakingly scrutinised the file copies of the Eldorado reports. Sooner or later, he knew, even the best tight-rope walker stumbles, even the best trapeze-artist fumbles. Sooner or later Eldorado had to attempt one of his famous triple backward somersaults and land on his famous Spanish ass. It was just a question of time. Wolfgang turned another page, read another paragraph, and twitched with excitement. There it was! The fatal flaw! He skimmed the next paragraph and grinned with delight: another beauty! He raced through the rest of the report and smacked his fist on the page with the third and greatest, deadliest error. 'I've *got* the bastard,' he breathed.

Otto Krafft, who was working at the other end of the room, looked around. 'Which bastard is that?' he asked.

'Both of them,' Wolfgang said. He took his hand from inside his shirt and flexed the fingers. Blood was pulsing through them, tingling the skin like fresh snow.

*

Julie found an accountant, a dapper man who actually enjoyed dealing with the *Ministerio da Fazenda* and who took an undisguised delight in dealing with Julie. He took care of registering Bradburn & Wedge, he took care of the complicated form, he took care of the baggy taxman. The only thing he couldn't take care of was selling one thousand American dollars' worth of lemonade crystals.

*

Major Schwarz was a liaison officer between *Abwehr* headquarters and the Fuehrer's office. When he visited Madrid on a working holiday, Brigadier Christian took the opportunity to polish his apples.

He began by introducing Otto Krafft, controller of Eagle. Schwarz remarked that he was impressed by Eagle's apparent freedom of movement in Britain.

'So am I, sir,' Otto said, with such fervency that they laughed. 'Of course, he has two great advantages: he's an American citizen, and his company trades with Britain, so he can justify his visits to ports or customers all over the island.'

'Invaluable,' Schwarz said.

'Eagle is an extremely reticent fellow . . .' Otto began.

'Like Gary Cooper,' Christian put in.

'. . . so we know next-to-nothing about his background, but reading between the lines of his reports I suspect that he spent some time at an English university. Perhaps even as a Rhodes Scholar. He has visited Oxford twice this summer.'

Schwarz snapped his fingers. 'That would explain some of his influential contacts. You know, by the way, that Operation Bandstand has been confirmed by a couple of other agents?'

'Has it really, sir?' Otto looked very impressed. 'Well, that's encouraging.'

'Yes. It wasn't always called "Bandstand" but that's not surprising: the British often change codenames during planning.'

'Yes, of course they do,' Otto said.

'And I heard just before I left that we've doubled our submarine patrols off Norway.'

'That's a pity,' Otto said, 'because I've just heard from Eagle that Bandstand's been cancelled.'

'Damnation!' Brigadier Christian smote his forehead. 'When did that come in?'

'Ten minutes ago, sir. I was just reading it when—'

'You can see what's happened, can't you?' Schwarz interrupted. 'Churchill's got cold feet! We move one piddling division into Norway and he calls the whole thing off. He knows we know.'

'What does Eagle think?' Christian asked.

As Otto Krafft opened his mouth, there was a knock on the door and Wolfgang Adler came in. He held up a folder. 'I have a special report for you to read, brigadier,' he said.

Christian waved it away. 'Not now.'

'It's urgent. It won't wait.'

Christian glanced at Schwarz with a God-help-us smile. 'It'll wait, Adler,' he said. 'It'll wait for ever, if necessary.'

'I take leave to doubt that, brigadier.' Wolfgang was pale with suppressed anger.

'Just take leave, Adler.'

There was a frozen moment while the two men stared.

Then Wolfgang turned and went out. As he closed the door he heard Christian's snort of amazement.

Later, Otto described the exchange for the benefit of the other controllers. 'It was quite extraordinary,' he said. 'He really hates the old man, for some reason.'

'Adler's a fool,' Franz Werth said. 'At this rate he'll end up cleaning the lavatories. D'you realise that, strictly speaking, he should have been next in line to be controller? He should have had Nutmeg. I bet Christian never gave him a thought.'

'Nutmeg? Who's Nutmeg?' Fischer asked.

'New sub-agent,' Otto told him. 'Eldorado just recruited him. Ex-Indian Army officer in Cambridge. Works for the Ministry of Food, hunting black marketeers. Hates Bolsheviks.'

'And who's controlling him?'

'Me,' said Franz.

'But you've got Seagull.'

'Well, now I've got Nutmeg too. '

'Good God!' Fischer exclaimed.

'You'll be next, I expect,' Otto said. 'Eagle's already sending as much material as two ordinary agents, so I'm fully occupied.'

'I wonder what Adler had in his magic folder?' Franz said.

'Sandwiches, I hope,' Otto said. 'He's got a long wait ahead of him.'

Chapter 52

Two Portuguese delivery-men carried in the new filing-cabinets, placed them next to the old ones, gave Luis the keys, got his signature and went out. They had also brought a Dictaphone system and three second-hand typewriters.

'Great idea,' said Julie from the door of her office. 'Now I can type three reports at once. I'd do four, but I need my left foot to beat time.'

Luis tapped a space-key until the machine rang its little bell. 'Different type-faces,' he said. 'It occurred to me that all the reports should look different, you see, especially now that

Garlic and Nutmeg are working. I got them cheap. Can you work them okay?'

She shrugged. 'I guess so.'

'If not I'll get some more. They're a deductible business expense.'

It was eleven in the morning on a day of autumnal crispness. Outside, the sky was a bowl of such pure blue that it looked as if it could be cracked with a spoon. A few gulls had wandered up from the Tagus and were flashing their extreme whiteness against the sky in a lazy display of flying skills. Down below, the red roofs and white walls of Lisbon stood out as sharply as the pop-up houses in a child's picture-book. It was, Julie thought, one hell of a day.

Luis stretched, and rubbed his eyes; he had been writing since 8 a.m. 'Shall we get ourselves organised?' he asked. He found a sheet of paper with a list of items. 'Let's start with Bradburn & Wedge.'

'I saw that guy Rodriguez again this morning.' She came over and sat on his desk. 'He says he's definitely bankrupt. He can't return the five hundred bucks'-worth of lemonade crystals because the guy he sold them to has gone away without paying.'

Luis grunted. 'No wonder he's bankrupt.'

'Rodriguez feels very bad about it all. He's offered to pay us back in de-greasing patents.'

Luis looked sideways at her. 'What are they?'

'God knows. But Rodriguez reckons they're worth eight hundred bucks, so I said yes.'

Luis crossed off item one. 'That still leaves us with half the crystals, doesn't it?'

'Maybe. Here's another reply to my ad in *Diario*.'

He scanned the letter she gave him. 'He's a German,' he said.

'That's just his name. Joachim von Klausbrunner. For all you know he comes from Nigeria.'

'He's got offices in Hamburg and Rome.' Luis raised his eyebrows. 'Why does he want lemonade crystals?'

'His secretary told me she thinks it's for export to Rommel's Afrika Korps.'

'Oh,' Luis said. 'Oh, oh.'

'Yeah. That about sums it up.' She swung her legs. Luis looked at them, and then looked away. 'They want all they can get,' she said. 'Twenty per cent above market price, too.'

'I don't suppose lemonade crystals can do the Afrika Korps all that much good, can they?' Luis asked. 'I mean, the really important thing is to get Bradburn & Wedge established. Isn't it?'

'I guess so.'

'It's a question of ends versus means.' He twitched his nose. 'Damn, damn.'

'Spin a coin,' Julie suggested.

Luis found an escudo. 'Heads we go ahead and sell them the stuff,' he said. It came down heads. 'Thank you, God, you can go home now.' He ticked lemonade crystals. 'Now, about Garlic. I think he ought to find out something to do with shipbuilding. Have you ever been to Glasgow?'

'Drove through it once. Grim.'

'Jasper Stembridge reckons they do a lot of shipbuilding in Glasgow.' He flipped open the book to a marked page. ' "*The deafening noise of countless hammers tells that men are busy at work building a vessel that soon will slide into the murky waters of the Clyde, and later speed across the seas*". I bet they're working night and day.'

'Sure. To make up for the U-boat sinkings.'

'Exactly . . .'

They talked about that, and about the four other items on Luis's list, involving Seagull, Knickers, Nutmeg and Eldorado. When he had crossed off the last one, Julie said: 'Okay, now let's get down to Any Other Business. The topic under discussion is sex.'

'Ah.' Luis adjusted the point of his propelling pencil. 'Sex.'

'Yes. Does it exist, has it a future, is there a place for it, and why can't that be in our bed?'

'I see what you mean. It has been rather a long time, I suppose.' He scratched his chin.

'It's been a week,' Julie said. 'A whole seven-day week.'

'As long as that? My goodness.'

'Your goodness is exactly what I need, Luis. Dammit, every night we stagger home, dead beat, and you fall into bed. And every morning you're up and crashing about, fully dressed, before dawn!'

'Seven o'clock.'

'Same thing. I mean, Seagull and Garlic and all those guys

334

are lovely people, Luis, but none of them has what you have. That is, assuming you still have it.'

'Mmm.' He nodded several times. She looked away. There was an awkward silence. 'The work takes up so much *time*,' he murmured.

'I can remember when we were in Madrid . . .' she began. She left it unfinished and went into her office. Soon Luis heard her start typing. He sighed and returned to his report.

There was another briefing letter waiting for him at the bank that afternoon. He scanned it, recognised Richard Fischer's style, and stuffed it into a pocket. That evening they worked until nine, and then went to a restaurant which overlooked the river. The view was deep and dark : blue-black sky and inky water. A few early stars gave depth to the night, and the yellow lights of ferries trickled to and from the far shore. There was lobster and watercress salad with a cool white wine. There was every fruit that Julie had ever seen and a few she hadn't, and a waiter who could carve a fat orange into the shape of a perfect waterlily without spilling a drop of juice. The coffee was like molten gold and the port was like molten grapes, except that it *was* molten grapes, but by that time Julie was too happy to conduct a careful analysis of her pleasures; she simply enjoyed them. 'You know, Luis,' she said, curling her leg inside his, 'for a dumb Spanish schmuck, you're not such a heel as you might be, even if you have got crumbs on your moustache.'

He reached for his handkerchief, and pulled the letter out with it. 'I forgot to tell you,' he said. 'Madrid is now interested in the economic planning of the British. It looks as if the war might last longer than was first thought. Isn't that encouraging?'

'Sure. What this world needs is another long war.'

'No, I mean it opens up a fresh area for us. I can feed them stuff about manpower and raw materials and budgets and . . .'

'And sex.'

'Well, growth of population is a factor. I mean, look at Russia.'

'Is there much sex in Russia?'

Luis sipped his port. Julie stroked the inside of his thigh.

335

'I wonder,' he said thoughtfully, 'I just wonder if it isn't all a matter of energy.'

'Tell you what. Let's go and find out.'

'Productive capacity, for instance. You get out what you put in.'

'It's worth trying,' she murmured. 'Who knows, we could be on the verge of a great discovery.'

Luis paid the bill and said nothing until they were outside. 'It really is a very promising development, you know, Julie,' he remarked. He was clicking his fingers and hoping from foot to foot as he searched for a taxi.

'Uh-huh,' she said.

'I mean, it offers us so many new opportunities, so many . . .' A taxi stopped. He held the door open while she got in, and he stood for a moment, twisting the handle back and forth. 'I'll tell you what: you go ahead. My mind's full of ideas. I'll just pop back to the office for a few minutes and dictate them into the machine. Otherwise I'm afraid I might forget them.'

'How long are you going to be?'

'Not long. I promise.'

He talked into the Dictaphone for half an hour, and then glanced through Jasper Stembridge to check a couple of facts. What he read about iron-smelting in the Middlesbrough district—'*By day smoke pours forth from the chimneys of many blast furnaces and steel factories, by night their lurid flames light the whole countryside*'—gave him new ideas about the effects of economic dislocation caused by black-out restrictions. He looked up Middlesbrough in the 1923 Michelin. It was very close to the North Sea, which made it highly vulnerable to bomber attack from Denmark. What would the British be doing about that? He put a fresh roll in the Dictaphone.

Julie was asleep when he got home; he was astonished to discover that it was three in the morning. Habit awoke him at seven; when he got up she stirred and blinked but fell asleep again. He was eager to be back at work, and he hurried his breakfast. She half-opened her eyes to see him getting dressed, and grunted. He paused and looked. 'See you later,' she mumbled. He squeezed her blanketed foot and walked softly away.

336

It was ten-thirty when she came into the office. There were two Portuguese men behind her, carrying a new divan bed and a package of sheets, pillows and blankets. They put it where she said. She tipped them. They went out. Luis watched with interest.

'Just a little idea I had last night while I was waiting for you to come home,' she said.

Luis tested the springs. 'Very comfortable. What a good idea. If I ever have to work really late—'

'I said it was for Bradburn & Wedge, so the store gave me twenty per cent discount.'

He nodded. 'I don't suppose it's a tax-deductible expense, but still . . .'

She watched him walk all around it.

'Don't forget to kick the tyres,' she said.

He smiled, and picked a loose thread from the mattress. She looked at him while he looked at the bed. Eventually he glanced up. 'A nice thought,' he said. 'Thank you.'

Julie held his gaze for perhaps five seconds. 'I'm pleased you're pleased,' she said, and went into her office.

They worked separately for about twenty minutes. Then she called out: 'What's this word "loins"?'

He frowned. 'I don't remember writing anything about loins.'

'Could it be "groins"?'

'No. Show me.'

She came in, smiling brightly and utterly naked. Her breasts swayed slightly in counterpoint to the easy swing of her hips. She looked very white and very lithe. Luis's head jerked as if someone had tugged his hair.

'Here it is.' She leaned gently against him and showed him the page of notes.

'That's not "loins",' he said. 'That's "dynamite".'

'Is there a difference?' She walked back to her office, taking the long way round. Her buttocks twinkled neatly.

Luis took a deep breath and picked up his work, but the words had lost their meaning. One minute later Julie was back. This time she drifted slowly over to his desk, walking on tip-toe and smoothing the back of her hair while she held a different sheet of paper at arm's length. In the reflected sunlight her skin had a sheen like new satin.

'Look,' she said, placing the paper in front of him. 'It must be jelly, cuz jam don't shake like that.'

She had ringed one word. 'That's "dynamite" again,' Luis said.

'Really?' She put her arm around his neck and leaned so that one nipple brushed his cheek and touched his lips. 'Dynamite, huh?'

'For God's sake!' Luis roared. He heaved himself out of his chair as she took her paper and walked away. Throwing off his coat and shirt and kicking off his shoes he followed her into her office, where she had already begun typing.

'Sorry if I disturbed you,' she said.

'Forget that,' he told her, dragging off his trousers with some difficulty. 'Come to bed.'

She paused with her hands on the keys, while he stood, panting and rampant. 'You do realise that it's not a tax-deductible expense,' she remarked.

'Oh, balls!' he cried.

'Well, if you put it that way,' she said, 'how can a lady refuse?'

They ripped open the packets of sheets and covered the bed. The cotton rustled stiffly against their bodies. One of the bedsprings squeaked. 'Did you really think I got this just for when you worked late?' Julie asked.

'Yes,' Luis said defiantly. He tucked his head under the sheet and blew a series of raspberries against her breasts until it made her laugh and she hugged him to stop it. 'Anyway,' he mumbled, 'when a woman arrives in your office with a bed at half-past ten in the morning, it's not easy to know exactly what to do next.'

'Poor Luis,' she said. 'Still, you seem to be getting the hang of it now, don't you?'

'Beginner's luck,' he said.

*

Luis slept for half an hour, and woke up to see Julie curled beside him, reading a Portuguese guide book. 'Let's go to Oporto,' she said. 'It's all green and blue up there. Lots of rivers and mountains. Have you ever been to Oporto?' He shook his head. 'Couple of hundred miles north,' she said.

He lay sideways and enjoyed watching her.

'Coimbra looks good too. And Santarém. Nazaré. Grandala. Beja. Loulé. Terrific old places, built by Moors and Romans. We should go take a look.'

'It would be nice.'

'Well, we can afford a week off.'

'Afford the money, yes. What about the time? What about the work?'

'It'll still be here when we come back.'

Luis almost laughed. 'Madrid wouldn't be very pleased to hear that the war has been adjourned for two weeks,' he said.

'Can't you cook something up? Tell them that Seagull's got mumps, Knickers got married, Garlic's working double-shifts at the hospital and Eldorado . . . I don't know, Eldorado's been run over by a bus.'

'That still leaves Nutmeg.'

'Jailed for shoplifting.'

Luis grunted, and looked away. 'They're easy enough to destroy,' he said, 'but they're damn difficult to create. In any case, I want to recruit a new man soon.'

Julie slowly raised her head and looked over the top of the guide book. 'Not another subagent, for heaven's sake?' she said.

'Certainly. He's a homosexual lecturer at the University of Birmingham. Codename "Wallpaper".'

She moved until she was kneeling and sitting on her heels, looking down at him. 'Luis, tell me something. Why are you doing all this?'

He shrugged. 'You know why.'

'No, I don't. I don't mean *how* did it happen, I mean what's the purpose of this whole damn great operation? Where is it getting you?'

'It's getting me rich, of course. What else?' He made a wide-open gesture.

'But you *are* rich, now.' She stared at him, determined to make him explain. 'How much do you make per year at the moment?'

'In dollars? About . . .' He worked it out. 'Maybe sixty or seventy thousand a year. That's *before* taxes and expenses,' he added hurriedly.

'Then I don't understand. What more do you want?'

'It's a business, Julie. You can't stop it growing if the market

339

wants it to grow. All I'm doing is meeting the demand.'

'What the hell are you talking about, Luis? You *create* the demand! You *create* all these nobodies! I mean, how many more do you need, for Pete's sake? What are you trying to do: make yourself the first spy millionaire?'

Luis looked at the ceiling and smoothed his moustache.

'Holy cow,' Julie said, in a voice flattened by amazement. 'I just aimed ten feet high and hit the target.'

Luis got out of bed, and stretched. 'Duty calls!' he said.

*

Luis successfully launched Wallpaper, hinting not only that his homosexuality was the lever which Eldorado had used to recruit him, but also that—in the decadence of Birmingham University—it won him access to secret research being done for the War Office. Wallpaper's first report was on experiments with hypnosis to reduce sexual tension among submarine crews. He ran up an impressive bill for entertaining his informants, which Madrid paid without question.

Bradburn & Wedge was also doing well. Julie sold a second consignment of lemonade crystals to the firm of Joachim von Klausbrunner. The degreasing patents which she had taken in payment from the bankrupt dealer lay on her desk for a while, until she advertised them in *Diario (Patentes Anti-Lubrificantes—Grande Utilidade—Oportunidade Exceptional)*. This brought an enquiry from a firm of engineers, who bought a five-year licence on the patents. Her accountant urged her to invest the money in Portuguese Government bonds; instead she spent it all on soap.

'Very American,' Luis said when she told him.

'Listen, you're more American than I am. At least I get some fun out of business. All you ever want to do is make money.'

'All I want to do is succeed. Would you prefer me to fail?'

'Oh, forget it.'

'The money comes afterwards. It's just a measurement of success, that's all.'

'Okay, you're rich! You're successful! So why can't we at least take a weekend in Oporto?'

Luis shook his head. 'We've been over that. You go, if you want to.'

'You're a goddam addict,' she said. 'Any time you're not making money you're afraid you're going to die. The more you get, the more you crave.'

He smiled, and steered her to the door. 'I always know when you're hungry,' he said, 'because that's when you stop making sense.'

It was drizzling and gloomy, so he took her to a restaurant made warm and cheerful by its charcoal fire. They ate grilled chicken made even hotter with *piri-piri* sauce, drank beer, and said little.

A man walked past their table, stopped, half-turned his head, and then came back. 'Hullo,' he said. 'This *is* a surprise.'

He was in his mid-thirties, with a plump, friendly face and hair that was thick but surprisingly grey. His suit was a smart and comfortable lovat tweed, and his manner was easy and confident. Luis went on chewing his chicken and looked at him warily. 'Is it?' he said.

'You're Luis Cabrillo. You don't remember me, do you?'

Luis's moustache briefly straightened in a polite smile. 'No, and I'm afraid you are mistaken.'

'You're not Luis Cabrillo?'

Luis handed him a business card. 'My name is Bradburn,' he said, 'and this is my partner, *Senhora* Wedge.'

'Jolly good.' He didn't even glance at the card. 'The last time we met, I was a very smelly deserter, you were driving a car, and Madrid was getting the daylights shelled out of it.' Luis leaned back and stared. 'Charles Templeton,' the man said.

'For heaven's sake.' Luis recognised traces of the haggard and ragged figure that he had once watched swigging brandy and chatting over-brightly to the newspapermen. 'Come and sit down. I thought you were dead. You look very well. How on earth did you get out of Spain?'

'The old-boy system, old boy. Met a chap I knew at school.' Templeton sat. 'I take it you're still in the skullduggery business?'

'What makes you think that?'

Templeton held up the card. 'Bogus name, old chap. I mean, it doesn't matter, I'm not *offended*, or anything.' He stopped a waiter and ordered more beer. 'It happens to be my line of work too, at the moment. If I may say so without offence, you don't look like a Miss Wedge.'

'I'm Julie Conroy,' she said. 'Luis is too cheap to get me a decent alias.'

'You look rather like Lauren Bacall.'

'Don't tell him that. The thought of the expense will give him palpitations.'

'What are you doing in Lisbon?' Luis asked.

'I'm with the British embassy. I got a job with the Secret Service, organising skullduggery.'

'But you were a *Communist*,' Luis said, 'you fought with the International Brigade, you were on the run—'

'Stand on your chair, Luis,' Julie said, 'the people at the back can't hear.'

Templeton laughed. 'That's all right, I've got diplomatic immunity nowadays.' The beer came. 'I suppose it must seem a bit odd to you,' he said. 'It's the old-boy system again. I met a chap I knew at school who was looking for chaps of the right sort, and here I am.'

They reminisced about the civil war, until Julie interrupted and told Templeton that Luis had met a colleague of his at the embassy. 'Yes?' Templeton said.

'Walter Witteridge,' Luis said.

'Oh, he's quite useless. He used to write books, I believe. You can't expect anything from a man who writes books for a living.'

'You used to paint pictures,' Luis pointed out.

'Ah, yes, but they didn't *sell*. I mean, nobody, *bought* them. Whereas Witteridge's stuff used to sell by the cartload. *Fearfully* popular man, he was. Did you find him useless?'

'Utterly.'

'There you are, then.' Templeton drank his beer with an air of satisfaction.

'Perhaps Luis should go and see someone else,' Julie said.

'About what?'

'Getting a job,' Luis said. 'You know, working for your people. I have certain . . . qualifications. *Special* qualifications.'

Templeton was shaking his head before Luis had finished. 'I can't honestly see it happening, old chap,' he said. 'It's not that you couldn't do a splendid job, I'm sure you'd be absolutely first-rate; but they have rather funny ideas in my

342

department. They rather like to have public-school chaps. I suppose it's to make sure we all understand each other.'

'I see.'

'Bloody silly, I know, but there you are.'

Templeton was returning to the embassy, and so he shared their taxi. 'I tell you what might make a difference,' he said. 'If you could find out something we wanted to know, that would be a sort of a foot in the door, at least.'

'I could try.'

Templeton looked at the driver and lowered his head. 'Our chaps have caught wind of an enemy agent called Eagle,' he whispered. 'He travels all over England but that's as much as we know. That and his code-name, Eagle.'

'All right,' Luis grunted. They straightened up. 'Awfully nice place, Lisbon,' Templeton said.

'Do you need any soap?' Julie asked.

'Well, I could always do with the odd bar, I suppose.'

'I've got half a ton.'

'Goodness. If I were you, I'd try the inhabitants of Jarama, in central Spain. The ones I met were always in desperate need of a bath.'

Julie wrinkled her nose. 'Waste of time. Only clean people buy soap.'

The remark saddened Templeton. He looked at the wet, black streets, and sighed. Soon they reached the embassy. He got out and waved goodbye.

As they drove on, Julie said: 'Now I know why Hitler decided not to invade England. He didn't go to the right school.'

Luis nodded, gloomily. 'He wouldn't have got along with the other chaps, poor devil.'

'Not that he wouldn't have done a splendid job.'

'Oh, I'm sure he'd have been absolutely first-rate.'

'Of course. It's just that . . .'

'Yes. I mean, how could one chap say to another chap, "Look here, old chap, I'd like you to meet a chap I knew at school, chap called Adolf Hitler"?'

'I can't honestly see it happening, old chap,' Julie said.

'Shitheads,' Luis muttered. 'They don't deserve to win.'

Chapter 53

The Russian winter began unusually early in 1941 : snow was falling near Leningrad in the first days of November. German commanders noticed its effects when their sentries, lacking winter clothing, froze to death at their posts. In Madrid, Brigadier Christian noticed that his office was surprisingly chilly in the mornings, and ordered a log fire.

When Otto Krafft brought in Eagle's report on the state of the British lightweight alloys industry, Christian read it while standing in front of the fire, one hand behind him to raise the flap of his hacking jacket.

He finished the last page and gave a snort of satisfaction. 'I very much doubt if the British Ministry of Aircraft Production could improve on that,' he said. 'It's complete, it's concise, and it reads like Hemingway.'

'Yes, sir. I suspect that Eagle is an admirer of Mr Hemingway, especially in view of Mr Hemingway's recent articles opposing American involvement in the war.'

Christian nodded, too pleased to pay much attention. 'The short, declarative sentence!' he said. 'So easy to translate. It helps them enormously in Berlin, I know. No damned subjunctives!'

'I'm afraid Eagle's travelling expenses are especially heavy this time,' Otto said. 'Southampton, Coventry, Newport—the one in South Wales, that is—Wolverhampton, Fort William in Scotland, and he even went to Northern Ireland for the bauxite works at Larne because—'

'Pay it.' Christian waved impatiently. 'We're lucky to have a man who has access to all these places. There's only one way to be sure, and that's to go and see for yourself. I know; I've done it.' He flourished the report like a flag. 'You don't gather intelligence of this calibre by sitting on your ass in London. There's only one tiny thing that puzzles me.'

Otto cocked his head and looked receptive.

'English spelling,' Christian said. 'Eagle spells "tyre" with a "y", not an "i". He writes "aluminium" instead of "alumi-num". Strange?' He hoisted his shaggy eyebrows.

'Yes and no, sir,' Otto said cautiously. 'After all, Eagle is getting all his information from English sources. He must be accustomed to talking about aluminium by now. And he *was* a Rhodes Scholar.'

'True.' Christian tossed him the report. 'Code it and forward it, top priority. Eagle gets a one-hundred-percent bonus and I want Dr Hartmann in here at once.'

Christian offered Hartmann a glass of dry sherry, sat him beside the fire, and together they reviewed Garlic's output. 'You know, it's time Garlic broadened his horizons,' Christian said. 'I want you to get him to concentrate on the lightweight alloys situation in Britain. Who makes them, where, how much : you know the sort of thing.'

'Yes sir. Is there a deadline?'

'No, but . . . Stir him up a bit. Hint that there's big bonus money available if . . . Wait a minute. You have to brief Garlic through Eldorado, don't you?'

'That's right.'

Christian thought for a moment. 'Let's see if we can't use Eagle to stimulate Eldorado. Tell Eldorado something about Eagle, not too much, just that Eagle's doing very well over there and as a result certain funds may have to be diverted from Eldorado or his subagents . . . Get the idea? Make it look like an act of courtesy on your part.'

'I gather the objective is to encourage a certain amount of healthy rivalry,' Hartmann said.

'You gather right,' Christian declared, 'and if it works, we shall all gather a rich reward.'

When Dr Hartmann went out, Wolfgang Adler was waiting at the door. This time he was not holding his folder. 'Request permission to see Captain Mullen,' he said before Christian could speak.

'I see.' Christian bared his teeth and scratched an incisor with the nail of his little finger. 'Well, you have a right to go over my head, I suppose. See Otto. He will arrange it.'

Ten minutes later Otto found Wolfgang staring out of a window. 'Two o'clock in Mullen's office,' he told him. Wolfgang grunted. 'Look, I think you're making a mistake,' Otto warned. 'I can easily cancel it, if you like.'

Wolfgang breathed deeply, in and out, until his shoulders slumped. 'Not me,' he said softly. 'The mistake is not mine.'

At three minutes to two, he took the lift to the top floor. He carried his folder. The fingers of his right hand were throbbing and his palms were sweating slightly.

Mullen's outer office was empty. Wolfgang knocked on the inner door and pushed it open. Waiting for him behind the big, curved, mahogany desk was Brigadier Christian. 'Come in, Adler,' he said. 'Mullen's gone, posted. I've got his job now. So what d'you want?'

Wolfgang was shocked but not beaten. He took some stapled papers from his folder and dropped them in front of Christian. 'That's a copy of an Eldorado report,' he said. 'It stinks with error and I can prove that. On page three he refers to St Pancras in central London in a context which suggests that he thinks it is a church. St Pancras is in fact a large railway station.' Chirstian linked his fingers behind his head and leaned back in his chair. 'The next paragraph,' Wolfgang went on, 'concerns supplies of coolant fluid for a certain radial-engined bomber. All radial engines are air-cooled.' Christian's eyelids drooped slightly. 'And worst of all, if you care to look on page six,' Wolfgang said in a voice flattened with anger, 'you will find Eldorado relating with enthusiasm the views of a supposedly experienced aeronautical engineer about an advanced version of the Hurricane fighter which he claims is fitted with no fewer than four cannon-guns. Four *seventy-five millimetre* cannon-guns.' Wolfgang saw that Christian had stopped listening, and his voice became higher and harsher. 'Such a machine is impossible! The recoil from the guns would stop it dead in mid-air! The wings would be torn off! The pilot would be hurled through the windscreen!' Christian stretched his neck to look at his desk diary. 'Look, I was an engineer!' Wolfgang cried. 'I studied in London, I know these things!'

'Finished?' Christian said. Wolfgang nodded. His leg was beginning to ache from standing. Christian straightened up. 'Three points,' he declared briskly. 'First, this report went to Berlin over a week ago. It's been sold and bought and paid for. The transaction is complete. Understand?'

He looked up and stared until Wolfgang nodded.

'Second point. You, Adler, have become more trouble than

you're worth. Just because Eldorado made a fool of you, you're obsessed with making a fool of him. That's no good to me. Understand?'

Another stare forced another nod.

'Third and last, you're posted. The *Abwehr* is forming new sections on the Russian Front. Berlin has requested the release of any personnel who are surplus to requirements, fighting fit and eager for a fresh start. You qualify on all three counts, Adler.'

Wolfgang felt the folder slip from his cold fingers. 'For God's sake, I don't want to go to bloody Russia,' he muttered.

'You want to grow up, don't you? Well, this is your big chance. You're posted to . . .' Christian's finger traced an entry in his desk diary. '. . . Novgorod. Now get out. And take that tosh with you.' The Eldorado report came spinning across the desk. Wolfgang grabbed at it and missed.

Chapter 54

The news that Eagle was not only an employee of Madrid *Abwehr* but also a serious rival to Eldorado came as a shock. When Luis got Dr Hartmann's briefing letter, with its hint that Eagle's success might oblige Madrid to redirect its funds, he became angry and depressed. 'Look at that, for Christ's sake,' he said disgustedly. 'After all the slaving and sweating I've done . . . I feel like telling them to go to hell.'

'Then why don't you?' Julie was unconcerned. 'If they're not going to pay you, why work? We can even go to Oporto.'

Luis turned away. They had been bickering for a week, on and off, about their way of life. She argued in favour of making money solely to enjoy the world; he argued that his work was what he enjoyed most, and that in any case they had obligations, commitments, deadlines . . . In this running quarrel, Oporto had come to symbolise, for her, an escape from endless money-making in Lisbon, while for him it represented a flimsy fantasy-world, an avoidance of responsibility. Escape versus escapism.

Meanwhile, it rained.

'We can go to Oporto in the spring,' he said. 'The weather in Oporto is rotten now.'

'The weather *here* is rotten now. Why can't we have rotten weather somewhere new?'

Luis read Dr Hartmann's letter again.

'I can't believe this bastard Eagle is really all that hot,' he muttered.

'You can always go to England and find out,' she suggested. 'I understand the weather there is no lousier than it is here.'

'Oh, go to hell,' he growled.

'Believe me, any change would be an improvement.' She went into her office and banged the door.

Luis forced himself to get down to work. Lightweight alloys. Where would Garlic go to find something about the British lightweight alloys industry? He reached for Jasper H. Stembridge and found the chapter on Scotland. Picture of Highland cattle. Picture of stag. Picture of golden eagle. He read: 'Little blue tarns lie half-hidden in the mountain, while through the rugged boulder-strewn glens that seam its sides dash foaming' (turn the page) 'torrents fed by the rains of this, one of the wettest districts in the British Isles. South of Fort William, lying at the head of the blue waters of Loch Leven, is Kinlochleven, where mountain falls are harnessed to generate electricity for the aluminium factory.'

And there was a picture to prove it: six huge pipes running down a mountainside and plugging themselves into a factory.

Terrific. A marvellous starting-point.

Luis took a fresh block of paper and a sharp pencil and prepared to make Eagle look stuffed.

Half an hour later he had the framework of a powerful report. Kinlochleven was the key to British alloy output. Production was up 73 per cent over 1940. Heavy rainfall (twelve inches above average) ensured record electricity output. New aluminium plants were being completed in secret at (see Michelin map 8) Fort Augustus, Inveraray and Drumnadrochit. For these plants, Canadian tunnelling experts had bored through three mountains to reach high-level water supplies. Luis chewed his pencil. *Drumnadrochit*, he thought. What a name!

He looked up and saw Julie standing in the doorway of her office, looking fairly bleak. He stopped chewing his pencil.

348

'You realise this is all a waste of time,' she said, holding up the report she was typing. Her voice had a harsh edge that he had not heard before. 'I mean, it doesn't mean anything. It's just marks on paper. You're just playing silly games.'

'Madrid believes in it.'

'So they're just playing silly games too. None of this makes any difference to anything.'

'It makes money.'

'Sure. But that doesn't mean anything either. That's just different marks on different pieces of paper. Bank shit. Eldorado shit. What's the difference?'

He looked down, determined not to give in and fight. His cheek twitched with suppressed rage. The door slammed.

Luis picked up his sheet of paper. *Bitch, bitch, bitch,* he thought. He wanted to smash something, but he knew that it would give her pleasure so he sat hunched over his optimistic report. After a while he tore it up. 'Kinlochleven,' he scribbled, 'is a disaster area. Drought, sabotage and managerial incompetence have dragged down aluminium output to a pathetic 23% of last year's figure. Attempts to rush construction of new plants have met with catastrophe. Last week, sixteen Polish tunnelling engineers died in explosions.' Rain lashed against the windows and briefly drowned the sound of typing next door. Luis crossed out 'sixteen' and wrote 'twenty-five'. He began to feel better.

*

'All right, who's wrong?' Brigadier Christian asked.

Dr Hartmann and Otto Krafft sat at each end of a large sofa and said nothing.

Christian was on the prowl around the room, rapping the wall with his knuckles as he went. Now that he had moved into Captain Mullen's office, he had greater scope for prowling. 'Look, I didn't get where I am by sending contradictory reports to Berlin,' he said. 'They don't buy guesses, they don't pay us to spin a coin, they want *facts*. You know what you've brought me? A salesman's catalogue. If I don't like it in blue you'll sell me something else in red. Choice! I don't want choice, I want the real thing!' He crashed the flat of his hand down on the nearest piece of furniture.

'It may be worth remembering, sir,' said Otto, cautiously,

349

'that Berlin has had Eagle's report for over a week now, and nobody there has queried it.'

'Not out loud, maybe.'

Dr Hartmann cleared his throat. 'Eldorado's team does have a remarkably good record, sir,' he observed. 'None of his sub-agents has ever let us down, Garlic least of all.'

Christian grunted. 'As far as we know, you mean. The fact remains that one or other of your geniuses has been spitting in his soup. The British light alloy industry cannot be going up and down at the same time, for God's sake. Eagle tells us it's booming, Garlic says it's going bust. Who's right?'

'On the face of it, sir,' Otto suggested, 'Eagle is better qualified to judge. He's an industrialist, whereas Garlic—'

'I know, I know. Don't you think I've considered all that?' Christian paused at a mirror, breathed heavily on his reflection, and prowled away. 'The point is, what do we do now?'

'Get a third opinion?' said Dr Hartmann.

'I don't want any more bloody *opinions*. I want the truth.' Christian reached the sofa and leaned on the back, making it rock. 'They'll have to fight it out between them, that's all. Send them both an order.' He prodded Otto on the shoulder and made him start. 'Make sure they know it's an *order*. Tell them to meet as soon as possible. How soon can they meet?'

Otto began: 'I really don't think . . .'

'Five days from now should be reasonable,' Hartmann said, 'allowing a day for delays.'

'Five days from now, then. Where?'

'Well, Manchester's midway between London and Glasgow,' Hartmann said. 'That's fair to both.'

'It may be fair, sir, but it's just not practical,' Otto protested. 'Eagle stressed when he joined us: no personal contact. It's the only way he can protect himself.'

'That's no damn good to me. Until I get an answer from both of them, how can I trust either? Tell Eagle that if he doesn't keep that rendezvous, he's fired. Tell Garlic the same. They rendezvous, they fight it out, they report back: who's right, who's wrong, and why. Got it?'

'Sir,' Otto said.

'Do it now. Sort out the details between you. Go.' He pointed to the door.

350

Chapter 55

Three days after he had posted Garlic's light-alloys report, Luis walked down to the bank to pick up his mail.

There was an unspoken agreement between him and Julie that he always went to the bank alone. It gave them a welcome break from each other, and he enjoyed the brisk walk down to the Rua do Comercio in the cool winter air.

The three-piece-suit saw him come in and was ready for him. There was only one letter, in the familiar square, brown envelope which Madrid *Abwehr* used. Luis signed for it. 'Your friend from the Spanish embassy would have collected it for you, Senhor Cabrillo,' the three-piece-suit said, 'but unfortunately he arrived too soon.'

'Ah,' Luis said. He blotted his signature to give himself time to think. 'That was when?'

'Oh, half an hour ago. The mail had not yet been sorted. You were not inconvenienced, I hope.'

'Not at all.' Luis slit open the envelope. He had an extraordinary sensation of *déjà vu*, of living a script that he had written. 'I'd like a word with him. Will he return, do you think?'

'I think so. He had to go back to the embassy to collect your written authorisation.'

'I see.' Luis was looking at the letter but not reading the words. 'He forgot that, did he? Silly fellow.'

The three-piece-suit gave a tiny, tolerant shrug.

'Excuse me a moment,' Luis said.

He found a quiet corner and made himself read his letter. It was bad news; the worst possible news. Christian ordered Garlic to rendezvous with Eagle at Manchester (Main Road) railway station on platform one, under the clock, at 3 p.m. by that clock, each man to carry a fountain pen in the left hand and have one shoelace undone . . . Luis skimmed through the rest, and then rested his head against the cold marble wall. Something had gone wrong. Evidently Garlic had made some

351

sort of blunder and now he was to be investigated by this terrible man Eagle. It was all going horribly wrong.

Luis forced himself back to the present. There were four days before the Manchester rendezvous; four days in which to avert disaster. Meanwhile a man was wandering around Lisbon pretending to be from the Spanish embassy so that he could get his hands on Luis's mail. That looked frighteningly as if someone had penetrated his cover. But if this weird someone knew all about Luis's set-up, he must also know that the Spanish embassy cover was mythical, was bogus. So why was he behaving as if it were real? And why did he want this particular letter?

There was only one way to find out. Luis got an envelope from a cashier, put the letter inside it and addressed the envelope to himself, exactly as Madrid *Abwehr* had done. Then he handed it to the three-piece-suit.

'Please give this to my friend from the Spanish embassy when he comes back,' he said, 'and don't worry if he hasn't found my authorisation. He's a terrible fellow for losing things.'

'Certainly, Senhor Cabrillo.'

'He even left his hat in my office.' Luis held up the big black hat. 'I had hoped to meet him here, so that . . .' Luis spun the hat on his forefinger, and smiled ruefully.

'Would you like me to give it to him?' the three-piece-suit asked.

Luis blinked, and widened his smile. 'Would you mind?' he said, handing it over.

He strolled up and down the street, watching the bank entrance. The longer he waited, the more he worried. Suppose the man never came back. Suppose he came back and refused to take the hat. Or he might accept the hat and then leave it inside the bank. Luis felt panic nibbling at his guts. He was enormously tempted to go back inside and keep watch, but commonsense insisted that that would be fatal: the three-piece-suit would notice him and, when the time came, would point him out. Luis stamped his feet and tried to decide how *he* would behave in the same situation. Would he realise that the hat was just a badge, a label? Would he think that it concealed a message? Would he, God forbid, fold it up and hide it in his pocket?

352

Luis suddenly stopped worrying. A man had come out of the bank and was examining the hat. He tried it on, and looked at himself in a shop window. Too big; far too big. He took it off, turned it inside-out, searched the lining, found nothing. He stood and thought. Finally he flattened the hat, rolled it up and shoved it into a briefcase. He began walking. Luis followed.

They turned south and crossed Black Horse Square. The traffic was busy—it was getting on for lunchtime—and they had to wait for a gap. Luis hung back, thought briefly about telephoning Julie, and abandoned the idea. His man seemed to be heading for the ferry terminal. The crowds were thick around here: Portuguese soldiers going on leave, people buying fruit from stallholders, lottery-ticket sellers, bootblacks, gypsies, police. A party of nuns got in the way. Luis lost him for a moment and had to hurry. He found him again, beyond the ferry, walking along the waterfront. As they passed below the Alfama, Luis heard a distant burst of accordion music. It sounded strange on such a grey and dreary day, with the wide Tagus slopping little black waves and the sky dirty with coming rain. They went across a small square, dodging taxis all the way, and into Santa Apolonia station. Luis hid behind a pillar while his man studied the departure board. He liked what he saw. Half a minute later he was on a train.

Luis ran back to the departure board. It was a fast train on the northern route, stopping at Santarém, Coimbra, Aveiro and Oporto. It was due to leave in ten minutes. He used up five of those minutes on finding the ticket office, standing in line, and buying a second-class one-way ticket to Oporto, which took nearly all his money. Hurrying to the train he saw an empty phone booth. He dialled the office. The number rang, then stopped. He shoved a coin into the slot but it refused to go: another coin was jammed inside. He hammered with his fist, bashed the side of the coin-box, punched the coin-release button again and again. Nothing happened. One minute left; somehow the time had raced away. He flung down the phone in disgust and ran to the barrier. They were slamming doors as he got aboard. Before he had caught his breath, the train was moving.

It turned out to be a long, tedious, anxious journey. His man was travelling first-class. Luis, as he swayed through the

353

first-class carriage, recognised him at once: thoughtful, clean-shaven, medium height, stocky build, about thirty-five. Dark blue suit. Belted raincoat neatly folded beside him. Briefcase. There were a million like him, but Luis knew this one immediately. He was staring at the rain which had begun to streak the window, and Luis knew what he was thinking. He was wondering why the hell anyone would want to give him a black hat.

The train was half-empty. Luis took a seat in the nearest second-class carriage. As they rattled northwards, the rain smearing the view, he chased one inadequate explanation after another around his brain. The probability was that some intelligence agency or counter-intelligence agency was involved, but the British had already told him they weren't interested, and why should the Germans want to steal their own letter? Moreover, this man behaved extremely clumsily. It was baffling. Luis gave up and began worrying about what he was going to do when the man got off. Any expert secret agent would have been trained to handle this kind of emergency. Madrid *Abwehr* had not included it in the curriculum. A pity.

At Santarém Luis was waiting and watching, but his man didn't move. After that there was a long haul of over a hundred kilometres to Coimbra. Luis sat and listened to his pleading stomach. Finally he gave in and spent almost all his remaining change on a cheese roll. He ate it slowly, taking very small bites.

The wooden slats of the second-class seats had numbed his backside long before the train clattered and jinked into Coimbra station. Again Luis watched his man stay put. As the train heaved its way back out into the worsening weather, his spirits sank. He was being carried steadily further from his base, he had no money, no coat, it was pouring with rain. Outside it would soon be dark, cold and miserable. He asked himself why on earth he was behaving in this crass, reckless, cock-eyed way? Just because the idiot in first class did stupid things, was that a reason why he should chase him to the black, wet ends of Portugal?

Aveiro station was dank and gloomy. Luis got up, kept watch, sat down again. Now he knew the worst. His man was going to Oporto.

The last leg of the journey was also the slowest. The train

kept finding reasons to squeal to a halt, usually in the middle of a stretch of wintry scrub. When it moved on, its pace was pessimistic. Luis was hunched in helpless boredom by the time it trundled unhurriedly onto the long bridge that spanned the Douro. He looked down at the broad, black waters, reflecting flickers of light from the city on the opposite bank, and wondered what Julie was thinking. He felt stiff, weary and depressed.

A minute later the train had grudgingly found its way into Campanha station. Luis stood and stretched until he saw his man walk by on the platform, and then he followed. The station seemed to be all boom and bustle after his cramped, dull journey, and the air on his face felt much colder than Lisbon's. Oporto sounded and smelt different: brisker, busier. His man stepped out confidently. Luis tracked him to the street outside and saw with dismay that he was getting into a taxi. *You might have guessed that, you bloody fool*, he told himself. At once the taxi moved off, its lights probing the gloom. Luis started to run. He had no plan, he only knew that he hadn't come all this way to lose everything so easily. He ran after the tail-lights of the taxi, pounding down the road, releasing all the stored-up frustration of the afternoon. He saw the taxi reach a corner and stop, and he put on a spurt. A vague shape loomed in front of him. He dodged but it turned across his path. Something heavy and woollen collided with his face, his knee struck metal, numbingly hard, and then he was diving, arms flung up to protect himself. There was a scraping crash as he landed hard on someone big and bony. One of Luis's hands skidded hotly across a wet cobblestone, the other banged against a greasy head. They lay for an instant, sprawled and stunned. A bicycle bell tinkled.

Luis heaved himself up. A car was approaching. By its lights he saw what he had run into: a railwayman, cycling to work. The car slowed. Luis looked for the taxi and found it just as it moved off. The railwayman was staggering to his feet, cursing. Luis seized his bicycle and dragged it around. He ran with it, got one foot on a pedal, gave a last, huge thrust, and swung his leg over the crossbar. Sounds of rage and pain followed him. His right kneecap ached like hell. He pedalled furiously.

The corner where the taxi had stopped was a junction with a main road. Luis didn't stop. He raced into the stream of traffic, heard the scream of car tyres behind him, and swung the bicycle into a long, fast curve. Horns blared in the night, but by then he was pedalling hard, threading between and across vehicles, praying that his wheels wouldn't get trapped in a tramline. His brakes didn't work. His lights didn't work. The saddle was far too low. And it was raining very hard.

He caught up with the cab just as he was losing hope, afraid that it had turned off. He got close enough to note its number-plate, then dropped back a length or two. They were on a wide avenue leading into the city but it was thick with traffic; keeping pace with the taxi was not difficult. He had a fright when they reached a large and un-square square with half-a-dozen exits: in the free-for-all, the taxi-driver zigged and zagged until Luis had to chase him through the narrowing gap between a bus and a delivery truck. He made it, at the price of more bellowing horns, and earned himself a straightforward run along another avenue. The rain plastered his hair and made him blink, and a traffic policeman shouted angrily. Luis concentrated grimly on staying with the taxi. They were both waiting at traffic lights when he saw that his trouser-leg was getting caught in the unguarded chain. He dragged the trouser free and tucked it inside his sock, fouling his hands with oil. Not just oil: there was blood too, from a cut finger. He sucked it and swallowed. The lights turned green.

Soon the taxi turned left, away from the shopping centre, and they went downhill, towards the river. The traffic was thinner here and Luis had to work harder; but without any brakes the only way he could stop was by letting both feet skid along the ground, so there was a danger in going fast, too. His legs and arms were aching when the taxi turned the last corner and pulled up outside a small stone building. The place stood on its own, on the uphill side of a street that had been terraced out of the slope. Luis turned his face away as he rattled past the taxi. Below was the chilly glitter of the Douro.

He rode on until he was safe in the darkness, stopped, and looked back. His man was unlocking the front door while the taxi U-turned and cruised away. The door shut. A breeze came wandering through the blackness and flicked invisible drops into Luis's face.

He knew one thing: whatever he did next, it had to be planned, calculated and methodical. Ever since they left the bank he had been acting on impulse, improvising. Now it was time to get organised.

For three minutes he stood in the wet and draughty night, reviewing the problem, analysing the known facts and preparing possible courses of action. After three minutes he was shivering and his teeth were chattering. All the possible courses of action appeared to be equally useless. He threw the bicycle behind some trees and walked briskly to the house.

It wasn't just a house; it was an office, or maybe a shop. It had a big front window with a closed Venetian blind, and a brass plate beside the door read C.A.P. Lda.

Luis rang the bell. It made a woolly sound, as if the rain had got into it. After five seconds he beat on the door. There was no porch to protect him. He hopped stiffly from foot to foot, and beat on the door again. A light came on and it occurred to him, too late, that other people might live here too. The door opened. It was his man, now coatless. '*Sim? O que é que deseja?*' he asked sharply.

'You have my letter,' Luis said in English.

The man stared. Luis stared back. Inside the house an enormous dog padded into view: some kind of mastiff or wolfhound.

'Who are you?' the man asked.

'Luis Cabrillo. Who are you?' Luis suddenly sneezed. He was shivering again. The dog came up and looked at him with interest.

'Good heavens, you're soaked to the skin. Have you had an accident?'

'Not yet,' Luis said. It wasn't an intelligent answer but it was the best he could do. The man's accent puzzled him: not English, but not Portuguese, either. The dog dropped its head and sniffed his hand. 'Well, you can't stand out there all night,' the man said. 'Come here, Bruno!'

Bruno escorted them into the house. They crossed a bare hallway and went into the front room. It extended the full depth of the building and everywhere Luis looked he saw a cutting instrument: axes, cleavers, billhooks, knives, scythes; they were stacked around the walls by the dozen, glinting and gleaming, brand new and alarmingly sharp. Luis hated sharp-edged tools. The very thought of a cut-throat razor made him fidget and hunch his shoulders. He felt horribly unsafe in this room. No matter where he stood, something sharp was pointing at his back.

'*What* name did you say?' the man asked. He seemed quite calm; just curious.

'Luis Cabrillo. I followed you from Lisbon. You have my letter, you took it from the bank, and I want to know why.' Luis kept turning as the man strolled across the room. There was something strange about his eyes. Luis had a feeling he had seen them before . . . No, not the eyes, but the expression.

'You *followed* me here? All the way from *Lisbon*?' He gave an astonished chuckle. 'And it's all about some *letter*, you say?'

'You took my letter. It's probably in your briefcase now.'

'You may well be right. I have a great number of letters in my briefcase, most of which I collected from my bank in Lisbon. I haven't even looked at them yet, but if yours is amongst them, Mr . . . uh . . .'

'Cabrillo.'

'Mr Cabrillo, then either it's an order for three dozen meat cleavers, or the bank has made a mistake.'

He smiled, took a handkerchief from his cuff, and blew his nose. Bruno got bored and went and sprawled in a corner.

Luis began to feel the rot of uncertainty eat into him. 'What were you doing in Lisbon?' he asked.

'Business. C.A.P. stands for *Cozinha, Agricultura e Pesca*. Cooking, farming and fishing. Each involves cutting things down or cutting things up. We supply the cutters. May I ask what *you* were doing in Lisbon, Mr . . .' He tapped his forehead to bring the name back. 'Sorry. Cabrillo.'

'You have my hat. Why did you take my hat?'

It sounded like a silly question, a simpleminded question. For a split second Luis's brain faltered and he couldn't remember why his hat mattered. He realised that he was very tired; he wanted to sit down, better yet to lie down; but he dared not move from the centre of this room. His clothes clung to him. He noticed that his right trouser leg was still tucked inside his sock. The lights seemed painfully bright.

'You're bleeding,' the man said. 'Have you hurt yourself?'

Luis remembered his finger and held it up. The end was

slippery with blood. 'It's nothing,' he said.

'It may be nothing to you but it's making a nasty mess of my carpet,' the man said. It was true: there were red drops soaking into the grey pile. 'You stay there,' he said, and trotted up an open staircase leading to the floor above. 'I really don't know what you're doing here,' he said as he went, 'but we can't let you go around like that.'

Luis held his palm underneath his finger to catch the drips, and yawned. He felt dreadful. If this man looked in his brief-case, found the letter and gave it back, the only course would be to apologise and agree that the bank had made a mistake, which was probably the case. The black hat meant nothing; quite possibly this man had lost a black hat, once, and when the bank said . . . Luis yawned again and looked at the display of weapons all around him. That was another thing: the fellow had had plenty of chance to grab a hatchet and brain him. Instead of which here he was, walking carefully downstairs so as not to spill the hot water on his tray of cut-finger treatments. 'Stay, Bruno,' he growled as the dog raised its head. 'You should have told me about that finger,' he said. 'I'm not terribly concerned about the carpet, but . . .' He put down the tray and picked up the hot water. 'No, it's not for you,' he told Bruno. 'He hasn't been fed yet,' he said. 'My fault. Now then, let's get the dirt out.'

Luis held his finger straight and braced himself for the sting of iodine. Only a sudden tightening of the man's finger-tips, and a sharp whiff of something harsher than iodine, saved Luis's eyes. He ducked as the contents of the bowl were hurled where his face had been. The stink of ammonia fouled the air.

The man was halfway up the stairs before Luis recovered and gave chase. Bruno charged after them both, baying deafeningly. Luis lashed out at the dog with his leg and missed. The man had disappeared when he got to the top but he heard a key rattle in a lock and flung himself at the door. It banged open and smashed the man in the face. He let out a croak of pain and staggered back. Luis barged in and grabbed for him, but Bruno, still baying hard, galloped between Luis's legs and he fell over.

The man ran to a metal desk. He was shouting something, an appeal or a threat, it was impossible to say which: he was gasping for breath and blood was splattering from his nose. Luis began heaving himself up as Bruno, in full, hoarse cry, completed a lap of the desk and collided with him and knocked him down again. By the time Luis had shoved the great hound aside, the man was dragging out desk drawers in a desperate search for something.

A terrible dread of what that something might be gave Luis a fresh burst of energy. The man dodged away from him, blood falling in a long, broken dribble, and seized a deep wooden tray, loaded with papers. As Luis closed in he flailed the tray with furious speed from side to side. Papers flew everywhere and the tray cracked Luis's knuckles. He roared. Bruno welcomed the competition and barked more thunderously than ever. As Luis backed away from the flailing tray, Bruno leaped up and tried to lick his face. Luis staggered under the weight and the man flung a glass inkpot. It struck just above the right eye, on the bone. The clammy fire of pain raged through his head.

For a second or two Luis was senseless. When Bruno's racket penetrated his brain it had a hysterical edge which kept repeating itself like a duplicate shriek. His head cleared and he saw that the man was on his knees, cursing, trying to force a very small key into the lock of a desk drawer. His fingers were wet with blood. It was a double nightmare now: Luis could see the key slipping and stumbling while his own body, drained of strength, refused to move. At last the key turned, the drawer was yanked out and dumped. The man gave a cry of despair which was straight from the jungle. Luis gaped. Bruno galloped joyously up and down the room, skidding on the turns. The man groped for the last desk drawer.

Luis watched him tug at the handle and felt himself hamstrung by fear. Then the drawer moved an inch, and Luis moved too, lurching forward as if wading. There was a big typewriter on the desk. He got both hands on it, raised it shoulder-high, and swung it at the man's bowed head. The machine crashed against his ear and knocked him sprawling until his knuckles touched the wall. He lay still, only the blood from his nostrils moving. After a while that stopped too.

Luis sat on the floor and rested his head on the desk. It was very quiet. He wondered why, and looked up. Bruno saw him look, and came padding across the room. Luis blinked into the dog's eyes. He was carrying something in his mouth, a gift. Luis let him drop it in his hand. It was the glass inkpot. Bruno's ears pricked and he gave one soft bark. He wanted Luis to throw it for him. 'Oh, for God's sake,' Luis muttered.

Bruno recognised the tone of voice. His ears drooped and he went away to sniff the bloody face by the wall.

When he felt strong enough, Luis crawled over there too. The man was dead; already the blood on his lips and chin was turning black and crusty. Luis crawled back to the desk. He and Bruno looked inside the last drawer. It contained a telephone. 'Oh Jesus,' Luis moaned. He had murdered a man who had simply been trying to call for help. It had all been a huge, appalling blunder. He tugged the drawer all the way out. Lying behind the telephone was an automatic pistol, a Luger. It was fully loaded. Luis closed his eyes and sagged with relief.

He took Bruno for a walk and found the bathroom. He stripped naked and washed off all the dust and sweat, the dirt and oil and blood. His finger began bleeding again, and there was a long cut over his eye. He found a medicine cabinet and stuck plaster dressings on the cuts. His right knee was swollen from the bicycle collision. Bruno licked it.

They padded into the bedroom. Luis got into fresh socks and underwear and put on a dressing gown. The other room was a kitchen, where he rewarded himself with a large brandy. Then back to the office.

The brandy turned out to have been a wise precaution. The first shock came when he searched the body and discovered that the dead man's name was Krafft. Alfred Krafft. Luis covered the lower half of the face and squinted at the eyes. Now that he knew what to look for, the likeness was unmistakable. Those were Otto Krafft's eyes. Good God Almighty.

Alfred Krafft's filing cabinets produced the second shock. One of them was half-full of carbon copies of intelligence reports. They were addressed to 'Tomcat' in Madrid, and they were signed 'Eagle'.

Luis made himself a couple of sandwiches, brought the brandy bottle, and read everything that Eagle had ever written. Bruno lay beside him, his massive head on his lap. One of the most recent reports was all about the British light-alloy industry and how well it was doing, especially in Scotland. Luis groaned. Bruno cocked an eye, in case he needed help.

So that was what it was all about. Luis heaved a sigh, and drank what was left in his glass in a toast to the sprawled corpse. Bad luck, Alfred. And bad luck, Otto.

There was an electric fire. Luis hung his suit in front of it to dry and stared at the glowing bars. He felt drowsy, so he went to sleep in Alfred Krafft's bed. It was three in the morning when he awoke. The rain had stopped. He shaved with Alfred's razor but drew the line at using Alfred's toothbrush. There was a yellow-and-blue bruise fattening one end of his forehead.

His suit wasn't completely dry, but it was dry enough. He cooked himself some eggs, and fed Bruno out of various boxes of dogfood. Alfred Krafft's raincoat was too small but it was better than nothing. Luis stuffed his dirty socks and underwear in the pockets. He collected the *Abwehr* letter and the big black hat from Alfred's briefcase, and wedged the front door open.

Still there was something he had overlooked. Luis stood in the doorway and patiently, carefully worked it out. Money. He had no money. He went back upstairs and cleaned out Alfred's wallet. Already the body was as stiff and cold as soap.

The bicycle was where he had left it. He dried the saddle with his handkerchief, tucked his right trouser-leg into Alfred's sock, and pedalled away. Bruno cantered happily alongside until Luis stopped and ordered him back. The hound wrinkled its huge brow, sat in the road, and miserably watched him go. Luis felt sorry for Bruno, so sorry that there were tears in his eyes.

He rode downhill until he reached the river, and then rode alongside it until he found a bridge. He pedalled across the bridge, heading south. There was no other traffic. The first signpost he met said that Aveiro was 68 kilometres away. He reckoned that it would be safer to catch a train from Aveiro than from Oporto. It took him four hours to get to Aveiro. The bicycle ended up leaning against a wall near the station, where he was fairly sure it would soon be stolen again. He was in Lisbon by noon.

362

Chapter 56

'Well, I thought you were dead,' Julie said.

'That's funny. So did I.'

He watched her cooking ham and eggs. There was an uncontrollable tremble in his right hand. He wondered whether he would be able to hold his knife. It would look silly if he had to ask her to cut up his food.

'I had to go to Oporto,' he said.

She looked over her shoulder. 'Oh, yes,' she said. 'I hope the weather was nice.'

'Not very nice. It poured with rain. I got wet.'

She put the ham and eggs on a plate.

'You didn't miss anything,' he said.

She put the plate in front of him and took a close look at the dramatic bruise over his right eye. 'Looks as if something didn't miss you,' she said.

'Luis began eating. He was ravenous. 'All a bit complicated,' he mumbled. 'I met this man at the bank and he went to Oporto and we had a fight.' His hand kept losing its grip on his knife. He gave the fingers a puzzled look. 'Something wrong there,' he said.

She took the knife and cut up his food. 'I thought you might telephone.'

Luis sat with his shoulders slumped and watched her work. 'Telephone,' he said. There was a good reason why he hadn't telephoned, but his brain had mislaid it. 'You'll never guess who it was,' he told her.

'Damn right I won't. So who was it?'

He began eating again. The dead man's name retreated as fast as his memory advanced on it. After a while he shook his head. 'Can't remember,' he said.

Julie sat on the other side of the kitchen table and watched him carefully. 'What can you remember?' she asked.

Luis stabbed his fork into some egg and pronged a bit of ham. 'We had a fight,' he said, nodding and frowning. He put the ham and egg into his mouth and chewed. 'Long fight.'

'And in the end?'

'In the end . . .' He swallowed. 'That's right. I killed him with a typewriter.'

Julie hid her face in her hands. After a while she looked up. 'You killed him?' she said. 'I mean, dead?'

Luis nodded. 'I had to.'

'You mean you hit him with a typewriter and . . .'

Again he nodded. 'I had to. You see, he was going for his telephone.'

He looked into her eyes for a long moment. 'That can't be right,' he said. 'Can it?'

'Oh, Luis . . .' She reached across and took his hand.

'I can't eat any more,' he said. 'I'm sorry.' His right hand was trembling more violently than ever. She helped him into the bedroom, helped him take off his clothes, helped him get into bed. She closed the curtains and went out. Five minutes later, when she looked in, he was asleep.

*

Otto Krafft looked dreadful. For a man who had always been so trim and chipper, the change was almost shocking. His eyes looked as if he hadn't slept for a week, he had no appetite, and his nerves were a mess. 'Look, old chap, you obviously can't carry on like this,' Richard Fischer told him. 'Go and see the doctor, for God's sake.'

Brigadier Christian noticed his changed condition, too. 'What's the trouble, Krafft?' he asked. 'Off your food, or something?'

'No, sir. I don't know, sir.' Otto's thumbs fretted against his forefingers. He looked thoroughly wretched.

'Well, I don't want you going around in that state. You make *me* feel tired. Why don't you take a couple of days off?'

Otto chewed his lip. 'I was just going to ask you if I might, sir.'

'Take a week. Get up in the mountains, do a bit of ski-ing. Hartmann can handle your work. Go on, get out of this dump.' Christian watched him trail out. 'Overwork,' he said to himself happily. He liked to see his staff trying too hard.

*

Luis slept the clock around. It was mid-afternoon by the time he had bathed and shaved and dressed, so he and Julie went out to have something to eat in one of the spacious tea rooms in the fashionable Rua Garrett, where the settees were comfortably cushioned and the waitresses were dressed in black and white like maids in an English stately home. Luis was hungry. They ordered hot sausage-rolls, pancakes with preserves, and pastries.

Julie was wearing a new dress of grey silk. It made every other woman in the room seem lumpy. Luis enjoyed looking at her.

'Listen, Luis,' she said, pouring tea, 'just give me the bare facts. Don't try and gussy it up. The bare facts are bound to be crazy enough anyway.'

He described what had happened at the bank and how he had followed Alfred Krafft to Oporto. He told her about the bicycle, the room full of sharp edges, Bruno, the ammonia, the chase, the fight, the typewriter. 'The silly part about it is that I never wanted to hurt him,' he said. 'If only he had explained, we could have arranged something, I'm sure of it. But when he threw the ammonia, I had no choice. As it was he damn near got his hands on the gun before I hit him.'

'So far, so bad,' Julie said. 'Now tell me what he could have explained. And keep it *simple*.'

'Oh, this was very simple. Alfred Krafft is related to Otto Krafft. You met Otto at the German embassy. Brothers, probably. When Otto saw how much money Eldorado was making, he reckoned there was room for two in this business, so he invented an agent called Eagle. Alfred was already in Oporto, running his little shop, so Alfred became Eagle, just like me.'

'Wait a minute . . . Otto didn't get this idea from you?'

'Certainly not. He still thinks Eldorado and company are in England. Otto dreamed up his swindle all on his own.'

'Coincidence.'

Luis shrugged. 'We both saw the same way to milk the *Abwehr*, that's all. Actually, the Krafft brothers had a far better system, because Otto could write to Alfred and tell him what to put in his reports. I saw the letters.'

'That's sweet,' Julie murmured. 'Sweet and neat and fool-proof. So what went wrong?'

'One of Eagle's reports contradicted one of Garlic's reports. When Christian heard about that, he ordered them to meet—in Manchester, for some reason—and straighten out the confusion.'

'Oh my God,' Julie said. 'Poor old Otto must have filled his pants.'

'Yes, he must. If he sent the order, Garlic would report that Eagle had failed to keep the rendezvous, and that would be the end of Eagle.'

'But he *had* to send the order.'

'Yes. And as soon as he'd sent it, he telephoned Alfred in Oporto, told him to get the first train to Lisbon and intercept that letter before my man Stork turned up from the Spanish embassy to collect it and send it on to London.'

Julie shook her head. 'That was pretty damn desperate, wasn't it?'

'It only *seems* desperate to us because we know better. All Alfred knew was what Otto had told him : that the letter was going to be claimed from the bank by someone who worked for the Spanish embassy.'

'I still think it was a hell of a gamble.'

'Maybe. But what would you have done?'

Julie sipped her tea.

'And look at it this way,' Luis went on. 'Suppose they'd succeeded. Suppose Alfred stole the letter and therefore Garlic never heard about the rendezvous. *Then* Eagle could safely report that Garlic failed to appear.'

'Eagle would be in the clear,' Julie said, 'and Eldorado would be in the soup.'

'It was worth the risk.'

He ate several sausage-rolls and a couple of pancakes.

'What now?' Julie asked. 'Will you tell Charles Templeton?'

'I think not,' Luis said. 'He would have to inform London. The British intercepted an *Abwehr* signal about Eagle. I don't want the *Abwehr* to intercept a British signal about Cabrillo. No, let's keep it a secret.'

'It won't be a secret in Madrid. They're going to know that Eagle's disappeared.'

'I've been thinking about that.' Luis brightened. 'Look, maybe I can help them. Suppose Garlic reports, via Eldorado, that Eagle kept the rendezvous but that he seemed very depressed and he talked of suicide. How's that?'

'Lousy,' Julie said. 'Suicidal for you. How can Garlic meet Eagle? As soon as Otto reads that, he'll know you're lying.'

'Good heavens!' Luis exclaimed. 'So he will. I never thought of that.'

'You'll just have to play it straight, Luis.'

'You're absolutely right.' He took her hand. 'I really didn't want to do it, you know,' he said. 'I thought of it over and over again, coming back on the train. I'm sure he would have shot me if I hadn't . . . you know . . .'

Julie linked her fingers with his, and squeezed.

'Doing it with a typewriter makes it worse, somehow,' he said. 'And in front of the damn dog, too.' He looked down, blinking. 'I hope someone looks after that dog,' he said.

'Yes.' She gave him a few moments to recover. 'Now let me tell you something. While you were having such an exciting time in Oporto, the Japs attacked America. So now we're in the war too.'

'This war?' Luis exclaimed. 'Europe?'

'Sure. Hitler declared war on the States. Don't worry, it's all legal. I thought that would make you happy.'

'War on five continents!' Luis cried. 'My God, what a business opportunity!'

*

Otto Krafft came back after a week's leave. He still looked tired, but his nerves were much more settled. The first person he went to see was Dr Hartmann.

'Welcome back!' Hartmann said, shaking his hand. 'Yes, the fresh air has done you good, I can see that. Do you feel better?'

'More or less. Has anything happened?' Otto's voice was flat, as if he found it hard to make an effort.

'The news is not good, I'm afraid. Yesterday we had a report from Garlic. Eagle failed to attend the rendezvous.'

Otto nodded. He seemed unsurprised. 'Let's go up and see Brigadier Christian,' he said.

Christian received them in the anteroom. 'My room's being redecorated,' he told them. 'Are you feeling better?'

'I've heard about Eagle,' Otto said.

Christian raised a warning finger. 'Let's not rush into judge-

367

ment. There may be special factors, unknown circumstances which we—'

'Eagle's dead.'

Christian buffed his moustache with the back of his hand. Hartmann stared at Otto's profile. There were slight hollows in the cheek, he noticed. 'You sound as if you know something, Krafft,' Christian said.

'I can't explain it all,' Otto said. 'When I left I kept worrying about Eagle. I knew there was something wrong. Perhaps I had a premonition. In the end I telephoned his branch office in Oporto.'

'Was that wise?' Christian asked softly.

'I said I was a customer. They said he'd disappeared in England, he was missing, they were getting worried. So I . . .' Otto swallowed a couple of times. 'So I went to Oporto.'

'Take your time.' Christian got up, stopped a rattling window, and sat down, carefully hitching his trousers. 'Now then: you went to Oporto.'

'Yes. The branch manager was . . . was . . .' Otto blew his nose while he searched for the word. 'Was shocked. He'd just heard that Eagle had been found dead. Head bashed in.'

Dr Hartmann recoiled.

'Where did this happen?' Christian asked.

'London. The police said it was robbery.'

'And what do you think?'

Otto rested his elbows on his knees and pressed his handkerchief against his eyes. 'I think MI5 killed him, sir,' he said, his voice breaking.

Christian nodded. 'It was not your fault, Otto,' he said. 'You did all you could. Don't feel guilty.'

Otto stood up, wiping his eyes. Christian gestured towards the door, and Otto went out.

The two men sat in sombre silence for a while. 'A remarkable demonstration of loyalty,' Christian remarked.

'Yes, indeed,' Hartmann agreed. The window rattled again, and Christian gave it a frown. This was obviously one of those days.

*

After the killing of Eagle, Julie Conroy stopped talking about going to Oporto. She had always been aware that what Luis did was risky; now the knowledge that it was murderously dangerous made her feel that any criticism would be petty. The danger did not come from the Portuguese police; reports of the murder dropped out of the newspapers after a couple of days, and Luis was certain that there was no way in which he could be linked with Alfred Krafft. But the whole affair emphasised even more violently that to work with the *Abwehr* was to take a ride on a tiger.

Luis's response was to work harder. In the first six weeks of 1942 the Eldorado Network added two more sub-agents: 'Haystack', who ran a hotel in London, and 'Pinetree', a British employee at the American embassy. This made a total of seven, plus Bluebird and Stork in the Spanish embassies at London and Lisbon. Luis was anxious to fill the vacuum left by Eagle. His enormous appetite for work always impressed Julie, and sometimes depressed her too: there seemed to be no limit to his ambition, yet—as far as she could tell—no purpose to it, either. Luis, it seemed, wanted to succeed because he enjoyed being a success. For him, the Second World War was a sales territory. She was reminded of her father, striving to sell more Coke in Indiana than ever before. Luis Cabrillo really did aim to become the first spy millionaire. It puzzled and annoyed her until it finally provoked her into challenging him again.

'What are you going to do with all this money, Luis?' she asked one day towards the end of February, when he was checking his bank statements.

He smiled, and dropped the statements into a file. 'What would you like me to do with it, Julie?'

'You mean you haven't any ideas?'

'Money is always useful.'

'Only if you spend it. The stuff's no good otherwise.'

'That's a very practical point of view. I don't think I'm practical. For me, business is a romantic thing.'

'Luis, you're about as romantic as a claw hammer.'

He nodded. 'The claw hammer is a very romantic tool. You can build anything with a claw hammer.'

'Maybe.' She looked around, at the desks and shelves and filing cabinets. 'But you're not actually building anything, are you? This is all nothing. It doesn't exist.'

He nodded happily. 'That's the whole point, Julie. I've

369

invented a way to make money out of war without actually hurting anyone.'

'Otto's brother wasn't hurt?'

'That was an accident. Self-defence.'

'Defending what, Luis? Your life, or your business?'

She could see that he was getting bored with this discussion. 'I don't see how one can be separated from the other,' he said, 'Do you?'

'I guess not. I just wish that . . .' She screwed up a paper, threw it at a waste-basket, and missed. 'I wish that we were helping the Allies, that's all.'

'Oh so do I. That was my original idea, remember. But they didn't seem to want me when I offered, and now they probably don't need me at all.'

Julie reluctantly accepted the force of his argument. Britain had massive allies in Russia and the U.S.A. Why should anyone bother about an eccentric freelance intelligence agent who traded exclusively in fiction from a neutral backwater?

She got on with her work, which included dealing in an ever wider range of commodities for Bradburn & Wedge. The income from the degreasing patents financed a brisk trade in impregnated papers, and when the first two shipments of lemonade crystals got torpedoed in the Mediterranean, von Klausbrunner came back for more. The war had created a seller's market; Julie bought almost anything she found : stocks of pencils, tablecloths, underwear, tennis rackets, candles, shoes. Bradburn & Wedge prospered, paid its taxes, and allowed Luis to get on with his work without interference from the Portuguese Government.

Nevertheless, one other worry troubled Julie, and it refused to go away.

Luis had been unlucky when his Garlic report contradicted Eagle's information, but it was the kind of bad luck that was always likely to happen; in fact it was increasingly likely, now that Eldorado was enlarging his team. It was amazing that he had got away with his inventions for so long, but surely someone in Berlin should have noticed discrepancies by now? The longer he survived, the more she worried. The *Abwehr* was a big, professional organisation with some very intelligent and hardnosed people at the top. Why were they so certain of Eldorado? Or—even more worrying—if they suspected

370

that Eldorado was cheating them, what were they doing about it?

Chapter 57

At first, Hitler's declaration of war against the United States slightly alarmed Brigadier Christian. He had visited a cousin in Minnesota in 1934, and he remembered Americans as a very energetic people. However he soon stopped worrying when, in the three months after Pearl Harbour, the Japanese captured a vast empire that stretched from the borders of India to the edge of Australia, and all at very little cost. Clearly the Americans would have more than enough to do in the Pacific. This was confirmed in Christian's mind when he heard that the U-boats had actually profited from America's entry into the war: they were sinking so many American vessels that the Allies were now losing ships faster than they could replace them.

In fact there seemed to be very little that the Americans could do to help anyone. In the spring of 1942 the Russians launched three counter-offensives; all failed disastrously; and the Americans watched helplessly as the German armies thrust east and south, aiming for the oilfields of the Caucasus. In North Africa, Rommel attacked suddenly, threw the British out of Libya and got within sixty miles of Alexandria; there was nothing the Americans could do about *that*, either. Nor was there much the British could do to harm Germany except revive the bombing offensive that had been such a failure in 1941. It soon became obvious that the R.A.F. was still incapable of precision bombing: bigger raids merely caused even more indiscriminate damage. Christian was angry when he heard about the first thousand-bomber raid, on Cologne in May. Two weeks later, he read with satisfaction in a secret *Abwehr* report that life in Cologne was virtually back to normal. 'Good,' he said to himself. 'Let the stupid British keep wasting their strength.'

Christian felt content. He enjoyed his work, and he enjoyed the approval of his superiors. Now that he was head of Madrid *Abwehr* they usually gave him anything he asked for: more men, more money, more office space. Reports reached him regularly from the Eldorado Network (now expanded to nine with the recruitment of new sub-agents in Plymouth and Belfast) and they were eagerly received in Berlin. The loss of Eagle had been a blow, but that damage was only temporary. For a while, Otto had withdrawn into a state of silent self-reproach. However, after Christian had given him control of one of the new sub-agents ('Hambone', a telephone operator in Belfast) he slowly brightened up, and everyone felt better.

Then Wolfgang Adler came back.

Christian found him sitting in the anteroom one afternoon when he returned from lunch. Wolfgang stood up respectfully. He was a wearing a new *Wehrmacht* officer's uniform, and his face was deeply windburned. He looked tired but composed.

'Well, well,' Christian said.

Wolfgang nodded, and gave a wry smile.

'You'd better come in,' Christian said. 'Is this an official visit, or what?' They went into his office and sat in his new armchairs.

'No, it's not official,' Wolfgang said. His voice had changed; it was deeper and easier. Christian noticed grey flecks in his hair, and creases radiating from his eyes. There were also new lines bracketing his mouth. He looked ten years older. 'I mean it's legal, I haven't deserted or anything.' Wolfgang gave a little laugh. 'That's one thing about the Russian Front: nobody deserts. Nowhere to desert to.'

Christian thought about that and decided to let it pass. 'What do you want here?' he asked.

'Nothing, really. The fact is, I'm on convalescent leave. They gave me a month to recuperate. Frostbite, mainly. You see?' he pointed to his left ear, half of which was missing. 'And a few toes. Also I got a shell splinter in the back, but mainly it was frostbite. They said I could go anywhere I liked to recuperate, and I couldn't think of anywhere else so I said Madrid. At least it's nice and warm here.'

'And when your leave is up? What then?'

'Oh, back to Novgorod. Provided Novgorod's still there.'

Christian nodded. 'I'm sorry to hear about your injuries, Adler.'

'Oh, well.' Wolfgang stretched his legs and placed the heel of one boot on the toe of the other. 'It wasn't as bad as it might have been. Funny thing: you remember my arm and leg used to hurt when I was here? Well, they stopped hurting as soon as I got to Russia. Odd, that.'

'Indeed. But at least you got some benefit from your experience in the east.'

'Oh yes, lots. It was an education. I learned things that I wouldn't have believed possible if I hadn't seen them.' Wolfgang took a bundle of photographs from his tunic pocket and offered them to Christian. 'For instance, you don't come across this kind of intelligence in Spain,' he said.

Christian leaned forward, glanced at the top photograph and leaned back without touching it. 'An S.S. execution, by the look of it.'

'Correct.'

'That has nothing to do with the *Abwehr*.'

'True. But it had a great deal to do with my education.' Wolfgang put the pictures away. 'That was why you sent me to Russia, remember? By the way, how is Eldorado? Thriving?'

'Eldorado is thriving and booming and making all our fortunes, Adler. And let me make one thing clear: if you do anything to disturb or upset that arrangement, I'll have you back in Russia so fast you'll bounce twice and land in Mongolia.'

Wolfgang smiled, and shook his head. 'I don't care two hoots about Eldorado, brigadier. I mention him only because when I passed through *Abwehr* headquarters the other day, *they* all seemed to be unusually interested in him.'

'They always are. He's an outstanding agent.'

'No, I mean strangely interested. They were dragging out files on Eldorado going back to his earliest days.'

Christian could sit still no longer. He got up and prowled over to a window. 'A special investigation, you mean? Did you ask why?'

'Yes, I asked why. They simply smiled their rather sinister smiles.'

Christian didn't like the sound of that. 'Berlin has no reason

373

to investigate Eldorado,' he said. 'Absolutely none. His work is beyond reproach. Exemplary. Immaculate.'

'Well, perhaps not quite immaculate,' Wolfgang murmured. Christian turned sharply. 'I beg your pardon, brigadier,' Wolfgang said. 'Please forget I spoke. It's really none of my business. I'm sure you know Eldorado far better than I do. Far better than Berlin does, come to that.'

'I ought to by now.' Christian scratched his chin and stared into space. Wolfgang could hear the faint rasp of stubble. For a while there was no other sound. 'Have they given you a room?' Christian asked.

'Not yet.'

'Well, go and tell them to give you one. Ask for anything you need, get yourself settled. Then come back here at six and have a drink.'

Christian cancelled his appointments for the rest of the afternoon. He telephoned an old friend at *Abwehr* headquarters who confirmed that a top-level report on Eldorado was being prepared; for whom, and why, he did not know. Christian paced his room and worried. Eldorado was much more than his best agent; he was his whole budget, his reputation, his career. On the other hand there was no future in riding on a bandwagon if it was about to crash.

Wolfgang came back at six. He asked for vodka but there was none so he settled for Scotch. 'Same difference,' he said. 'I just think of it as brown vodka.'

They sat in the armchairs again.

'You never trusted Eldorado, did you?' Christian said. 'You always thought he was a crook.'

'I can't remember exactly what I thought, but I certainly knew he made mistakes. Although perhaps I was only looking for the mistakes. I don't know. I'm sure he's improved enormously since then.'

'I'd like you to do something for me, Adler. Please feel absolutely free to say no, if you'd rather not. After all, you are on leave.'

Wolfgang gestured his willingness.

'I'd like you to sort of browse through the Eldorado files and just jot down anything that seems odd. Anything that strikes you as ... uh ... questionable.'

'Anything that doesn't add up, so to speak.'

374

'That's right. I know everybody makes mistakes, but . . .'

'But some mistakes are more mistaken than others.'

'Exactly. What I'd like you to do, Adler, is act as a sort of devil's advocate.'

'I see.' Wolfgang finished his Scotch. 'Well, that could be an interesting exercise, couldn't it?'

'Does it appeal to you?'

'Oh yes,' Wolfgang said, 'it appeals.'

'Good, I'm glad. Have they given you a decent room? Is there anything particular you need?'

'More brown vodka, please,' Wolfgang said. Christian got the bottle.

Chapter 58

Luis returned from getting a haircut. 'Just as well you didn't go to England,' he said. 'They've cut the rations again, it says here.' He held up a newspaper.

Julie failed to think of an answer, and so there was an awkward silence. She sat and looked at her typewriter. He stood and looked at the papers on his desk.

During the last couple of weeks the old, pre-Oporto tensions had crept back. They had not quarrelled, they hadn't even argued; but they both felt the continual presence of hidden disapproval. She resented his obsession with Eldorado. He interpreted this as weakness, perhaps even jealousy. Julie sensed the mounting futility of it all, and felt trapped. She knew it couldn't go on, and yet what else was there?

'Templeton called,' she said.

'Charles? What did he want?'

'You.'

'Oh. Did he say why?'

Julie shook her head. Luis stood and worried for a moment. Then he telephoned the British embassy and talked to Templeton.

'He won't say what it's about,' he told her. 'I'd better go and see him.'

She nodded. He got his hat.

'You might say goodbye,' he said.

'All right. Goodbye.'

Oh, bloody stinking hell! Luis said to himself as he ran down the stairs.

Templeton met him in the embassy lobby. 'Things have changed a bit, Luis,' he said. 'Between you and me, a few heads have rolled. Witteridge got the shove—sent to Mozambique. One of the new chaps is a man called Meredith. He's come from Madrid. Ever met him? Commander Meredith.'

'The name means nothing.'

'Royal Navy type, something of a fire-eater. The thing is, he went through Witteridge's files, read about you, and now I think he wants to talk business.'

'I see.' Part of Luis's mind was still back in the office, silently fighting Julie.

'Word of advice, old boy,' Templeton said, leading him along a corridor. 'Don't take up too much of his time. He gets impatient.' Luis gave a snort of surprise. 'We can work out all the details later,' Templeton whispered as he tapped on a door.

'Come!' boomed a voice. Templeton went in first. 'Mr Cabrillo, sir,' he said, and gave Luis a reassuring smile as he went out.

Commander Meredith was writing. He raised one hand and, without looking up, pointed to a chair. Luis saw a cup and saucer in the middle of it. He picked them up and sent them crashing into a metal waste-bin. He sat and crossed his legs.

Meredith raised his head an inch. A pair of baggy, overworked eyes examined Luis. He sniffed, and went back to his writing.

The minutes passed. Luis began thinking of the urgent work waiting for him in his office. Finally Meredith blotted the last sheet and straightened up.

'Right, let's get on with it,' he said. He had a hard, nasal voice. 'Correct me if I'm wrong, but you need a job.'

'You're wrong,' Luis said.

Meredith exercised his jaws in a little demonstration of annoyance. 'What's that supposed to mean?' he snapped.

'I have a job. I don't *need* anything from anybody.'

'You came here asking for employment, for God's sake.'

376

Meredith thumped the file in front of him.

'Rubbish. I offered to co-operate with British intelligence, to let your people use my channels of communication with the *Abwehr*. Nobody was interested and so—'

'Oh, never mind all that,' Meredith said brusquely. 'The point is, your one-man band is now in the way. Frankly, it's become a damn nuisance. The time has come for it to be absorbed into the overall system.'

'Oh, yes?' Luis said nastily. 'And how is that supposed to happen?'

'You'll join my department and operate under the super-vision of my men. We shall soon be setting up major projects of strategic deception in order to mislead the enemy. Your amateur effort will be integrated with our professional or-ganisation.' Luis made a sour face. 'Oh, don't worry,' Meredith added wearily, 'you'll get paid for your time, for God's sake.'

'I'm already paid for my time,' Luis retorted, 'and paid bloody well. What happens to that?'

'You mean the *Abwehr* income? It will be credited to His Majesty's Government, of course.'

'No,' Luis said. Meredith made an amused snuffle. 'I'll say it again so that you can wet yourself laughing,' Luis snapped. 'No!'

'You don't understand, Cabrillo,' Meredith said. 'These deception projects are crucial. Your involvement is required. You have no choice.'

Luis heaved himself out of his chair. 'You ask me to join in your famous fight for freedom?' he said. 'And then you tell me I have no choice?'

'Right.'

'Think again! You're not talking to one of your thick Anglo-Saxon peasants. I am not a mechanic from Wolver-hampton. I am Luis Cabrillo, I am a Spaniard, and I do as I damn well please.'

'I'll tell you what you are,' Meredith said, sorting through his papers. 'You're a cocky little dago crook who's taken a free ride inside the machinery of war. So far you've been lucky. You say you want a choice: very well, I'll give you a choice. Either you do as you're bloody well told, or I'll make damn sure you get trapped in the works and squashed flat.' He opened another file and began reading.

'Your stupidity is exceeded only by your boorish manners,' Luis told him.

'You've got a week to decide,' Meredith said. The meeting was over.

Luis was still grim with anger when he got back to the office. Julie listened in silence to his account. 'So much for democracy!' he scoffed at the end. 'So much for liberty! For justice!'

'Well, they're fighting for their lives,' she said. 'What are you fighting for, Luis?'

He gestured at his surroundings. 'You should know,' he exclaimed. 'What does it look like?'

'Sometimes it looks like vanity, selfishness and greed,' she said, 'but I've been wrong before.'

'Look, I fight a separate war,' he told her fiercely. 'I owe nothing to anybody.'

'Yeah? I've a feeling it's not as easy as that,' she said. 'And I don't think you're really fighting at all. I think you're just playing with your toys.'

*

Brigadier Christian finished reading the last sheet of notes, shuffled the pages together, and banged a staple through the corner. 'That turned out to be quite a considerable exercise for you, Adler,' he said.

Wolfgang stirred his Scotch with his forefinger. 'There was a lot to read,' he said.

'And a lot to write.' Christian rapped the bundle of pages with his knuckles. 'You've done a remarkable job. I'm grateful.'

'My pleasure.'

'Of course I don't pretend to understand all the points you raise. Some are rather technical and . . .'

'Oh well. I expect I made a few mistakes myself.'

They chuckled, and examined their drinks.

'Any word from Berlin?' Wolfgang asked.

'Yes,' Christian said. 'Yes, by a coincidence it came today, just a little while ago.' He looked and sounded very serious, even stern. Wolfgang waited and watched, but Christian said no more about Berlin.

'Well, that's something, anyway,' Wolfgang remarked.

378

Christian nodded. He turned and flicked the pages of his desk diary. 'How would you like to come and meet Eldorado?' he asked.

Wolfgang tried to read Christian's expression and failed. 'Is this business or pleasure?' he inquired.

'Let's say it's a surprise party.'

'Ah.' Wolfgang smiled. 'Well, nobody deserves it more.'

*

The message which Julie had been dreading arrived the next day. Luis came back from the bank with a letter from Madrid *Abwehr*. Brigadier Christian wanted to see him. The rendezvous was to take place in Lisbon in four days. This allowed Eldorado time to get a flight from London on a neutral airline. He was to take a room in a central hotel, telephone his whereabouts to a certain number at the German embassy, and wait.

Julie's reaction was immediate. 'Beat it,' she said. 'Get out while you can. You've had a damn good run and you're lucky to get your notice in writing. Pack up and scram.'

'Perhaps he just wants a conference,' Luis said. He felt very nervous; the last thing in the world he wanted was a conference with Christian. 'If it's just a conference and I don't turn up, he'll mistrust everything.'

'So what? Who cares? Cash in, and get out.'

'Damn it, *I* care. All these months of work . . . The business is running beautifully, it's going like a factory. If we keep expanding at our current rate, we'll be turning over half a million dollars in the financial year 1942! D'you realise that? I'm not going to just . . . chuck it all away.'

'You don't need to chuck it all away. Transfer it to the British.'

Luis glared. 'So they make a profit out of my work? Not on your life.'

'It's *your* life, you great Spanish dope, and any day now some big hairy kraut is going to put an end to it!'

'You said that six months ago.'

'So now the odds are even shorter. You want to be a millionaire corpse? Go ahead. I'll have you cremated over a nice hot fire of greenbacks.'

'I will not work for that bastard Meredith,' Luis said firmly.

379

'Never. I thought the British had style. Meredith is a boor. He makes Attila the Hun look like Cary Grant. I won't work for that bastard, ever.'

'Style,' Julie said. She sucked her teeth. 'Is that what this war's all about, style?'

He refused to argue. 'I've made up my mind,' he said.

The next three days were tense and gloomy. Lisbon co-operated with a spell of cloudy, muggy weather which from time to time made an attempt to rain but never got beyond a half-hearted drizzle. Luis went on working; there was nothing else he could think to do. Julie found reasons to go out on business for Bradburn & Wedge. She spent a lot of the time walking the wet streets and worrying.

On the fourth day Luis took a room in the Hotel São Jorge and telephoned the German embassy. He was glad the waiting was over but he was also scared. Hidden in his briefcase was the hefty Colt revolver, now cleaned and oiled. Whether or not he would be able to get it out in time was very uncertain.

He sat in the room all morning. At 12.30 the phone rang and his heart kicked his ribs. He took several deep breaths and picked up the receiver.

'Is that you?' It was Julie.

'Yes, it's me,' he said. 'Nobody's come yet.'

'Jesus . . . Listen, I can't stand it here. I'm coming over. I'll wait downstairs, in the bar.' She hung up before he could speak.

Just before three o'clock, Brigadier Christian opened the door. Luis got to his feet. He felt curiously blank, as if he were about to undergo an unavoidable major operation. 'Hullo,' he said. Christian walked in without a word. Behind him came Wolfgang Adler, wearing a new brown suit, bought off-the-peg in Madrid. 'Hullo,' Luis said again.

Christian cleared his throat. He was holding a typewritten statement, and he began reading from it. '*Acting on the in-structions of Admiral Canaris, head of the Abwehr, under the authority given him by the Fuehrer, the Third Reich,*' he said rapidly, and looked up to make sure Luis was listening.

Christ, Luis thought, *it's a death warrant.* His left knee was refusing to lock into place; it kept twitching forward.

' "After a full and thorough review of your operational activities," ' Christian went on, forcefully, ' "which have taken place in an area that is not only highly sensitive but also militarily vital . . ." ' He looked up again, chin out-thrust, and glanced at Wolfgang. Wolfgang was standing with his right hand inside his bulging jacket-pocket. Luis knew that he had no hope of reaching the briefcase, let alone the gun. 'Plus a good deal more which needn't concern us,' Christian said. 'What matters is that you have been awarded the Iron Cross, Second Class.' He had it in his hand, strung on a ribbon. He hung it around Luis's neck. 'Congratulations,' he said.

Luis reached up and gripped the ribbon as if it were a lifebelt. 'Thank you very much indeed,' he said.

Christian gave Wolfgang a sidelong look. 'Now what d'you think of that, Adler?' he asked.

Wolfgang took his hand from his pocket. 'I'm too full to speak, sir,' he said.

*

They stayed for an hour, just chatting. Christian talked most; Wolfgang said very little. After they left, Luis watched from the window until he saw them walk across the forecourt and drive away in an embassy car. Then he telephoned the bar and told Julie to come up.

When she came in he was slumped in a chair, arms dangling.

'I brought a bottle,' she said, showing it. 'After all, what's a wake without booze?'

'I could do with a drink.'

'They didn't shoot you too much, then. You don't look too dead.'

'They gave me a bloody medal, Julie.' He swung it until the ribbon wound around his finger. 'I got the Iron Cross, Second Class.'

She pulled the cork and looked for glasses. 'I'll say one thing for the Third Reich,' she said. 'They recognise mediocrity when they see it.'

They worked their way through the bottle and Luis had another sent up. Julie had heard all about the meeting—Christian's warmth and confidence, Wolfgang's curious silence—and it was beginning to seem funny. As they started on the second bottle, it became even funnier. 'You know I'm not even supposed to have this thing?' he said, whirling the medal above his head. 'I mean, it's strictly illegal.'

'Luis, you wouldn't do anything *crooked*,' Julie said. 'You wouldn't get Bradburn & Wedge flung out of Rotary.'

'It's supposed to be only for Germans. I'm not a German.'

'Hell, no. You're the king of Albania.'

'Right! *And* I am also now a cavalry lieutenant in the Spanish Blue Division, in action somewhere on the Russian Front! Aren't you proud?'

'That deserves a drink.' They drank.

'Apparently it was the only way Christian could get the award past the lawyers,' Luis explained. 'You see, the *Abwehr* had me commissioned retrospectively . . .' He stopped and looked puzzled. 'Ret-ro-spect-ively,' he said. 'Very peculiar word.'

'I can't even pronounce it,' Julie told him. 'Retrospectively is one of the many words I just cannot pronounce.'

'Like corrugated iron,' Luis said. 'A very hard word, corrugated iron.'

'Not as hard as psychic phenomena.'

'I thought psychic phenomena were soft. And mysterious. And . . .' Luis kissed her on the neck and began undoing buttons. 'I don't know what else. The correct word escapes me.'

'How about "indescribable"?' She was tugging his shirt out. 'That's a good three-dollar word. House-trained, washable. One size fits all.' She slipped out of her dress.

'Yes, maybe.' Luis kicked off his shoes. 'It has an indefinable *je ne sais quoi.*'

'You couldn't put it better.'

'Well, I'm going to try.'

He was down to his boxer shorts and she was getting out of her slip when someone knocked on the door. They froze.

'For Pete's sake!' Julie whispered.

'It can't be room service, can it?' he asked softly.

'The hell with them.'

They stood motionless, waiting for the sound of someone going away. Instead the door opened and Wolfgang Adler came in.

'Hullo?' Luis said.

'Hullo. Is there anything left in that bottle? May I have some?'

They watched him fill a glass and drink most of it. He

topped up the glass and found himself an armchair. 'That's much better,' he said. 'Excellent stuff.'

'*Periquita*,' Luis said. 'They make it in Setubal. Quite drinkable, isn't it?'

Wolfgang took another big swig and breathed deeply. 'Sorry about my awful manners,' he said to Julie. 'I've been in Russia, you see. The main problem is the cold. Were you going to bed?'

She shrugged. 'It's a movable feast, I guess. Is this Wolfgang?' she asked Luis.

Luis nodded. He was putting on his shirt and looking for his socks. 'Wolfgang Adler, Julie Conroy . . . Did you . . .' He coughed, nervously. 'Did you forget something, or something?'

'What do you think of the war?' Wolfgang asked.

'The war? Well, it's going splendidly,' Luis said. 'I mean, look at Rommel. Look at the U-boats. Look at Russia.' He found his socks. 'That's more or less what you've been doing, isn't it?'

'And America, Mrs Conroy?'

Julie did her best to sneer. 'You can forget America.'

'By the way, Mrs Conroy is a close associate of mine,' Luis said, putting his trousers on. 'She knows all about my work. You can speak freely.'

'Ah,' Wolfgang said. He drank more wine.

'Americans aren't going to get involved in Europe,' Julie told him. 'They've got their hands full in the Pacific. My money's on Hitler, always has been.' Her voice was muffled as she pulled her dress over her head.

'I see,' Wolfgang said.

Julie tugged the dress straight and gave Luis a what-the-hell-is-going-on? look. He made a brief, baffled lift of the eyebrows.

'And Britain?' Wolfgang asked.

'Oh, finished,' Luis said. 'Blockaded, demoralised and isolated. Britain is irrelevant.' He amazed himself by the clarity of his speech. He was suddenly very sober.

Wolfgang sat nodding gently. Luis saw how tired he looked, how emotionally spent. 'Let me tell you the way it really is,' Wolfgang said. 'Hitler cannot defeat Stalin. The Russians will not be beaten. We shall have to kill them all. That's a lot of

Russians, you know. Maybe two hundred million. Of course the S.S. is doing its best. They carry out about ten thousand executions a day, I reckon.'

'Good Christ,' Julie said.

'But at that rate it will take fifty-four years, ten months and ten days to kill them all,' Wolfgang said. 'I have worked it out, you see. And by that time the Fuehrer will be a hundred and seven.'

'Oh dear,' Luis said.

'In fact it's worse than that. While the S.S. executes ten thousand a day, the rest are still breeding! At a rate of five per cent per annum! That means the Fuehrer must live an extra seventeen-and-a-half years to see final victory. He'd have to be a hundred and twenty-four.'

'That old, huh?' Julie said.

'It's asking a lot of the man,' Wolfgang said. 'I doubt if he can do it.'

'Look, Wolfgang,' Luis said, 'I'm delighted to see you, of course, but . . . Why have you come back? Is there something you want?'

Wolfgang drank from the bottle. 'I want to go over to the British,' he said. 'I know a lot, and I want to tell them everything. I thought you could help.'

Chapter 59

Luis telephoned room service and ordered two more bottles of *Periquita*.

'I think we should be quite sure that we don't misunderstand each other,' he said. 'So perhaps you had better tell me again.'

Wolfgang pulled three chairs up to a small table. They sat down. 'To start at the beginning,' he said. 'Why is Germany at war?'

Luis rubbed his eyes, and thought.

'So as to beat the Allies, I guess,' Julie said.

Wolfgang wrinkled his nose: a disarmingly schoolboyish

384

act. 'That's a consequence of *going* to war. It's not an aim of *making* war.'

'Does that matter any more?' Luis asked. 'Once you start fighting, all that matters is to win.'

'Then let me put it another way. How will Hitler know that he has won?'

'When the other side gives in,' Julie said. Wolfgang gave her a sad smile. 'You've got a point,' she said. 'I can't see it happening, either.'

'It took me a long time to realise that Germany is now at war for the sake of being at war,' Wolfgang said. 'We have no other aim. Therefore, since we have no other aim, how can we possibly know when to stop?'

'All right,' Luis said. 'Suppose that's true, for the sake of argument. What next?'

'I can show you that.' Wolfgang took out a small, square packet. 'I discovered something in Russia. I discovered that people *must* have a reason for making war, and if they are not given a reason then they invent one. I made this discovery in a small village about twenty miles from Kharkov. There had just been a very big counter-offensive by the Russians. The fighting was quite ferocious. Lots of dead on both sides. In the end the Russians lost, and I was in this little village when some German soldiers brought in a few hundred prisoners and shot them.'

'That happened in Spain all the time,' Luis said.

'Yes, it's not unusual. I don't think anyone was surprised. But afterwards the soldiers were not satisfied. Remember, they had just fought a terrible battle, seen their friends blown to bits, and for what? Not to conquer new land. They had gone through all that horror merely to stay where they were—in a thoroughly unpleasant, wretched village, a long way from home.'

'And that wasn't enough for them,' Julie said.

'Oh, nowhere near enough. So they shot all the men in the village, about twenty of them. Then they shot the women. I think they found fifty women. After that they shot all the very old people. Perhaps a dozen.'

'They went berserk,' Luis said. 'That happens, too.'

'Not berserk,' Wolfgang told him. 'They were very orderly, very controlled, very systematic. They worked their way through that village three times: first the men, then the women, then the old folk. I was watching and to me it made complete sense. They had given themselves a reason for winning: so that they could shoot Russians. I could almost smell the satisfaction in the air.'

'That's very interesting,' Luis said.

'Then they found the children.' Wolfgang opened the package but did not empty it. 'They'd been hiding under floorboards and so on. The soldiers went through the village again and winkled them out, but you know what children are like: they won't keep still for a minute. They kept breaking loose and running around. The soldiers had the devil's own job killing them. It was very messy.' He tipped a bundle of black-and-white photographs onto the table. 'And *that* was when the soldiers lost their tempers,' he said. 'They started smashing and kicking and using bayonets. I watched them, all these educated, trained, disciplined Germans, slipping and falling about in the mud, chasing a bunch of ragged-assed ten-year-olds, and I realised that these men didn't know why they were fighting this war. They had no reason. You can see it in their faces.' He pushed the pictures across the table.

The room-service waiter brought the wine while they were looking at the pictures. Wolfgang took it and topped up the glasses.

'I saw some terrible things in the Civil War,' Luis said, 'but I never saw anything like that.' His voice was curiously flat.

Julie said nothing. She was too close to tears.

'The children kept *wriggling*, you see,' Wolfgang said. He drank down his wine and poured some more. 'Now, the important thing is that I know all about the *Abwehr*. Not just Madrid—the whole organisation. I can tell the British where all our agents are and what they've been reporting, and a lot more besides. So you must go to British intelligence at once and arrange for my reception. Tell them I won't move unless my safety is guaranteed.'

'Why me?' Luis protested. 'Damn it all, Wolfgang, I'm working for the *Abwehr* too, remember.'

Wolfgang flinched as if he had been hurt. He looked from Luis to the scattered photographs and back again. 'You intend to go on taking German money?' he asked.

386

Luis knew that Julie was watching him. 'All right,' he said. 'I suppose I'd better go.'

*

Charles Templeton met him in the lobby of the British embassy.

'Don't ask me a lot of questions,' Luis said. 'The main thing is I've got a fairly senior *Abwehr* man called Wolfgang Adler and he wants to change sides.'

'Where is he now?'

'Not far away. But he must be sure that you'll protect him.'

'I see. You'd better come and wait in my office.'

Luis sat on a hard chair and watched Templeton's secretary work at her typewriter. He felt mentally battered and emotionally bruised. Too much had happened to him; he had been running hard for many months, and at last his stamina was beginning to fade. The endless pecking of the typewriter made it hard to think. He felt a great desire *not* to think : to let others solve his problems.

Templeton opened the door and beckoned him out.

'I've had a word with Meredith,' he said, 'and the decision is that we don't want him.'

'What d'you mean, you don't want him?' Luis said. Exasperation swelled inside him like a balloon. 'Of course you want the bastard. He's *Abwehr*, for Christ's sake.'

'Makes no difference, old boy. He's no use to us.'

'But that's bloody ridiculous. You must be insane.'

Templeton shook his head. He was quite untroubled. 'As I said, old chap, the decision's been made. Sorry.'

'But what am I going to tell him?'

'Tell him to go home.'

Luis walked away, beating his fists against his sides. He came back and gave Templeton a long, defeated look. 'I give in,' he said. 'What the hell is going on?'

'Dear oh dear,' Templeton sighed. 'I was afraid you might ask that.'

'Well, now I have bloody asked.'

Templeton's tongue sought a bit of food from a back tooth. He nibbled it and swallowed. 'I suppose I owe you a favour from the old days, Luis,' he said. 'The fact is, we don't need Adler because we already know everything he knows.

387

You mustn't tell *him* that, of course.'

It took Luis a moment to comprehend this. 'You mean you know how the *Abwehr* operates?' he said. 'The names of all their agents? It's not possible. How *can* you know?'

'Ah . . .' Templeton smiled ruefully. 'I'm afraid I'm not allowed to reveal that, old boy.'

He escorted Luis down to the street. 'Thanks for letting us know, all the same,' he said. 'You won't waste your sympathy on Adler, will you? Remember, he didn't want to change sides until he thought Hitler was losing.' He waved goodbye.

*

Luis found a telephone and called the hotel. He was lucky: Julie answered. 'Where is he?' he asked.

'On the john, I think. His plumbing's in trouble.'

'Meet me downstairs in five minutes.'

The Hotel São Jorge had an English-style Palm Court Room with plenty of plants in tubs and a string trio punishing Franz Lehar. Luis found Julie waiting at a corner table which was half-hidden by foliage. She gave him no chance to speak.

'Luis, you can't do it,' she said. 'I realised as soon as you'd gone: the very minute that sonofabitch upstairs joins the British, the whole Eldorado network goes up in flames.'

'Wait a minute, wait a minute.' Luis screwed up his face in an effort of concentration. 'What do you mean?'

'Sure! It's inevitable!' She shook his arm, impatiently. 'Look, the *Abwehr* will know he's gone, right? Or they'll suspect it, which is just as bad. They're bound to assume he's gone over to the British and betrayed everything he knows. Can't you see that?'

'Yes.' Luis slumped. 'I see it. Why didn't I think of it? Anyway, it doesn't matter. The British don't want him.'

'They *don't*?' She was amazed and relieved. 'Good God. Why not?'

'Oh . . . he's no good to them. They know all about him, and he's worthless, or something.'

'Gee.' She relaxed, and they sat in silence. A waiter came. Luis ordered tea and cakes. 'I'm starving,' he said. 'I didn't get any lunch.'

'What are you going to tell him?' she asked.

'I don't know exactly. He'll have to go back to Madrid, that's obvious.'

Julie gave him a curious, twisted smile. 'I'm glad it's worked out this way,' she said. 'I was afraid that when you knew what would happen to Eldorado, you might try and stop Adler.'

'Talk him out of it, you mean.'

'No, I mean stop him. Like you stopped Alfred Krafft.'

'Oh.' That possibility disturbed Luis. 'No, I don't think I could do that,' he said. 'I haven't got a typewriter.'

'But you did bring this lousy cannon.' She held up the briefcase.

'That thing. I can't see myself shooting anyone with that, not even to save Eldorado.'

'Good.'

'You can shoot him, if you want to.'

'No thanks.'

'I suppose I might shove him off a cliff, if no one were looking,' Luis said gloomily. 'That's painless, isn't it?'

'As long as you don't sprain your wrist, it is.'

'You know what I mean.' He propped his head on his hand and gazed wearily at the string trio, which was now attacking Vincent Youmans. 'I wish the damn food would come . . . Is he all right upstairs, d'you think?'

'Well, I left him a note saying . . .' Julie stopped, and craned her neck. 'Forget it,' she said. 'Here comes tea and here comes Wolfgang, too.'

The German sat down at their table as the waiter began unloading his tray. 'My apologies,' he said. 'I forgot that you would wish to have tea. It became very lonely in that room. Since Russia I don't like to be alone.'

'Well, that's understandable,' Julie said.

'Although now that I have changed sides, I suppose I shall always be alone.' He sat hunched forward, with his hands grasped between his knees.

'I wanted to talk to you about that,' Luis said. He poured himself some tea. Wolfgang watched closely.

'It's good that you put the milk in second,' Wolfgang said. 'Christian put the milk in first. I told him that was wrong but he made a joke of it. He was a stupid man.'

The waiter brought them an extra cup and saucer, and went away.

'I saw the British,' Luis said. He took a bite out of a small cake and gestured with the rest of it. 'They're very excited, of course.'

'Good.'

'But they can't take you now. They want you to go back to Madrid and find out more—'

'No, no, no. I can't go to Madrid. I can't go anywhere except to England.'

'Surely you can if you go *now*,' Luis urged. 'I mean, nobody else knows.'

Wolfgang took a sugar-cube and dipped it into Luis's tea. They watched the liquid soak up through the grains until the cube collapsed between his fingers. 'Everybody knows,' Wolfgang said. 'You see, before I came back to see you, I killed Brigadier Christian.'

'Christ Almighty,' Julie breathed.

'Oh no,' Luis said. 'Why on earth did you do that?'

Again, Wolfgang wrinkled his nose in that casual, boyish way. 'It's not important any more,' he said.

'But where is he?'

'In the German embassy, I expect. We went into the lavatories. I hit him on the head with a bottle of disinfectant and strangled him with his tie.' He licked sugar from his fingertips.

'And he's really dead?' Julie said. 'I mean, sometimes—'

'Please. I killed him. I know he is dead. When you have finished your tea,' Wolfgang said to Luis, 'we should go to the British embassy again.'

Luis chewed his cake and failed to think of an alternative. He swallowed, and licked his lips. 'I'm ready now,' he said.

As they walked across the room, Wolfgang suddenly checked. 'Excuse me,' he said. 'Where is the toilet?' Luis pointed.

They waited for him in the lobby.

'Do you think he really killed Christian?' Luis asked.

'He sounded pretty convincing,' Julie said. 'Mind you, he also sounds pretty crazy.'

'Yes. Did you know I pushed him out of a window once? Maybe he landed on his head.'

Around them, the usual endless hotel-lobby traffic came and went.

'I still have to pay for the room,' Luis said. 'Don't let me forget the receipt. It's deductible.'

'What are we going to do, Luis?' Julie asked.

'I wish I really hated him,' he said. 'Maybe I could kill him if I really hated him.'

'Do you want to kill him?'

'Sometimes. When I think that he stands between me and a million dollars, yes, I'd like to be able to kill him. Painlessly.'

'Where's the nearest cliff?' she asked.

'We haven't got time for cliffs. It's got to be done now, within the next hour, or not at all. The German embassy must know he's missing. If he doesn't turn up soon they'll assume the worst, won't they?'

'I guess so.'

'If Adler lives, Eldorado dies. That's what it comes down to. Then I'll be no use to anyone, not even the British.' Luis took a quick look inside his briefcase. 'I wonder if I could shoot him? Maybe if I thought hard about it I could . . . you know . . . sort of work myself up to it.' He sighed. 'Damn it all. Why didn't he stay in bloody Russia where he belonged?'

'That revolver makes such a hell of a noise,' Julie said.

'Yes. You're sure you wouldn't like to do it?'

'No *thanks.*'

'You needn't sound so righteous. You keep wanting me to join the British and fight for freedom, don't you? Well, he's ruining all your plans too, remember. I thought you were very keen on bashing the enemy.'

Julie had no answer to that. She looked away. Luis glanced at his watch. 'Strangling people seems to have a disastrous effect on Adler's bowels,' he muttered.

Julie suddenly turned back to him and snapped her fingers. 'We must be crazy!' she said. 'It's not our job to get rid of him, for Pete's sake. The goddam German embassy already *wants* him, for murder! All we have to do is tell them where he is!'

Hope revived Luis like a whiff of pure oxygen. He looked for a telephone and saw Wolfgang striding across the lobby. 'Too damn late,' he said. 'Still, maybe they're already out looking for him. If we stay in the open—'

'We go?' Wolfgang called.

'Look, you two don't really need me,' Julie began.

391

'On the contrary!' Without stopping, Wolfgang took her arm and headed for the exit. 'I think we must hurry,' he called to Luis.

Chapter 60

It was the end of the afternoon. The sun filtered through the overcast and gave the city a strangely sallow look. The air had the empty smell that comes with the fading of a long, hard day, and the streets were full of people trudging home.

'Taxi?' Wolfgang suggested.

'It's not worth it,' Luis said. 'The embassy isn't far. Besides, in this traffic it would take forever.' He began to walk, but Wolfgang still hesitated. 'If we take a taxi I shall be sick,' Luis said firmly. 'I need some fresh air.'

Wolfgang reluctantly followed. Luis headed towards the centre of Lisbon, wondering if it might be possible to pretend to be lost and perhaps go into a bar to ask directions so that Julie could slip away to a telephone . . . He glanced at Wolfgang. Wolfgang smiled back. Luis thought of Brigadier Christian lying on the lavatory floor with his eyes popping and his tongue sticking out, and returned a smile that felt more like a nervous grin. This wasn't the first time he had been frightened recently, but he knew that fear could make people behave stupidly. He was afraid of Adler and he was even more afraid of killing Adler. Above all he was terrified of doing something foolish and thereby hurting Julie. He felt stiff and clumsy and unbrave.

They walked three abreast until the street narrowed and the crowd thickened. Then Wolfgang kept Julie on his arm while Luis walked behind. Eventually the street led to a long flight of stone steps that curved down to feed into one of the avenues. The steps were uneven, and Wolfgang had to watch his footing. Luis got his right hand inside the briefcase and took hold of the gun.

Because Wolfgang was always a step below, the gun was pointing at the middle of his back. Would that kill him?

Would the bullet go through and kill someone else? The noise would be awful, but so would the confusion. All the same someone might see him fire, might even grab him. Luis glanced around. The crowd was mostly women, shop-assistants or office workers by the look of them. That would help: more screaming, more panic. On the other hand it made him conspicuous: the only man. If he were ever going to do it, it had to be now, on these steps, in this crowd, before they reached the wide, exposed avenue. He hitched up the briefcase with his left hand and stretched his fingers around the butt until his forefinger found the cold curve of the trigger. An extra-wide step surprised him and made him stumble. There was sweat on his brow and his legs wobbled like an infant's. He could see the end now, see the traffic on the avenue. Wolfgang turned his head to ask something, was jostled, and gave a little gasp, hardly more than an exhalation. He stopped. Luis had to stop too, and he braced himself against the knocks of people walking into him. Wolfgang's hand slid down Julie's arm and he collapsed, slowly, like an old dancer going down too far in a curtsey and unable to get up again.

By the time Luis had got in front of him, Wolfgang's head was resting between his knees. Luis kneeled and took his face in his hands. All around, people had stopped to watch. Others bumped into them; there was much scuffling and apologising. The face in Luis's hands was warm but the eyes were dead. He looked up and saw Julie staring at him, frowning a little. At last his sluggish brain caught up and he turned to look for the jostler, but already the crowd had changed, had moved on; it could have been any one of thirty people. Even as he looked they were moving away, disappearing.

He took his hands from the face. Wolfgang sat on the steps and parted the flow of pedestrians like a rock in a stream. Luis grabbed Julie's hand and hurried her down the steps as fast as he could. They went along the avenue, fast, not going anywhere, simply escaping. Charles Templeton was waiting at the first corner. 'I have a car,' he said. 'Why don't you come with me? You don't want to hang around here, do you?'

They got into his car. 'Right-ho, George,' Templeton told the driver.

'I should have guessed,' Luis said. He felt drained of energy and will. 'It was you, wasn't it?'

393

'Not exactly,' Templeton said, 'but more or less.'

*

They went first to Templeton's office, where they drank his Portuguese brandy while he made some telephone calls.

'Well now, Luis,' he said, when he had finished. 'In terms of human gore it didn't compare with Jarama, did it? All the same I expect you're glad it's over.'

'True,' Luis said.

'Jarama is where we first met,' Templeton explained to Julie. 'A lot of fighting over a rather boring hill, I can't remember why.'

'Honour and glory,' Luis said.

'Is that what it was? No wonder I never understood. Anyway, today's nonsense is now behind us, and that's the main thing, isn't it?'

'No question,' Luis said.

'You may think I'm buttering you up,' Templeton went on, pouring more brandy, 'but I really am looking forward immensely to working with you. I'm sure it will be most enjoyable.'

'What on earth makes you think we're going to work together?' Luis asked.

'My dear chap, after today's experience surely even you can see . . . I mean, you've had a jolly good innings but . . .'

'Be your age, Luis,' Julie said. 'It's time to grow up and play with the big boys.'

'I fail to see,' Luis said stiffly, 'how today's events make it necessary for me to change my plans. On the contrary, now that certain obstacles have been removed—'

'You're crazy,' Julie said. 'He's crazy,' she told Templeton. 'He wants to take the *Abwehr* for a million bucks. If the war doesn't last long enough he's going to sue Churchill.'

Luis hunched his shoulders and glowered at a framed photograph of the Royal Family in kilts.

'Honestly, it's not on, old boy,' Templeton said. 'Our chaps can't have chaps like you running independent sideshows. You might spoil the big attraction, if you see what I mean.'

'No,' Luis said.

Templeton grunted sadly. 'I think we'd better go upstairs,' he said.

394

They went upstairs, and trooped into Commander Meredith's office. Luis leaned against a wall and sneered. Meredith looked as if he hadn't left his desk since the last time they met.

'I'm not a man to hold a grudge, Cabrillo,' he said. 'I intend to forget your extraordinary carry-on at our previous meeting . . .' He did his best to suppress a glare. '. . . and recommence with a clean sheet.'

'Do what you like,' Luis muttered.

Meredith released the full force of his glare at Templeton, but Templeton was fully occupied with adjusting the crease in his trousers.

'Just for Christ's sake listen to what they have to say, Luis,' Julie said.

'I have no intention of attempting to *persuade* you,' Meredith said. 'The facts alone are enough, and the facts are that we cannot allow you to continue operating independently.'

'You can't stop me, either.'

'That is a stupid remark,' Meredith said, 'particularly after what you observed less than an hour ago.'

Luis looked at Julie, and scoffed. 'You see what I mean? Threats. Big mouth, small brain. No style.'

'I can live without style,' she said. 'I can even live without *your* style.'

That silenced him. He folded his arms and looked at the carpet.

'The truth is we can all live without you, Cabrillo,' Meredith said. 'Don't flatter yourself that this department eliminated Adler for your benefit. Far from it.'

Luis raised his head, and sniffed sharply. 'Then why did you do it?' he demanded.

'None of your business.'

Luis walked to the door. 'And my business is none of your business,' he said.

'You'll come a cropper, old boy,' Templeton warned him. 'Honestly you will.'

'Luis, listen to them,' Julie pleaded. 'You can't go on forever on your own.'

'Why should I do as *he* says?' Luis jerked his head towards Meredith.

'Because you've got no damn choice,' Meredith snapped.

'That's not good enough.'

Julie turned away. 'I can't go on like this,' she said. 'You're on your own now, Luis.'

For a moment the air was sour with stalemate. Then the telephone rang. Templeton answered it. 'The Director would like to see you,' he said to Luis and Julie.

'Tell him to write for an appointment,' Luis said.

'You maniac!' Julie shouted. She went over and punched him in the eye. He hit her in the mouth. 'Please, *please*,' Templeton said, pulling them apart. 'Try to control yourselves. There's a war on, remember.'

'She started it,' Luis complained. Already his eye felt like a blood-orange.

'If that's what he means by style,' Meredith said to Templeton, 'I think I'm better off without it. Get him out of here.'

Templeton led them down the corridor and into another and bigger office. 'Mrs Conroy and Mr Cabrillo, sir,' he said.

'Do sit down,' the Director said. He was a short, comfortably built man with a pleasant, rubbery face. Julie, sucking a split lip, took an armchair. Luis took another and held his handkerchief against his eye. 'Be a dear chap and open that champagne, Charles,' the Director said. 'This is something of a special occasion for me.'

He picked up a sheet of paper from his desk, went over to Luis, and squatted on his haunches so that they could both read it. 'You probably recognise this,' he murmured.

Luis squinted at it through his one good eye. 'Yes,' he said. 'That's part of my report on the new British "crusher" tank.'

'Excellent stuff,' the Director said. 'I did enjoy it. What a pity the tank doesn't exist. Mind you, we may develop it one day.'

'How did you get hold of this?' Luis asked.

'We intercepted it. We intercept a lot of *Abwehr* signals, frightfully dull stuff most of it, but this . . . Ah, well done, Charles.' Glasses of champagne arrived. The Director took a mouthful, and perched on the arm of Luis's chair. 'You see that bit *there*,' he said. 'Delightful turn of phrase; I wish I'd written it . . . Now tell me, Mr Cabrillo: am I wrong, or has your style been influenced by the novels of Graham Greene?'

Luis was startled and pleased. 'Well, naturally I admire

Greene's writing,' he said. 'Can you really tell?'

'Heavens, yes.' The Director stood up. 'If you've got a minute,' he said, 'I'd be most interested in your opinion about a passage that rather intrigued me . . .' He took Luis over to his desk.

For the next half-hour they talked books and writers. Luis responded more and more willingly to the Director's slightly diffident questions until the conversation was flowing quite freely. Meanwhile Templeton chatted quietly with Julie.

Eventually Luis and the Director strolled back to the arm-chairs. Templeton refilled everyone's glass. 'Of course you know that Graham Greene is here,' the Director said.

'No, I didn't.' Luis's functioning eye opened wide with surprise. 'You mean he's working here?'

'In my department. Would you like to meet him some time? I know he'd be fascinated to meet you. My goodness, yes.'

Luis simply nodded. Julie sipped champagne through the undamaged corner of her mouth and watched discreetly. Was he hooked? Would he let himself be caught?

'I'm awfully glad you dropped in,' the Director said. 'There's another problem that's been bothering me.'

'Anything I can do,' Luis said generously.

'I hoped you'd say that.' The Director led him over to a wall-map of Europe. 'I expect you've guessed that the Allies are going to invade somewhere, sooner or later,' he said, gesturing vaguely at the entire Continent.

'It's no secret.'

'No, of course not. The only secret is when and where. Now, just suppose we knew that one area where the invasion will definitely not take place is, for instance, Greece.'

Luis nodded.

'In your opinion,' the Director said, 'would it be possible, using a team of agents such as your own Eldorado team, to feed a stream of misinformation to the enemy until he became persuaded that Greece *must* be the invasion site?'

'Nothing is certain,' Luis said, 'but it would probably be worth a try.'

'I see. Of course the entire operation would have to be carefully orchestrated so as to harmonise with all our other deception plans.'

'That goes without saying,' Luis agreed.

'And the price of success would be the eventual sacrifice of the entire Eldorado team.'

Luis shrugged. 'The *Abwehr* would have to know that they had been deceived,' he said, 'or there would be no deception.'

There was a moment of silent satisfaction, like the pause between the last note and the first applause.

'Good,' the Director said. 'Shall we drink to that?'

They drank. 'Now then, what about the money?' Luis said briskly.

'My dear chap, you've had such a long and trying day. Why don't we leave the technicalities to another—'

'Not on your life. A deal is a deal.'

Julie groaned. She looked away in despair.

The Director licked up a drip of champagne that was running down the outside of his glass. 'What were you thinking of?' he asked.

'I work for you, free of charge, and keep what the *Abwehr* pays me. When Eldorado collapses, you compensate me for my lost earnings.'

'That sounds like rather a lot of money.'

'Yes, it is. It adds up to a million dollars.'

The Director nodded. 'Well, a million dollars, in the context of this war, is nothing much. It wouldn't pay for the squadron of bombers we lost last week, or one quarter of the ship that gets torpedoed in the Atlantic every day. No, I can see that yours is a minor expense, Mr Cabrillo, and if it were up to me I should authorise it without thinking twice. As it is, such matters are decided by my masters in London, a notoriously tightfisted and narrowminded crew. Regrettable, of course; inefficient and inflexible and crass and all those other sterling qualities which have made British Intelligence the crippled beast which it is. On the other hand, what am I to do?'

'In that case the deal's off,' Luis announced.

'What a pity,' the Director said. 'Here we have an opportunity to shorten the war, to save thousands of lives—perhaps tens or even hundreds of thousands of lives—and all for a million dollars. What a great, *great* pity.'

'Rotten shame,' Templeton murmured.

'The point is,' Luis said, 'you can always have another war, but this is my only chance to make a million dollars. You see what I mean?'

Julie suddenly turned and said: 'Here, catch.' Something hit Luis in the chest and fell to the floor. He picked it up: a key. 'What's this?' he asked.

'Key to the office. I shan't need it any more.'

He stared at her, and saw that she was forcing down the corners of her eyes and compressing her lips to keep back the tears. He felt genuinely perplexed. 'Why do you take it so seriously?' he asked her. 'It's just business, that's all.'

'Go to hell,' she mumbled.

Luis rubbed the key against the side of his nose. 'You definitely need Eldorado?' he said to the Director.

'To be sure of success, yes, we do.'

'The operation is very important?'

'Tremendously important. Crucial.'

'Then it's worth a million dollars.'

The Director finished his champagne and gave the glass to Templeton. He walked over to his desk and unlocked a drawer. He took out a chequebook, wrote in it, blotted it, detached the cheque, got up, and gave it to Luis. 'I advise you to cash it quickly,' he said. 'The Treasury is not terribly well-off at the moment.'

Luis carefully read the cheque, ending with the signature. 'Thank you, Mr Philby,' he said. 'I've always wanted one of these.'

He turned and held it out to Julie. 'Would you look after it for me?' he asked. 'And the key, too?'

For a moment she sat and stared at his outstretched hands. Then she stood up and took the key and the cheque. 'Can you give me a light?' she asked Templeton.

He produced a lighter.

They all watched while she set fire to the cheque. The flames stretched and shrank and stretched again as she turned the paper. Templeton held out a large ashtray and she let the last corner drop into it.

'What an extraordinary thing flame is,' Luis said. 'Have you noticed? It has colour but no substance. Its shape is always changing, so it has no shape. You can see through it. It has no independent existence. It depends on something else for its existence, and then it destroys the very thing that created it. Isn't that strange?'

'Load of bullshit,' Julie said.

'Such a pleasure meeting you both,' the Director said. 'I look forward enormously to a long and fruitful relationship, Luis.'

'Thank you, Mr Philby.' They shook hands.

'Please call me Kim,' the Director said. 'All my friends do.'

Templeton took Luis and Julie down to the lobby.

'Nice chap,' Luis said.

'I think he's brilliant,' Templeton told him. 'And so does everybody else here. There's no reason why he shouldn't go right to the very top.' He pushed open the front door. 'I've laid on a car for you. The driver knows where to go.'

It was an old, comfortable Daimler. Julie curled up in a corner of the deep back seat and watched the bright lights drift by. She was lightheaded with stress, alcohol and fatigue. 'Why must you always be such an obstinate bastard, Luis?' she asked.

He stretched his legs, and linked his hands behind his head.

'You knew what I'd do to that cheque, didn't you?' she said. 'That's why you gave it to me. You're a maniac.'

'It made a beautiful flame,' he said.

Templeton went back upstairs and found Philby talking to Meredith.

'I was afraid I might have done permanent damage to his blasted Spanish honour,' Meredith said.

'No, no. You softened him up nicely,' Philby said.

'I've put a man outside their apartment, sir,' Templeton told him. 'And I'll collect them personally in the morning.'

Philby smiled his thanks. 'I rather like the fellow. I'm glad he agreed to help us.'

'Supposing he hadn't agreed?' Meredith said. 'You could never have turned him loose again. Not with what he knows.'

'Dear me no.' Philby found some champagne dregs in a bottle and poured them out. 'Mr Cabrillo just saved his own life. Now it will be interesting to see if he can help us save ours.' He sipped, and made a face. 'Flat,' he said.

Chapter 61

Next morning, Luis and Julie moved out of their apartment and went to live in the British embassy. Luis protested briefly against the shift but Templeton soon made him see that it was essential, both for efficiency and for security.

While they were packing, Julie said to Templeton: 'What happened to Wolfgang? Or shouldn't I ask?'

'It's no secret, in fact it's in all the papers. The poor chap had a heart attack while he was walking back to the German embassy. I'm told the embassy took possession of the body last night.'

'Funny heart attack,' Luis said. 'I saw blood on his shirt.'

'Haemorrhage,' Templeton said.

'Ah.'

'I'll tell you what I don't understand,' Julie said. 'What did your boss Meredith mean when he said Adler wasn't removed for Luis's benefit?'

'Did he say that?' Templeton asked.

'You heard him,' Luis said.

'Dear me. He really shouldn't have said that.'

'Answer the question,' Julie said. 'If you didn't do it for Luis, why did you do it?'

They both stopped packing and stared at him.

'Oh . . . *Must* you know?' he said wretchedly.

'Give!' Julie cried. 'We're all on the same side now, remember?'

Templeton thought about it, his eyes shifting nervously. At last he said: 'Very well, since you insist. The fact is that there was another reason, an extremely urgent reason.'

'What?' she asked.

Templeton changed his mind. 'I can't say.'

'You clod,' Luis said.

'It's just too soon. In due course, perhaps . . .'

'Oh, garbage,' Julie snapped.

In the afternoon Luis was introduced to the controllers with whom he would be working. Templeton and Julie went over to the office and began the process of putting Bradburn & Wedge into voluntary liquidation. By the end of the day, all the Eldorado files had been moved to the embassy and Luis had finished drafting his first report to Madrid under the guidance of British intelligence. Within a week the entire Eldorado Network was in action again, and the personality of a new sub-agent—the eighth—was taking shape.

Luis worked an eight-hour day and a seven-day week for the rest of the summer and the whole of the autumn of 1942. He and Julie shared a flat on the top floor of the embassy; Templeton had arranged a job for her in the Press Office. In many ways life was easier for Luis: he had a skilled team advising him and directing him, checking his reports, doing his research. But it wasn't like the old days. 'It's not so much fun,' he complained to Julie. 'They're all so damned efficient, they take all the sport out of it.'

'It's not supposed to be fun,' she said. 'It's supposed to work. Is it going to work?'

He shrugged. 'Only Madrid knows that.'

In the short crisis that followed the deaths of Christian and Adler, Richard Fischer had been appointed temporary head of Madrid *Abwehr*. He made a good job of it, and the appointment became permanent in September.

A couple of weeks later, during his weekly meeting of controllers, he suddenly interrupted Franz Werth's report on Seagull. It was unknown for Fischer to interrupt a report. Everyone was very surprised. Fischer looked quite agitated, too, which was unlike him.

'Never mind Seagull,' he said. 'Never mind Knickers or Wallpaper or Haystack or what any *individual* agent is saying. Put it all together! Look at the *overall* picture! Where does it point?'

The controllers looked blank.

'It's obvious!' Fischer exclaimed. 'All that stuff from Seagull about fleets of ships getting sent round the Horn to Suez and not coming back.'

'But that was a month ago,' Franz said.

'Exactly! And three weeks ago Knickers heard about those crated Spitfires and Hurricanes with Syrian lettering on the crates.'

'*En route* to Russia, we decided,' said Otto Krafft.

'Then why weren't the crates lettered in Russian? And what about Nutmeg's report on that special secret training centre for the British Army Catering Corps in wherever-it-was—'

'Harrogate,' Dr Hartmann said. 'They taught rather exotic cooking, as I recall. Goats and stuffed squid and so on.'

'And we all thought it meant desert warfare, eating Arab food,' Fischer said. 'Wrong again!'

'What, then?' Otto asked.

'Look at last week's report from Garlic. Massive Commando training in the Western Islands of Scotland. Endless amphibious landings. Now where do you find terrain like that in Europe?'

'You mean rocky islands?' Franz asked. 'Mountains and sea and stuff? Norway?'

'With *goats*, for God's sake!' Fischer cried. 'Goats that live within flying distance of Syria and sailing distance of Suez! And if that isn't enough we've been staring at a dozen other clues every time we open an Eldorado report!'

'Good heavens. It must be Greece,' Dr Hartmann said.

'*Of course* it's Greece,' Fischer told him.

'They're going to invade Greece?' Otto asked, but Fischer was no longer listening. 'You're in charge until I get back,' he told Franz. 'I'm on the first plane to Berlin. How could we be so blind?'

*

Six weeks later, British and American forces landed in Morocco and Algeria. They were not opposed.

The news surprised and dismayed everyone in Madrid *Abwehr*. It surprised Luis too. He and Julie met the Director in his office on the day the landings were announced. Philby was very pleased. 'Complete success,' he said. 'The enemy was quite convinced it was going to be somewhere else. Well done.'

'I thought it was going to be Norway,' Luis said. 'I had convinced myself it would be Norway.'

'Hell, everyone tips Norway,' Julie said. 'Norway's been done to death.'

'Of course. That's why I thought it was a good bet, because it's become unfashionable, everyone's so bored with Norway, so—'

'Shall we have a drink?' Philby asked. He rang a little brass bell and a secretary came in. 'Now that Eldorado and his friends have sacrificed themselves so nobly,' he said, 'there's something you deserve to know. It goes back to your poor friend Adler, and why he had to have his heart attack. Actually, it goes back a lot further than that, but Adler's death was the point at which you became involved.'

He waited while his secretary found out what they wanted, and gave it to them, and went out.

'Adler didn't die simply to protect and preserve your operation,' Philby said. 'Good health.'

'So I was told,' Luis said. 'Cheers.'

'The fact is that *we* couldn't allow him to defect, either. If the *Abwehr* believed that he had betrayed all their secret agents to us, they would obviously cease trusting those agents. That was the last thing we wanted, since every one of their agents had long ago been intercepted by us and turned around.'

'What?' Julie stared. 'You mean all the *Abwehr* agents in England are working for you? That's incredible.'

'Yes, isn't it?' Philby said. 'Presumably that's why the *Abwehr* goes on accepting and endorsing their reports. Perhaps I shouldn't claim that *all* their agents are working for us. Some of them refused, some were temperamentally unsuitable, some were too stupid, but when that happened we simply replaced the man with one of our own chaps and kept sending reports in the original fellow's name, using his style and technique. The point is that everything the *Abwehr* gets out of Britain comes from us.'

'Let's get this straight,' Luis said. 'You British are actually running all German intelligence operations in Britain?'

'It's a highly successful business,' Philby said. 'Naturally the enemy keeps paying all his agents, and so we get that money. Managing double agents is an expensive affair, but we expect to show a profit at the end of the year.'

'Now I know how you got away with it for so long, Luis,' Julie said. 'I could never understand why the *Abwehr* didn't see through Eldorado,' she told Philby. 'I kept thinking of all those real agents in England sending back genuine reports, and I knew that sooner or later someone had to notice that Eldorado's stuff was always different. But if there never *were* any real agents . . .'

404

'Occasionally we had enquiries from the *Abwehr*,' Philby said. 'You know : requests to such-and-such an agent to check this set of figures or that location. Sometimes we recognised items that had appeared recently in Eldorado reports, reports that we'd intercepted.'

'Just as well I never knew *that* was going on,' Luis said.

'Oh, we always radioed back that your information was good,' Philby told him. 'After all, none of it was correct, so there was no point in denying it, was there?'

Luis finished his drink. Philby gave him another. 'What now?' Luis asked. 'Now that the balloon's burst, I mean.'

'I think you should keep on sending them your misinformation until they stop paying you, Luis. Paying *us*, that is. I don't suppose they'll sack you overnight. We've found that the *Abwehr* is remarkably reluctant to acknowledge its mistakes.'

'Luis isn't just a mistake,' Julie said. 'Luis is a total disaster.'

Philby chuckled, and they all drank to that.

*

As it happened, Eldorado was neither a disaster nor a mistake. After a prolonged and painstaking review of the events leading up to the Anglo-American landings in North Africa, Madrid *Abwehr* came to the conclusion that the Eldorado Network had honestly and accurately reported a series of actions that had been carefully and deliberately contrived by Allied Counter-Intelligence in order to divert German attention to Greece and the Balkans as a probable invasion area.

'Eldorado did a good job,' Richard Fischer decided. 'He and his team saw what there was to see, and reported it accurately. The fact that what they saw was part of a major diversionary exercise by the enemy can hardly be blamed on them. The whole point of such a deception is that it should look like the real thing. The Eldorado team would have been at fault if they had *not* reported what they found. As it is, my confidence in their diligence, skill and courage is renewed.'

'Bad luck, old boy,' Charles Templeton said when he heard that the *Abwehr* payments were continuing. 'Looks as if you're going to be with us for rather a long time. Will you find it too awfully boring?'

Julie laughed when she heard the news. 'Terrific,' she said.

'You can't quit and they won't fire you. What will you do now?'

Luis wondered. Julie was standing by the window, and the way the light shone through her dress was especially attractive. He went over and put his arm around her. 'I'll just have to go all the way and become a myth, I suppose,' he said.

Afterword

You may, perhaps, have found this novel rather fanciful, even unbelievable. In fact it was suggested by a true story.

Luis Cabrillo is based upon a Spaniard who, after spending two years hidden in a house during the Civil War, in January 1941 offered himself to the British as an intelligence agent, was rejected, and thereupon joined the Germans—with the deliberate intention of double-crossing them because he calculated that this would greatly improve his prospects of employment by the British.

The Germans codenamed him 'Arabel', and after training he left Madrid in July 1941, having arranged to travel to Britain on a Spanish diplomatic mission which would provide cover for his spying activities.

In fact Arabel went no further than Lisbon. For the next nine months he wrote long and lively letters to German intelligence in Madrid, all supposedly sent from Britain. Arabel had never in his life set foot in Britain. He had only a few elementary documents to help his work—a Blue Guide, a map of England, an obsolete railway-timetable and the like. Nevertheless, such was his skill, imagination and daring that the Germans came to value his reports highly, and he soon created three subagents to help expand his operations.

Once established, Arabel again tried to join the British. Again they rejected him. However in February 1942 British intelligence learned from other sources that the enemy was wasting considerable effort on intercepting a non-existent convoy from Liverpool to Malta. Arabel had invented it. At last his value was recognised. He was smuggled to England and joined MI5, where he was codenamed 'Garbo'.

For the rest of the war Garbo/Arabel worked with a prolific skill that verged on genius. By 1944 he headed, so the Germans believed, an organisation in Britain of fourteen active agents and eleven valuable contacts. By then his organisation had sent them about four hundred secret letters and transmitted about two thousand radio reports, for which they had paid some £20,000.

Perhaps the greatest achievement of the Garbo network was to help persuade the Germans that the main D Day landings would take place in the Pas de Calais area, and that the Normandy attack was only a diversion. The German Secret Service not only believed this; it went on believing it. Three days *after* D Day, Garbo sent an urgent warning that the real assault was now about to strike the Pas de Calais area. Immediately, two Panzer Divisions were sent there. At least seven German divisions which might have been expected to be sent to Normandy were kept in the Pas de Calais area for two weeks after D Day. To the end, it seems, the Germans were convinced that the only reason why the Pas de Calais attack never took place was because the Normandy landings were unexpectedly successful. This explains the Germans' continued trust in Garbo's reports. In December, 1944, when the British decorated him with the M.B.E., the Germans were trying hard (despite the obstacle of his Spanish nationality) to award him the Iron Cross, Second Class.

Garbo was only one—although perhaps the outstanding one —of many double-agents controlled by the British Secret Service. Astonishingly, MI5 was so successful in intercepting enemy agents and immediately 'turning them around' that before long all German agents in Britain were double-agents, transmitting misinformation to the *Abwehr*.

In his excellent book, *The Double-Cross System, 1939-1945,* J. C. Masterman writes : 'by means of the double-agent system *we actively ran and controlled the German espionage system in this country.*' (Masterman's italics.) He goes on : 'This is at first blush a staggering claim and one which in the nature of things could not be advanced until late in the history of the war.' According to Masterman, MI5 controlled about 120 double-agents, 39 of whom were important enough to be described in his book. It is a totally convincing account of a brilliant triumph.

Other characters in my story were also suggested by real people or events. 'Eagle' was based on an individual codenamed 'Ostro', one of several Germans living in the Iberian Peninsula who supplied information to the *Abwehr* which (so they claimed) came from agents in England; in fact their reports were invented. Wolfgang Adler's fate emerged as the logical conclusion of a threat to the Double-Cross System that was, in fact, posed by certain *Abwehr* officials when they attempted to desert the German cause. If they had succeeded, the *Abwehr* would naturally have expected its agents to be betrayed and arrested; thus the defection had to be prevented at all costs—a response which must have considerably depressed and bewildered the would-be defectors.

The man in charge of British counter-espionage in Spain and Portugal for most of the war was Kim Philby, then chief assistant of Section V in MI6. His staff included Graham Greene and Malcolm Muggeridge, and Philby was outstandingly good at his job. I have juggled history by actively involving Philby in the Double-Cross System, which was not his department, and by installing him in Lisbon: he visited Portugal but his office was in England.

As for the earlier episodes in my story: the references to the Visions at Fatima and the account of the Battle of Jarama are substantially accurate, as are the descriptions of the bombings of Durango and Guernica. Everything else I made up; which is not to say that it could not have happened.

D.R.